The Catholic Tradition

REV. CHARLES J. DOLLEN
DR. JAMES K. McGOWAN
DR. JAMES J. MEGIVERN
EDITORS

The Catholic Tradition

Social Thought
Volume 1

A Consortium Book

Library of Congress Card Catalog Number: 79-1977
ISBN: 0-8434-0730-1
ISBN: 0-8434-0725-5 series

The publisher gratefully acknowledges permission to quote from the following copyrighted sources. In cases where those properties contain scholarly apparatus such as footnotes, such footnotes have been omitted in the interest of the general reader.

BENZIGER BROTHERS
Rerum Novarum by Pope Leo XIII, copyright 1943. Reprinted by permission of Benziger, a division of Glencoe Publishing Co., Inc.

WALTER J. BLACK, INC.
"Book Two" from *The Utopia* of Sir Thomas More, copyright 1947. Reprinted by permission of Walter J. Black, Inc.

BURNS OATES & WASHBOURNE LTD.
Pages 104-135 from the *Summa Theologica* of St. Thomas Aquinas, Part II translated by Fathers of the English Dominican Province, 1929.

CAMBRIDGE UNIVERSITY PRESS
Selection from *Origen: Contra Celsum*, translated by Henry Chadwick, 1953. Reprinted by permission of Cambridge University Press.

THE CATHOLIC UNIVERSITY OF AMERICA PRESS, INC.
"Works and Almsgiving" from *The Fathers of the Church*, Volume 36, *St. Cyprian: Treatises*, translated by Roy J. Deferrari, copyright © 1958; Chapters 4-17 from *The Fathers of the Church*, Volume 24, *St. Augustine: The City of God*, Book XIX, translated by Gerald G. Walsh, S.J. and Daniel J. Honan, copyright 1954; "Sermons" from *The Fathers of the Church*, Volume 17, *St. Peter Chrysologus: Selected Sermons*, translated by George E. Ganss, S.J., copyright 1953. Reprinted by permission of The Catholic University of America Press, Inc.

SISTER EMILY JOSEPH DALY, C.S.J.
"Apology" and "To Scapula" from *The Fathers of the Church*, Volume 10, *Tertullian: Apologetical Works* translated by Rudolph Arbesmann, O.S.A., Sister Emily Joseph Daly, C.S.J., Edwin A. Quain, S.J.

WM. B. EERDMANS PUBLISHING COMPANY
"Who Is the Rich Man That Shall Be Saved?" by Clement of Alexandria from *The Ante-Nicene Fathers*, 1967.

HOWARD FERTIG, INC.
Chapter 13 from *The Genius of Christianity* by Chateaubriand. Howard Fertig, Inc. Edition 1976.

GARLAND PUBLISHING, INC.
"Book One" from *Monarchy and Three Political Letters* by Dante Alighieri, 1972. Reprinted by permission of Garland Publishing, Inc.

HARPER & ROW, PUBLISHERS, INC.
"On the Perfection of Poverty" (pp 15–52) from *St. Francis of Assisi* translated by Leo Sherley-Price. Copyright © 1959 by A. R. Mowbray & Co., Limited. Reprinted by permission of Harper & Row, Publishers, Inc.

D. H. McBRIDE & CO.
Selection from *The Church and Modern Society* by John Ireland, copyright 1903.

THE MISSIONARY SOCIETY OF ST. PAUL THE APOSTLE IN THE STATE OF NEW YORK
Bartolomé de Las Casas selection from *Readings in Church History*, Volume 1, edited by Colman J. Barry, O.S.B. Copyright © 1960 by The Newman Press. Reprinted by permission of The Paulist Press.

P. O'SHEA
"Political Tendencies" from *The American Republic* by O. A. Brownson, LL.D., 1866.

ESTATE OF EDWIN A. QUAIN, S.J.
"Apology" and "To Scapula" from *The Fathers of the Church*, Volume 10, *Tertullian: Apologetical Works* translated by Rudolph Arbesmann, O.S.A., Sister Emily Joseph Daly, C.S.J., Edwin A. Quain, S.J. Copyright 1950, The Catholic University of America Press, Inc. Copyright renewed 1978 by Sr. Emily Joseph Daly, C.S.J., and Edwin A. Quain, S.J. Reprinted by permission of Sister Emily Joseph Daly, C.S.J. and the Estate of Edwin A. Quain, S.J.

Table of Contents

THE CATHOLIC TRADITION: Social Thought

Introduction

The Catholic Tradition is a 14 volume anthology of excerpts from the great Catholic writers from antiquity to the present day. *The Catholic Tradition* is intended for the armchair reader who has not studied theology or church history and has not time to struggle unassisted through 198 books. The publisher's intention is to provide such a reader with a compact home library that will permit him to familiarize himself with the great Catholic writers and their works. The works included in *The Catholic Tradition* are all religious in subject. The publisher did not include fiction or nonfiction books on secular subjects written by Catholic authors.

The Catholic Tradition arranges the writings according to religious subjects. There are seven religious subjects, each of which is covered in two volumes: The Church; Mass and the Sacraments; Sacred Scripture; The Saviour; Personal Ethics; Social Thought; and Spirituality. Within each subject, the writings are arranged in chronological order, which permits the reader to follow the development of Catholic thought across 2000 years.

Each excerpt in *The Catholic Tradition* is preceded by a brief biographical and explanatory introduction to help the reader understand the world in which the writer lived and wrote, and the problems with which he was dealing.

The selection of the excerpts and the writing of the introductions has been a long and difficult process. The task of making the final selections was particularly arduous (as such choices always are); the most modern authors, about whose writing there is yet no final judgment provoking the most debate. The selection of authors was made originally in the publisher's offices and then submitted to the three editors of the series who refined the selection. The editors submitted their selection to an unofficial board of scholars who very kindly made constructive comments.

The process of assembling the many hundreds of books from which to make the final selection was in itself a vast task. Many of the books under consideration were very scarce and not available in bookstores or libraries. The work of collecting the books and then making selections among them stretched over a three year period, and many books were selected for inclusion and later rejected after careful scrutiny and reflection.

The editing of *The Catholic Tradition* was a long and difficult job because the literature of Roman Catholicism is a vast and complex body. Of all the Christian denominations, the Roman Catholic Church is by far the oldest and largest. Its ranks include a tremendous number of saints and scholars, writers and thinkers, mystics and preachers: many of whom felt so strongly about their faith that they were willing to die for it. They have left an incomparably rich legacy of art and writing. Selecting from it is not simple.

The selections that we made are representative of the best of mainstream Catholic writing. Generally, they should be intelligible to a thoughtful layman. Some however, may prove more technical than others, and some of the very recent writers may seem controversial. The reader should bear in mind that some theological questions simply do not admit of facile answers, and that some of the earlier writers were considered controversial in their own days. It is also well to remember that the writings gathered here, brilliant and revered as their authors may be, are not necessarily official statements of Church policy. But they are, all of them, solidly part of the Catholic tradition.

The writers are all Catholics, many of them clergymen, some of them converts to Catholicism. They all wrote as loyal servants of the Church and from a Catholic point of view. When they wrote on personal ethics they proceeded from the assumption that man's goal was to imitate Christ, not simply to follow a secular set of ethical rules. When they wrote on social problems they expressed the need to solve social problems because they loved their neighbors, not for the material enrichment of society. Their writings on Christ reflect an intense struggle to bend human language to divine definition. Taken together, their writings form a literary tradition that is Roman Catholic at heart. That tradition has certain ingredients that are not present in the literary traditions of the other Christian denominations. Particularly, the heritage of liturgical ceremony and mystical contemplation have left an incomparable treasure of literature that is here presented in the volumes entitled *Mass and the Sacraments,* and *Spirituality.*

The whole corpus of Catholic thinking and writing, distilled here in *The Catholic Tradition,* is generally considered by scholars to have three important periods: the ancient, or patristic, period; the high middle-ages, which is the era of St. Thomas Aquinas and sometimes called the scholastic period; finally the time in which we live today, the last 100 years. These three epochs are golden ages of Catholic writing. They are separated from each other by the generally unproductive eras of the dark ages and the Reformation.

Through all these epochs the great Catholic writers have preserved and developed the Christian message: love God; love your fellow man. Each writer wrote conscious of the tradition behind him, conscious that he was building on the work of men before him, adapting their work to changed conditions or continuing their work on the outer edges of human speculation.

The present day writers, those of the third great era of Catholic writing, are the most important part of *The Catholic Tradition.* Here for the first time their thinking is presented along with the work of their predecessors; here can be seen the stunning achievement of today's Catholic writing, and how it follows logically from the writing of the patristic and scholastic thinkers.

The present day writers presented in *The Catholic Tradition* number 114, over half of the total number of writers chosen.

Their writing will probably prove more intelligible to the average reader because they write in today's idiom and they address contemporary problems.

Oddly enough, many if not most of the modern writers are not familiar to the average Catholic. St. Augustine, and St. Thomas Aquinas are household names, but only serious Catholic readers today are familiar with the masterful writings of Karl Rahner, Edward Schillebeeckx, Raymond Brown, and Gustavo Gutiérrez. None the less, these men are representative of a great historical flowering of Catholic writing today and their names may well echo down the ages.

THE PUBLISHER

Clement of Alexandria
150-215

Very little information is available on this Father of the Church who is second only to Origen as a representative of the early development of theology in Alexandria. Clement was well instructed in Greek philosophy, which he used generously in his theological writings. A convert to Christianity, he conducted a school of Christian instruction in Alexandria. He left that city around 202, during a persecution of the Christians. He seems to have spent time in Antioch and Cappadocia before his death.

Clement was highly respected in Christian antiquity for his holiness and learning. He is one of the major contributors to early Christian literature. Perhaps one of Clement's greatest achievements is the ease with which he blended Greek philosophical thought and Christian biblical faith into a complementary whole.

His three most important works are The Exhortation to the Heathen, Christ The Educator *and* The Stromata. *The Exhortation, designed to lead pagans to the Christian faith, is an excellent example of how the spirit of philosophy and of the gospel can be brought together.* Christ The Educator *is a guide to Christian life. The aim of* The Stromata *(tapestries, miscellanies) is to supply the Christian community with ample material to construct a rich Christian philosophy.*

Besides these three works, Clement wrote several treatises. The treatise chosen for inclusion here is Who is the rich man that shall be saved? *It is reproduced in its entirety.*

Among the questions that had to be resolved by the early Christians was that of material possessions. The ideal of poverty is one of the most attractive themes of Christianity. But it becomes troublesome as soon as some of the members of the community possess noticeable wealth. What is to be done? Does the wealthy person simply and literally give up what he has? Does he place it at the service of the community? Can he hope to be saved if he remains wealthy? The gospel story of the rich young man who asked what he must do to be saved and then went away disappointed when challenged to give up his goods and follow Christ seems to suggest that salvation is particularly difficult for the wealthy.

Clement recognizes that material possessions can be a real obstacle to the Christian. But he insists that external goods, in themselves, cannot hurt. It is the Christian's disposition of soul that makes the difference. Thus, he who seriously sees his possessions for the good of his brother and who is capable of rising above his possessions with a spirit of detachment, is truly blessed by the Lord and is poor in spirit. Faith, love, brotherliness, meekness, humility and truthfulness are among the qualities essential to resolving the tension between the life of the spirit and material goods.

The same question haunts the Christian community today. How does the individual, the family, and the Church work out a healthy attitude toward wealth? Social injustice is the inevitable outcome of a poor balance. This brief treatise can be of great value to the Christian who seeks to establish his resolution of the question on evangelical principles.

WHO IS THE RICH MAN THAT SHALL BE SAVED?

T hose who bestow laudatory addresses on the rich appear to me to be rightly judged not only flatterers and base, in vehemently pretending that things which are disagreeable give them pleasure, but also godless and treacherous; godless, because neglecting to praise and glorify God, who is alone perfect and good, "of whom are all things, and by whom are all things, and for whom are all things," they invest with divine honours men wallowing in an execrable and abominable life, and, what is the principal thing, liable on this account to the judgment of God; and treacherous, because, although wealth is of itself sufficient to puff up and corrupt the souls of its possessors, and to turn them from the path by which salvation is to be attained, they stupefy them still more, by inflating the minds of the rich with the pleasures of extravagant praises, and by making them utterly despise all things except wealth, on account of which they are admired; bringing, as the saying is, fire to fire, pouring pride on pride, and adding conceit to wealth, a heavier burden to that which by nature is a weight, from which somewhat ought rather to be removed and taken away as being a dangerous and deadly disease. For to him who exalts and magnifies himself, the change and downfall to a low condition succeeds in turn, as the divine word teaches. For it appears to me to be far kinder, than basely to flatter the rich and praise them for what is bad, to aid them in working out their salvation in every possible way; asking this of God, who surely and sweetly bestows such things on His own children; and thus by the grace of the Saviour healing their souls, enlightening them and leading them to the attainment of the truth; and whosoever obtains this and distinguishes himself in good works shall gain the prize of everlasting life. Now prayer that runs its course till the last day of life needs a strong and tranquil soul; and the conduct of life needs a good and righteous disposition, reaching out towards all the commandments of the Saviour.

Perhaps the reason of salvation appearing more difficult to the rich man than to poor men, is not single but manifold. For some, merely hearing, and that in an off-hand way, the utterance of the Saviour, "that it is easier for a camel to go through the eye of a needle than for a rich man to enter into the kingdom of heaven," despair of themselves as not destined to live, surrender all to the world, cling to the present life as if it alone was left to them, and so diverge more from the way to the life to come, no longer inquiring either whom the Lord and Master calls rich, or how that which is impossible to man becomes possible to God. But others rightly and adequately comprehend this, but attaching slight importance to the works which tend to salvation, do not make the requisite preparation for attaining to the objects of their hope. And I affirm both of these things of the rich who have learned both the Saviour's power and His glorious salvation. With those who are ignorant of the truth I have little concern.

Those then who are actuated by a love of the truth and love of their brethren, and neither are rudely insolent towards such rich as are called, nor, on the other hand, cringe to them for their own avaricious ends, must first by the word relieve them of their groundless despair, and show with the requisite explanation of the oracles of the Lord that the inheritance of the kingdom of heaven is not quite cut off from them if they obey the commandments; then admonish them that they entertain a causeless fear, and that the Lord gladly receives them, provided they are willing; and then, in addition, exhibit and teach how and by what deeds and dispositions they shall win the objects of hope, inasmuch as it is neither out of their reach, nor, on the other hand, attained without effort; but, as is the case with athletes—to compare things small and perishing with things great and immortal—let the man who is endowed with worldly wealth reckon that this depends on himself. For among those, one man, because he despaired of being able to conquer and gain crowns, did not give in his name for the context; while another, whose mind was inspired with this hope, and yet did not submit to the appropriate labours, and diet, and exercises, remained uncrowned, and was balked in his expectations. So also let not the man that has been invested with worldly wealth proclaim himself excluded at the outset from the Saviour's lists, provided he is a believer and one who contemplates the greatness of God's philanthropy; nor let him, on the other hand, expect to grasp the crowns of immortality without struggle and effort, continuing untrained, and without contest. But let him go and put himself under the Word as his trainer, and Christ the President of the contest; and for his prescribed food and drink let him have the New Testament of the Lord; and for exercises, the commandments; and for elegance and ornament, the fair dispositions, love, faith, hope, knowledge of the truth, gentleness, meekness, pity, gravity: so that, when by the last trumpet the signal shall be given for the race and departure hence, as from the stadium of life, he may with a good conscience present himself victorious before the Judge who confers the rewards, confessedly worthy of the Fatherland on high, to which he returns with crowns and the acclamations of angels.

May the Saviour then grant to us that, having begun the subject from this point, we may contribute to the brethren what is true, and suitable, and saving, first touching the hope itself, and, second, touching the access to the hope. He indeed grants to those who beg, and teaches those who ask, and dissipates ignorance and dispels despair, by introducing again the same words about the rich, which become their own interpreters and infallible expounders. For there is nothing like listening again to the very same statements, which till now in the Gospels were distressing you, hearing them as you did without examination, and erroneously through puerility: "And going forth into the way, one approached and kneeled, saying, Good Master, what good thing shall I do that I may inherit everlasting life? And Jesus saith, Why callest thou Me good? There is none good but one, *that is,* God. Thou knowest the commandments. Do not commit adultery, Do not kill, Do not steal, Do not bear false witness, Defraud not, Honour thy father and thy mother. And he answering saith to Him, All these have I observed. And Jesus, looking upon him, loved him, and said, One thing thou lackest. If thou wouldest be perfect, sell what thou hast and give to the poor, and thou shalt have treasure in heaven: and come, follow Me. And he was sad at

5

that saying, and went away grieved: for he was rich, having great possessions. And Jesus looked round about, and saith to His disciples, How hardly shall they that have riches enter into the kingdom of God! And the disciples were astonished at His words. But Jesus answereth again, and saith unto them, Children, how hard is it for them that trust in riches to enter into the kingdom of God! More easily shall a camel enter through the eye of a needle than a rich man into the kingdom of God. And they were astonished out of measure, and said, Who then can be saved? And He, looking upon them, said, What is impossible with men is possible with God. For with God all things are possible. Peter began to say to Him, Lo, we have left all and followed Thee. And Jesus answered and said, Verily I say unto you, Whosoever shall leave what is his own, parents, and brethren, and possessions, for My sake and the Gospel's, shall receive an hundred-fold now in this world, lands, and possessions, and house, and brethren, with persecutions; and in the world to come is life everlasting. But many that are first shall be last, and the last first."

These things are written in the Gospel according to Mark; and in all the rest correspondingly; although perchance the expressions vary slightly in each, yet all show identical agreement in meaning.

But well knowing that the Saviour teaches nothing in a merely human way, but teaches all things to His own with divine and mystic wisdom, we must not listen to His utterances carnally; but with due investigation and intelligence must search out and learn the meaning hidden in them. For even those things which seem to have been simplified to the disciples by the Lord Himself are found to require not less, even more, attention than what is expressed enigmatically, from the surpassing superabundance of wisdom in them. And whereas the things which are thought to have been explained by Him to those within—those called by Him the children of the kingdom—require still more consideration than the things which seemed to have been expressed simply, and respecting which therefore no questions were asked by those who heard them, but which, pertaining to the entire design of salvation, and to be contemplated with admirable and supercelestial depth of mind,

6

we must not receive superficially with our ears, but with application of the mind to the very spirit of the Saviour, and the unuttered meaning of the declaration.

For our Lord and Saviour was asked pleasantly a question most appropriate for Him,—the Life respecting life, the Saviour respecting salvation, the Teacher respecting the chief doctrines taught, the Truth respecting the true immortality, the Word respecting the word of the Father, the Perfect respecting the perfect rest, the Immortal respecting the sure immortality. He was asked respecting those things on account of which He descended, which He inculcates, which He teaches, which He offers, in order to show the essence of the Gospel, that it is the gift of eternal life. For He foresaw as God, both what He would be asked, and what each one would answer Him. For who should do this more than the Prophet of prophets, and the Lord of every prophetic spirit? And having been called "good," and taking the starting note from this first expression, He commences His teaching with this, turning the pupil to God, the good, and first and only dispenser of eternal life, which the Son, who received it of Him, gives to us.

Wherefore the greatest and chiefest point of the instructions which relate to life must be implanted in the soul from the beginning,—to know the eternal God, the giver of what is eternal, and by knowledge and comprehension to possess God, who is first, and highest, and one, and good. For this is the immutable and immoveable source and support of life, the knowledge of God, who really is, and who bestows the things which really are, that is, those which are eternal, from whom both being and the continuance of it are derived to other beings. For ignorance of Him is death; but the knowledge and appropriation of Him, and love and likeness to Him, are the only life.

He then who would live the true life is enjoined first to know Him, "whom no one knows, except the Son reveal (Him)." Next is to be learned the greatness of the Saviour after Him, and the newness of grace; for, according to the apostle, "the law was given by Moses, grace and truth came by Jesus Christ;" and the gifts granted through a faithful servant are not equal to those bestowed by the true Son. If then the law of Moses had been sufficient to confer eternal life, it were to no purpose for the Saviour Himself to come and suffer for us, accomplishing the course of human life from His birth to His cross; and to no purpose for him who had done all the commandments of the law from his youth to fall on his knees and beg from another immortality. For he had not only fulfilled the law, but had begun to do so from his very earliest youth. For what is there great or pre-eminently illustrious in an old age which is unproductive of faults? But if one in juvenile frolicsomeness and the fire of youth shows a mature judgment older than his years, this is a champion admirable and distinguished, and hoary pre-eminently in mind.

But, nevertheless, this man being such, is perfectly persuaded that nothing is wanting to him as far as respects righteousness, but that he is entirely destitute of life. Wherefore he asks it from Him who alone is able to give it. And with reference to the law, he carries confidence; but the Son of God he addresses in supplication. He is transferred from faith to faith. As perilously tossing and occupying a dangerous anchorage in the law, he makes for the Saviour to find a haven.

Jesus, accordingly, does not charge him with not having fulfilled all things out of the law, but loves him, and fondly welcomes his obedience in what he had learned; but says that he is not perfect as respects eternal life, inasmuch as he had not fulfilled what is perfect, and that he is a doer indeed of the law, but idle at the true life. Those things, indeed, are good. Who denies it? For "the commandment is holy," as far as a sort of training with fear and preparatory discipline goes, leading as it did to the culmination of legislation and to grace. But Christ is the fulfilment "of the law for righteousness to every one that believeth;" and not as a slave making slaves, but sons, and brethren, and fellow-heirs, who perform the Father's will.

"If thou wilt be perfect." Consequently he was not yet perfect. For nothing is more perfect than what is perfect. And divinely the expression "if thou wilt" showed the self-determination of the soul holding converse with Him. For choice depended on the man as being free; but the gift on God as the Lord. And He gives to those who are willing and and are exceedingly earnest, and ask, that so their salvation may become their

8

own. For God compels not (for compulsion is repugnant to God), but supplies to those who seek, and bestows on those who ask, and opens to those who knock. If thou wilt, then, if thou really willest, and art not deceiving thyself, acquire what thou lackest. One thing is lacking thee,—the one thing which abides, the good, that which is now above the law, which the law gives not, which the law contains not, which is the prerogative of those who live. He forsooth who had fulfilled all the demands of the law from his youth, and had gloried in what was magnificent, was not able to complete the whole with this one thing which was specially required by the Saviour, so as to receive the eternal life which he desired. But he departed displeased, vexed at the commandment of the life, on account of which he supplicated. For he did not truly wish life, as he averred, but aimed at the mere reputation of the good choice. And he was capable of busying himself about many things; but the one thing, the work of life, he was powerless, and disinclined, and unable to accomplish. Such also was what the Lord said to Martha, who was occupied with many things, and distracted and troubled with serving; while she blamed her sister, because, leaving serving, she set herself at His feet, devoting her time to learning: "Thou art troubled about many things, but Mary hath chosen the good part, which shall not be taken away from her." So also He bade him leave his busy life, and cleave to One and adhere to the grace of Him who offered everlasting life.

What then was it which persuaded him to flight, and made him depart from the Master, from the entreaty, the hope, the life, previously pursued with ardour?—"Sell thy possessions." And what is this? He does not, as some conceive off-hand, bid him throw away the substance he possessed, and abandon his property; but bids him banish from his soul his notions about wealth, his excitement and morbid feeling about it, the anxieties, which are the thorns of existence, which choke the seed of life. For it is no great thing or desirable to be destitute of wealth, if without a special object,—not except on account of life. For thus those who have nothing at all, but are destitute, and beggars for their daily bread, the poor dispersed on the streets, who know not God and God's righteousness, simply on account of their extreme want and destitution of subsistence, and lack even of the smallest things, were most blessed and most dear to God, and sole possessors of everlasting life.

Nor was the renunciation of wealth and the bestowment of it on the poor or needy a new thing; for many did so before the Saviour's advent,—some because of the leisure (thereby obtained) for learning, and on account of a dead wisdom; and others for empty fame and vainglory, as the Anaxagorases, the Democriti, and the Crateses.

Why then command as new, as divine, as alone life-giving, what did not save those of former days? And what peculiar thing is it that the new creature the Son intimates and teaches? It is not the outward act which others have done, but something else indicated by it, greater, more godlike, more perfect, the stripping off of the passions from the soul itself and from the disposition, and the cutting up by the roots and casting out of what is alien to the mind. For this is the lesson peculiar to the believer, and the instruction worthy of the Saviour. For those who formerly despised external things relinquished and squandered their property, but the passions of the soul, I believe, they intensified. For they indulged in arrogance, pretension, and vainglory, and in contempt of the rest of mankind, as if they had done something superhuman. How then would the Saviour have enjoined on those destined to live for ever what was injurious and hurtful with reference to the life which He promised? For although such is the case, one, after ridding himself of the burden of wealth, may none the less have still the lust and desire for money innate and living; and may have abandoned the use of it, but being at once destitute of and desiring what he spent, may doubly grieve both on account of the absence of attendance, and the presence of regret. For it is impossible and inconceivable that those in want of the necessaries of life should not be harassed in mind, and hindered from better things in the endeavour to provide them somehow, and from some source.

And how much more beneficial the opposite case, for a man, through possessing a competency, both not himself to be in straits about money, and also to give assistance to those to whom it is requisite so to do! For if no one had anything, what room would be left among men for giving? And how can this dogma fail to be found plainly opposed to and conflicting with many other excellent teachings of the Lord? "Make to yourselves friends of the mammon of unrighteousness, that when ye fail, they may receive you into the everlasting habitations." "Acquire treasures in heaven, where neither moth nor rust destroys, nor thieves break through." How could one give food to the hungry, and drink to the thirsty, clothe the naked, and shelter the houseless, for not doing which He threatens with fire and the outer darkness, if each man first divested himself of all these things? Nay, He bids Zaccheus and Matthew, the rich tax-gathers, entertain Him hospitably. And He does not bid them part with their property, but, applying the just and removing the unjust judgment, He subjoins, "To-day salvation has come to this house, forasmuch as he also is a son of Abraham." He so praises the use of property as to enjoin, along with this addition, the giving a share of it, to give drink to the thirsty, bread to the hungry, to take the houseless in, and clothe the naked. But if it is not possible to supply those needs without substance, and He bids people abandon their substance, what else would the Lord be doing than exhorting to give and not to give the same things, to feed and not to feed, to take in and to shut out, to share and not to share? which were the most irrational of all things.

Riches, then, which benefit also our neighbours, are not to be thrown away. For they are possessions, inasmuch as they are possessed, and goods, inasmuch as they are useful and provided by God for the use of men; and they lie to our hand, and are put under our power, as material and instruments which are for good use to those who know the instrument. If you use it skilfully, it is skilful; if you are deficient in skill, it is affected by your want of skill, being itself destitute of blame. Such an instrument is wealth. Are you able to make a right use of it? It is subservient to righteousness. Does one make a wrong use of it? It is, on the other hand, a minister of wrong. For its nature is to be subservient, not to rule. That then which of itself has neither good nor evil, being blameless, ought not to be blamed; but that which has the power of using it well and ill, by reason of its possessing voluntary choice. And this is the mind and judgment of man, which has freedom in itself and self-determination in the treatment of what is assigned to it. So let no man destroy wealth, rather than the passions of the soul, which are incompatible with the better use of wealth. So that, becoming virtuous and good, he may be able to make a good use of these riches. The renunciation, then, and selling of all possessions, is to be understood as spoken of the passions of the soul.

I would then say this. Since some things are within and some without the soul, and if the soul make a good use of them, they also are reputed good, but if a bad, bad;—whether does He who commands us to alienate our possessions repudiate those things, after the removal of which the passions still remain, or those rather, on the removal of which wealth even becomes beneficial? If therefore he who casts away worldly wealth can still be rich in the passions, even though the material [for their gratification] is absent,—for the disposition produces its own effects, and strangles the reason, and presses it down and inflames it with its inbred lusts,—it is then of no advantage to him to be poor in purse while he is rich in passions. For it is not what ought to be cast away that he has cast away, but what is indifferent; and he has deprived himself of what is serviceable, but set on fire the innate fuel of evil through want of the external means [of gratification]. We must therefore renounce those possessions that are injurious, not those that are capable of being serviceable, if one knows the right use of them. And what is managed with wisdom, and sobriety, and piety, is profitable; and what is hurtful must be cast away. But things external hurt not. So then the Lord introduces the use of external things, bidding us put away not the means of subsistence, but what uses them badly. And these are the infirmities and passions of the soul.

The presence of wealth in these is deadly to all, the loss of it salutary. Of which, making the soul pure,—that is, poor and bare,—we must hear the Saviour speaking thus, "Come, follow Me." For to the pure in heart He now becomes the way. But into the impure soul the grace of God finds no entrance. And that (soul) is unclean which is rich in lusts, and is in the throes of many worldly affections. For he who holds possessions, and gold, and silver, and houses, as the gifts of God; and ministers from them to the God who gives them for the salvation of men; and knows that he possesses them more for the sake of the brethren than his own; and is superior to the possession of them, not the slave of the things he possesses; and does not carry them about in his soul, nor bind and circumscribe his life within them, but is ever labouring at some good and divine work, even should he be necessarily some time or other deprived of them, is able with cheerful mind to bear their removal equally with their abundance. This is he who is blessed by the Lord, and called poor in spirit, a meet heir of the kingdom of heaven, not one who could not live rich.

But he who carries his riches in his soul, and instead of God's Spirit bears in his heart gold or land, and is always acquiring possessions without end, and is perpetually on the outlook for more, bending downwards and fettered in the toils of the world, being earth and destined to depart to earth,— whence can he be able to desire and to mind the kingdom of heaven,—a man who carries not a heart, but land or metal, who must perforce be found in the midst of the objects he has chosen? For where the mind of man is, there is also his treasure. The Lord acknowledges a twofold treasure,—the good: "For the good man, out of the good treasure of his heart, bringeth forth good;" and the evil: for "the evil man, out of the evil treasure, bringeth forth evil: for out of the abundance of the heart the mouth speaketh." As then treasure is not one with Him, as also it is with us, that which gives the unexpected great gain in the finding, but also a second, which is profitless and undesirable, an evil acquisition, hurtful; so also there is a richness in good things, and a richness in bad things, since we know that riches and treasure are not by nature separated from each other. And the one sort of riches is to be possessed and acquired, and the other not to be possessed, but to be cast away.

In the same way spiritual poverty is blessed. Wherefore also Matthew added, "Blessed are the poor." How? "In spirit." And again, "Blessed are they that hunger and thirst after the righteousness of God." Wherefore wretched are the contrary kind of poor, who have no part in God, and still less in human property, and have not tasted of the righteousness of God.

So that (the expression) rich men that shall with difficulty enter into the kingdom, is to be apprehended in a scholarly way, not awkwardly, or rustically, or carnally. For if the expression is used thus, salvation does not depend on external things, whether they be many or few, small or great, or illustrious or obscure, or esteemed or disesteemed; but on the virtue of the soul, on faith, and hope, and love, and brotherliness, and knowledge, and meekness, and humility, and truth, the reward of which is salvation. For it is not on account of comeliness of body that any one shall live, or, on the other hand, perish. But he who uses the body given to him chastely and according to God, shall live; and he that destroys the temple of God shall be destroyed. An ugly man can be profligate, and a good-looking man temperate. Neither strength and great size of body makes alive, nor does any of the members destroy. But the soul which uses them provides the cause for each. Bear then, it is said, when struck on the face; which a man strong and in good health can obey. And again, a man who is feeble may transgress from refractoriness of temper. So also a poor and destitute man may be found intoxicated with lusts; and a man rich in worldly goods temperate, poor in indulgences, trustworthy, intelligent, pure, chastened.

If then it is the soul which, first and especially, is that which is to live, and if virtue springing up around it saves, and vice kills; then it is clearly manifest that by being poor in those things, by riches of which one destroys it, it is saved, and by being rich in those things, riches of which ruin it, it is killed. And let us no longer seek the cause of the issue elsewhere than in the state and disposition of the soul in respect of obedience to God and purity, and in respect of transgression of the commandments and accumulation of wickedness.

He then is truly and rightly rich who is rich in virtue, and is capable of making a holy and faithful use of any fortune; while he is spuriously rich who is rich, according to the flesh, and turns life into outward possession, which is transitory and perishing, and now belongs to one, now to another, and in the end to nobody at all. Again, in the same way there is a genuine poor man, and another counterfeit and falsely so called. He that is poor in spirit, and that is the right thing, and he that is poor

14

in a worldly sense, which is a different thing. To him who is poor in worldly goods, but rich in vices, who is not poor in spirit and rich toward God, it is said, Abandon the alien possessions that are in thy soul, that, becoming pure in heart, thou mayest see God; which is another way of saying, Enter into the kingdom of heaven. And how may you abandon them? By selling them. What then? Are you to take money for effects, by effecting an exchange of riches, by turning your visible substance into money? Not at all. But by introducing, instead of what was formerly inherent in your soul, which you desire to save, other riches which deify and which minister everlasting life, dispositions in accordance with the command of God; for which there shall accrue to you endless reward and honour, and salvation, and everlasting immortality. It is thus that thou dost rightly sell the possessions, many are superfluous, which shut the heavens against thee by exchanging them for those which are able to save. Let the former be possessed by the carnal poor, who are destitute of the latter. But thou, by receiving instead spiritual wealth, shalt have now treasure in the heavens.

The wealthy and legally correct man, not understanding these things figuratively, nor how the same man can be both poor and rich, and have wealth and not have it, and use the world and not use it, went away sad and downcast, leaving the state of life, which he was able merely to desire but not to attain, making for himself the difficult impossible. For it was difficult for the soul not to be seduced and ruined by the luxuries and flowery enchantments that beset remarkable wealth; but it was not impossible, even surrounded with it, for one to lay hold of salvation, provided he withdrew himself from material wealth,—to that which is grasped by the mind and taught by God, and learned to use things indifferent rightly and properly, and so as to strive after eternal life. And the disciples even themselves were at first alarmed and amazed. Why were they so on hearing this? Was it that they themselves possessed much wealth? Nay, they had long ago left their very nets, and hooks, and rowing boats, which were their sole possessions. Why then do they say in consternation, "Who can be saved?" They had heard well and like disciples what was spoken in parable and obscurely by the Lord, and perceived the depth of the words. For they were sanguine of salvation on the ground of their want of wealth. But when they became conscious of not having yet wholly renounced the passions (for they were neophytes and recently selected by the Saviour), they were excessively astonished, and despaired of themselves no less than that rich man who clung so terribly to the wealth which he preferred to eternal life. It was therefore a fit subject for all fear on the disciples' part; if both he that possesses wealth and he that is teeming with passions were the rich, and these alike shall be expelled from the heavens. For salvation is the privilege of pure and passionless souls.

But the Lord replies, "Because what is impossible with men is possible with God." This again is full of great wisdom. For a man by himself working and toiling at freedom from passion achieves nothing. But if he plainly shows himself very desirous and earnest about this, he attains it by the addition of the power of God. For God conspires with willing souls. But if they abandon their eagerness, the spirit which is bestowed by God is also restrained. For to save the unwilling is the part of one exercising compulsion; but to save the willing, that of one showing grace. Nor does the kingdom of heaven belong to sleepers and sluggards, "but the violent take it by force." For this alone is commendable violence, to force God, and take life from God by force. And He, knowing those who persevere firmly, or rather violently, yields and grants. For God delights in being vanquished in such things.

Therefore on hearing those words, the blessed Peter, the chosen, the pre-eminent, the first of the disciples, for whom alone and Himself the Saviour paid tribute, quickly seized and comprehended the saying. And what does he say? "Lo, we have left all and followed Thee." Now if by all he means his own property, he boasts of leaving four oboli perhaps in all, and forgets to show the kingdom of heaven to be their recompense. But if, casting away what we were now speaking of, the old mental possessions and soul diseases, they follow in the Master's footsteps, this now joins them to those who are to be enrolled in the heavens. For it is thus that one truly follows the Saviour, by aiming at sinlessness and at His perfection, and adorning and composing the soul before it as a mirror, and arranging everything in all respects similarly.

"And Jesus answering said, Verily I say unto you, Whosoever shall leave what is his own, parents, and children, and wealth, for My sake and the Gospel's, shall receive an hundredfold." But let neither this trouble you, nor the still harder saying delivered in another place in the words, "Whoso hateth not father, and mother, and children, and his own life besides, cannot be My disciple." For the God of peace, who also exhorts to love enemies, does not introduce hatred and dissolution from those that are dearest. But if we are to love our enemies, it is in accordance with right reason that, ascending from them, we should love also those nearest in kindred. Or if we are to hate our blood-relations, deduction teaches us that much more are we to spurn from us our enemies. So that the reasonings would be shown to destroy one another. But they do not destroy each other, nor are they near doing so. For from the same feeling and disposition, and on the ground of the same rule, one loving his enemy may hate his father, inasmuch as he neither takes vengeance on an enemy, nor reverences a father more than Christ. For by the one word he extirpates hatred and injury, and by the other shamefacedness towards one's relations, if it is detrimental to salvation. If then one's father, or son, or brother, be godless, and become a hindrance to faith and an impediment to the higher life, let him not be friends or agree with him, but on account of the spiritual enmity, let him dissolve the fleshly relationship.

Suppose the matter to be a law-suit. Let your father be imagined to present himself to you and say, "I begot and reared thee. Follow me, and join with me in wickedness, and obey not the law of Christ;" and whatever a man who is a blasphemer and dead by nature would say.

But on the other side hear the Saviour: "I regenerated thee who wert ill born by the world to death. I emancipated, healed, ransomed thee. I will show thee the face of the good Father God. Call no man thy father on earth. Let the dead bury the dead; but follow thou Me. For I will bring thee to a rest of ineffable and unutterable blessings, which eye hath not

THE CATHOLIC TRADITION: Social Thought

seen, nor ear heard, nor have entered into the heart of men;
into which angels desire to look, and see what good things God
hath prepared for the saints and the children who love Him."
I am He who feeds thee, giving Myself as bread, of which he
who has tasted experiences death no more, and supplying day
by day the drink of immortality. I am teacher of supercelestial
lessons. For thee I contended with Death, and paid thy death,
which thou owedst for thy former sins and thy unbelief towards
God."

Having heard these considerations on both sides, decide
for thyself and give thy vote for thine own salvation. Should a
brother say the like, should a child, should a wife, should any
one whosoever, in preference to all let Christ in thee be conqueror. For He contends in thy behalf.

You may even go against wealth. Say, "Certainly Christ
does not debar me from property. The Lord does not envy."
But do you see yourself overcome and overthrown by it?
Leave it, throw it away, hate, renounce, flee. "Even if thy
right eye offend thee," quickly "cut it out." Better is the kingdom of God to a man with one eye, than the fire to one who
is unmutilated. Whether hand, or foot, or soul, hate it. For if
it is destroyed here for Christ's sake, it will be restored to life
yonder.

And to this effect similarly is what follows. "Now at this
present time not to have lands, and money, and houses, and
brethren, with persecutions." For it is neither penniless, nor
homeless, nor brotherless people that the Lord calls to life,
since He has also called rich people; but, as we have said above,
also brothers, as Peter with Andrew, and James with John the
sons of Zebedee, but of one mind with each other and Christ.
And the expression "with persecutions" rejects the possessing
of each of those things. There is a persecution which arises
from without, from men assailing the faithful, either out of
hatred, or envy, or avarice, or through diabolic agency. But the
most painful is internal persecution, which proceeds from each
man's own soul being vexed by impious lusts, and diverse
pleasures, and base hopes, and destructive dreams; when,
always grasping at more, and maddened by brutish loves, and
inflamed by the passions which beset it like goads and stings,

it is covered with blood, (to drive it on) to insane pursuits, and to despair of life, and to contempt of God.

More grievous and painful is this persecution, which arises from within, which is ever with a man, and which the persecuted cannot escape; for he carries the enemy about everywhere in himself. Thus also burning which attacks from without works trial, but that from within produces death. War also made on one is easily put an end to, but that which is in the soul continues till death.

With such persecution, if you have worldly wealth, if you have brothers allied by blood and other pledges, abandon the whole wealth of these which leads to evil; procure peace for yourself, free yourself from protracted persecutions; turn from them to the Gospel; choose before all the Saviour and Advocate and Paraclete of your soul, the Prince of life. "For the things which are seen are temporary; but the things which are not seen are eternal." And in the present time are things evanescent and insecure, but in that to come is eternal life.

"The first shall be last, and the last first." This is fruitful in meaning and exposition, but does not demand investigation at present; for it refers not only to the wealthy alone, but plainly to all men, who have once surrendered themselves to faith. So let this stand aside for the present. But I think that our proposition has been demonstrated in no way inferior to what we promised, that the Saviour by no means has excluded the rich on account of wealth itself, and the possession of property, nor fenced off salvation against them; if they are able and willing to submit their life to God's commandments, and prefer them to transitory objects, and if they would look to the Lord with steady eye, as those who look for the nod of a good helmsman, what he wishes, what he orders, what he indicates, what signal he gives his mariners, where and whence he directs the ship's course. For what harm does one do, who, previous to faith, by applying his mind and by saving has collected a competency? Or what is much less reprehensible than this, if at once by God, who gave him his life, he has had his home given him in the house of such men, among wealthy people, powerful in substance, and pre-eminent in opulence? For if, in consequence of his involuntary birth in wealth, a

19

man is banished from life, rather is he wronged by God, who created him, in having vouchsafed to him temporary enjoyment, and in being deprived of eternal life. And why should wealth have ever sprung from the earth at all, if it is the author and patron of death?

But if one is able in the midst of wealth to turn from its power, and to entertain moderate sentiments, and to exercise self-command, and to seek God alone, and to breathe God and walk with God, such a poor man submits to the commandments, being free, unsubdued, free of disease, unwounded by wealth. But if no, "sooner shall a camel enter through a needle's eye, than such a rich man reach the kingdom of God."

Let then the camel, going through a narrow and strait way before the rich man, signify something loftier; which mystery of the Saviour is to be learned in the "Exposition of first Principles and of Theology."

Well, first let the point of the parable, which is evident, and the reason why it is spoken, be presented. Let it teach the prosperous that they are not to neglect their own salvation, as if they had been already fore-doomed, nor, on the other hand, to cast wealth into the sea, or condemn it as a traitor and an enemy to life, but learn in what way and how to use wealth and obtain life. For since neither does one perish by any means by fearing because he is rich, nor is by any means saved by trusting and believing that he shall be saved, come let them look what hope the Saviour assigns them, and how what is unexpected may become ratified, and what is hoped for may come into possession.

The Master accordingly, when asked, "Which is the greatest of the commandments?" says, "Thou shalt love the Lord thy God with all thy soul, and with all thy strength;" that no commandment is greater than this (He says), and with exceeding good reason; for it gives command respecting the First and the Greatest, God Himself, our Father, by whom all things were brought into being, and exist, and to whom what is saved returns again. By Him, then, being loved beforehand, and having received existence, it is impious for us to regard ought else older or more excellent; rendering only this small tribute of gratitude for the greatest benefits; and being unable to imagine anything else whatever by way of recompense to God, who needs nothing and is perfect; and gaining immortality by the very exercise of loving the Father to the extent of one's might and power. For the more one loves God, the more he enters within God.

The second in order, and not any less than this, He says, is, "Thou shalt love thy neighbour as thyself," consequently God above thyself. And on His interlocutor inquiring, "Who is my neighbour?" He did not, in the same way with the Jews, specify the blood-relation, or the fellow-citizen, or the proselyte, or him that had been similarly circumcised, or the man who uses one and the same law. But He introduces one on his way down from the upland region from Jerusalem to Jericho, and represents him stabbed by robbers, cast half-dead on the way, passed by by the priest, looked sideways at by the Levite, but pitied by the vilified and excommunicated Samaritan; who did not, like those, pass casually, but came provided with such things as the man in danger required, such as oil, bandages, a beast of burden, money for the inn-keeper, part given now, and part promised. "Which," said He, "of them was neighbour to him that suffered these things?" and on his answering, "He that showed mercy to him," (replied), Go thou also, therefore, and do likewise, since love buds into well-doing.

In both the commandments, then, He introduces love; but in order distinguishes it. And in the one He assigns to God the first part of love, and allots the second to our neighbour. Who else can it be but the Saviour Himself? or who more than He has pitied us, who by the rulers of darkness were all but put to death with many wounds, fears, lusts, passions, pains, deceits, pleasures? Of these wounds the only physician is Jesus, who cuts out the passions thoroughly by the root,—not as the law does the bare effects, the fruits of evil plants, but applies His axe to the roots of wickedness. He it is that poured wine on our wounded souls (the blood of David's vine), that brought the oil which flows from the compassions of the Father, and bestowed it copiously. He it is that produced the ligatures of health and of salvation that cannot be undone,—Love, Faith, Hope. He it is that subjected angels, and principalities, and powers, for a great reward to serve us. For they also shall be delivered from the vanity of the world through the revelation of the glory of the sons of God. We are therefore to love Him equally with God. And he loves Christ Jesus who does His will and keeps His commandments. "For not every one that saith unto Me, Lord, Lord, shall enter into the kingdom of heaven; but he that doeth the will of My Father." And "Why call ye Me Lord, Lord, and do not the things which I say?" "And blessed are ye who see and hear what neither righteous men nor prophets" (have seen or heard), if ye do what I say.

He then is first who loves Christ; and second, he who loves and cares for those who have believed on Him. For whatever is done to a disciple, the Lord accepts as done to Himself, and reckons the whole as His. "Come, ye blessed of My Father, inherit the kingdom prepared for you from the foundation of the world. For I was an hungered, and ye gave Me to eat: I was thirsty, and ye gave Me to drink: and I was a stranger, and ye took Me in: I was naked and ye clothed Me: I was sick, and ye visited Me: I was in prison, and ye came to Me. Then shall the righteous answer, saying, Lord, when saw we Thee hungry, and fed Thee? or thirsty, and gave Thee drink? And when saw we Thee a stranger, and took Thee in? or naked, and clothed Thee? Or when saw we Thee sick, and visited Thee? or in prison, and came to Thee? And the King answering, shall say to them, Verily I say unto you, inasmuch as ye have done it unto one of the least of these My brethren, ye have done it unto Me."

Again, on the opposite side, to those who have not performed these things, "Verily I say unto you, inasmuch as ye have not done it unto one of the least of these, ye have not done it to Me." And in another place, "He that receiveth you, receiveth Me; and he that receiveth not you, rejecteth Me."

Such He names children, and sons, and little children, and friends, and little ones here, in reference to their future greatness above. "Despise not," He says, "one of these little ones; for their angels always behold the face of My Father in heaven." And in another place, "Fear not, little flock, for it is your Father's good pleasure to give you the kingdom of heaven." Similarly also He says that "the least in the kingdom of heaven" that is His own disciple "is greater than John, the greatest

22

among those born of women." And again, "He that receiveth a righteous man or a prophet in the name of a righteous man or a prophet, shall receive their reward; and he that giveth to a disciple in the name of a disciple a cup of cold water to drink, shall not lose his reward." Wherefore this is the only reward that is not lost. And again, "Make to you friends of the mammon of unrighteousness, that, when ye fail, they may receive you into everlasting habitations;" showing that by nature all property which a man possesses in his own power is not his own. And from this unrighteousness it is permitted to work a righteous and saving thing, to refresh some one of those who have an everlasting habitation with the Father.

See then, first, that He has not commanded you to be solicited or to wait to be importuned, but yourself to seek those who are to be benefited and are worthy disciples of the Saviour. Excellent, accordingly, also is the apostle's saying, "For the Lord loveth a cheerful giver;" who delights in giving, and spares not, sowing so that he may also thus reap, without murmuring, and disputing, and regret, and communicating, which is pure beneficence. But better than this is the saying spoken by the Lord in another place, "Give to every one that asketh thee." For truly such is God's delight in giving. And this saying is above all divinity,—not to wait to be asked, but to inquire oneself who deserves to receive kindness.

Then to appoint such a reward for liberality,—an everlasting habitation! O excellent trading! O divine merchandise! One purchases immortality for money; and, by giving the perishing things of the world, receives in exchange for these an eternal mansion in the heavens! Sail to this mart, if you are wise, O rich man! If need be, sail round the whole world. Spare not perils and toils, that you may purchase here the heavenly kingdom. Why do transparent stones and emeralds delight thee so much, and a house that is fuel for fire, or a plaything of time, or the sport of the earthquake, or an occasion for a tyrant's outrage? Aspire to dwell in the heavens, and to reign with God. This kingdom a man imitating God will give thee. By receiving a little here, there through all ages He will make thee a dweller with Him. Ask that you may receive; haste; strive; fear lest He disgrace thee. For He is not commanded to receive, but thou to give. The Lord did not say, Give, or bring, or do good, or help, but make a friend. But a friend proves himself such not by one gift, but by long intimacy. For it is neither the faith, nor the love, nor the hope, nor the endurance of one day, but "he that endureth to the end shall be saved."

How then does man give these things? For I will give not only to friends, but to the friends of friends. And who is it that is the friend of God? Do not you judge who is worthy or who is unworthy. For it is possible you may be mistaken in your opinion. As in the uncertainty of ignorance it is better to do good to the undeserving for the sake of the deserving, than by guarding against those that are less good to fail to meet in with the good. For though sparing, and aiming at testing, who will receive meritoriously or not, it is possible for you to neglect some that are loved by God; the penalty for which is the punishment of eternal fire. But by offering to all in turn that need, you must of necessity by all means find some one of those who have power with God to save. "Judge not, then, that ye be not judged. With what measure ye mete, it shall be measured to you again; good measure, pressed and shaken, and running over, shall be given to you." Open thy compassion to all who are enrolled the disciples of God; not looking contemptuously to personal appearance, nor carelessly disposed to any period of life. Nor if one appears penniless, or ragged, or ugly, or feeble, do thou fret in soul at this and turn away. This form is cast around us from without, the occasion of our entrance into this world, that we may be able to enter into this common school. But within dwells the hidden Father, and His Son, who died for us and rose with us.

This visible appearance cheats death and the devil; for the wealth within, the beauty, is unseen by them. And they rave about the carcase, which they despise as weak, being blind to the wealth within; knowing not what a "treasure in an earthen vessel" we bear, protected as it is by the power of God the Father, and the blood of God the Son, and the dew of the Holy Spirit. But be not deceived, thou who hast tasted of the truth, and been reckoned worthy of the great redemption. But contrary to what is the case with the rest of men, collect for thyself an unarmed, an unwarlike, a bloodless, a passionless, a stainless host, pious old men, orphans dear to God, widows armed with meekness, men adorned with love. Obtain with thy money such guards, for body and for soul, for whose sake a sinking ship is made buoyant, when steered by the prayers of the saints alone; and disease at its height is subdued, put to flight by the laying on of hands; and the attack of robbers is disarmed, spoiled by pious prayers; and the might of demons is crushed, put to shame in its operations by strenuous commands.

All these warriors and guards are trusty. No one is idle, no one is useless. One can obtain your pardon from God, another comfort you when sick, another weep and groan in sympathy for you to the Lord of all, another teach some of the things useful for salvation, another admonish with confidence, another counsel with kindness. And all can love truly, without guile, without fear, without hypocrisy, without flattery, without pretence. O·sweet service of loving [souls]! O blessed thoughts of confident [hearts]! O sincere faith of those who fear God alone! O truth of words with those who cannot lie! O beauty of deeds with those who have been commissioned to serve God, to persuade God, to please God, not to touch thy flesh! to speak, but to the King of eternity dwelling in thee.

All the faithful, then, are good and godlike, and worthy of the name by which they are encircled as with a diadem. There are, besides, some, the elect of the elect, and so much more or less distinguished by drawing themselves, like ships to the strand, out of the surge of the world and bringing themselves to safety; not wishing to seem holy, and ashamed if one call them so; hiding in the depth of their mind the ineffable mysteries, and disdaining to let their nobleness be seen in the world; whom the Word calls "the light of the world, and the salt of the earth." This is the seed, the image and likeness of God, and His true son and heir, sent here as it were on a sojourn, by the high administration and suitable arrangement of the Father, by whom the visible and invisible things of the world were created; some for their service, some for their discipline, some for their instruction; and all things are held together so long as the seed remains here; and when it is gathered, these things shall be very quickly dissolved.

For what further need has God of the mysteries of love? And then thou shalt look into the bosom of the Father, whom God the only-begotten Son alone hath declared. And God Himself is love; and out of love to us became feminine. In His ineffable essence He is Father; in His compassion to us He became Mother. The Father by loving became feminine: and the great proof of this is He whom He begot of Himself; and the fruit brought forth by love is love.

For this also He came down. For this He clothed Himself with man. For this He voluntarily subjected Himself to the experiences of men, that by bringing Himself to the measure of our weakness whom He loved, He might correspondingly bring us to the measure of His own strength. And about to be offered up and giving Himself a ransom, He left for us a new Covenant-testament: My love I give unto you. And what and how great is it? For each of us He gave His life,—the equivalent for all. This He demands from us in return for one another. And if we owe our lives to the brethren, and have made such a mutual compact with the Saviour, why should we any more hoard and shut up worldly goods, which are beggarly, foreign to us and transitory? Shall we shut up from each other what after a little shall be the property of the fire? Divinely and weightily John says, "He that loveth not his brother is a murderer," the seed of Cain, a nursling of the devil. He has not God's compassion. He has no hope of better things. He is sterile; he is barren; he is not a branch of the ever-living supercelestial vine. He is cut off; he waits the perpetual fire.

But learn thou the more excellent way, which Paul shows for salvation. "Love seeketh not her own," but is diffused on the brother. About him she is fluttered, about him she is soberly insane. "Love covers a multitude of sins." "Perfect love casteth out fear." "Vaunteth not itself, is not puffed up; rejoiceth not in iniquity, but rejoiceth in the truth; beareth all things, believeth all things, hopeth all things, endureth all things. Love never faileth. Prophecies are done away, tongues cease, gifts of healing fail on the earth. But these three abide, Faith, Hope, Love. But the greatest of these is Love." And rightly. For Faith departs when we are convinced by vision, by seeing God. And Hope vanishes when the things hoped for come. But Love comes to completion, and grows more when that which is perfect has been bestowed. If one introduces it into his soul, although he be born in sins, and has done many forbidden things, he is able, by increasing love, and adopting a pure repentance, to retrieve his mistakes. For let not this be left to despondency and despair by you, if you learn who the rich man is that has not a place in heaven, and what way he uses his property.

If one should escape the superfluity of riches, and the difficulty they interpose in the way of life, and be able to enjoy the eternal good things; but should happen, either from ignorance or involuntary circumstances, after the seal and redemption, to fall into sins or transgressions so as to be quite carried away; such a man is entirely rejected by God. For to every one who has turned to God in truth, and with his whole heart, the doors are open, and the thrice-glad Father receives His truly repentant son. And true repentance is to be no longer bound in the same sins for which He denounced death against Himself, but to eradicate them completely from the soul. For on their extirpation God takes up His abode again in thee. For it is said there is great and exceeding joy and festival in the heavens with the Father and the angels when one sinner turns and repents. Wherefore also He cries, "I will have mercy, and not sacrifice." "I desire not the death, but the repentance of the sinner." "Though your sins be as scarlet wool, I will make them white as snow; though they be blacker than darkness, I will wash and make them like white wool." For it is in the power of God alone to grant the forgiveness of sins, and not to impute transgressions; since also the Lord commands us each day to forgive the repenting brethren. "And if we, being evil, know to give good gifts," much more is it the nature of the Father of mercies, the good Father of all consolation, much pitying, very merciful, to be long-suffering, to wait for those who have turned. And to turn is really to cease from our sins, and to look no longer behind.

Forgiveness of past sins, then, God gives; but of future, each one gives to himself. And this is to repent, to condemn the past deeds, and beg oblivion of them from the Father, who only of all is able to undo what is done, by mercy proceeding from Him, and to blot out former sins by the dew of the Spirit. "For by the state in which I find you will I judge," also, is what in each case the end of all cries aloud. So that even in the case of one who has done the greatest good deeds in his life, but at the end has run headlong into wickedness, all his former pains are profitless to him, since at the catastrophe of the drama he has given up his part; while it is possible for the man who formerly led a bad and dissolute life, on afterwards repenting, to overcome in the time after repentance the evil conduct of a long time. But it needs great carefulness, just as bodies that have suffered by protracted disease need regimen and special attention. Thief, dost thou wish to get forgiveness? steal no more. Adulterer, burn no more. Fornicator, live for the future chastely. Thou who hast robbed, give back, and give back more than [thou tookest]. False witness, practise truth. Perjurer, swear no more, and extirpate the rest of the passions, wrath, lust, grief, fear; that thou mayest be found at the end to have previously in this world been reconciled to the adversary. It is then probably impossible all at once to eradicate inbred passions; but by God's power and human intercession, and the help of brethren, and sincere repentance, and constant care, they are corrected.

Wherefore it is by all means necessary for thee, who art pompous, and powerful, and rich, to set over thyself some man of God as a trainer and governor. Reverence, though it be but one man; fear, though it be but one man. Give yourself to hearing, though it be but one speaking freely, using harshness, and at the same time healing. For it is good for the eyes not to continue always wanton, but to weep and smart sometimes, for greater health. So also nothing is more pernicious to the soul than uninterrupted pleasure. For it is blinded by melting away, if it remain unmoved by bold speech. Fear this man when angry; be pained at his groaning; and reverence him when making his anger to cease; and anticipate him when he is deprecating punishment. Let him pass many sleepless nights for thee, interceding for thee with God, influencing the Father with the magic of familiar litanies. For He does not hold out against His children when they beg His pity. And for you he will pray purely, held in high honour as an angel of God, and grieved not by you, but for you. This is sincere repentance. "God is not mocked," nor does He give heed to vain words. For He alone searches the marrow and reins of the heart, and hears those that are in the fire, and listens to those who supplicate in the whale's belly; and is near to all who believe, and far from the ungodly if they repent not.

And that you may be still more confident, that repenting thus truly there remains for you a sure hope of salvation, listen to a tale, which is not a tale but a narrative, handed down and committed to the custody of memory, about the Apostle John. For when, on the tyrant's death, he returned to Ephesus from the isle of Patmos, he went away, being invited, to the contiguous territories of the nations, here to appoint bishops, there to set in order whole Churches, there to ordain such as were marked out by the Spirit.

Having come to one of the cities not far off (the name of which some give), and having put the brethren to rest in other matters, at last, looking to the bishop appointed, and seeing a youth, powerful in body, comely in appearance, and ardent, said, "This (youth) I commit to you in all earnestness, in the presence of the Church, and with Christ as witness." And on his accepting and promising all, he gave the same injunction and testimony. And he set out for Ephesus. And the presbyter taking home the youth committed to him, reared, kept, cherished, and finally baptized him. After this he relaxed his stricter care and guardianship, under the idea that the seal of the Lord He had set on him was a complete protection to him. But on his obtaining premature freedom, some youths of his age, idle, dissolute, and adepts in evil courses, corrupt him. First they entice him by many costly entertainments; then afterwards by night issuing forth for highway robbery, they take him along with them. Then they dared to execute together something greater. And he by degrees got accustomed; and from greatness of nature, when he had gone aside from the right path, and like a hard-mouthed and powerful horse, had taken the bit between his teeth, rushed with all the more force down into the depths. And having entirely despaired of salvation in God, he no longer meditated what was insignificant, but having perpetrated some great exploit, now that he was once lost, he made up his mind to a like fate with the rest. Taking them and forming a band of robbers, he was the prompt captain of the bandits, the fiercest, the bloodiest, the cruelest.

Time passed, and some necessity having emerged, they send again for John. He, when he had settled the other matters on account of which he came, said, "Come now, O bishop, restore to us the deposit which I and the Saviour committed to thee in the face of the Church over which you preside, as witness." The other was at first confounded, thinking that it was a false charge about money which he did not get; and he could neither believe the allegation regarding what he had not, nor disbelieve John. But when he said "I demand the young man, and the soul of the brother," the old man, groaning deeply, and bursting into tears, said, "He is dead." "How and what kind of death?" "He is dead," he said, "to God. For he turned wicked and abandoned, and at last a robber; and now he has taken possession of the mountain in front of the church, along with a band like him." Rending, therefore, his clothes, and striking his head with great lamentation, the apostle said, "It was a fine guard of a brother's soul I left! But let a horse be brought me, and let some one be my guide on the way." He rode away, just as he was, straight from the church. On coming to the place, he is arrested by the robbers' outpost; neither fleeing nor entreating, but crying, "It was for this I came. Lead me to your captain;" who meanwhile was waiting, all armed as he was. But when he recognised John as he advanced, he turned, ashamed, to flight. The other followed with all his might, forgetting his age, crying, "Why, my son, dost thou flee from me, thy father, unarmed, old? Son, pity me. Fear not; thou hast still hope of life. I will give account to Christ for thee. If need be, I will willingly endure thy death, as the Lord did death for us. For thee I will surrender my life. Stand, believe; Christ hath sent me."

And he, when he heard, first stood, looking down; then threw down his arms, then trembled and wept bitterly. And on the old man approaching, he embraced him, speaking for himself with lamentations as he could, and baptized a second time with tears, concealing only his right hand. The other pledging, and assuring him on oath that he would find forgiveness for himself from the Saviour, beseeching and falling on his knees, and kissing his right hand itself, as now purified by repentance, led him back to the church. Then by supplicating with copious prayers, and striving along with him in continual fastings, and subduing his mind by various utterances of words, did not depart, as they say, till he restored him to the Church, presenting in him a great example of true repentance and a great token of regeneration, a trophy of the resurrection for which we hope; when at the end of the world, the angels, radiant with joy, hymning and opening the heavens, shall receive into the celestial abodes those who truly repent; and before all, the Saviour Himself goes to meet them, welcoming them; holding forth the shadowless, ceaseless light; conducting them to the Father's bosom, to eternal life, to the kingdom of heaven.

Let one believe these things, and the disciples of God, and God, who is surety, the Prophecies, the Gospels, the Apostolic words; living in accordance with them, and lending his ears, and practising the deeds, he shall at his decease see the end and demonstration of the truths taught. For he who in this world welcomes the angel of penitence will not repent at the time that he leaves the body, nor be ashamed when he sees the Saviour approaching in His glory and with His army. He fears not the fire.

But if one chooses to continue and to sin perpetually in pleasures, and values indulgence here above eternal life, and turns away from the Saviour, who gives forgiveness; let him no more blame either God, or riches, or his having fallen, but his own soul, which voluntarily perishes. But to him who directs his eye to salvation and desires it, and asks with boldness and vehemence for its bestowal, the good Father who is in heaven will give the true purification and the changeless life. To whom, by His Son Jesus Christ, the Lord of the living and dead, and by the Holy Spirit, be glory, honour, power, eternal majesty, both now and ever, from generation to generation, and from eternity to eternity. Amen.

Origen
185-253

Origen is one of the most fascinating personalities of early
Christianity. His intellectual abilities and accomplishments are
astounding; his apostolic zeal knew no bounds. He received an
excellent education in the city of his birth, Alexandria. By the
age of eighteen he was the head of that city's catechetical
school. Throughout his lifetime he journeyed widely, to places
such as Rome, Arabia, Cappadocia, Palestine. Wherever he went,
his objective was to clarify and communicate his understanding
of the Word of God.

It is difficult to say what stands out as Origen's greatest
contribution to the Christian tradition. He is best known for his
scholarly work in Scripture, his theological writings and his
wide use of philosophy, particularly Platonism, to develop
Christian doctrine. Sustaining and enriching both his biblical
scholarship and his theological speculation was a life of prayer.
Origen was an unusually devout Christian. He spent his life seeking the unknowable depths of the love of God. His insatiable
drive, anchored in prayer, to penetrate the divine mystery gave
direction to his intellectual and apostolic life. It also enabled
him, a few years before his death, to withstand brutal torture
for the name of Christ during the persecution of Emperor
Decius.

Origen wrote the Contra Celsum *(Against Celsus) as a reply to a book by the pagan Celsus, which was entitled* The True Doctrine. *Celsus's document was a rather severe attack on Christianity and was established primarily on intellectual grounds. Origen's refutation consists of eight books. The reading below is taken from the eighth book. It reveals Origen's thinking around the relationship of the Christian to the emperor.*

Three particularly difficult questions are contained in this brief selection, questions which Christians of every century must face: (1) How is the Christian to look up to the temporal ruler? (2) What is the Christian attitude toward war? (3) To what degree should the Christian be involved in public service?

Celsus claimed that Christians were not good citizens because they did not properly honor the emperor. Origen replies that they very definitely do honor him and in a way that goes beyond the honor afforded the emperor by non-Christians. They pray for the emperor; they try to live their lives as citizens as well as possible; they work for harmony, even in Asia, Europe, Libya, and among Greeks and barbarians; they go the extra step and speak well of their enemies. Thus, the Christians honor the emperor by helping build up the empire. On the negative side, under no condition will they make the mistake of deifying the emperor.

The Christian does not fight for the emperor or go to war for him as an ordinary soldier does. Rather, Christians constitute a special army of piety which prays that everything which is opposed and hostile to those who act rightly may be destroyed. Piety offers greater service to the emperor than the soldier who kills all the enemies he can find.

Finally, if Christians seem to avoid public service, it is only that they might serve in the church of God for the salvation of men. As an aside, Origen mentions the requisites for true service: competence, soundness of doctrine and life, no love of power, and great humility.

AGAINST CELSUS

BOOK VIII

A fter all that Celsus has said about daemons needing burnt-offering and blood, he seems to come, I think, to making a wicked recantation when he says: *We ought rather to think that the daemons do not long for anything and need nothing, but are pleased with people who perform acts of devotion to them.* If he thought this was true, either he ought not to have made his earlier statements or he should have deleted this. However, human nature has not been entirely abandoned by God and His only-begotten truth. That is why Celsus spoke the truth in his words about the burnt-offering and blood for which daemons long. But again by his characteristic wickedness he sank down to falsehood comparing the daemons to men who strictly perform what is right even if no one acknowledges their gratitude to them, while to people who do return thanks they do acts of kindness.

He seems to me to be confused on this subject. Sometimes his mind is distracted by the daemons, and sometimes, when he recovers his senses a little from the irrationality which the daemons produce, he gets a glimpse of the truth. For again he continues: *But we ought never to forsake God at all, neither by day nor by night, neither in public nor in private. In every word and deed, and in fact, both with them and without them, let the soul be continually directed towards God.* I understand his words *with them* to mean *in public* and *in every deed* and *in every word.*

Then again, as if wrestling in mind against the distractions caused by the daemons and being for the most part overcome, he goes on to say: *If this is the case, what is dreadful in propiti-ating the powers on earth, both the others and the rulers and emperors among men, since not even they hold their position without the might of the daemons?* Earlier he did all he could to bring our soul down to the level of daemons. But now he wants us to propitiate also the rulers and emperors among men. Of these life and history are full, and I have not thought it necessary to quote any examples now.

64. We ought, then, to propitiate the one supreme God and to pray that He may be gracious, propitiating Him by piety and every virtue. But if Celsus also wants us to propitiate others besides the supreme God, let him realize that, just as a moving body is followed by the movement of its shadow, in the same way if the supreme God is propitiated it follows that all the angels who are dear to Him, and souls, and spirits, are kindly disposed as well. For they perceive who are worthy of God's kindness; and they not only become kindly disposed themselves to those who are worthy, but also work together with people who wish to worship the supreme God; and they are propitiated and pray and intercede together with them. Consequently we dare to say that for men who of set purpose put forward higher things when they pray to God, there are praying with them countless sacred powers who have not been invoked, assisting our mortal race. And, if I may say so, they strive without us because of the daemons whom they see fighting and working against the salvation especially of those who dedicate themselves to God and pay no attention to the hostility of daemons, if they savagely attack the person who avoids worshipping them by burnt-offering and blood and who in every way by words and deeds earnestly attempts to draw close and be united to the supreme God through Jesus. For he overthrew countless daemons when he went about healing and converting those who were under the power of the devil.

65. We ought to despise the kindly disposition of men and of emperors if to propitiate them means not only that we have to commit murders and acts of licentiousness and savagery, but also that we have to blaspheme the God of the universe or make some servile and cringing utterance, alien to men of bravery and nobility who, together with the other virtues, wish to possess courage as the greatest of them. Here we are doing nothing contrary to the law and word of God. We are not *mad*, nor do we *deliberately rush forward to arouse the wrath of an emperor or governor which brings upon us blows and tortures and even*

death. For we have read the precept: 'Let every soul be subject to the higher powers; for there is no power except by God's permission; the powers that be are ordained of God; so that those who resist the power resist the ordinance of God.' In our commentary on the epistle to the Romans we have studied these words at length to the best of our ability, and given various interpretations. But now with a view to our present task we have followed the more usual interpretation, and taken them more simply, since Celsus says: *Not even they hold their position without the might of daemons.*

The doctrine concerning the institution of emperors and rulers is profound. Many questions are raised on this subject by the existence of those who have ruled savagely and tyrannically, or of those who have drifted from exercising rule into debauchery and wantonness. On this account we here omit any discussion of the problem. However, we certainly do not *swear by the fortune (genius) of the emperor*, in the same way as we do not swear by any other supposed god. For if, as some have said, fortune is only a mode of expression like an opinion or a disagreement, we do not swear by something which does not exist as though it were a god, or as if it were a certain reality and had the power to do something, lest we apply the force of an oath to the wrong things. Or if, as some think who say that people who swear by the genius of the Roman emperor are swearing by his daemon, the so-called genius of the emperor is a daemon, in this case also we ought rather to die than to swear by a wicked and faithless daemon which often commits sin with the man to whom it has been assigned, or sins even more than he does.

66. Then again, like those who sometimes recover from daemonic possession and then once more have a relapse, as if he were sober Celsus says something to this effect: *If you happen to be a worshipper of God and someone commands you either to act blasphemously or to say some other disgraceful thing, you ought not to put any confidence in him at all. Rather than this you must remain firm in face of all tortures and endure any death rather than say or even think anything profane about God.* Then again because he is ignorant of our doctrine and, in addition to this, because he is muddled about all these things, he says: *But if anyone tells you to praise Helios or with a noble*

paean to speak in enthusiastic praise of Athena, in so doing you will appear much more to be worshipping the great God when you are singing a hymn to them. For the worship of God becomes more perfect by going through them all.

Our answer is that we do not wait for anyone to tell us to praise Helios since we have learnt to speak well not only of those which are subordinate to God's ordering but even of our enemies. We praise Helios (the sun) as a noble creation of God, which keeps God's laws and hears the saying, 'Praise the Lord, sun and moon', and with all its power praises the Father and Creator of the universe. But the traditions of the Greeks have concocted a legend about Athena, whom he puts with Helios, and, whether with or without some secret meaning, assert that she was born armed from the head of Zeus. And they say that she was chased at that time by Hephaestus who desired to ruin her virginity. She escaped from him, but loved and brought up the seed resulting from his lust which fell to the earth, and called the child Erichthonios whom, they say, Athena

The daughter of Zeus brought up, an offspring of the grain-giving earth.

So we see that anyone who addresses worship to Athena, the daughter of Zeus, must accept many myths and fictitious stories which would not be accepted by anyone who avoids myths and seeks the truth.

67. But supposing that Athena is given an allegorical interpretation, and is said to be Intelligence, let anyone show that she has a real and substantial existence and that her nature conforms to this allegorical meaning. But if Athena was some person who lived in ancient times and received honour because those who desired to have her name praised among men as if she were a goddess declared secret rites and mysteries to those who were in their power, how much rather ought we to avoid singing hymns of praise to Athena and glorifying her as a goddess if, in fact, it is not even right for us to worship the mighty sun, though we may speak well of it?

Celsus then says that we appear to worship the great God much more if we sing praise to Helios and Athena. We know that the reverse is the case. We address our hymns of praise to the supreme God alone and to His only-begotten Son, the divine Logos. And we sing praise to God and His only-begotten Son, as also do the sun, moon, and stars, and all the heavenly host. For all these form a divine choir and with just men sing the praise of the supreme God and His only-begotten Son.

We observed earlier that we ought not to swear by the emperor among men, nor by what is called his genius. It is therefore unnecessary for us to reply again to this: *Even if some one tells you to take an oath by an emperor among men, that also is nothing dreadful. For earthly things have been given to him, and whatever you receive in this life you receive from him.* But in our judgment it is certainly not true that all earthly things have been given to him; nor do we receive from him whatever we receive in this life. Whatever we receive that is right and good we have from God and His providence, such as cultivated crops and bread 'that strengthens man's heart', and the pleasant vine and 'wine that gladdens the heart of man'. From the providence of God we also have the fruits of the olive 'to make the face shine with olive-oil'.

68. Then Celsus next says that *we ought not to disbelieve the ancient man who long ago declared*

Let there be one king, him to whom the son of crafty
Kronos gave the power.

And he continues: *For, if you overthrow this doctrine, it is probable that the emperor will punish you. If everyone were to do the same as you, there would be nothing to prevent him from being abandoned, alone and deserted, while earthly things would come into the power of the most lawless and savage barbarians, and nothing more would be heard among men either of your worship or of the true wisdom.*

Let there be one ruler, one king,

I agree, yet not

Him to whom the son of crafty Kronos gave the power,

but the one whose power was given by Him who 'appoints and changes kings and from time to time raises up a useful man on the earth'. Kings are not appointed by the son of Kronos who drove his father from his rule and, as the Greek myths say, cast him down to Tartarus, not even if anyone were to interpret the story allegorically; but by God who governs all things and knows what He is doing in the matter of the appointment of kings.

Accordingly we do *overthrow the doctrine* of the words

To whom the son of crafty Kronos gave the power

because we are convinced that a God or the Father of a God would have no crafty or crooked designs. But we do not overthrow the doctrine of providence, and of the things which are produced by it, either as those which are primarily intended or as those which are the product of certain consequences. Moreover, it is not *probable* that an emperor would punish us for asserting that the son of crafty Kronos did not give him the power to reign, but that it was He who 'changes and appoints kings'. Let *all men do just the same* as I. Let them deny the Homeric doctrine, while keeping the doctrine of the divine right of the king and observing the command 'Honour the king.' Yet on such a basis as this neither would the emperor be left alone, nor would he be deserted, nor would earthly things be in the power of the most lawless and savage barbarians. For if, as Celsus has it, every one were to do the same as I, obviously the barbarians would also be converted to the word of God and would be most law-abiding and mild. And all other worship would be done away and only that of the Christians would prevail. One day it will be the only one to prevail, since the word is continually gaining possession of more souls.

69. Then as Celsus did not understand himself, his remarks are inconsistent with his words *For if every one were to do the same as you*, when he says: *You will surely not say that if the Romans were convinced by you and were to neglect their customary honours to both gods and men and were to call upon your Most High, or whatever name you prefer, He would come down and fight on their side, and they would have no need for any other defence. In earlier times also the same God made these promises and some far greater than these, so you say, to those who pay regard to him. But see how much help he has been to both them and you. Instead of being masters of the whole world, they have been left no land or home of any kind.*

Origen

*While in your case, if anyone does still wander about in secret,
yet he is sought out and condemned to death.*

He raises the question of what would happen if the Romans
were to become convinced by the doctrine of the Christians,
and neglect the honours paid to the supposed gods and the old
customs observed among men, and were to worship the Most
High. Let him hear, then, what our opinion is on these matters.
We believe that if two of us agree on earth as touching any thing,
if they pray for it, it shall be given to them by the heavenly
Father of the righteous. For God rejoices when the rational
beings agree and turns away when they disagree. What must we
think if it is not only, as now, just a few who agree but all the
Roman Empire? For they will be praying to the Logos who *in
earlier times* said to the Hebrews when they were being pursued
by the Egyptians: 'The Lord will fight for you, and you shall
keep silence.' And if they pray with complete agreement they
will be able to subdue many more pursuing enemies than those
that were destroyed by the prayer of Moses when he cried to
God and by the prayer of his companions. If God's promises
to those who keep the law have not come to pass, this is not
because God tells lies, but because the promises are made on
condition that the law is kept and that men live in accordance
with it. If the Jews, who received the promises upon these
conditions, have neither land nor home left, the reason for that
is to be found in all their transgressions of the law and especially
in their crime against Jesus.

70. However, if as Celsus suggests all the Romans were
convinced and prayed, they would be superior to their enemies,
or would not even fight wars at all, since they would be protected by divine power which is reported to have preserved five
entire cities for the sake of fifty righteous men. For the men of
God are the salt of the world, preserving the permanence of
things on earth, and earthly things hold together so long as the
salt does not turn bad. For if the salt has lost its savour, it is of
no further use either for the earth or for the dunghill, but is
cast out and trodden under foot by men. Let him who has ears
to hear, understand what this means. We, moreover, are only
persecuted when God allows the tempter and gives him authority
to persecute us. And when it is not God's will that we should

41

suffer this, even in the midst of the world that hates us by a miracle we live at peace, and are encouraged by him who said: 'Be of good cheer, I have overcome the world.' And he really has overcome the world, so that the world prevails only in so far as he who overcame it wills, for he received from his Father the victory over the world. And by his victory we are encouraged.

If it is his will that we should again wrestle and strive for our religion, let antagonists come forward. To them we will say: 'I can do all things by Christ Jesus our Lord who strengthens me.' For, though sparrows are sold, as the Bible has it, at two for a farthing, 'one does not fall into a snare against the will of the Father in heaven'. And to such an extent has divine providence included everything that not even the hairs of our head have escaped being numbered by Him.

71. Then again, as usual with Celsus, he gets muddled, and in his next remarks says things which none of us has written. This is what he says: *It is quite intolerable of you to say that if those who now reign over us were persuaded by you and were taken prisoner, you would persuade those who reign after them, and then others, if they too are taken prisoner, and others after them until, when all who are persuaded by you are taken prisoner, there will be a ruler who, being a sensible man and foreseeing what is happening, will utterly destroy you all before you destroy him first.* Reason does not require us to speak about these remarks; for none of us says of those who now reign that if they are persuaded and taken prisoner, we will then persuade their successors, and if they are taken prisoner we will in turn persuade those who follow them. And how did he come to remark that if the last in the succession are persuaded by us and are taken prisoner because they fail to defend themselves against their enemies, there will be a ruler who, being a sensible man and foreseeing what is happening, will utterly destroy us? In these words he seems to be putting together nonsensical statements and to have shrieked out stuff he invented out of his own head.

72. After this he utters a sort of wish: *Would that it were possible to unite under one law the inhabitants of Asia, Europe, and Libya, both Greeks and barbarians even at the furthest limits.* As if he thought this impossible he continues that *he*

42

who thinks this knows nothing. If I must say something about this subject which needs much study and argument, I will say a little in order to make it clear that his remark about uniting every rational being under one law is not only possible but even true. The Stoics say that when the element which, as they think, is stronger than the others becomes dominant, the conflagration will take place and all things change into fire. But we believe that at some time the Logos will have overcome the entire rational nature, and will have remodelled every soul to his own perfection, when each individual simply by the exercise of his freedom will choose what the Logos wills and will be in that state which he has chosen. And we hold that just as it is unlikely that some of the consequences of physical diseases and wounds would be too hard for any medical art, so also it is unlikely in the case of souls that any of the consequences of evil would be incapable of being cured by the rational and supreme God. For since the Logos and the healing power within him are more powerful than any evils in the soul, he applies this power to each individual according to God's will, and the end of the treatment is the abolition of evil. But to teach whether or not the consequence is that it can under no circumstances be allowed any further existence, is not relevant to the present discussion.

The prophecies say much in obscure terms about the total abolition of evils and the correction of every soul. But it is enough now to quote the passage from Zephaniah which reads as follows:

> Get ready and wake up early; all their small grapes are destroyed. On this account wait patiently for me, saith the Lord, in the day when I rise up for a witness; for my decision is to assemble the peoples to receive the kings, to pour out upon them all the anger of my wrath. For in the fire of my zeal all the earth shall be consumed. Then I will turn to the peoples a language for its generation, that they may all call upon the name of the Lord and serve him under one yoke. From the furthest rivers of Ethiopia they shall offer sacrifices to me, in that day thou shalt not be ashamed of all thy habits which thou hast impiously practised against me. Then I will take away from thee

the contempt of thy pride, and thou shalt no longer continue to boast upon my holy mountain. And I will leave in you a people meek and humble, and the remnants of Israel shall fear the name of the Lord, and they shall not do wickedness nor say foolish things, and a crafty tongue shall not be found in their mouth. Wherefore they themselves shall feed and lie down and there shall be none to make them afraid.

Anyone who has the ability to enter into the meaning of the scripture and has understood all these statements may show the explanation of the prophecy, and, in particular, may study what is the meaning of the words that when all the earth is consumed there will be turned to the people 'a language for its generation', which corresponds to the state of affairs before the Confusion. And let him understand what is the meaning of the words 'That all men may call upon the name of the Lord, and may serve him under one yoke', so that 'the contempt of their pride' is taken away and there is no more wickedness nor foolish words nor crafty tongue.

I have thought it right to quote this passage, with an ordinary interpretation and without a careful discussion, because of the remark of Celsus who thinks that it is impossible for the inhabitants of Asia, Europe, and Libya, both Greeks and barbarians, to be agreed. And it is probably true that such a condition is impossible for those who are still in the body; but it is certainly not impossible after they have been delivered from it.

73. Then Celsus next exhorts us to *help the emperor with all our power, and cooperate with him in what is right, and fight for him, and be fellow-soldiers if he presses for this, and fellow-generals with him.* We may reply to this that at appropriate times we render to the emperors divine help, if I may so say, by taking up even the whole armour of God. And this we do in obedience to the apostolic utterance which says: 'I exhort you, therefore, first to make prayers, supplications, intercessions, and thanksgivings for all men, for emperors, and all that are in authority.' Indeed, the more pious a man is, the more effective he is in helping the emperors—more so than the soldiers who go out into the lines and kill all the enemy troops that they can.

We would also say this to those who are alien to our faith and ask us to fight for the community and to kill men: that it is also your opinion that the priests of certain images and wardens of the temples of the gods, as you think them to be, should keep their right hand undefiled for the sake of the sacrifices, that they may offer the customary sacrifices to those who you say are gods with hands unstained by blood and pure from murders. And in fact when war comes you do not enlist the priests. If, then, this is reasonable, how much more reasonable is it that, while others fight, Christians also should be fighting as priests and worshippers of God, keeping their right hands pure and by their prayers to God striving for those who fight in a righteous cause and for the emperor who reigns righteously, in order that everything which is opposed and hostile to those who act rightly may be destroyed? Moreover, we who by our prayers destroy all daemons which stir up wars, violate oaths, and disturb the peace, are of more help to the emperors than those who seem to be doing the fighting. We who offer prayers with righteousness, together with ascetic practices and exercises which teach us to despise pleasures and not to be led by them, are cooperating in the tasks of the community. Even more do we fight on behalf of the emperor. And though we do not become fellow-soldiers with him, even if he presses for this, yet we are fighting for him and composing a special army of piety through our intercessions to God.

74. If Celsus wishes us to be generals for our country, let him realize that we do this; but we do not do so with a view to being seen by men and to being proud about it. Our prayers are made in secret in the mind itself, and are sent up as from priests on behalf of the people in our country. Christians do more good to their countries than the rest of mankind, since they educate the citizens and teach them to be devoted to God, the guardian of their city; and they take those who have lived good lives in the most insignificant cities up to a divine and heavenly city. To them it could be said: You were faithful in a very insignificant city; come also to the great city where 'God stands in the congregation of the gods and judges between gods in the midst', and numbers you even with them, if you no longer 'die like a man' and do not 'fall like one of the princes'.

75. Celsus exhorts us also to *accept public office in our country if it is necessary to do this for the sake of the preservation of the laws and of piety.* But we know of the existence in each city of another sort of country, created by the Logos of God. And we call upon those who are competent to take office, who are sound in doctrine and life, to rule over the churches. We do not accept those who love power. But we put pressure on those who on account of their great humility are reluctant hastily to take upon themselves the common responsibility of the church of God. And those who rule us well are those who have had to be forced to take office, being constrained by the great King who, we are convinced, is the Son of God, the divine Logos. And if those who are chosen as rulers in the church rule well over God's country (I mean the church), or if they rule in accordance with the commands of God, they do not on this account defile any of the appointed civic laws.

If Christians do avoid these responsibilities, it is not with the motive of shirking the public services of life. But they keep themselves for a more divine and necessary service in the church of God for the sake of the salvation of men. Here it is both necessary and right for them to be leaders and to be concerned about all men, both those who are within the Church, that they may live better every day, and those who appear to be outside it, that they may become familiar with the sacred words and acts of worship; and that, offering a true worship to God in this way and instructing as many as possible, they may become absorbed in the word of God and the divine law, and so be united to the supreme God through the Son of God, the Logos, Wisdom, Truth, and Righteousness, who unites to Him every one who has been persuaded to live according to God's will in all things.

76. You have here, holy Ambrose, the end of the task that you set me, according to the ability possessed by and granted to me. We have concluded in eight books everything which we have thought fit to say in reply to Celsus' book entitled *The True Doctrine.* It is for the reader of his treatise, and of our reply against him, to judge which of the two breathes more of the spirit of the true God and of the temper of devotion towards

Him and of the truth attainable by men, that is, of sound doctrines which lead men to live the best life.

Observe, however, that Celsus promises to compose *another
treatise* after this, in which he has promised to *teach those who
are willing and able to believe* him *the right way to live*. If he
did not write the second book which he promised, we may well
be content with the eight books written in reply to his argument. But if he began the second book and finished it, search
out and send the treatise that we may make to that also the
reply that is given to us by the Father of the truth, and may
refute the false opinions in that as well. If in any place he makes
some true statement, we shall bear witness that he is right in
this respect without seeking occasion for disagreement.

Tertullian
160-220

Quintus Septimus Florens Tertullianus was one of the
greatest Christian writers of the early church. He was born
around 160, most probably in Carthage. After receiving an excellent education, he practiced law at Rome. Sometime around
195, Tertullian became a Christian. He immediately oriented
both his strong personality and his unusual talents toward the
building up of the church. He served as an instructor of cate-
chumens and put his genius for writing to good use, particularly
as an apologist. Gradually he was attracted toward a heretical
group known as the Montanists. He joined them in 212 or 213.
Tertullian lived the remainder of his life in Carthage. He died
sometime after 220.

Several of Tertullian's personal characteristics worked their
way into his writing. He was an unusually honest man with very
strong convictions and moral principles. In the face of opposition or moral weakness, he was intolerant and impatient. He
had little time for the person who did not stand wholeheartedly
by what he professed. His treatises were well known for their
sarcasm, bitter humor and straightforward criticism. Yet, his
creativity, his imagination and his capacity to coin lasting
phrases ranks him as one of the great Latin writers of his time.

Of the many treatises he wrote, thirty-one are extant. They
are traditionally classified as apologetical, polemical and disci-

plinary. The selections below are taken from his apologetical writings. Tertullian, along with other early Christian authors, took on the responsibility of demonstrating the validity of the Christian way of life. Negatively, he refuted the many false reports about Christians; positively he argued that the Christian is actually the best of all citizens within the state.

Tertullian's Apology, *written in 197, is considered a classic in Christian literature. It is a passionate plea for social justice. The Christian has the same right as any other citizen to a fair hearing, yet the worst criminal is treated better than the best Christian. Tertullian shows that the Christians support the emperor, especially by their prayers, their respect and their loyalty. He describes the lifestyle of the Christian community and explains the why of it. Few documents have more powerfully exposed the blindness of human prejudice toward truth.*

To Scapula, *written more than a decade later, is a brief open letter to the governor of proconsular Africa. In it, Tertullian defends the principle of freedom of conscience. Every person has the right to worship as he so chooses. "It is the law of mankind and the natural right of each individual to worship what he thinks proper, nor does the religion of one man either help or hinder another. But, it is not proper for religion to compel men to religion, which should be accepted on one's own accord, not by force." (Chapter 2)*

Both treatises are excellent examples of Tertullian's capacity to bring the written word to life. They also reveal the social conditions and problems that the Christian of the early third century had to face. The same questions, viz., social injustice and freedom of conscience, continue to disturb the Christian world. Though circumstances have changed, the basic insights of Tertullian remain valid. However, in some situations today, it may be the Christian who must be reminded of the principles of social justice and freedom of conscience.

APOLOGY AND
TO SCAPULA

CHAPTER 1

APOLOGY

Magistrates of the Roman Empire, seated as you are before the eyes of all, in almost the highest position in the state to pronounce judgment: if you are not allowed to conduct an open and public examination and inquiry as to what the real truth is with regard to the Christians; if, in this case alone your authority fears or blushes to conduct a public investigation with the diligence demanded by justice; if, in fine—as happened lately in the private courts—hatred of this group has been aroused to the extent that it actually blocks their defense, then let the truth reach your ears by the private and quiet avenue of literature.

Truth makes no appeal on her own behalf, because she does not wonder at her present condition. She knows that she plays the role of an alien on earth, that among strangers she readily discovers enemies, but she has her origin, abode, hope, recompense, and honor in heaven. Meanwhile, there is one thing for which she strives: that she be not condemned without a hearing. As for the laws, supreme in their own realm, what have they to lose if she be given a hearing? Or shall their power be glorified the more for *this*, that they condemn her without a hearing? But, if they condemn her without a hearing, they will incur the stigma of acting unjustly; in addition, they will deserve the suspicion of realizing to some extent their injustice, in that they refuse to hear a case on which they would be unable to pass adverse judgment once it was heard.

This, then, is the first grievance we lodge against you, the injustice of the hatred you have for the name of Christian. The motive which appears to excuse this injustice is precisely that which both aggravates and convicts it; namely ignorance. For, what is more unjust than that men should hate what they do not know, even though the matter itself deserves hatred? Only when one knows whether a thing deserves hatred does it deserve it. But, when there is no knowledge of what is deserved, how is the justice of hatred defensible? Justice must be proved not by the fact of a thing's existence, but by knowledge of it. When men hate because they are in ignorance of the nature of the object of their hatred, what is to prevent that object from being such that they ought not to hate it? Thus we counterbalance each attitude by its opposite: men remain in ignorance as long as they hate, and they hate unjustly as long as they remain in ignorance.

The proof of their ignorance, which condemns while it excuses their injustice, is this: In the case of all who formerly indulged in hatred [of Christianity] because of their ignorance of the nature of what they hated, their hatred comes to an end as soon as their ignorance ceases. From this group come the Christians, as a result, assuredly, of their personal experience. They begin now to hate what once they were and to profess what once they hated; and the Christians are really as numerous as you allege us to be. Men cry that the city is filled with Christians; they are in the country, in the villages, on the islands; men and women, of every age, of every state and rank of life, are transferring to this group, and this they lament as if it were some personal injury.

In spite of this fact, men's minds are not directed to the consideration of some underlying good. They cannot guess more accurately; they do not choose to investigate more closely. Here only does the curiosity of mankind lack its keenness. They delight in their ignorance, while others rejoice in their knowledge. How much more fault would Anacharsis have found with those who, though lacking in insight, pass judgment on those who have it than he did in the case of those unskilled in music judging musicians! They prefer to remain ignorant because they are already filled with hatred. Consequently, they form a preconceived idea with regard to that of which they are ignorant. Yet, if they knew it, they could not hate it; because, if no ground for their hatred be found, it would certainly be best to cease their unjust hatred. On the other hand, if it is justly deserved, then their hatred, far from losing anything, even by the authority of justice itself, actually gains more reason for its continuance.

'But,' says one, 'a thing is not considered good simply because it wins many converts: How great a number of men are given thorough training for evil! How many go astray into ways of perversity!' Who denies that? Yet, if a thing is really evil, not even those whom it attracts dare to defend it as good. All evil is drenched with fear or shame by nature. For example, evildoers are anxious to remain in hiding. They shun the light. They tremble when caught; they deny when accused. Even under torture they do not easily or always confess. When condemned beyond all hope, they lament. They tell of the attacks upon themselves of an evil spirit; their moral weaknesses they impute to fate or to the stars. What they recognize as evil they do not want to acknowledge as their own. In what respect is the Christian like this? No one of them is ashamed, no one has any regrets, except that he was not a Christian earlier. If a charge is brought against him, he glories in it. If he is accused, he offers no defense. When questioned, he confesses of his own accord. For the word of condemnation he gives thanks. What kind of evil is this that has none of the natural signs of evil— fear, shame, subterfuge, repentance, lament? What crime is this for which the accused rejoices, when the accusation is the object of his prayer and the condemnation his joy? *You* cannot call this madness, you who stand convicted of knowing nothing about it.

CHAPTER 2

If, then, it is decided that we are the most wicked of men, why do you treat us so differently from those who are on a par with us, that is, from all other criminals? The same treatment ought to be meted out for the same crime. When others are charged with the same crimes as we, they use their own lips and the hired eloquence of others to prove their innocence. There is full liberty given to answer the charge and to cross-question, since it is unlawful for men to be condemned without defense or without a hearing. Christians alone are permitted to say nothing that would clear their name, vindicate the truth, and aid the judge to come to a fair decision. One thing only is what they wait for; this is the only thing necessary to arouse public hatred: the confession of the name of Christian, not an investigation of the charge. Yet, suppose you are trying any other criminal. If he confesses to the crime of murder, sacrilege, incest, or treason—to particularize the indictments hurled against us—you are not satisfied to pass sentence immediately; you weigh the attendant circumstances, the character of the deed, the number of times it was committed, the time, the place, the witnesses, and the partners-in-crime. In our case there is nothing of this sort. No matter what false charge is made against us, we must be made to confess it; for example, how many murdered babies one has devoured, how many deeds of incest one has committed under cover of darkness, what cooks and what dogs were on hand. Oh, what glory for that governor who should have discovered someone who had already consumed a hundred infants!

On the other hand, we find that it has been forbidden to search us out. For when Pliny the Younger was in charge of his province and had condemned certain Christians and had driven others from their established position, he was so disturbed because of the numbers involved that he consulted Trajan, emperor at the time, as to what he should do thereafter. He explained that, except for their obstinate refusal to offer sacrifice, he had learned nothing else about their religious rites except that they met before daybreak to sing to Christ and to God and to bind themselves by oath to a way of life which forbade murder, adultery, dishonesty, treachery, and all other crimes. Trajan wrote back that men of this kind should not be sought out, but, when brought to court, they should be punished.

Oh, how unavoidably ambiguous was that decision! He says that they should not be sought—as though they were innocent; then prescribes that they should be punished—as though they were guilty! He spares them, yet vents his anger upon them; he pretends to close his eyes, yet directs attention toward them! Judgment, why do you thus ensnare yourself? If you condemn them, why not also search for them? If you do not search for them, why not also acquit them? Throughout the provinces troops of soldiers are assigned to track down robbers. Against traitors and public enemies each individual constitutes a soldier: the search is extended even to comrades and accomplices. Only the Christian may not be sought out—but he may be brought to court. As though a search were intended to bring about something else than his appearance in court! So, you condemn a man when he is brought into court, although no one wanted him to be sought out. He has earned punishment, I suppose, not on the ground that he is guilty, but because he was discovered for whom no search had to be made.

Then, too, when you deal with us in this matter, you do not follow the procedure prescribed for judging criminals. To others who deny their guilt you apply torture to force them to confess; to Christians alone, to force them to deny. Yet, if it were something evil, we would certainly go on denying it, and you would try to force us, by torture, to confess. For you would not think that an investigation of our crimes was unnecessary on the ground that you were sure they were committed because of the mere confession of the name. Why, to this very day, after the confession of a murderer, you, who know what murder is, nevertheless extract by torture the details of the crime from him who has confessed it. Much more perverse is your treatment when you take it for granted from the confession of the name that our crimes have been committed and then, by torture, compel us to add a confession. You intend that by one and the same act we deny both our name and the crimes which you had taken for granted were committed merely from the confession of the name.

It is not your wish, I suppose, that we, whom you believe the most utterly worthless of creatures, should perish. You are in the habit of saying to a murderer: 'Deny it!' If one accused of sacrilege persists in confessing his guilt, you bid him be tortured [till he denies it]. If you do not act thus toward the guilty, then you indicate that you consider us absolutely innocent; you do not wish us, being absolutely innocent, to persist in a confession of that which you realize you must condemn, not out of justice, but of necessity. A man proclaims: 'I am a Christian.' He says what he is; you want to hear what he is not. You, who preside as judges to extract the truth, in our case alone take pains to hear a lie. 'I am,' says one, 'what you ask if I am. Why do you torture me into lying? I confess, and you torture me! What would you do if I were to deny?' Certainly, when others deny, you do not readily believe them; if we deny, you immediately believe us!

Let this perversity of yours lead you to suspect that there is some secret underlying power which uses you as tools against the form and nature of exercising justice, and, in fact, against the very laws themselves. Unless I am mistaken, the laws demand that evil-doers be brought to light, not concealed; they prescribe that confessed criminals be condemned, not acquitted. This is what senatorial decrees and imperial rescripts clearly set down. This empire, of which you are the ministers, is a government controlled by free citizens, not by tyrants. Under tyrants, torture was employed in place of punishment; under you, it is restricted to examination only. Keep your law in so far as torture is necessary to effect a confession, and then, if it is forestalled by confession, torture will be unnecessary; sentence is then required. The guilty must be freed by, not freed from, paying the punishment which is his due.

Finally, no one makes an effort to acquit *him*. He cannot even entertain a desire for this; that is why no one is forced into a denial. In the case of the Christian, you regard him as guilty of every crime, the enemy of the gods, rulers, laws, morals, and all nature. Yet you force him into a denial that you may acquit him, although you could not possibly acquit him unless he were to deny. You are making a sham of the laws; you want him to deny that he is guilty, so that you may *make* him guiltless—and this, really, against his will! Now, you say, he is no longer responsible for his past. Whence comes this perversity of yours, that you should fail to realize that a voluntary confession is more to be trusted than a forced denial? Or [should you not fear] that one who has been forced into a denial may have made his denial without good faith, and, being acquitted, may immediately after the trial laugh at your malevolence and become once again a Christian?

Since, then, you treat us differently from other criminals in every respect, having in mind one object only, that we may be cut off from that name—for we are cut off only if we do what non-Christians do—you can understand that there is no crime at all in our case; it is a question merely of a name. This name a certain power of a rival agency persecutes, making this its first and foremost aim, that men may be unwilling to obtain certain knowledge about that of which they are certain they have no knowledge. Hence it is that they believe stories about us which are not proved and they do not want any investigation, lest it be proved that the stories which they prefer to have believed are not true. It follows that the name, an object of enmity to that rival agency, is condemned by its mere admission because of crimes presumed, not proved. Therefore, if we confess, we are tortured; if we persevere, we are punished; if we deny, we are acquitted, because it is an attack on a name.

Finally, why do you read from your indictment that so-and-so is a Christian? Why not also that he is a murderer, if the Christian is a murderer? Why not adulterer, also, or whatever else you believe us to be? In our regard alone is it a cause of shame and annoyance to report us with the specification of our crimes? If the term 'Christian' involves in itself no element of guilt, it is extremely ridiculous that the charge is one of name only.

CHAPTER 3

What should one say of the fact that many shut their eyes and force themselves to such hatred of the name that, even when they speak favorably of someone, they insert some hateful remark about this name? 'Caius Seius is a good man, except that he is a Christian.' Similarly, someone else says: 'I am surprised that Lucius Titius, otherwise a man of sense, has suddenly become a Christian!' No one stops to think whether Caius is good and Lucius sensible because he is a Christian, or is a Christian because he is sensible and good! Men praise what they know and find fault with what they do not know. They contaminate their knowledge with their ignorance, although it would be more correct to form a preconceived idea with regard to what is unknown from what is known than to condemn beforehand what is known because of what is unknown.

Others censure those whom they knew in the past, before they acquired this name, as vagrant, good-for-nothing scoundrels, and they censure them in the very act of praising them. In the blindness of their hatred they stumble into favorable criticism. 'That woman! How dissolute and frivolous she was! And that young man, how much more prodigal and debauched he used to be! They have become Christians.' Thus, the name which was responsible for their reformation is set down as a charge against them. Some, even, at the expense of their own advantage, bargain with their hatred, satisfied to suffer a personal loss, provided that their home be freed from the object of their hatred. A wife who has become chaste is cast out by her husband now that he is relieved of his jealous suspicions of her. A son, now docile, is disowned by a father who was patient with him in the past. A servant, now trustworthy, is banished from the sight of a master who was formerly indulgent. To the degree that one is reformed under the influence of the name he gives offense. The Christians' goodness is outweighed by the hatred borne them.

Well, then, if it is simply the name that is hated, what guilt can attach to names? What fault can be found with words except that something in the word sounds rough or unlucky or abusive or immodest? The term 'Christian,' on the other hand, as far as its etymology goes, is derived from 'unction.' Even when you mispronounce it 'Chrestian'—for your knowledge of the word itself is uncertain—it is made up of 'sweetness' or 'kindness.' Hence, in harmless men even a harmless name is hated.

But, I suppose, the religion is hated in the name of its founder. Is it anything new that some way of life gives to its followers the name of its teacher? Are not philosophers called Platonists, Epicureans, Pythagoreans after their founders? Are not the Stoics and Academics so called from the places of their meetings and assemblies? In the same way, are not doctors named after Erasistratus, grammarians after Aristarchus, and even cooks after Apicius? No one takes offense at the profession of a name which has been handed down by a teacher together with his teaching. Of course, if anyone will prove that a school is bad and its founder likewise bad, he will prove also that the name is bad and deserves hatred because of the worthless character of the school and its founder. Consequently, before hating a name, it is fitting to examine first the character of the school with reference to its founder or the character of the founder with reference to his school. But, in this case, investigation and knowledge of both are neglected. The name is seized upon; the name is subjected to punishment; although this religion and its founder are unknown, a word alone condemns them in advance because of the name they bear, not because they are convicted of anything.

CHAPTER 4

Now that I have set down these remarks as a preface, as it were, to stigmatize the injustice of the public hatred against us, I shall take the stand to defend our innocence. Not only shall I refute the charges which are brought against us, but I shall even hurl them back upon those who make them, so that men may thereby know that among the Christians those crimes do not exist which they are not unaware exist among themselves; and that, at the same time, they may blush when, as utter reprobates, they accuse—I do not say the most righteous of men—but, as they themselves would have it, their equals. We shall reply to each charge individually: to those which we are said to commit in secret, and to those which we are found to be committing before the eyes of all—charges on the basis of which we are held to be criminals, deceivers, reprobates, and objects of ridicule.

Inasmuch as truth, which is on our side, answers all charges, in the last resort the authority of the law is hurled against it in such a way that either there is nothing to be said by way of retracting after the law has been appealed to, or, to your regret, the necessity of obedience takes precedence with you to regard for the truth. Therefore, I shall first discuss with you the question of the law, inasmuch as you are its protectors. In the first place, then, when you harshly lay down the law and say: 'Your existence is illegal!' and when you make this charge without any further investigation—which would certainly be more humane—you make profession of violence and of an unjust, tyrannical domination, if you are saying that Christianity is illegal simply because that is your will, not because it really ought to be illegal. On the other hand, if you want a thing to be illegal because it ought to be, unquestionably that ought to be illegal which is evil. And, assuredly, from this very fact it is a foregone conclusion that what is good is legal. If I find that something is good which a law of yours has forbidden, is the law not powerless to keep me, in view of that previous conclusion, from doing that which, if it were evil, the law with full right would forbid? If a law of yours has erred, it is, I presume, because it was conceived by man; it certainly did not fall from heaven.

Is it any wonder to you that a man may have erred in making a law or that he recovered his senses and rejected it? Why, consider even the laws of Lycurgus himself, revised by the Spartans: did they not inflict such sorrow upon their author that he condemned himself to solitary starvation? And what about yourselves? As your research daily throws more light upon the darkness of former days, do you not cut and hew all that old, overgrown forest of laws with the new axes of imperial rescripts and edicts? Consider the Papian laws which oblige men to beget children at an earlier age than the Julian laws oblige people to contract marriage. Were they not, in spite of the weight of authority due to their old age, just a short time ago annulled by Severus, the most conservative of emperors, on the ground that they were utterly devoid of sense? Again, the law used to be that those found guilty of bankruptcy might be cut in pieces by their creditors. Yet, by common consent, this cruel stipulation was later abrogated, and capital punishment was exchanged for a mark of disgrace. Proscription of a man's goods was intended to bring the blood to his cheeks rather than to shed it.

How many of your laws lie hidden which still need to be reformed—laws which are not recommended by length of years or the high position of him who framed them, but solely by their profession of justice! On this ground, when they are recognized as being unjust, they deserve to be condemned, even when they themselves condemn. How is it that we call them unjust? As a matter of fact, if it is merely a name they are punishing, they are actually stupid. On the other hand, if it is a question of actions, why do they depend solely on the name in punishing actions, whereas in the case of others these deeds are punished when it has been proved that they were committed, and not merely because of a name? I am, they say, an adulterer. Why do they not question me? I am guilty of child murder. Why do they not wring a confession from me? I commit some crime against the gods, against the Caesars. Why am I not given a hearing, since I have an answer which will clear my name? There is no law which forbids an investigation of the crime it prohibits, because a judge does not punish justly unless he knows that some illegal act has been committed, nor does a citizen faithfully observe a law if he is ignorant of what kind of crime the law punishes. No law has to render an account of its own justice solely to itself, but to those from whom it expects observance. Besides, a law is under suspicion if it refuses to submit to examination, whereas it is worthless if it demands obedience without examination.

CHAPTER 5

Let us consider to some extent the origin of laws of this sort. There was an ancient decree that no god should be consecrated by a victorious general without the approval of the Senate. M. Aemilius is well aware of this law in connection with his god, Alburnus. It likewise carries weight for our cause, that among you divinity depends on human judgment. Unless a god please man, he simply will not be a god; man will have to be well-disposed toward the god! So Tiberius, in whose reign the name of Christian entered the world, hearing from Palestine in Syria information which had revealed the truth of Christ's divinity, brought the matter before the Senate, with previous indication of his own approval. The Senators, on the ground that they had not verified the facts, rejected it. Caesar maintained his opinion and threatened dire measures against those who brought accusations against the Christians. Consult your histories: you will find in them that Nero was the first to rage with the imperial sword against this religion which was just at that particular time coming to life at Rome. We actually glory that such a person took the lead in condemning us. For, whoever knows him can understand that nothing save some magnificent good was ever condemned by Nero. Domitian, too, somewhat of a Nero in cruelty, made some attempts. But—being also, to a certain degree, human—he soon put a halt to what he had initiated and even recalled those whom he had exiled. Such have always been our persecutors, unjust, wicked, depraved men whom you yourselves are accustomed to condemn, while you have regularly recalled those whom they have condemned.

But, of so many emperors from that time down to our own day who were wise in matters divine and human, show me one who persecuted the Christians! On the contrary, we can point out our protector, if you will examine the letters of the most venerable emperor, Marcus Aurelius. In these letters he attests that the great drought in Germany was relieved by rain which fell in answer to the prayers of the Christians who happened to be in his army. Although he did not openly revoke the edict of persecution from these men, yet in another way he openly counteracted its effect, by threatening their persecutors with a sentence which was actually more horrible. What sort of laws, then, are those which are set in operation against us only by emperors who are wicked and devoid of justice, base and impious, deceptive and mentally deranged? These are the laws which Trajan nullified in part by forbidding that a search be made for Christians, laws which no Hadrian—eager investigator though he was of all that attracted his inquisitive mind, no Vespasian—conqueror though he was of the Jews, no Pius, no Verus ever enforced! Assuredly, the worst of men would be more readily adjudged worthy of utter extermination by the best of emperors as being their natural enemies than by men of their own kind!

CHAPTER 6

Now, I should like the most scrupulous guardians and avengers of the laws and institutions of our forefathers to answer with regard to their loyalty, their respect, and their obedience toward the decrees of their ancestors: whether they have been faithful to all of them; whether they have in no respect deviated from any of them, or caused any necessary and appropriate matters of discipline to be forgotten. What has become of those laws which restrained extravagance and bribery? which forbade the spending of more than a hundred asses on a supper, or the serving of more than one hen—and that an unfattened one? which removed a patrician from the Senate because he had ten pounds of silver, on the serious pretext of too lofty ambition? which destroyed theaters just as soon as they were erected, as tending to corrupt morals? which did not permit the marks of dignity and noble lineage to be usurped rashly or with impunity? I observe that suppers now have to be called 'centenarian' because of the 100,000 sesterces expended on them. Silver from the mines is even being converted into dishes—not for the use of Senators, which would be a mere trifle—but rather for freedmen or those whip-crackers whose backs are even yet breaking the whips. I see, too, that a single theater is not sufficient, or one without an awning. For, lest winter weather cast a chill upon their impure pleasures, the Spartans were the first to conceive the idea of a mantle for the games. I see, too, that there is no difference left between honorable matrons and prostitutes, as far as their dress is concerned.

As a matter of fact, as regards women, those customs of our ancestors which protected their modesty and sobriety have fallen into disregard. Why, no woman was acquainted with any gold except that on the one finger which her spouse had pledged to himself with the engagement ring. Women abstained so completely from wine that one who had unlocked the cupboard of the wine cellar was forced by her own family to die of starvation. In fact, under Romulus, a woman who had merely touched wine was put to death with impunity by her husband Metennius. That is the reason, too, why women had to offer a kiss to their relatives, that they might judge their breath. What has become of that conjugal happiness so fostered by high moral living that for nearly six hundred years after Rome was founded no home sued for a divorce? Look at women now. Every limb is weighed down with gold; because of wine, no kiss is freely given. Yes, and now it is a divorce which is prayed for, as though that were the natural issue of marriage!

Even the decrees which your fathers had prudently passed respecting your very gods, you, their most dutiful sons, have abolished. The consuls, with full approval of the Senate, drove Father Bacchus and his mysteries not only from Rome but from all Italy. During the consulship of Piso and Gabinius, men who were by no means Christians, it was forbidden to have Serapis, Isis, and Harpocrates with his dog-headed Anubis admitted into the Capitoline temple; that is, they were expelled from the solemn assembly of the gods. Their shrines were overthrown and they were banished. Thus did the consuls check the evils of these base and hateful superstitions. These gods *you* have restored, conferring upon them the utmost dignity.

Where is your religious feeling? Where is that reverence which you owe your ancestors? By your dress, your food, your manner of living, your attitude of mind, in fine, by your very speech, you have renounced your forefathers. You are forever praising bygone days, but in a far different manner do you live your everyday life. From this it is clear that, in departing from the laudable customs of your ancestors, you retain and preserve those which you should not, while those which you should have preserved, you have not. Consider the traditions of your fathers which you appear to be keeping most faithfully, wherein, principally, you have deemed Christians guilty of transgression (I refer to your devotedness in worshipping the gods, a matter in which men of old most grievously erred). Though you have re-erected altars to Serapis, become by now a Roman, though you offer your licentious orgies to Bacchus, now a naturalized Italian, I will show in its proper place that these traditions are being despised, neglected, and destroyed by you in contradiction to the precedent set by your ancestors. I will now reply to that infamous charge about our clandestine crimes, that I may clear my path for those which are more manifest.

CHAPTER 7

We are spoken of as utter reprobates and are accused of having sworn to murder babies and to eat them and of committing adulterous acts after the repast. Dogs, you say, the pimps of darkness, overturn candles and procure license for our impious lusts. We are always spoken of in this way, yet you take no pains to bring into the light the charges which for so long a time have been made against us. Now, either bring them into the light, if you believe them, or stop believing them, inasmuch as you have not brought them to light! Because of your hypocrisy, the objection is made against you that the evil does not exist which you yourselves dare not bring to light. Far different is the duty you enjoin upon the executioner against the Christians, not to make them state what they do, but to make them deny what they are.

The origin of this religion, as we have already said, dates from the time of Tiberius. Truth and hatred came into existence simultaneously. As soon as the former appeared, the latter began its enmity. It has as many foes as there are outsiders, particularly among Jews because of their jealousy, among soldiers because of their blackmailing, and even among the very members of our own household because of corrupt human nature. Day by day we are besieged; day by day we are betrayed; oftentimes, in the very midst of our meetings and gatherings, we are surprised by an assault. Who has ever come upon a baby wailing, as the accusation has it? Who has ever kept for the judge's inspection the jaws of Cyclopes and Sirens, bloodstained as he had found them? Who has ever found any traces of impurity upon [Christian] wives? Who has discovered such crimes, yet concealed them or been bribed to keep them secret when dragging these men off to court? If we always keep under cover, whence the betrayal of our crimes?

Rather, who could have been the traitors? Certainly not the accused themselves, since the obligation of pledged silence is binding upon all mysteries by their very nature. The mysteries of Samothrace and of Eleusis are shrouded in silence; how much more such rites as these which, if they were made public, would provoke at once the hatred of all mankind—while God's wrath is reserved for the future? If, then, Christians themselves are not the betrayers, it follows that outsiders are. Whence do outsiders get their knowledge, since even holy initiation rites always ban the uninitiated and are wary of witnesses? Unless you mean that the wicked are less afraid.

The nature of rumor is well known to all. It was your own poet who said: 'Rumor, an evil surpassing all evils in speed.' Why call rumor an evil? Because it flies? Because it testifies? Or because it generally lies? Even when it has a modicum of truth in it, rumor is not free from some taint of falsehood; it detracts from, adds to, or deviates from the truth. What of the fact that it exists only on this condition, that it may not continue in existence unless it lies, and its life endures only so long as there is no proof? Of course, when proof comes, rumor ceases to exist; having, as it were, fulfilled its office of reporting the news, it passes it on as a fact. From then on the story is considered a fact, and called a fact. For example, no one says: 'They say that such a thing has happened at Rome,' or: 'The story is that so-and-so was assigned to a province,' but: 'So-and-so was assigned to a province,' and: 'Such a thing happened at Rome.'

Rumor, a word designating uncertainty, has no place where there is certainty. But does anyone except the unthinking believe rumor? One who is wise surely does not heed uncertainty. Everyone can reflect that however great the zeal with which the tale has been spread, however strong the assertion with which it was fabricated, it necessarily started at some time or other from one source. Thence it creeps gradually along the grapevine of tongues and ears, and a defect in the tiny seedling so overshadows the other details of the rumor that no one reflects whether the first mouth sowed the seed of falsehood, as often happens, from a spirit of envy or a suspicious thought or from the pleasure some derive from lying—a pleasure not new-born, but inborn.

It is well that time brings all things to light, as even your own proverbs and sayings testify, in accordance with the design of nature which has so ordained things that nothing remains a secret for long, even though rumor has not spread it abroad. Rightly, then, is rumor alone for so long a time aware of the crimes of Christians; this is the witness you bring forth against us. What it has sometime or other spread abroad and over such an interval of time hardened into a matter of opinion, it has not yet been able to prove, so that I call upon the steadfastness of nature itself against those who assume that such accusations are credible.

CHAPTER 8

Look! we set up a reward for these crimes: they promise eternal life. For the time being, believe it! On this point I have a question to ask: If you believed it, would you consider the acquisition of eternal life worth attaining with such a [troubled] conscience? Come, bury your sword in this baby, enemy though he is of no one, guilty of no crime, everybody's son; or, if that is the other fellow's job, stand here beside this [bit of] humanity, dying before he has lived; wait for the young soul to take flight; receive his fresh blood; saturate your bread in it; partake freely! Meanwhile, as you recline at table, note the place where your mother is, and your sister; note it carefully, so that, when the dogs cause darkness to fall, you may make no mistake—for you will be guilty of a crime unless you commit incest!

Initiated and sealed in such mysteries as these, you live forever! I wish you would tell me if eternity is worth such a price; if it isn't, these crimes should not be believed. Even if you believed them, I tell you you would not want to commit them. Even if you wanted to, I tell you you couldn't. How is it, then, that others can commit them, if you cannot? Why cannot you, if others can? We, I suppose, have a different nature, being Cynopennae or Sciapodes; we have a different arrangement of teeth, different muscles for incestuous lust! You who believe these crimes about any other man can commit them, too; you are a man yourself, just as a Christian is. If you cannot do these things, you ought not to believe them of Christians. For a Christian, too, is a man even as you are.

'But, without realizing it, they are deceived and imposed upon.' They were unaware that anything of the sort was asserted of Christians—and that they should examine and investigate the matter with all vigilance. Yet, I suppose, it is customary for those who wish to be initiated to approach first the father of the sacred rites to arrange what must be prepared. Then he says, 'Now, you need a baby, still tender, one who does not know what death means, and one who will smile under your knife. You need bread, too, with which to gather up his juicy blood; besides that, candlesticks, lamps, some dogs, and bits of meat which will draw them on to overturn the lamps. Most important of all, you must come with your mother and sister.' But, what if the latter are unwilling to come, or you do not have any? What about the Christians who are without relatives? A man cannot really be a Christian, I suppose, unless he is someone's brother or son. Now, what if all those preparations are made without the foreknowledge of those concerned? At any rate, after once experiencing it, they know of it and support and condone the procedure. 'They are afraid of being punished if they make it known.' Well, how can they deserve to be defended, since they would prefer to die outright rather than live with such crimes upon their conscience? Come now, granted that they are afraid, why do they persevere? The logical conclusion is that you no longer would want to be that which you would not have been at all, had you known ahead of time what it was.

CHAPTER 9

To refute these points at greater length, I will point out that you yourselves commit these very crimes—sometimes openly, sometimes secretly—and that, perhaps, is the reason why you have believed them also of us. In Africa, babies used to be sacrificed publicly to Saturn even down to the proconsulate of Tiberius. He impaled the priests themselves on the very trees overshadowing their temple. The crosses were votive offerings to expiate their crimes. As witness of this there is the army of my own country, which performed this task for this very proconsul. Even now this holy crime is continued in secret. Christians are not alone in despising you; no crime is wiped out forever, or else some god is changing his ways. Since Saturn did not spare his own sons, surely he did not insist on sparing the children of others, who, for example, were offered to him by their very own parents. They gladly complied and they fondled their babies so that they would not be crying when they were sacrificed. Yet, there is considerable difference between murder and parricide!

Among the Gauls, an older person was sacrificed to Mercury. I leave to their theaters the stories of the Taurians. Look at conditions in that city of the pious race of Aeneas, a city renowned for its religious worship! There is a certain Jupiter whom they bathe in human blood during the games held in his honor. 'But it is the blood of a beast-fighter,' you say. That, I suppose, is something of less value than the blood of a man! Or is it not worse because it is the blood of a bad man? At any rate, it is blood shed in murder. Oh, what a Christian Jupiter! He is his father's only son as far as cruelty goes!

But, with regard to infanticide, since it makes no difference whether it is committed for a religious purpose or according to one's own choosing—although there is a difference between murder and parricide—I will turn to the people. How many, do you suppose, of those here present who stand panting for the blood of Christians—how many, even, of you magistrates who are so righteous and so rigorous against us—want me to touch their consciences for putting their own offspring to death? If there is some distinction in kind between one act of murder and another, it is certainly more cruel to kill by drowning or by exposure to cold, hunger, and the dogs; for an older person would prefer to die by the sword. But, with us, murder is forbidden once for all. We are not permitted to destroy even the fetus in the womb, as long as blood is still being drawn to form a human being. To prevent the birth of a child is a quicker way to murder. It makes no difference whether one destroys a soul already born or interferes with its coming to birth. It is a human being and one who is to be a man, for the whole fruit is already present in the seed.

As for bloody food and such tragic dishes, read—I think it is related by Herodotus, but I am not sure—how, among some tribes, blood was taken from the arms and tasted by both parties in forming a treaty. Something was tasted, too, under Catiline. And they say that it was a custom among certain tribes of Scythians for every deceased member to be eaten by his relatives. But I am going too far afield. Today, right here among you, to mark the devotees of Bellona, a thigh is slashed, the blood is taken in the hand and given them for their benefit. Again, consider those who with greedy thirst, at a show in the arena, take the fresh blood of wicked criminals as it runs down from their throats and carry it off to heal their epilepsy. What about them? And what about those who make a meal on the flesh of wild beasts taken from the arena, who prefer the meat of boar or stag? That boar has licked the blood off him whom he has spattered with blood in the struggle. The stag has rolled in the blood of a gladiator. The very bellies of the bears, still stuffed with undigested human flesh, are the object of their search. Thence does man belch forth flesh that was nourished with human flesh. You who eat these animals, how far removed are you from the banquets of the Christians?

And do those who lust after human flesh, with a beastly passion, commit less grievous crimes because they devour something that is living? Are they less polluted with human blood and less dedicated to lewdness because they lap up that which is to turn into blood? No, they, of course, do not feast on babies, but rather on adults. Let your unnatural ways blush before the Christians. We do not even have the blood of animals at our meals, for these consist of ordinary food. This is why we refrain from eating the meat of any animals which have been strangled or that die of themselves, lest we be in any way contaminated with blood, even if it is hidden in the flesh.

At the trials of Christians you offer them sausages filled with blood. You are convinced, of course, that the very thing with which you try to make them deviate from the right way is unlawful for them. How is it that, when you are confident that they will shudder at the blood of an animal, you believe they will pant eagerly after human blood? Is it, perchance, that *you* have found the latter more to your taste? Human blood, then, and nothing else is certainly the very thing that ought to be employed as the touchstone of Christians, like fire or the incense box. Then they would be proved Christians by their appetite for human blood, just as they are at present by their refusal to offer sacrifice. On the other hand, they would have to be declared non-Christians if they did not taste it, just as if they had offered sacrifice. And, of course, you would have no shortage of human blood provided at the examination and condemnation of prisoners.

Another point—Who are more expert at practising incest than those whom Jupiter himself has instructed? Ctesias relates that the Persians have intercourse with their own mothers. The Macedonians, too, were suspected of it because, the first time they attended the tragedy of *Oedipus,* they mocked the grief of the incestuous son, saying: 'He lay with his mother!' Well, now! Consider how great chance there is for incestuous unions occasioned by mistaken identity. The promiscuousness of your wanton living affords the opportunity. In the first place, you expose your children to be taken up by some passerby out of the pity of a stranger's heart; or you release them from your authority to be adopted by better parents. Sooner or later, the memory of the alienated family necessarily fades away. As soon as a mistake has occurred, the transmission of incest goes on, the stock spreading together with its crime. Finally, then, wherever you are, at home, abroad, across the sea, your lust travels as your companion, and its outbursts everywhere—or even some slight indulgence—can easily beget children for you any place at all, though you may not know it. The result is that a brood thus scattered through illicit human intercourse may fall in with its own kindred and in blind ignorance fail to recognize it as begotten of incestuous blood.

As for us, an ever-watchful and steadfast chastity shields us from such an occurrence and, in so far as we refrain from adultery and every excess after marriage, we are safe, too, from the danger of incest. Some are even more secure, since they ward off the entire violence of this error by virginal continence, and as old men are still [as pure as] boys.

If you would realize that these sins exist among yourselves, then you would perceive clearly that they do not exist among Christians. The same eyes would tell you the facts in both cases. But, a two-fold blindness easily imposes itself, so that those who do not see what does exist seem to see what does not. I will point out that this is true in everything. Now I will speak of the more manifest crimes.

CHAPTER 10

'You do not worship the gods,' you say, 'and you do not offer sacrifice for the emperors.' It follows that we do not offer sacrifices for others for the same reason that we do not do it even for ourselves—it follows immediately from our not worshipping the gods. Consequently, we are considered guilty of sacrilege and treason. This is the chief accusation against us— in fact, it is the whole case—and it certainly deserves investigation, unless presumption and injustice dictate the decision, the one despairing of the truth, the other refusing it.

We cease worshipping your gods when we find out that they are non-existent. This, then, is what you ought to demand, that we prove that those gods are non-existent and for that reason should not be worshipped, because they ought to be worshipped only if they were actually gods. Then, too, the Christians ought to be punished if the fact were established that those gods do exist whom they will not worship because they consider them non-existent. 'But, for us,' you say, 'the gods do exist.' We object and appeal from you to your conscience. Let this pass judgment on us, let this condemn us, if it can deny that all those gods of yours have been mere men. But, if it should deny this, it will be refuted by its own documents of ancient times from which it has learned of the gods. Testimony is furnished to this very day by the cities in which they were born, and the regions in which they left traces of something they had done and in which it is pointed out that they were buried.

And now, shall I quickly run through the list of deities, one by one, numerous and important as they are, the new and the old, barbarian and Greek, Roman and foreign, captive and adopted, private and public, male and female, belonging to the country, the city, the sailor, the soldier? It would be wearisome even to call the roll! To sum up the whole situation—and this, not that you may become informed for the first time, but that you may recall what you already know (for you certainly act as though you had forgotten it)—before the advent of Saturn there was no god among you. With him starts the roster of all your divinities, or at least of those who are more powerful and better known. Hence, whatever is established about their beginnings will apply also to their posterity. As for Saturn, as far as literature tells us, neither Diodorus the Greek, nor Thallus, nor Cassius Severus, nor Cornelius Nepos, nor any other writer on antiquities of this sort has pronounced him other than a mere man. As far as arguments drawn from fact go, I find none more trustworthy than this: right in Italy itself, where Saturn finally took his abode after much traveling to and fro, and after enjoying the hospitality of Attica, he was welcomed by Janus— or, as the Salii wish to call him, Janes. The mountain which he made his home was called the Saturnian. The city which he founded is called, even to the present day, Saturnia. Finally, all Italy, after being called Oenotria, was named Saturnia after him.

The art of writing was first established there by him and coins were struck with his image. Hence, he presides over the treasury.

However, if Saturn was a man, he certainly was born of man, and, because conceived by man, he was certainly not the child of Heaven and Earth. But, if his parents were unknown, it was easy for him to be called the child of those from whom all of us too may claim birth. For, who would not call heaven his father and earth his mother to pay them respect and honor? Even according to the custom all of us have, persons who are unknown, or even those who make an unexpected appearance, are said to have dropped from the sky. Therefore, inasmuch as Saturn suddenly appeared everywhere, he happened to be called the 'Heavenly One,' for in popular speech people whose parentage is uncertain are called 'sons of Earth.' I make no comment upon the actions of men who were still so uncivilized that they were moved by the quasi-divine appearance of some newcomer, since today men who by this time are civilized apotheosize human creatures who a few days before, with public mourning, they confessed were dead! That is enough now about Saturn, brief though it is. We shall also prove that Jupiter was every bit as much a man, inasmuch as he was born of man, and thereafter the whole stock of his family was as mortal as the seed from which it came.

CHAPTER 11

While you dare not deny that the gods were once men, yet you have made it your practice to affirm that after their death they became gods. Let us go back over the causes which have brought this about. In the first place, you have to grant that there is some god more sublime, one who has, as it were, a rightful title to divinity, who has made gods out of men. The gods could not have assumed to themselves a divinity which they did not possess, nor could anyone supply it to them when they did not possess it, unless he had it in his own right. On the other hand, if there were no one to make gods, you are offering a vain presumption that gods were made, while at the same time you do away with the maker. At all events, if they could have made gods of themselves, there never would have remained men with this power over a superior state of being.

So, if there is someone who could make gods, I come back to examine the reasons why anyone would make gods out of men. I find no other reason except that the great god desired ministers and assistants in his divine functions.

But, in the first place, it would be beneath his dignity to need the services of anyone—least of all, a dead man! It would be more fitting for him to have made some god right from the start, if in due time he was going to need the services of a dead man. I fail to see what service is needed. For, this whole fabric of the universe, whether it be unborn or unmade (as Pythagoras taught), or whether (as Plato believed born or made, was certainly arranged, equipped, ordered once and for all in its construction, and supplied with the complete guidance of reason. That which has perfected all things could not be imperfect. Nothing awaited Saturn and Saturnia's tribe. Men would be fools if they were not convinced that from the beginning rain fell from the sky, the stars were bright, light shone, thunder rolled, and Jupiter himself trembled in fear of the thunderbolts which *you* place in his hand; if they were not certain that all crops came forth in abundance from the earth before Liber, Ceres, and Minerva, in fact, even before the first man (whoever he was), for nothing designed for the sustenance and preservation of man could be introduced after man. Finally, the gods are said to have discovered, not devised, those things necessary to sustain life. But, whatever is discovered, was already in existence, and what was in existence is not to be considered the property of him who discovered it but of him who devised it; it existed before it could be discovered. Now, if Liber is a god because he demonstrated the use of the vine, Lucullus fared badly in not having been deified as the originator of a new fruit, inasmuch as he was the discoverer of it; for it was he who first introduced the cherry from Pontus to Italy. Therefore, if from the beginning the universe has stood devised and arranged with fixed laws for exercising its functions, the argument from this viewpoint for admitting men into the ranks of divinity is void, because the positions and powers which you have attributed to them were in existence from the beginning, just as they would have been even if you had not made them gods.

But, you turn your attention to another argument and reply that the conferring of divinity was a means of rewarding their services. On this point you grant, I suppose, that the god who makes gods possesses justice in a superior degree, since he has not recklessly nor undeservedly nor extravagantly bestowed such a great reward. I would like to review these services, then, to see whether they are of a kind that would exalt these men to heaven and not rather plunge them into the abyss of Tartarus. (Such is the name you use, when it pleases you, for the prison of infernal punishment.) It is there that the dead are relegated— those who are shameless toward their parents, who commit incest with their sisters, who seduce married women, rape young girls, and defile young boys, who commit sins of cruelty, murder, robbery, and fraud: all who are like anyone of your gods. No one of these, unless you deny that he was a man, can you prove to be free from crime or vice.

Yet, just as you could not deny that they were once men, so these disgraceful marks upon them are an additional reason for our not believing that they afterwards became gods. For, if you sit in judgment to punish such persons, if such of you as are upright scorn fellowship, intercourse, intimacy with the wicked and depraved, while, on the other hand, it is men on their same level whom that god of yours has joined to himself to share in his majesty, why, then, do you condemn men whose associates you idolize? Your injustice is an affront to heaven. Make all the worst reprobates into gods, that you may please your gods! It is an honor for them to have their equals deified.

But—to omit further discussion of this disgraceful matter— supposing they were upright, blameless, and good! Yet, what a number of better men you have left in the underworld! For instance, a Socrates, renowned for wisdom, an Aristides for justice, a Themistocles for military ability, an Alexander for distinction, a Polycrates for good fortune, a Croesus for wealth, a Demosthenes for eloquence! Which one of those gods of yours is more venerable or wiser than Cato, more just or more highly endowed with military prowess than Scipio? Who surpasses Pompey in distinction, or Sulla in fortune, or Crassus in wealth, or Tully in eloquence? With how much more dignity might that god have waited to take such men as these into the ranks of the gods, since he surely knew ahead of time of their better qualifications! He acted hastily, I think, and closed the gates of heaven once and for all; he now blushes as the better men grumble about it in the world of the dead.

CHAPTER 30

For, in our case, we pray for the welfare of the emperors to the eternal God, the true God, the living God, whom even the emperors themselves prefer to have propitious to them before all other gods. They know who has given them power; they know—for they are men—who has given them life; they feel that He is the only God in whose power alone they are, commencing with whom they are second, after whom they stand first, who is before all and above all gods. Why not?—since they are above all men; since, as living beings, they surpass, at any rate, the dead. They consider to what extent power of empire avails and thus they come to understand God; against Him they cannot avail, through Him they know they do avail. Let the emperor [have a mind to] war against heaven, lead heaven in chains in his triumph, send his sentries to heaven, and on heaven impose his tax! He cannot do it. So he is mighty, because he is less than heaven, for he is himself the property of Him to whom heaven and every creature belong. From Him comes the emperor, from whom came the man, also, before he became the emperor; from Him comes the emperor's power and his spirit as well. Looking up to Him, we Christians—with hands extended, because they are harmless, with head bare because we are not ashamed, without a prayer leader because we pray from the heart—constantly beseech Him on behalf of all emperors. We ask for them long life, undisturbed power, security at home, brave armies, a faithful Senate, an upright people, a peaceful world, and everything for which a man or a Caesar prays. Such petitions I cannot ask from any other save from Him, and I know that I shall obtain them from Him, since He is the only One who supplies them and I am one who ought to obtain my request. For, I am His servant; I alone worship Him; for His teaching I am put to death; I offer Him the rich—and better—sacrifice which He Himself has commanded, the prayer sent up

Tertullian

from a chaste body, an innocent heart, and a spirit that is holy; not grains of incense worth a mere penny, or tears of the Arabic tree, or two drops of wine, or the blood of a worthless ox that is longing for death, and, in addition to all this filth, a polluted conscience—so that I wonder when, among you, victims are examined by the most vicious of priests, why it is the hearts of the slain animals are examined rather than those of the priests themselves. So, then, as we kneel with arms extended to God, let the hooks dig into us, let the crosses suspend us, the fires lick us, the swords cut our throats, and wild beasts leap upon us: the very posture of a Christian in prayer makes him ready for every punishment. Carry on, good officials, torture the soul which is beseeching God on behalf of the emperor! Here will lie the crime, where there reigns truth and devotion to God!

CHAPTER 31

Well, now, we have been flattering the emperor and have lied about the prayers we said just to escape rough treatment! That ingenious idea of yours is certainly of advantage to us, for you permit us to prove whatever we allege in our defense. If you think that we have no interest in the emperor's welfare, look into our literature, the Word of God. We ourselves do not keep it concealed; in fact, many a chance hands it over to outsiders. Learn from this literature that it has been enjoined upon us, that our charity may more and more abound, to pray to God even for our enemies, and to beg for blessings for our persecutors. Now, who are any greater enemies and persecutors of Christians than those on whose account we are charged with the crime of treason? But it is clearly and expressly said: 'Pray for kings, for princes and for rulers, that all may be peaceful for you!' For, when the empire is shaken, and its other members are shaken, we, too, although we are considered outsiders by the crowd, are naturally involved in some part of the disaster.

CHAPTER 32

There is also another, even greater, obligation for us to pray for the emperors; yes, even for the continuance of the empire in general and for Roman interests. We realize that the

77

tremendous force which is hanging over the whole world, and the very end of the world with its threat of dreadful afflictions, is arrested for a time by the continued existence of the Roman Empire. This event we have no desire to experience, and, in praying that it may be deferred, we favor the continuance of Rome.

Then, too, we take an oath not by the '*genii* of the emperors,' but by their prosperity—which is more august than any *genius* at all. Are you not aware that *genii* are evil spirits and, thence, to use a diminutive term, are called *daemonia?* We respect in the emperors the decision of God, since He has placed them over the people. We know that in them is that which God has willed, and so we wish that what God has willed be safe and sound, and we consider this an important oath. As for evil spirits, that is, *genii,* we are in the habit of exorcising them in order to drive them out of men, but not to swear by them in a manner that would confer upon them the honor of divinity.

CHAPTER 33

Why should I say more about the respect and the loyalty of Christians toward the emperor? We are under obligation to look up to him as one whom our Lord has chosen. So, I might well say: 'Caesar belongs more to us, since he has been appointed by our God.' And so, as he is mine, I do more for his welfare, not only because I pray for it to Him who can really grant it, or because I am such that I deserve to be heard, but also because, as I set the dignity of Caesar below that of God, I commend him the more to God to whom alone I subordinate him. However, I do subordinate him to God; I do not make him His equal. I will not call the emperor God, either because I do not know how to lie, or because I dare not make fun of him, or because even he himself does not want to be called God. If he is a man, it is to his interest as a man to yield precedence to God. Let him consider it enough to be called emperor. That, indeed, is a title of dignity which God has given him. One who says he is God says he is not the emperor; unless he were a man he could not be emperor. Why, even during his triumph, right in his lofty chariot, he is reminded that he is a man. For, someone behind him whispers: 'Look behind you! Remember you are a man!' And certainly, he rejoices all the more in this, that he shines forth in such great glory that he needs a reminder of his condition. He would be of less importance were he then called 'God,' because it would not be true. He is of greater importance who is called to look back, lest he think that he is God.

CHAPTER 34

Augustus, who formed the empire, did not even want to be called 'Lord'; for this title, too, belongs to God. Of course, I will call the emperor Lord, but only in the customary meaning of the word, if I am not forced to call him Lord in place of God. So far as he is concerned, I am a free man. For, I have one Lord, the omnipotent and eternal God, the same who is his Lord, too. As for the one who is 'Father of his country,' how can he be its Lord? Yet, this title is an acceptable one, too, implying paternal responsibility rather than power. Even in the family, we speak of 'fathers' rather than 'lords.' All the more improper is it that the emperor should be called God, which is unthinkable save in terms of a most disgraceful and pernicious flattery. Just as if you already had an emperor and were to call another man by that name, would you not incur the severe and inexorable displeasure of the real emperor whom you had, a displeasure which must be feared even by him whom you called emperor? Be reverential toward God if you wish Him to be propitious to the emperor. Stop believing in another god and, so, stop calling this one god who has need of God. If flattery like this, which addresses a man as god, does not blush for its hypocrisy, let it at least have fear of misfortune. It is blasphemous to call Caesar god before his apotheosis.

CHAPTER 35

So, this is why Christians are public enemies, because they do not proclaim meaningless, false, and wanton honors for the emperors; for, as men who belong to the true religion, they celebrate the feasts of the emperors with realization rather than with self-gratification. There is no question about it: it is a splendid ceremony to bring out in public the braziers and banquet couches, to dine in the streets, to make the city smell like a tavern, to make mud with the wine, to chase around in bands

in order to commit crimes, effrontery, and the seductive pleasures of lust. Is it in such fashion that the public expresses its
delight, with public degradation? Are such actions as these
becoming on solemn festivals of the emperors, though they
are not becoming on other days? Are those who keep order out
of respect for the emperor to abandon it because of the emperor? And shall their immoral licentiousness be considered
loyalty; the opportunity for excessive indulgence, religious
respect? Oh, how rightly are we to be condemned! Why do we
perform our ceremonies and express our joys for the Caesars in
a way that is chaste, sober, and decent? Why, on a festive day,
do we not overshadow our doorposts with laurel branches and
infringe upon the daylight with lamps? It is an honorable
practice, indeed, when a public festival demands that you deck
out your home with the appearance of a new brothel!

Now, on this question of religious worship rendered to a
less august majesty, the point on which action is brought against
us Christians as a second charge of sacrilege, inasmuch as we
do not celebrate with you the festivals of the emperors in a
manner which neither modesty, self-respect, nor virtue permits,
a manner urged by the opportunity for self-indulgence rather
than any worthy motive—in this regard I would like to point
out your loyalty and sincerity, in case here, too, those who
want us to be considered not Romans, but enemies of the
Roman emperors, may prove, perchance, to be worse than
Christians. It is the Romans themselves, the very people born
and bred on the Seven Hills, that I arraign: does that Roman
tongue spare any emperor of its own? As witness, there is the
Tiber, and the training schools for wild beasts. If only nature
had enclosed our breasts with some kind of glass-like material
to make them transparent, whose heart would not appear
engraved with the scene of one new Caesar after another pre-
siding over the distribution of the dole, even in that hour when
they shout in applause: 'From our years may Jupiter multiply
for thee thine own!' A Christian can no more make such remarks than he can hope for a new emperor.

'But, that's the rabble,' you say. Perhaps it is the rabble;
still, they are Romans, and none is more clamorous in their
demands for punishment of the Christians than the rabble.

Yes, of course, the other classes of society are conscientiously loyal, as their position of authority requires. There is never a hostile whisper from the Senate, the knights, the camp, or the palace itself. Whence come men like Cassius and Niger and Albinus? Whence, those who between the two laurels lay hands on Caesar? Whence, those who practise the art of wrestling in order to choke him to death? Whence, those who burst into the palace in arms, bolder than any Sigerius or Parthenius? From the ranks of the Romans, unless I am mistaken—that is, from among non-Christians. And so, all of them, right until the very outbreak of their disloyalty, offered sacrifices for the well-being of the emperor and swore by his *genius,* some publicly, others privately; naturally, they gave Christians the name of public enemies.

But, even those who now are being brought to light each day as associates or acclaimers of the criminal parties, the gleanings which are left after a whole harvest of parricides—how they used to deck their doorposts beforehand with the freshest and fullest laurel branches! How they used to shadow their halls with the loftiest and brightest lamps! How they apportioned the forum among themselves with the most elegant and magnificent couches! And all this, not to celebrate an occasion of public joy, but to express what was already their own wish on the festivity of another emperor and to set up the model and image of the object of their own hopes, while changing the name of the emperor in their hearts. The same type of service is rendered by those who consult astrologers, soothsayers, fortune-tellers, and magicians regarding the life of the emperors. But these wiles, which have been made known by the rebel angels and which are forbidden by God, Christians do not use even in their own personal affairs. Moreover, who has to inquire about the emperor's health except one who is plotting or desiring something against it, or who is hoping for or expecting something after his death? For, it is not with the same attitude of mind that one seeks information regarding his loved ones and his masters! There is one kind of concern shown in uneasiness about one's family; another, about one's enslavement.

CHAPTER 36

If such is the case, and those who once were called Romans are now found to be enemies, why is it that we who are considered enemies are refused the name of Romans? It cannot be that we are non-Romans because we are enemies, since it is discovered that those are really enemies who once were considered Romans. Furthermore, the loyalty, the reverence, the fidelity due the emperors consists not in such services as even hostile minds can render to cloak their thoughts, but, on the contrary, it consists in that moral behavior which God demands be shown the emperor just as truly as necessarily is to be shown to all men. These indications of good will are not due on our part to the emperors alone. In no good that we perform do we show preference for certain persons, since we actually are doing it for ourselves; we are striving for a just recompense either of praise or of reward not from man, but from God who demands and repays goodness that is impartial. We are the same toward the emperors as we are toward our neighbors. For, to desire evil, to do evil, to speak evil, to think evil of anyone—all are equally forbidden to us. Whatever we may not do to the emperor, we may not do to anyone else; whatever is forbidden with regard to anyone is, perhaps even to a greater degree, forbidden with regard to that one who, through God, is so great a personage.

CHAPTER 37

If, as I have said above, we are commanded to love our enemies, who is there for us to hate? Likewise, if we are forbidden to return an injury, lest, through our action, we become wrong-doers like them, who is there for us to injure? Examine yourselves on this point! How often do you rage furiously against the Christians, partly in response to your own feelings, partly out of respect for the laws? How often, too, has a hostile mob, without consulting you, attacked us on their own initiative, with stones and torches in their hands? Why, with the very fury of Bacchanals, they spare not even the corpses of Christians, but drag them from the repose of the grave, from that resting place, as it were, of death; although they are already changed and by now rotting in corruption, they cut them into bits and tear them limb from limb. Yet, what fault do you ever find with people who are bound together by such intimate ties, what retaliation for injury do you ever experience from those who are so disposed even to death, though even a single night, with a few little torches, could produce such rich vengeance, if it were permitted us to requite evil with evil? But, far be it from us that our God-given religion avenge itself with human fire or that it grieve to endure the suffering whereby it is put to the test.

If we wanted to act as open enemies and not merely as secret avengers, would we lack the strength of numbers and troops? Take the Moors and Marcomani and the Parthians themselves or any tribes at all who, even if they are numerous, still live in one place and inhabit their own territories—are they really more numerous than the Christians who are scattered over the whole world? We are but of yesterday, yet we have filled every place among you—cities, islands, fortresses, towns, marketplaces, camp, tribes, town councils, the palace, the senate, the forum; we have left nothing to you but the temples of your gods. For what war would we not have been fit and ready, even though unequally matched in military strength, we who are so ready to be slain, were it not that, according to our rule of life, it is granted us to be killed rather than to kill?

Even unarmed and without any uprising, merely as malcontents, simply through hatred and withdrawal, we could have fought against you. For, if such a multitude of men as we are had broken loose from you and had gone into some remote corner of the earth, the loss of so many citizens, of whatever kind they might be, would certainly have made your power blush for shame; in fact, it would even have punished you by this very desertion. Without a doubt, you would have been exceedingly frightened at your loneliness, at the silence of your surroundings, and the stupor, as it were, of a dead world. You would have had to look around for people to rule; there would have been more enemies than citizens left to you. For, now, the enemies whom you have are fewer because of the number of Christians, inasmuch as nearly all the citizens you have in nearly all the cities are Christians. But, you have preferred to call them the enemies of the human race rather than of human error.

But, who would snatch you away from those secret enemies that are constantly destroying your spiritual and bodily health—I mean, from the attacks of demons which we ward off from you without any reward and without pay? This alone would have been sufficient revenge for us, if from then on you were left open and exposed to the possession of the impure spirits. Furthermore, instead of thinking of any compensation for so great a protection, you have preferred to consider as enemies a class of men, who, far from being a troublesome burden to you, are actually indispensable. To tell the truth, we are enemies, not, however, of the human race, but rather of human error.

CHAPTER 38

Accordingly, ought not this religion to be regarded with somewhat milder judgment among those societies which cannot legally exist? Its members commit no such crimes as are regularly feared from illegal associations. For, unless I am mistaken, the motive for prohibiting associations rests on the prudent care for public order, lest the state be split into parties, a situation which would easily disturb voting assemblies, council meetings, the Senate, mass meetings, and even public entertainments by the clash of rival interests, since by now men have even begun to make a business of their violence, offering it for sale at a price. But, for us who are indifferent to all burning desire for fame and honor, there is no need of banding together. There is nothing more unfamiliar to us than politics. There is only one state for all which we acknowledge—the universe.

Likewise, we renounce your public shows just as we do their origins which we know were begotten of superstition, while we are completely aloof from those matters with which they are concerned. Our tongues, our eyes, our ears have nothing to do with the madness of the circus, the shamelessness of the theater, the brutality of the arena, the vanity of the gymnasium. How, then, do we offend you? If we prefer different pleasures, if, in fine, we do not want to be amused, that is our loss—if loss there be—not yours. We reject the things that please you. And ours give you no pleasure. But the Epicureans were allowed to decide upon a different truth regarding the nature of pleasure, namely, tranquillity of mind.

CHAPTER 39

Now I myself will explain the practices of the Christian Church, that is, after having refuted the charges that they are evil, I myself will also point out that they are good. We form one body because of our religious convictions, and because of the divine origin of our way of life and the bond of common hope. We come together for a meeting and a congregation, in order to besiege God with prayers, like an army in battle formation. Such violence is pleasing to God. We pray, also, for the emperors, for their ministers and those in power, that their reign may continue, that the state may be at peace, and that the end of the world may be postponed. We assemble for the consideration of the Holy Scriptures, [to see] if the circumstances of the present times demand that we look ahead or reflect. Certainly, we nourish our faith with holy conversation, we uplift our hope, we strengthen our trust, intensifying our discipline at the same time by the inculcation of moral precepts. At the same occasion, there are words of encouragement, of correction, and holy censure. Then, too, judgment is passed which is very impressive, as it is before men who are certain of the presence of God, and it is a deeply affecting foretaste of the future judgment, if anyone has so sinned that he is dismissed from sharing in common prayer, assembly, and all holy intercourse. Certain approved elders preside, men who have obtained this honor not by money, but by the evidence of good character. For, nothing that pertains to God is to be had for money.

Even if there is some kind of treasury, it is not accumulated from a high initiation fee as if the religion were something bought and paid for. Each man deposits a small amount on a certain day of the month or whenever he wishes, and only on condition that he is willing and able to do so. No one is forced; each makes his contribution voluntarily. These are, so to speak, the deposits of piety. The money therefrom is spent not for banquets or drinking parties or good-for-nothing eating houses, but for the support and burial of the poor, for children who are without their parents and means of subsistence, for aged men who are confined to the house; likewise, for shipwrecked sailors, and for any in the mines, on islands or in prisons. Provided only it be for the sake of fellowship with God, they become entitled to loving and protective care for their confession. The practice of such a special love brands us in the eyes of some. 'See,' they say, 'how they love one another'; (for *they* hate one another), 'and how ready they are to die for each other.' (They themselves would be more ready to kill each other.)

Over the fact that we call ourselves brothers, they fall into a rage—for no other reason, I suppose, than because among them every term of kinship is only a hypocritical pretense of affection. But, we are your brothers, too, according to the law of nature, our common mother, although you are hardly men since you are evil brothers. But, with how much more right are they called brothers and considered such who have acknowledged one father, God, who have drunk one spirit of holiness, who in fear and wonder have come forth from the one womb of their common ignorance to the one light of truth! Perhaps this is why we are considered less legitimate brothers, because no tragic drama has our brotherhood as its theme, or because we are brothers who use the same family substance which, among you, as a rule, destroys brotherhood.

So, we who are united in mind and soul have no hesitation about sharing what we have. Everything is in common among us—except our wives. In this matter—which is the only matter in which the rest of men practise partnership—we dissolve partnership. They not only usurp the marriage rights of their friends, but they even hand over their own rights to their friends with the greatest equanimity. This results, I suppose, from the teaching they have learned from those who were older and wiser, the Greek Socrates and the Roman Cato, who shared with their friends the wives whom they had married, so that they could bear children in other families, too. As a matter of fact, perhaps the wives were not exactly unwilling. For, why should they care about a chastity which their husbands had so readily given away? Oh, what an example of Attic wisdom and Roman dignity! The philosopher a pander, and the censor, too!

86

Why wonder, then, if such dear friends take their meals together? You attack our modest repasts—apart from saying that they are disgraced by crimes—as being extravagant. It was, of course, to us that Diogenes' remark referred: 'The people of Megara purchase supplies as if they were to die tomorrow, but put up buildings as though they were never to die.' However, anyone sees the bit of straw in another's eye more easily than a mote in his own. With so many tribes, courts, and sub-courts belching, the air becomes foul: if the Salii are going to dine, someone will have to give a loan; the city clerks will have to count up the cost of the tithes and extravagant banquets in honor of Hercules; for the festival of the Apaturia, for the Dionysiac revels, for the mysteries of Attica, they proclaim a draft of cooks; at the smoke of a feast of Serapis the firemen will become alarmed. But, only about the repast of the Christians is any objection brought forth.

Our repast, by its very name, indicates its purpose. It is called by a name which to the Greeks means 'love.' Whatever it costs, it is gain to incur expense in the name of piety, since by this refreshment we comfort the needy, not as, among you, parasites contend for the glory of reducing their liberty to slavery for the price of filling their belly amidst insults, but as, before God, greater consideration is given to those of lower station. If the motive of our repast is honorable, then on the basis of that motive appraise the entire procedure of our discipline. What concerns the duty of religion tolerates no vulgarity, no immorality. No one sits down to table without first partaking of a prayer to God. They eat as much as those who are hungry take; they drink as much as temperate people need. They satisfy themselves as men who remember that they must worship God even throughout the night; they converse as men who know that the Lord is listening. After this, the hands are washed and lamps are lit, and each one, according to his ability to do so, reads the Holy Scriptures or is invited into the center to sing a hymn to God. This is the test of how much he has drunk. Similarly, prayer puts an end to the meal. From here they depart, not to unite in bands for murder, or to run around in gangs, or for stealthy attacks of lewdness, but to observe the same regard for modesty and chastity as people do who have partaken not only of a repast but of a rule of life.

Such is the gathering of Christians. There is no question about it—it deserves to be called illegal, provided it is like those which are illegal; it deserves to be condemned, if any complaint is lodged against it on the same ground that complaints are made about other secrets societies. But, for whose destruction have we ever held a meeting? We are the same when assembled as when separate; we are collectively the same as we are individually, doing no one any injury, causing no one any harm. When men who are upright and good assemble, when the pious and virtuous gather together, the meeting should be called not a secret society but a senate.

CHAPTER 1

TO SCAPULA

We, are, indeed, neither dismayed nor greatly disturbed at the persecutions which we suffer from ignorant men, since we joined this way of life with the understanding that we pledged ourselves to enter into the present conflicts at the risk even of our lives, wishing to obtain those things which God promises in return, and fearing to suffer those things which He threatens for any contrary course of life. Accordingly, we battle against all your cruelty, even rushing voluntarily to the contest, and we rejoice more when condemned than when acquitted. We have therefore presented this petition to you, not fearing for ourselves, and by no means for our friends, but for you and for all our enemies. For, we are commanded by the teachings of our religion to love even our enemies and to pray for those who persecute us: so that our goodness may be perfect and peculiar to us, and not that of the run of the world. To love friends is the custom for all men, but to love enemies is customary only for Christians. We, then, who are saddened by your ignorance, have compassion on human error, and look ahead into the future, seeing signs of it threatening daily—we, I say, must proceed to set before you in this way what you do not wish to hear openly.

CHAPTER 2

We worship one God, whom you all know, since nature is your teacher, at whose lightning and thunder you tremble, at whose benefits you rejoice. The rest you yourselves think to be gods, but we know to be demons. It is the law of mankind and the natural right of each individual to worship what he thinks proper, nor does the religion of one man either harm or help another. But, it is not proper for religion to compel men to religion, which should be accepted of one's own accord, not by force, since sacrifices also are required of a willing mind. So, even if you compel us to sacrifice, you will render no service to your gods. They will not desire sacrifices from the unwilling unless they are quarrelsome—but a god is not quarrelsome. Finally, He who is the true God bestows all His gifts equally— on the unholy as well as on His own. This is why He also appointed an eternal judgment for those who are thankful and for those who are not. You have never caught us, whom you consider sacrilegious, in theft; much less, in committing sacrilege. But, all those who rob the temples both swear by the gods and worship the same; they are not Christians, yet they are caught in committing sacrilege. It would be tedious to relate in what other ways all the gods are ridiculed and despised, even by their own worshippers.

So, too, we are defamed regarding the majesty of the emperor, yet never could the followers of Albinus, or of Niger, or of Cassius be found among the Christians; but, those same men who, up to the very day before, had sworn by the genii of the emperors, who had both offered up and vowed sacrifices for their health, who had often condemned the Christians, were found to be enemies of the emperors. A Christian is an enemy of no one, much less of the emperor. Since he knows him to be appointed by his own God, he must love, reverence, honor, and wish him well, together with the whole Roman Empire, as long as the world shall last. For, so long the Roman Empire will last. In this way, then, do we honor the emperor, as is both lawful for us and expedient for him, as a man next to God: who has received whatever he is from God; who is inferior to God alone. This, too, he himself will desire. For, in this way he is greater than all, since he is inferior only to the true God. Thus, he is even greater than the gods themselves, since they, too, are also in his power. This is why we also offer sacrifice for the welfare of the emperor, but to God, who is our God and his— and in the way God commanded us, with pure prayer. God, the Maker of the universe, does not need any odor or blood. These are the food of demons. And the demons we not only reject, but convict; we daily expose them, and cast them out of men, as is well known to many. Therefore, we pray in a better way for the welfare of the emperor, asking it from Him who is able to give it. Surely, it can be sufficiently clear to you that we act according to the teachings of godly patience, when, as such a great multitude of men—almost the majority in every city—we live in silence and loyalty, known, perhaps, more as individuals than as a group, and knowable in no other way than by the reformation of our former vices. For far be it from us to take it ill that we suffer things for which we long, or to plot of ourselves any vengeance which we await from God.

CHAPTER 3

Nevertheless (as we have said before), we must grieve, because no city will go unpunished for the shedding of our blood, as was the situation under the governorship of Hilarian, when they had cried out concerning our burial grounds: 'Let them have no *areae*—no burial grounds!' But, the result was that they themselves had no *areae*—no threshing-floors: they did not gather their harvest. Moreover, with regard to the rains of the past year, it has become clear of what they have reminded mankind, namely, that there was a deluge in ancient times because of the unbelief and wickedness of men. What the fires which lately hung all night over the walls of Carthage threatened is known to those men who were eye witnesses. Of what message the sounds of the preceding thunders were portents is known to those men who hardened themselves against them. All these are signs of the impending wrath of God, which we must, in whatever way we can, both announce and proclaim, and in the meanwhile pray that it may be only local. The universal and final wrath will be felt in due time by those who interpret these samples of it in another fashion. The well-known strange appearance of the sun, when its light was almost extinguished, during the meeting of the court at Utica, also was an omen, inasmuch as the sun could not have suffered this from an ordinary eclipse, since it was situated in its own height and abode in the heavens. You have astrologers; consult them about it.

We can likewise call to your attention deaths of certain governors who at the close of their lives realized that they had sinned by tormenting the Christians. Vigellius Saturninus, who was the first to draw his sword against us in this province, lost his eyesight. In Cappadocia, Claudius Lucius Herminianus, taking it ill that his wife had become a convert to our mode of life, had treated the Christians cruelly. Left alone in his palace, and wasted by the plague, even to the point of breaking out with worms, he said while still alive: 'Let no one know it, lest the Christians rejoice and Christian wives conceive new hopes.' Afterwards, he recognized his error in having caused some to fall away from their resolution because of torture, and died, almost a Christian. Caecilius Capella, during the well-known doom which overtook Byzantium, cried out: 'Christians, rejoice.' But, even those persecutors who believe that they have gone unpunished will come to the day of divine judgment. To yourself, also, we wish it may have been only as a warning that, after you condemned Mavilus of Hadrumetum to the beasts, this recent calamity immediately followed. And, now, this hemorrhage of yours is for the same reason. But, think of the future.

CHAPTER 4

We who are without fear ourselves do not wish to frighten you, but I would that we could save all men by warning them 'not to fight against God.' You can perform the duties of your office as a judge, yet keep in mind the rights of humanity—even if for no other reason than that you are also under the law of the sword. For, what other command do you have than to condemn the guilty who confess, and to bring to torture those who deny? You see, then, how you yourselves act against your orders by forcing those who have confessed to deny. By this, you confess that we are innocent, whom you are willing to condemn at once from our own confession. But, if you strive to destroy us, it is our innocence that you are attacking.

How many governors, more determined and cruel than you, have made allowances in order to rid themselves of such cases! Cincius Severus did so, who himself furnished a plan of escape at Thysdrus, whereby the Christians might make such an answer that they would be set free; so did Vespronius Candidus, who, in order to satisfy the wishes of his citizens, first punished a Christian as a disturber of the peace and then dismissed him; so did Asper, who, when a man was slightly tortured and immediately fell from the faith, did not compel him to offer sacrifice, for he had previously declared in the presence of the advocates and assessors that he was sorry that he had come upon this case. Pudens also dismissed a Christian who had been sent to him, perceiving from the indictment that the man was the victim of a vexatious countercharge. He tore up this very indictment, saying that according to his instructions he was not to hear a man without an accuser.

All these things you may learn from the officials on your staff, from the same advocates who themselves have benefitted from the Christians, although in court they vote as they like. For, the secretary of a certain gentleman, when he was suffering from falling sickness caused by a demon, was freed from it; so also were a relative of some of the others and a certain little boy. And heaven knows how many distinguished men, to say nothing of common people, have been cured either of devils or of their sicknesses. Even Severus himself, the father of Antoninus, graciously remembered the Christians. He searched for Proculus— a Christian whose surname was Torpacion, a manager in the employ of Euhodia—who had cured him once by means of oil, and kept him in his palace until his death. Antoninus also knew him very well, brought up as he was on Christian milk. Moreover, Severus did not harm prominent women and prominent men, even though he was aware that they belonged to our group. Even more, he honored them by his own testimony and openly resisted the populace when they were raging against us. Marcus Aurelius, during his German expedition, after prayers had been offered to God by his Christian soldiers, also obtained rain during the well-known drought. When have droughts failed to be removed by our kneelings and fastings? Then, too, the people cried to the God of gods who alone is mighty and gave testimony to our God, though they did so under the name of Jupiter.

Besides this, we do not misuse any trust funds deposited with us, we defile the marriage of none, we treat our orphans affectionately, we succor the needy, to no one do we return evil for evil. What does it matter that there are some who falsely claim to belong to our religion and whom we ourselves disown? Finally, who makes a complaint in court against us on other grounds? What other trouble does a Christian suffer, except that which comes to him because of his religion? And no one in all this time has proved this religion to be marred by incest and cruel deeds. It is for so much innocence, for so much upright-ness, for justice, for chastity, for faith, for love of truth, for the living God, that we are burned at the stake: a punishment which you are wont to inflict neither on those guilty of sacrilege, nor on real public enemies, nor on those guilty of high treason. Even now, this name of Christian is persecuted by the governors of Numidia and Mauretania, though, in pronouncing death sentences, they limit them to beheading, that is, to that kind of punishment which from the very beginning was officially ordered to be inflicted on the Christians. But, the greater the contests, the greater the rewards to follow.

CHAPTER 5

Your cruelty is our glory. Only, see to it whether, just be-cause we endure such things, we do not appear to burst out for this one purpose alone, namely, to prove that we do not fear these things, but willingly call them down upon ourselves. When Arrius Antoninus was carrying out a vehement persecution in Asia, all the Christians of the city appeared in a body before his tribunal. After ordering a few to be led away to execution, he said to the rest: 'Wretched men, if you wish to die, you have precipices and ropes to hang yourselves.' If it should come into our mind to do the same thing here, also, what will you do with so many thousands of human beings, so many of both sexes—men and women—of every age, of every station, giving them-selves up to you? How many stakes, how many swords, will you need? What will Carthage itself endure, which you will have to decimate, when every man will recognize his own relatives and companions among them, when, perhaps, he will see even men of your own rank among them, noble ladies, and all the outstanding persons of the city, and the relatives or friends of your own friends? Spare yourself, then, if not us. Spare Carthage, if not yourself. Spare the province which, when your intention became manifest, fell victim to the vexatious accusations both of the soldiers and each man's private enemies.

We have no master but God alone. He, to whom you can do nothing, is before you and cannot be hidden. But, those whom you regard as masters over you are men, and they themselves one day will die. Our religion, however, which you know is growing stronger at the very moment when it seems to be cut down, will never perish. For, whoever beholds such noble endurance will first, as though struck by some kind of uneasiness, be driven to inquire what is the matter in question, and, then, when he knows the truth, immediately follow the same way.

St. Cyprian
200-258

St. Cyprian, bishop of Carthage, ended his active career as a martyr during the Valerian Persecution. Exactly when he was born is not known. He was converted to Christianity in 246 and only three years later was the bishop of Carthage. His excellent education, his public speaking talents and his strong leadership abilities contributed to the rapidity with which he rose to such an important position in the church. Cyprian guided his people through the Decian Persecution (250-251). There were times when his outspokenness lead to serious tensions between himself and the bishop of Rome. After contributing his talents so generously to the development of the early Church, he went to his death, in imitation of the Word of God, in silence. His great worth was quickly recognized and honored, for his name was listed among the martyrs specifically mentioned in the liturgical canon.

Cyprian is best known for his concept of the Church. He was convinced of the basic unity of the Church and applied this conviction at various levels, viz., the city of Carthage, the region of Africa and the Church universal. There could be but one faith and one charity, and all members were held together in the Holy Spirit. Episcopal collegiality was essential to the living out of church unity. All members of the church, through baptism and *the other sacraments, were one in Christ and were called to live out that unity in their daily lives.*

A pestilence that struck Carthage around 252-254 provided the Christian community with an opportunity to live out these basic concepts in a particular way. Sensitive leader and pastor that he was, Cyprian called upon the Christians in his city to help the sick and the dying, and the many people who had been impoverished by the plague. His treatise, Works and Almsgiving, *interprets human suffering and need in the light of faith and offers a theological foundation for coming to the aid of one's fellowman in time of need.*

The human condition is itself sick, needy and poor. It could become nothing were it not for the fact that God, in his divine goodness through Christ came to the rescue of the human with justice and mercy. Because of this, it is the Christian's responsibility to return thanks to God in a concrete manner by helping his fellowman.

Cyprian obviously ran into opposition. He responds simply and beautifully to several reasons why the more fortunate members of the community do not give alms, e.g., if one gives too much, one can be reduced to penury, or one has a responsibility to one's own household first. The answer is straightforward: you have grown cold; you refuse to come to the aid of your brothers. But there are no acceptable excuses. By selfishness and greed, you cut yourselves off from truly celebrating the Lord's feast. Cyprian appealed to the example of the first Christian community, "when the faith of believers was warm with a fervor of faith still new." The original spirit was one of selling everything and gladly distributing the proceeds to the poor.

Cyprian's treatise both raises questions and suggests directions for twentieth century man whose complicated society, laden with problems such as poverty and sickness, must still contend with the simplicity of the primitive Christian spirit.

WORKS AND ALMSGIVING

CHAPTER 1

Many and great, most beloved brethren, are the divine blessings by which the abundant copious clemency of God the Father and of Christ has both worked and is always working for our salvation, because the Father has sent His son to preserve us and to quicken us that He might be able to restore us, and because the son wished to be sent and to be called the son of man that He might make us the sons of God. He humbled Himself that He might raise up the people who before were prostrate; He was wounded that He might cure our wounds; He served that He might draw those served away to liberty. He underwent death that He might hold forth immortality to mortals. These are the many and great gifts of divine mercy. But still further, what providence and what great clemency that is, that we are provided for by a plan of salvation so that more abundant care is taken for man's salvation who has already been redeemed! For when the Lord had come and healed the wounds which Adam had borne and had cured the old poisons of the serpent, He gave him when made whole a law not to sin anymore lest something more serious happen to him in his sinning. We were restricted and shut within a narrow limit by the prescription of innocence. And the infirmity of human frailty would have no resource nor accomplish anything, unless again divine goodness came to the rescue and by pointing out the works of justice and mercy opened a way to safeguard salvation, so that by almsgiving we may wash away whatever pollutions we later contract.

CHAPTER 2

The Holy Spirit speaks in the Scriptures, saying: 'By alms and by faith sins are cleansed.' Surely not those sins which had been contracted before, for they are purged by the blood and sanctification of Christ. Likewise again he says: 'As water quenches fire, so do alms quench sin.' Here also it is shown and proved that just as with laver of the waters of salvation the fire of Gehenna is extinguished, so by almsgiving and good works the flame of sins is quenched. And because the remission of sins is once granted in baptism, constant and continuous labor acting in the manner of baptism again bestows the indulgences of God. This does the Lord also teach in the Gospel. For when it was noted that His disciples were eating without first having washed their hands, He replied and said: 'He who made the inside made also the outside. Truly give alms, and behold all things are clean to you,' that is, teaching and showing that not the hands but the heart ought to be washed and that the foulness within rather than without ought to be taken away, but that he who cleanses what is within has cleansed also what is without and when the mind has been made clean he has begun to be clean in skin and body. But furthermore advising and showing how we can be pure and cleansed, He added that alms must be given. The merciful One advises that mercy be shown, and, because He seeks to save those whom He redeemed at a great price, He teaches that those who have been polluted after the grace of baptism can be cleansed again.

CHAPTER 3

So, most beloved brethren, let us acknowledge the saving gift of divine indulgence by cleansing and purging our sins; let us, who cannot be without some wound of conscience, care for our wounds with spiritual remedies. Let no one so flatter himself on his pure and immaculate heart that relying on his innocence he think that medicine should not be applied to his wounds, since it is written: 'Who shall boast that he has a pure heart or who shall boast that he is clean from sins?' and since again John lays down and says in his Epistle: 'If we say that we have no sin, we deceive ourselves and the truth is not in us.' But if no one can be without sin, and whoever says that he is without fault is either proud or foolish, how necessary, how kind is the divine clemency which, since it knows that certain later wounds are not lacking to those already healed, gave salutary remedies for the care and healing of the wounds anew.

CHAPTER 4

Finally, most beloved brethren, never has the divine admonition failed and been silent in the Old as well as the New Testament in always and everywhere urging the people of God to works of mercy, and, as the Holy Spirit prophesies and exhorts, in ordering everyone, who is being instructed unto hope of the heavenly kingdom, to practice almsgiving. The God of Isaias commands and orders: 'Cry out in strength,' he says, 'and spare not; lift up thy voices as with a trumpet; announce to my people their sins, and to the house of Jacob their crimes.' And when He had ordered their sins to be charged upon them and when He had set forth their iniquities with the full force of His indignation, and had said that they could not make satisfaction for their sins, not even if they resorted to prayers, nor even if they rolled in sackcloth and ashes could they soften God's anger, yet in the last part showing that God can be placated by almsgiving alone, he added saying: 'Break thy bread with the hungry and bring into thy house those who lack a roof. If you see one naked, clothe him, and thou shalt not despise the offspring of thy seed. Then shalt thy light break forth seasonably, and thy garments shall speedily arise, and thy justice shall go before thee and the brightness of God shall surround thee. While you shall yet speak, He shall say 'Lo, here I am.'

CHAPTER 5

The remedies for propitiating God have been given in the words of God himself; divine instructions have taught that God is satisfied by just works, that sins are cleansed by the merits of mercy. And in Solomon we read: 'Shut up alms in the heart of the poor, and it shall obtain help for thee against all evil.' And again: 'He that stoppeth his ears lest he hear the weak, shall himself call upon God, but there will be none to hear him.' For he will not be able to merit the mercy of God who himself has not been merciful, nor will gain any request from the divine love by his prayers, who has not been humane toward the prayer of the poor. This likewise the Holy Spirit declares in the Psalms and proves, saying: 'Blessed is he who thinks of the needy and the poor; the Lord will save him in the evil day:' Mindful of these precepts Daniel, when king Nebuchodonosor being frightened by an unfavorable dream was worried, gave a remedy for averting evils by obtaining divine help, saying: 'Wherefore, O king, let my counsel be acceptable to thee, and redeem thy sins with alms, and thy iniquities with works of mercy to the poor, and God will be patient with thy sins.' When the king did not obey him, he suffered the misfortunes and trouble which he had seen, which he might have escaped and avoided, if he had redeemed his sins by almsgiving. The angel Raphael also testifies likewise, and urges that almsgiving be practiced freely and generously, saying: 'Prayer is good with fasting and alms, for alms delivereth from death, and itself purges away sins.' He shows that our prayers and fastings are of less avail, unless they are aided by almsgiving, that entreaties alone are able to obtain little, unless they are made sufficient by the addition of deeds and works. The angel reveals and makes manifest and confirms that our petitions are made efficacious by almsgiving; that by almsgiving life is redeemed from dangers; that by almsgiving souls are freed from death.

CHAPTER 6

Most beloved brethren, we do not so bring forth these things, so as not to approve by the testimony of truth what the angel Raphael said. In the Acts of the Apostles faith in the fact is established, and it is discovered by the proof of the accomplished and fulfilled fact that by almsgiving souls are freed not only from the second but also from the first death. When Tabitha who had been very much given to just works and almsgiving fell sick and died, Peter was summoned to the body of the lifeless one. And when he had come quickly in accord with apostolic charity, there stood around him widows weeping and beseeching, showing the cloaks and tunics and all the garments which they had previously received, and praying for the deceased not by their words but by her own works. Peter felt that what was sought in this way could be obtained and that Christ's help would not be lacking the widows as they pleaded, since He Himself was clothed in the clothing of widows. So when, falling on his knees, he had prayed and as a proper advocate of the widows and the poor had brought the prayers entrusted to him to the Lord, turning to the corpse which already washed lay on the bier, he said: 'Tabitha, arise in the name of Jesus Christ.' Nor did He fail to bring aid to Peter at once, who had said in His Gospel that whatever should be asked in His name was granted. Therefore, death is suspended and the spirit is restored and, as all marvelled and were amazed, the body is revived and quickens for the light of this world anew. So powerful were the merits of mercy, so much did just works avail! She who had conferred upon suffering widows the assistance for living deserved to be recalled to life by the petition of widows.

CHAPTER 7

Thus in the Gospel the Lord, the Teacher of our life and Master of eternal salvation, quickening the populace of believers, and providing for them forever when quickened, among His divine mandates and heavenly precepts, commands and prescribes nothing more frequently than that we continue in almsgiving and not depend on earthly possessions but rather lay up heavenly treasures. 'Sell,' He says, 'Your possessions, and give alms'; and again: 'Do not lay up for yourselves treasures on earth, where rust and moth consume, and where thieves break in and steal; but lay up for yourselves treasures in heaven where neither rust nor moth consumes and where thieves do not break in. For where thy treasure is, there also will be thy heart.' And when He wished to show the man who had been made perfect and complete by the observance of the law, He said: 'If you wish to be perfect, go, sell all that you have, and give to the poor, and thou shalt have treasure in heaven, and come follow me.' Likewise in another place He says that a merchant of heavenly grace and a purchaser of eternal salvation, after ridding himself of all his possessions, ought to purchase from the amount of his patrimony the precious pearl, that is eternal life, precious by the blood of Christ. He says: 'The kingdom of heaven is like a merchant seeking good pearls. When he finds a pearl of great price, he goes and sells all that he has and buys it.'

CHAPTER 8

Finally also He calls those sons of Abraham, whom He perceives active in abiding and nourishing the poor. For when

Zachaeus said: 'Behold I give one-half of my possessions to the poor, and if I have defrauded anyone of anything, I restore it four-fold,' Jesus replied: 'Today salvation has come to this house, since he, too, is a son of Abraham.' For if Abraham believed in God, and it was accounted to him unto righteousness, surely he who gives alms according to the precept of God believes in God; and he who possesses the truth of faith keeps the fear of God; moreover, he who keeps the fear of God considers God in showing mercy to the poor. For so he labors, because he believes in God, because he knows that those things are true which have been predicted in the words of God, and that holy Scripture cannot lie, that unfruitful trees, that is, sterile men, are cut off and cast into the fire, that the merciful are called to the kingdom. He also in another place calls the laborious and fruitful faithful, but to the unfruitful and sterile he denies the faith, saying: 'If in the wicked mammon you have not been faithful, who will entrust to you what is true? And if in the case of what belongs to another you have not been faithful, who will give you what is your own?

CHAPTER 9

But you are afraid and you fear lest, if you begin to act very generously, your patrimony come to an end because of your generous action and you perchance be reduced to penury; be undisturbed on this score, be secure. That cannot be ended, whence expenditure is made in the service of Christ, whence the heavenly work is celebrated. I do not promise you on my own authority but I vouch for it on the faith of holy Scriptures and on the authority of the divine promise. The Holy Spirit speaks through Solomon and says: 'He that giveth to the poor shall never be in want; but he that turns away his eyes shall be in great want,' showing that the merciful and those who do good can never be in want, that rather the sparing and the sterile later come to want. Likewise the blessed apostle Paul full of the grace of the Lord's inspiration says: 'He who provides seed for the sower, also will give bread to eat and will multiply your seed and will increase the growth of the fruits of your justice, so that in all things you may be enriched.' And again: 'The administration of this service not only will supply what the saints lack but will abound also through much action of gratitude in the Lord,' because, while the action of thanks is directed to God by the prayer of the poor for our almsgiving and good works, the wealth of him who does good is increased by the retribution of God. And the Lord in the Gospel, already considering the hearts of such men and denouncing the faithless and unbelievers with prescient voice, bears witness and says: 'Be not anxious, saying: 'What shall we eat or what shall we drink or what shall we put on?' For after all these things the Gentiles seek. For your Father knows that you have need of all these things. But seek first the kingdom and the justice of God, and all these things shall be added to you.' He says that all things are added and given over to those who seek the kingdom and the justice of God; for the Lord says that, when the day of judgment shall come they, who have labored in His Church, are admitted to receive the kingdom.

CHAPTER 10

You fear lest your patrimony perchance fail you, if you begin to do good generously from it, and you do not know, wretched man that you are, that, while you are afraid lest your personal wealth be failing, life itself, and salvation fail, and, while you are anxious lest any of your possessions be diminished, you do not take notice that you youself, a lover of mammon rather than of your soul, are being diminished, and, while you are afraid lest for your own sake you lose your patrimony, you yourself perish for the sake of your patrimony. Therefore, the Apostle well exclaims, saying: 'We brought nothing into this world, and we can take nothing out. Therefore, having food and clothing, with these let us be content. But those who seek to become rich fall into temptation and a snare, and into many harmful desires which plunge a man into destruction and damnation. For covetousness is the root of all evils and some seeking wealth have made shipwreck of their faith and have involved themselves in many troubles.'

CHAPTER 11

Do you fear lest your patrimony perchance fail, if you begin to act generously from it? For when did it happen that resources could fail a just man, when it is written: 'The Lord will not afflict the soul of the just with famine.' Elias in the desert is fed by ministering ravens, and a meal is prepared in heaven for Daniel when he was inclosed in a den of lions by order of the king; and you fear lest food be lacking for you while you do good and deserve well of the Lord, when He Himself in the Gospel bears witness for a reproach of those of doubtful mind and little faith and says: 'Look at the birds of the air; they do not sow or reap, or gather into barns; yet your heavenly Father feeds them. Are not you of more value than they?' God feeds the fowls, and daily sustenance is furnished the sparrows, and to those creatures who have no sense of things divine neither drink nor food is lacking. Do you think that to a Christian, do you think that to a servant of God, do you think that to one devoted to good works, do you think that to one dear to the Lord anything will be lacking?

CHAPTER 12

Unless you think that he who feeds Christ is not himself fed by Christ, or that earthly things will be lacking to those upon whom heavenly and divine things are bestowed, whence this incredulous thinking, whence that impious and sacrilegious contemplation? What is a faithless heart doing in a home of faith? Why is he called and spoken of as Christian who does not believe in Christ at all? The name of pharisee is more befitting you. For when the Lord in the Gospel was discoursing about almsgiving, and forewarned faithfully and for our salvation that we should make friends for ourselves of our earthly lucre by provident good works, the Scripture added after this the following words: 'Now the Pharisees, who were very fond of money, were listening to all these things, and they were sneering at him.' Certain persons like these we now see in the Church, whose closed ears and blinded hearts admit no light from the spiritual and saving warnings, of whom we should not marvel that they contemn the servant in his discourses, when we see that the Lord Himself is contemned by such.

CHAPTER 13

Why do you give approbation to yourself with these empty and foolish thoughts, as if you were withheld from good works by fear and solicitude for the future? Why do you hold forth certain shadows and illusions of a vain excuse? By all means confess what is the truth, and, since you cannot deceive those who know, set forth the hidden and secret things of your mind. The shadows of sterility have besieged your mind, and with the withdrawal from it of the light of truth the deep and profound darkness of avarice has blinded your carnal heart. You are the captive and slave of your money; you are tied by the chains and bonds of avarice, and you whom Christ had already freed are bound anew. You save money which, when saved, does not save you; you accumulate a patrimony which burdens you with its weight; and you do not remember what God replied to the rich man who boasts with foolish glee over the abundance of his abounding harvest. 'Thou fool,' He said, 'this night thy soul is demanded. Therefore, the things that thou hast provided, whose will they be?' Why do you alone watch over your riches? Why do you pile up the burden of your patrimony, that the richer you have been in the sight of the world, the poorer you may become in the sight of God? Divide your returns with your God; share your gains with Christ; make Christ a partner in your earthly possessions, that He also may make you co-heir of His heavenly kingdom.

CHAPTER 14

You err and are deceived, whoever think yourself rich in the world. Hear the voice of your Lord in the Apocalypse as He rebukes such men with just reproaches. He says: 'You say: "I am rich and have grown wealthy and I have need of nothing," and you do not know that you are wretched and poor and blind and naked. I counsel you to buy of me gold refined by fire, that you may become rich, and that you may put on a white garment, and that the shame of your nakedness may not appear; and anoint your eyes with eye-salve that you may see.' You, therefore, who are wealthy and rich buy for yourself from Christ gold that has been tried by fire, that you can be pure gold, when your impurities have been burnt out as if by fire, if you are cleansed by almsgiving and just works. Buy for yourself a white garment, that you, who according to Adam had been naked and were before frightful and unseemly, may be clothed in the white raiment of Christ. And you who are a rich and wealthy matron anoint your eyes not with the stibium of the devil but with the eye-salve of Christ, that you can come to see God, when you merit God by character and good works.

CHAPTER 15

But you, who are such, cannot do good works in the Church; for your eyes suffused with blackness and covered with the shadows of night do not see the needy and the poor. Do you, rich and wealthy, think that you celebrate the Lord's Feast, who do not at all consider the offering, who come to the Lord's Feast without a sacrifice, who take a part of the sacrifice which the poor man offered? Behold in the Gospel the widow mindful of the heavenly precepts, doing good in the very midst of the pressures and hardships of poverty, casting two mites which were her only possessions into the treasury; and when the Lord noticed and saw her, considering and weighing her good work not as from a patrimony but as from the heart, He answered and said: 'Truly I say to you that this widow has put more than all into the offering for God. For all these out of their abundance have put in as gifts to God, but she out of her want has put in all that she had to live on.' A greatly blessed and glorious woman, who even before the day of judgment merited to be praised by the voice of the Judge. Let the rich man be ashamed of his sterility and his misfortunes. A widow, that is, a poor widow is found with an offering, and, although all things that are given are conferred upon orphans and widows, she gives who ought to receive, that we may know what punishment awaits the rich man, when by this teaching the poor also should do good. And that we may understand that these works are given to God and that he, whoever does these, deserves well of God, Christ calls this 'gifts of God' and points out that the widow has placed two mites among the gifts of God, that it can be more and more manifest that he who pities the poor lends to God.

CHAPTER 16

Let not this fact, dearest brethren, restrain and recall the Christian from good and just works, that anyone think that he can be excused for the benefit of his children, since in spiritual contributions we should consider Christ who has professed that He receives them and not prefer our fellow-servants to our children but the Lord, for he instructs and warns us, saying: 'He who loves father or mother more than me is not worthy of me, and he who loves son or daughter more than me is not worthy of me.' Likewise in Deuteronomy for the strengthening of the faith and the love of God, similar things are written. He says: 'Those who say to their father and mother: "I do not know you," and who have not known their children, these have kept thy precepts and observed thy covenant.' For if we love God with our whole heart, we should prefer neither parents nor children to God. This also John lays down in his Epistle, that there is no love of God in those whom we see unwilling to do good to the poor. He says: 'He who has the goods of this world and sees his brother in need and closes his heart to him, how does the love of God abide in him?' For if by almsgiving to the poor God is made our debtor, and when it is given to the least it is given to Christ, there is no reason for anyone preferring earthly things to heavenly, nor placing human things before divine.

CHAPTER 17

Thus when the widow in the third Book of Kings, after all had been consumed in the drought and the famine, had made a cake upon the ashes from the little meal and oil that was left, and after this had been eaten was about to die with her children, Elias came and asked that there first be given him to eat and that she with her children then eat what was left of this. She did not hesitate to obey nor did the mother put her children before Elias in the famine and want. Rather, there is done in the sight of God what pleases God; promptly and gladly what was sought is offered, and a portion is not given out of the abundance but the whole from a little, and another is fed before her hungry children, and in poverty and hunger food is not considered before mercy, so that while in a saving work life according to the flesh is contemned the soul spiritually is preserved. Thus Elias, playing the part of Christ, and showing that he returns to each according to his mercy, replied and said: 'Thus saith the Lord: the pot of meal shall not fail, nor the curse of oil diminish until the day wherein the Lord will give rain upon the earth.' According to her faith in the divine promise what she promised was multiplied and heaped high for the widow, and, as her just works and merits of mercy took on growth and increase, her vessels of meal and oil were filled. Nor did the mother deprive her children of what she gave Elias, but rather she conferred upon her children what she did kindly and piously. But she did not yet know Christ; not yet had she heard his precepts; she did not, as one redeemed by His cross and His passion, repay food and drink for His blood, so that from this it is apparent how much he sins in the world, who, placing himself and his children before Christ, preserves his wealth, and does not share his plentiful patrimony with the indigent poor.

CHAPTER 18

But yet there are many children in the house, and the number of offspring prevents you from applying yourself to good works. Still by this very fact you ought the more to do good works, since you are the father of many pledges. There are more for whom you beseech the Lord; the sins of many must be redeemed; the consciences of many must be purged; the souls of many must be freed. As in this unholy life the greater the number of your children the greater is the expense for their nourishment and sustenance, so too in the spiritual and heavenly life the greater the abundance of your children, the greater also should be the outlay of good works. Thus Job offered numerous sacrifices for his children, and as great as was the number of pledges in his home, so great a number of victims also was offered to God. And since daily there cannot be lacking some sinning in the sight of God, daily sacrifices were not lacking with which the sins could be wiped away. Scripture proves this when it says: 'Job, a true and just man, had seven sons and three daughters, and he cleansed them by offering for them sacrifices to God according to their number, and for their sins one calf.' If then you truly love your sons, if you show them the full and paternal sweetness of love, you should do good works more that you may commend your sons to God by your righteous works.

CHAPTER 19

Do not consider him the father of your children who is both temporary and weak, but obtain Him who is the eternal and strong Father of spiritual children. Assign to Him your wealth which you are keeping for your heirs; let Him be your children's guardian, their caretaker, their protector with his divine majesty against all worldly injuries. When your patrimony is entrusted to God, the state does not seize it, nor does the tax-collector assail it, nor any forensic calumny overturn it. The inheritance is placed in safety, which is kept under God's care. This is to provide for the future of your dear charges; this is to provide for your future heirs with paternal love according to the faith of the holy Scripture which says: 'I have been younger and I have grown old, and I have not seen the just man forsaken nor his seed begging bread. All the day he shows mercy and lends, and his seed shall be blessed.' And again: 'He who lives without reproach in justice shall leave behind him blessed children.' So you as a father are a transgressor and a betrayer, unless you look out faithfully for the welfare of your children, unless you attend to their salvation with religious and true love. Why are you eager for earthly rather than heavenly patrimony? Why do you prefer to commend your children to the devil rather than to Christ? You sin twice and commit a twofold and double crime both because you do not make ready the help of God the Father for your children and because you teach your children to love their patrimony more than Christ.

CHAPTER 20

Be to your children such a father as was Tobias. Give useful and salutary precepts to your pledges such as he gave to his son; command your children as he too commanded saying: 'And now, sons, I command you, serve God in truth, and do before Him what pleases Him; and command your children that they do justice and almsdeeds, and that they be mindful of God, and bless His name on every occasion.' And again: 'And all the days of thy life, son, have God in mind, and do not transgress His commandments. Do justice all the days of thy life, and do not walk the way of iniquity, for when you act truthfully there will be respect of your works. Give alms out of thy substance, and turn not away thy face from any poor person, for so shall it come to pass that the face of the Lord shall not be turned from thee. As you have, my son, so give: if you have an abundant supply, give alms the more from that. If you have a little, give a share from that little. Have no fear when you bestow an alms; you are storing up for yourself a good reward for the day of necessity, for alms delivers from death and does not suffer one to go into darkness. Alms provides a great confidence for all who do it before the most high God.'

CHAPTER 21

What sort of gift is it, dearest brethren, whose setting forth is celebrated in the sight of God? If in a gift of the Gentiles it seems grand and glorious to have proconsuls or emperors present, and the preparation and the expense on the part of the givers is greater that they may be able to please greater personages, how much more illustrious and greater is the glory of the giver to have God and Christ as spectators; how much richer in this case is the preparation, and extensive the expense to be set forth, when the powers of heaven assemble for the spectacle, all the angels assemble, when not a four-horsed chariot or a consulship is sought for the giver, but eternal life is presented, nor is the empty and temporary favor of the mob laid hold of, but the everlasting reward of the heavenly kingdom is received.

CHAPTER 22

And that the lazy and the sterile and those doing nothing about the fruit of salvation because of their covetousness for many may be more ashamed, that the blush of their shame and disgrace may the more strike upon their sordid conscience, let each one place before his eyes the devil and his servants, that is, with the people of perdition and of death springing forth into the midst, the people of Christ, with Him present and judging, calling forth in a contest of comparison, as he says: 'I, for those whom you see with me have neither received blows nor have I undergone stripes, nor carried the cross, nor poured forth blood, nor have I redeemed my family at the cost of suffering and blood; moreover, neither do I promise them a heavenly kingdom nor, after restoring immortality, do I again recall them to paradise; and what precious, what grand gifts, sought out with what excessively long labor do they prepare for me with the most sumptuous devices, after mortgaging or selling their possessions; and unless a respectable demonstration follows, they are cast out with reproaches and hissings, and sometimes they are almost stoned to death by the fury of the populace. Point out such almsgivers of yours, O Christ, those rich men, those men affluent with abounding wealth, whether in the Church where you preside and watch they give forth a gift of this kind, after pawning and distributing their possessions, rather after transferring them to heavenly treasures by exchanging what they possess for something better. By those transitory and earthly gifts of mine no one is fed, no one is clothed, no one is sustained, by the solace of any food or drink. Everything in the midst of the madness of the giver and the mistake of the spectator are perishing because of the prodigious and foolish vanity of frustrating pleasures. There among your poor You are clothed and You are fed; You promise those who give alms eternal life; and scarcely are Your people, who are honored by You with divine wages and heavenly rewards, made equal to mine.'

CHAPTER 23

What do you reply to all this, dearest brethren? In what manner do we defend the sacrilegious sterilities and the minds of the rich covered by a kind of night of shadows; by what excuse do we clear them, we who are less than the servants of the devil, so as not to repay Christ even in small measure for the price of His passion and blood? He has given us precepts; He has taught what His servant should do; promising a reward to those who give alms and threatening punishment to the sterile; He has set forth His sentence; He has foretold what His judgment would be. What excuse can there be for him who ceases to do so; what defense for the sterile? Unless it be that, unless the servant does what is commanded, the Lord will do what He threatens. He even says: 'When the Son of man shall come in His majesty, and all angels with Him, then He will sit on the throne of His glory; and before Him will be gathered all the nations, and He will separate

111

them one from another, as the shepherd the sheep from the goats, and He will set the sheep on His right hand, but the goats on the left. Then the king will say to those who are on His right hand: "Come, ye blessed of my Father, take possession of the kingdom prepared for you from the foundation of the world; for I was hungry and you gave me to eat; I was thirsty and you gave me to drink; I was a stranger and you took me in; naked and you covered me; I was sick and you visited me; I was in prison and you came to me." Then the just will answer Him saying: "Lord, when did we see hungry, and feed thee; or thirsty, and give thee drink? And when did we see thee a stranger, and take thee in; or naked, and clothe thee? Or when did we see thee sick, or in prison, and come to thee?" Then the king answering will say to them, "Amen I say to you, as long as you did it for one of these, the least of my brethren, you did it for me." Then he will say of those who are on His left hand: 'Depart from me, accursed ones, into the everlasting fire which my Father has prepared for the devil and his angels. For I was hungry and you did not give me to eat; I was thirsty and you gave me no drink; I was a stranger and you did not take me in; naked, and you did not clothe me; sick, and in prison, and you did not visit me." Then they also will answer and say to Him: "Lord, when did we see Thee hungry, or thirsty, or a stranger, or naked, or sick, or in prison, and did not minister to Thee?" And He will answer them: "Amen, I say to you, as long as you did not do it for one of these least ones, you did not do it for me." And these will go away into everlasting fire, but the just into everlasting life." What greater declaration could Christ have made to us? How more could He have stimulated the works of our justice and mercy than by having said that whatever is offered to the poor and the needy is offered to Him, and by having said that He is offended unless offering is made to the needy and the poor? So that he in the Church, who is not moved by consideration of his brother, may indeed be moved by contemplation of Christ, and he who does not give thought to his fellow servant in trouble and in need may indeed give thought to the Lord abiding in that very one whom he despises.

CHAPTER 24

And so, most beloved brethren, let us whose fear is inclined toward God, and whose minds, after spurning and trampling upon the world, are turned to heavenly and divine things to deserve well of the Lord, offer obedience with full faith, devoted minds, and continual good works. Let us give Christ earthly garments that we may receive heavenly clothing. Let us give worldly food and drink that together with Abraham and Isaac and Jacob we may come to the heavenly banquet. Lest we reap little, let us sow very much. While there is time, let us take thought for security and eternal salvation, as Paul, the Apostle, advises saying: 'Therefore, while we have time, let us do what is good to all men, but especially to those who are of the household of faith. And in doing good let us not grow tired, for in due time we shall reap.'

CHAPTER 25

Let us consider, most beloved brethren, what the assemblage of believers did under the Apostles, when at the very beginning the mind flourished with greater virtues, when the faith of believers was warm with a fervor of faith still new. Then they sold their homes and estates, and gladly and generously offered the proceeds to the Apostles for distribution among the poor, by selling and distributing their earthly patrimony transferring their estates there where they might receive the fruits of an eternal possession, there preparing homes where they might begin to live always. Such was their abundance in good works then as was their unity in love, as we read in the Acts of the Apostles: 'Now the multitude of those who believed were acting with one soul and one mind, nor was there any discrimination among them, nor did they judge anything their own of the goods that they had, but they had all things in common.' This is truly to become a son of God by spiritual birth; this is to imitate the equity of God by the heavenly law. For whatever belongs to God, belongs to all by our appropriation of it, nor is anyone kept from his benefits and gift, nor does anything prevent the whole human race from equally enjoying God's goodness and generosity. Thus the day illuminates equally; the sun radiates, the rain moistens; the wind blows, and for those who sleep there is one sleep; and the splendor of the stars and the moon is common. With this example of equality the possessor on the earth who shares his returns and fruits, while he is fair and just with his gratuitous bounties, is an imitator of God the Father.

CHAPTER 26

What, dearest brethren, will be that glory of the charitable; how grand and consummate the joy, when the Lord begins to number His people, and, distributing the rewards for our merits and works, to grant heavenly things for the earthly, everlasting for the temporal, great for small, to offer us to the Father to whom he restored us by His sanctification, to bestow eternal immortality on us, for which He has prepared us by the quickening of His blood, to bring us back again to paradise, to open up the kingdom of heaven by the faith and truth of His promise! Let these things cling firmly in our thoughts; let these things be understood with a full faith; let these things be lived with a whole heart; let these things be redeemed by the magnanimity of unceasing good works. Dearest brethren, a glorious and divine thing is the work of salvation [charity], a grand solace for believers, a salutary safeguard of our security, a bulwark of hope, a safeguard of faith, a cure for sin, something placed in the power of the doer, a grand and easy thing, a crown of peace without the danger of persecution, a true and very great gift of God, necessary for the weak, glorious for the strong, aided by which the Christian bears spiritual grace, deserves Christ as judge, and accounts God his debtor. Let us strive gladly and promptly for this palm of the works of salvation; let us all run in the contest of justice as God and Christ look on, and let us, who already have begun to be greater than this life and this world, not slacken our course by a desire for this life and this world. If the day of reward or of persecution comes upon us ready and swift as we run in this contest of good works, the Lord will never fail to give a reward for our merits; in peace He will give to those who conquer a white crown for their good works; in persecution He will give a second crown, a purple one, for our passion.

St. Augustine
354-430

Aurelius Augustine is one of those exceptional human beings who seem to be beyond the barriers of space and time. Yet his autobiography reveals a humanness that makes the reader feel at ease with him immediately. The general lines of his life are well known. He was born in 354 in Tagaste, North Africa, to a pagan father and Christian mother, was well-educated, lived a life of sensual pleasures for several years, was constantly searching for truth and intellectual fulfillment, underwent a dramatic conversion process, and developed into the most influential theologian in the western Christian tradition. He died as Bishop of Hippo, Africa, in 430. His was a life that voyaged through darkness and light, that knew joy and sorrow, that drifted downward into the abyss of sin and soared up to unimaginable heights of graceful union with God. Augustine's brilliant intellect explored the depths of the human soul in an effort to capture its mysterious origins. This was the search that led him to exclaim, "You have made us for yourself, and our heart is restless until it rests in you." (Confessions I.1).

The City of God is Augustine's greatest work. In the year 410, the barbarian Goths invaded and conquered the imperial city of Rome. Looking for some explanation for this catastrophe, the pagan citizens of Rome tended to blame the Christians for the collapse of the empire. In 413, Augustine started writing his *masterpiece in response to this false accusation. When he finally completed* The City of God *fourteen years later (427), Augustine had gone far beyond a mere response. Of the work's twenty-two books, the first ten constitute the reply to the pagan charge against the Christians. They are also an invaluable source of information on the early history of mankind and the social structures of the pagan world.*

Beginning with Book 11, Augustine develops his thesis of the two cities in human history, treating successively their origin (Books 11 to 14), their development (Books 15 to 18) and their ends (Books 19 to 22).

If two cities exist, and they do, then they are the product of two loves, love of God and love of the world. For Augustine, these two loves explain all history: "These are two loves, the one of which is holy, the other, unholy; one social, the other individualist; one takes heed of the common utility because of the heavenly society, the other reduces even the commonweal to its own ends because of a proud lust of domination; the one is subject to God, the other sets itself up as a rival to God . . . Tell me what a people loves and I shall tell you what it is."

The following selection is from Book 19. It includes Chapter 4 and Chapters 11 to 18. Augustine discusses the supreme good and supreme evil in Chapter 4. Chapter 11 introduces the theme of peace, for which mankind ceaselessly yearns. After exploring various aspects of earthly peace, Augustine declares that the only true peace is the perfectly ordered and harmonious communion of those who find their joy in God and in one another in God.

This concept, so foreign to contemporary peace efforts established on weapons and balance of power, deserves renewed and serious reflection on the part of modern man.

116

THE CITY OF GOD

I f I am asked what stand the City of God would take on the issues raised and, first, what this City thinks of the supreme good and ultimate evil, the answer would be: She holds that eternal life is the supreme good and eternal death the supreme evil, and that we should live rightly in order to obtain the one and avoid the other. Hence the Scriptural expression, 'the just man lives by faith'—by faith, for the fact is that we do not now behold our good and, therefore, must seek it by faith; nor can we of ourselves even live rightly, unless He who gives us faith helps us to believe and pray, for it takes faith to believe that we need His help.

Those who think that the supreme good and evil are to be found in this life are mistaken. It makes no difference whether it is in the body or in the soul or in both—or, specifically, in pleasure or virtue or in both—that they seek the supreme good. They seek in vain whether they look to serenity, to virtue, or to both; whether to pleasure plus serenity, or to virtue, or to all three; or to the satisfaction of our innate exigencies, or to virtue, or to both. It is in vain that men look for beatitude on earth or in human nature. Divine Truth, as expressed in the Prophet's words, makes them look foolish: 'The Lord knows the thoughts of men' or, as the text is quoted by St. Paul: 'The Lord knows the thoughts of the wise that they are vain.'

For, what flow of eloquence is sufficient to set forth the miseries of human life? Cicero did the best he could in his *Consolatio de morte filiae,* but how little was his very best? As for the primary satisfactions of our nature, when or where or how can they be so securely possessed in this life that they are not subject to the ups and downs of fortune? There is no pain of body, driving out pleasure, that may not befall the wise man; no anxiety that may not banish calm. A man's physical integrity is ended by the amputation or crippling of any of his limbs; his beauty is spoiled by deformity, his health by sickness, his vigor by weariness, his agility by torpor and sluggishness. There is not one of these that may not afflict the flesh even of a philosopher. Among our elementary requirements we reckon a graceful and becoming erectness and movement; but what happens to these as soon as some sickness brings on palsy or, still worse, a spinal deformity so severe that a man's hands touch the ground as though he were a four-footed beast? What is then left of any beauty or dignity in a man's posture or gait? Turn, now, to the primary endowments of the soul: senses to perceive and intelligence to understand the truth. How much sensation does a man have left if, for example, he goes deaf and blind? And where does the reason or intelligence go, into what strange sleep, when sickness unsettles the mind? We can hardly hold back our tears when mad men say or do extravagant things—things wholly unlike their customary behavior and normal goodness. To witness such things, even to recall them, makes a decent man weep. Still worse is the case of those possessed by demons. Their intelligence seems driven away, not to say destroyed, when an evil spirit according to its will makes use of their body and soul. And who can be sure that even a philosopher will not be such a victim at some time in his life?

Further, what is to be said of our perception of the truth, at the very best? What kind of truth and how much of it can we reach through our bodily senses? Do we not read in the truth-speaking Book of Wisdom: 'For the corruptible body is a load upon the soul, and the earthly habitation presseth down the mind that museth upon many things'?

And what of the urge and appetite for action—*hormé*, as the Greeks call it—which is reckoned among the primary goods of our nature? Is not this the root, too, of those restless energies of the madmen who fill us with tears and fears when their senses deceive them and their reason refuses to function?

So much for the elementary endowments of nature. Look, now, at virtue herself, which comes later with education and claims for herself the topmost place among human goods. Yet, what is the life of virtue save one unending war with evil inclinations, and not with solicitations of other people alone, but with evil inclinations that arise within ourselves and are our very own.

I speak especially of temperance—*sōphrosynē*, as the Greeks call it—which must bridle our fleshly lusts if they are not to drag our will to consent to abominations of every sort. The mere fact that, as St. Paul says, 'the flesh is at war with the spirit,' is no small flaw in our nature; and virtue is at war with this evil inclination when, in the same Apostle's words, 'the spirit lusts against the flesh.' These are opposed to each other to such a degree that 'we do not the things that we would.' And when we seek final rest in the supreme good, what do we seek save an end to this conflict between flesh and spirit, freedom from this propensity to evil against which the spirit is at war? Yet, will as we may, such liberty cannot be had in mortal life.

This much, however, we can do with the help of God—not yield by surrender of the spirit and be dragged into sin willingly. Meanwhile, we must not fondly imagine that, so long as we wage this inward war, we may achieve that longed-for beatitude which can be solely the prize of the victor. For there lives no man so perfected in wisdom as not to have some conflict with excessive desires.

Take, next, the virtue called prudence. Is not this virtue constantly on the lookout to distinguish what is good from what is evil, so that there may be no mistake made in seeking the one and avoiding the other? So it bears witness to the fact that we are surrounded by evil and have evil within us. This virtue teaches that it is evil to consent to desires leading to sin and good to resist them. And what prudence preaches temperance puts into practice. Yet, neither prudence nor temperance can rid this life of the evils that are their constant concern.

Finally, there is justice. Its task is to see that to each is given what belongs to each. And this holds for the right order within man himself, so that it is just for the soul to be subordinate to God, and the body to the soul, and thus for body and soul taken together to be subject to God. Is there not abundant evidence that this virtue is unremittingly struggling to effect this internal order—and is far from finished? For, the less a man has God in his thoughts, the less is his soul subject to God; the more the flesh lusts counter to the spirit, the less the flesh is subject to the soul. So long, then, as such weakness, such moral sickliness remains within us, how can we dare to say that we are out of danger; and, if not yet out of danger, how can we say that our happiness is complete?

Look, now, at the great virtue called fortitude. Is not its very function—to bear patiently with misfortune—overwhelming evidence that human life is beset with unhappiness, however wise a man may be? It is beyond my comprehension how the Stoics can boldly argue that such ills are not really ills, meanwhile allowing that, if a philosopher should be tried by them beyond his obligation or duty to bear, he may have no choice but to take the easy way out by committing suicide. So stultifying is Stoic pride that, all evidences to the contrary, these men still pretend to find the ultimate good in this life and to hold that they are themselves the source of their own happiness. Their kind of sage—an astonishingly silly sage, indeed—may go deaf, dumb and blind, may be crippled, wracked with pain, visited with every imaginable affliction, driven at last to take his own life, yet have the colossal impertinence to call such an existence the happy life! Happy life, indeed, which employs death's aid to end it! If such a life is happy, then I say, live it! Why pretend that evils are not evils, when they not only overcome the virtue of fortitude and force it to yield to evil, but make a man so irrational as to call one and the same life both happy and unlivable? How can anyone be so blind as not to see that if life is happy it should not be shunned? Yet, the moment sickness opens her mouth they say one must choose a way out. If so, why do they not bow their stiff necks and admit life's unhappiness? Now, let me ask: Was it courage or cowardice that made their hero Cato kill himself? Certainly, he would not have done what he did had he not been too cowardly to endure the victory of Caesar. Where, then, was his fortitude? It was a fortitude that yielded, that surrendered, that was so beaten that Cato ran away, deserted, abandoned the happy life. Or, maybe it was no longer the happy life? In that case, it was unhappy. If so, how can anyone deny that the ills that made Cato's life unhappy and unlivable were real evils?

From this it follows that those who admit that such things are evils, so do the Aristotelians and those of the Old Academy whom Varro defends, are nearer the truth than the Stoics, even though Varro also makes the egregious mistake of maintaining that this life is still the happy life in spite of evils so grievous that, for one who suffers them, suicide becomes imperative. 'The pains and afflictions of the body,' Varro admits, 'are evils; and the worse the pains, the greater the evil. To escape them you should end your life.' I ask: Which life? He answers: 'This life which is made grievous by so many evils.' Life, then, is the happy life in the midst of evils which drive a man to escape from life? Is it, perhaps, the happy life precisely because you are allowed to escape its unhappiness by death? Suppose you should be bound by a divine law to remain in its evils and be permitted neither to die nor ever to be free from such misfortunes? Then, at least, you would have to say that such a life would be unhappy. And, surely, if you admit it would be unhappy if unending, you cannot say that it is not unhappy just because there is a quick way out. You cannot maintain that just because unhappiness is short-lived it is really not unhappiness at all; or, what is more preposterous, that because unhappiness is short-lived it deserves to be called happiness.

No, these ills of life must be very real indeed if they can drive even a sage of their type to take his life. For, these philosophers say—and rightly say—that the first and most fundamental command of nature is that a man should cherish his own human life and, by his very nature, shun death; that a man should be his own best friend, wanting and working with all his might and main to keep himself alive and to preserve the union of his body and soul. These ills must be very real indeed if they can subdue the very instinct of nature that struggles in every possible way to put death off; overwhelm it so utterly that death, once shunned, is now desired, sought, and, when all else fails, is self-inflicted. Yes, very real, when they can turn courage into a killer, if, indeed, there be any question of genuine courage, when this virtue, devised to support and steel a man, is so battered down by misfortune that—having failed to sustain him—it is driven, against its very function, to finish him off. It is true, of course, that a philosopher should face death as well as all other trials, with fortitude, but that means death coming upon him from without.

If then, as these philosophers held, even a wise man must yield to suicide, they ought logically to admit that there are evils—even insufferable evils—that account for this tragic compulsion; and that a life so burdensome, so exposed to fortune's ebb and flow, should not be called happy! Nor would those who talk of 'the happy life' ever have called life happy if they had yielded to the truth and the cogency of reason in their search for the happy life as readily as they yield to unhappiness and the weight of evils when they lose their life by suicide; and if, further, they had given up the idea that they could enjoy the supreme good in this mortal life. They would have realized that man's very virtues, his best and most useful possessions, are the most solid evidences of the miseries of life, precisely because their function is to stand by him in perils and problems and pains.

For, when virtues are genuine virtues—and that is possible only when men believe in God—they make no pretense of protecting their possessors from unhappiness, for that would be a false promise; but they do claim that human life, now compelled to feel the misery of so many grievous ills on earth, can, by the hope of heaven, be made both happy and secure. If we are asked how a life can be happy before we are saved, we have the answer of St. Paul: 'For in hope were we saved. But hope that is seen is not hope. For how can a man hope for what he sees? But if we hope for what we do not see, we wait for it with patience.'

Of course, the Apostle was not speaking of men lacking prudence, fortitude, temperance, and justice, but of men whose virtues were true virtues because the men were living by faith. Thus, as 'we are saved by hope,' so we are made happy by hope. Neither our salvation nor our beatitude is here present, but 'we wait for it' in the future, and we wait 'with patience,' precisely because we are surrounded by evils which patience must endure until we come to where all good things are sources of inexpressible happiness and where there will be no longer anything to endure. Such is to be our salvation in the hereafter, such our final blessedness. It is because the philosophers

122

will not believe in this beatitude which they cannot see that
they go on trying to fabricate here below an utterly fraudulent
felicity built on virtue filled with pride and bound to fail them
in the end.

CHAPTER 11

Thus, we may say of peace what we have said of eternal
life—that it is our highest good; more particularly because
the holy Psalmist was addressing the City of God (the nature
of which I am trying, with so much difficulty, to make clear)
when he said: 'Praise the Lord, O Jerusalem; praise thy God,
O Sion. Because he hath strengthened the bolts of thy gates,
he hath blessed thy children within thee. He hath placed peace
in thy borders.' For, when the bolts of that city's gates will
have been strengthened, none will enter in and none will issue
forth. Hence, its borders [fines] must be taken to mean that
peace which I am trying to show is our final good. Note, too,
that Jerusalem, the mystical name which symbolizes this City,
means, as I have already mentioned, 'the vision of peace.'

However, the word 'peace' is so often applied to conditions
here on earth, where life is not eternal, that it is better, I think,
to speak of 'eternal life' rather than of 'peace' as the end or
supreme good of the City of God. It is in this sense that St. Paul
says: 'But now being made free from sin, and become servants
of God, you have your fruit unto sanctification, and the end
life everlasting.'

It would be simplest for all concerned if we spoke of
'peace in eternal life,' or of 'eternal' or of 'eternal life in peace,'
as the end or supreme good of this City. The trouble with the
expression 'eternal life' is that those unfamiliar with the Scriptures might take this phrase to apply also to the eternal loss of
the wicked, either because, as philosophers, they accept the
immortality of the soul, or even because, as Christians, they
know by faith that the punishment of the wicked has no end
and, therefore, that they could not be punished forever unless
their life were eternal.

The trouble with 'peace' is that, even on the level of earthly and temporal values, nothing that we can talk about, long
for, or finally get, is so desirable, so welcome, so good as

peace. At any rate, I feel sure that if I linger a little longer on this topic of peace I shall tire very few of my readers. After all, peace is the end of this City which is the theme of this work; besides, peace is so universally loved that its very name falls sweetly on the ear.

CHAPTER 12

Any man who has examined history and human nature will agree with me that there is no such thing as a human heart that does not crave for joy and peace. One has only to think of men who are bent on war. What they want is to win, that is to say, their battles are but bridges to glory and to peace. The whole point of victory is to bring opponents to their knees—this done, peace ensues. Peace, then, is the purpose of waging war; and this is true even of men who have a passion for the exercise of military prowess as rulers and commanders.

What, then, men want in war is that it should end in peace. Even while waging a war every man wants peace, whereas no one wants war while he is making peace. And even when men are plotting to disturb the peace, it is merely to fashion a new peace nearer to the heart's desire; it is not because they dislike peace as such. It is not that they love peace less, but that they love their kind of peace more. And even when a secession is successful, its purpose is not achieved unless some sort of peace remains among those who plotted and planned the rebellion. Take even a band of highwaymen. The more violence and impunity they want in disturbing the peace of other men, the more they demand peace among themselves. Take even the case of a robber so powerful that he dispenses with partnership, plans alone, and single-handed robs and kills his victims. Even he maintains some kind of peace, however shadowy, with those he cannot kill and whom he wants to keep in the dark with respect to his crimes. Certainly in his own home he wants to be at peace with his wife and children and any other members of his household. Of course, he is delighted when his every nod is obeyed; if it is not obeyed, he rages, and scolds, and demands peace in his own home and, if need be, gets it by sheer brutality. He knows that the price of peace in domestic society is to have everyone subject in the home to some head—in this instance, to himself.

Suppose, now, a man of this type were offered the allegiance of a larger society, say of a city or of a nation, with the pledge that he would be obeyed as he looks to be obeyed under his own roof. In this case, he would no longer hide himself away in a darksome robber's den; he would show himself off as a high and mighty king—the same man, however, with all of his old greed and criminality. Thus it is that all men want peace in their own society, and all want it in their own way. When they go to war what they want is to make, if they can, their enemies their own, and then to impose on them the victor's will and call it peace.

Now let us imagine a man like the one that poetry and mythology tell us about, a being so wild and anti-social that it was better to call him half-human than fully a man. He was called Cacus, which is Greek for 'bad.' His kingdom was the solitude of a dreadful cave and it was his extraordinary wickedness that gave him his name. He had no wife to exchange soft words with him; no tiny children to play with; no bigger ones to keep in order; no friend whose company he could enjoy, not even his father, Vulcan—than whom he was at least this much luckier that he had never begotten a monster like himself! There was no one to whom he would give anything, but whenever and from whomsoever he could he would take whatever he wanted and whenever he wanted it.

Nevertheless, all alone as he was in a cave that was always 'warm with the blood of some recent victim,' his sole longing was for peace in which no force would do him harm and no fear disturb his rest. Even with his own body he wanted to be at peace, and he was at ease only when peace was there. Even when he was bidding his members to obey him and was seizing, killing, and devouring his victims, his purpose was peace—the speediest possible peace with his mortal nature, driven by its needs to rebellion, and with his hunger, in sedition, clamoring for the breakup of the union of body and soul. Brutal and wild as he was and brutal and wild as were his ways, what he wanted was to have his life and limbs in peace. So much so that, had he been as willing to be at peace with his neighbors as he was active in procuring peace within himself and in his cave, no one would have called him wicked, nor a monster, nor even sub-human; or, at least, despite the shape of his body and the smoke and fire that issued from his mouth and kept all neighbors at a distance, people would have said that what looked like injustice, greed, and savagery were merely means to self-preservation. The truth is, of course, that there never existed any such being, or at least, none just like the foil the poets' fancy invented to glorify Hercules at the expense of Cacus. As is the case with most poetic inventions, we need not believe that any such creature, human or sub-human, ever lived.

I turn now to real wild beasts (from which category the animal part of the so-called half-beast, Cacus, was borrowed). They, too, keep their own particular genus in a kind of peace. Their males and females meet and mate, foster and feed their young, even though many of them by nature are more solitary than gregarious, like lions, foxes, eagles, and owls—as contrasted with deer, pigeons, starlings, and bees. Even a tigress purrs over her cubs and curbs all her fierceness when she fondles them. Even a falcon which seems so lonely when hovering above its prey mates and builds a nest, helps to hatch the eggs and feed the young, and makes every effort to maintain with the mother falcon a peaceful domestic society.

It is even more so with man. By the very laws of his nature, he seems so to speak, forced into fellowship and, as far as in him lies, into peace with every man. At any rate, even when wicked men go to war they want peace for their own society and would like, if possible, to make all men members of that society, so that every one and every thing might be at the service of one head. Of course, the only means such a conqueror knows is to have all men so fear or love him that they will accept the peace which he imposes. For, so does pride perversely copy God. Sinful man hates the equality of all men under God and, as though he were God, loves to impose his sovereignty on his fellow men. He hates the peace of God which is just and prefers his own peace which is unjust. However, he is powerless not to love peace of some sort. For, no man's sin is so unnatural as to wipe out all traces whatsoever of human nature. Anyone, then, who is rational enough to prefer right to wrong and order to disorder can see that the kind of peace that is based on injustice, as compared with that which is based on justice, does not deserve the name of peace.

Of course, even disorder, in whole or in part, must come to some kind of terms either with the situation in which it finds itself or with the elements out of which it takes its being—otherwise it would have no being at all.

Take a man hanging upside down. Certainly his members are in disorder and the posture of the body as a whole is unnatural. The parts which nature demands should be above and below have become topsy-turvy. Such a position disturbs the peace of the body and is therefore painful. Nevertheless, the soul remains at peace with the body and continues to work for its welfare. Otherwise, the man would not live to feel the agony. And even if the soul is driven from the body by excess of pain, nevertheless, so long as the limbs hold together, some kind of peace among these parts remains. Otherwise, there would be no corpse to go on dangling there. Further, the fact that by gravity the corpse, made out of earth, tends to fall to the ground and pulls at the noose that holds it up proves that there is some order in which it seeks peace, and that its weight is, as it were, crying out for a place where it can rest. Lifeless and insensible though the body now is, it does not renounce that appropriate peace in the order of nature which it either has or seeks to have.

So, too, when a corpse is treated to embalming, to prevent dissolution and decay, there is a kind of peace which holds the parts together while the whole is committed to the earth, its proper resting place, and, therefore, a place with which the body is at peace. If, on the other hand, embalming is omitted and nature is allowed to take its course, the corpse remains a battleground of warring exhalations (that attack our senses with the stench we smell) only until such time as they finally fall in with the elements of this world and, slowly, bit by bit, become indistinguishable in a common peace.

Even afterward, however, the law and ordering of the Creator who is supreme in the whole cosmos and the regulator of its peace are still in control. Even when tiny bacteria spring from the corpse of a larger animal, it is by the same law of the Creator that all these minute bodies serve in peace the organic

127

wholes of which they are parts. Even when the flesh of dead animals is eaten by other animals, there is no change in the universal laws which are meant for the common good of every kind of life, the common good that is effected by bringing like into peace with like. It makes no difference what disintegrating forces are at work, or what new combinations are made, or even what changes or transformations are effected.

CHAPTER 13

The peace, then, of the body lies in the ordered equilibrium of all its parts; the peace of the irrational soul, in the balanced adjustment of its appetites; the peace of the reasoning soul, in the harmonious correspondence of conduct and conviction; the peace of body and soul taken together, in the well-ordered life and health of the living whole. Peace between a mortal man and his Maker consists in ordered obedience, guided by faith, under God's eternal law; peace between man and man consists in regulated fellowship. The peace of a home lies in the ordered harmony of authority and obedience between the members of a family living together. The peace of the political community is an ordered harmony of authority and obedience between citizens. The peace of the heavenly City lies in a perfectly ordered and harmonious communion of those who find their joy in God and in one another in God. Peace, in its final sense, is the calm that comes of order. Order is an arrangement of like and unlike things whereby each of them is disposed in its proper place.

This being so, those who are unhappy, in so far as they are unhappy, are not in peace, since they lack the calm of that Order which is beyond every storm; nevertheless, even in their misery they cannot escape from order, since their very misery is related to responsibility and to justice. They do not share with the blessed in their tranquility, but this very separation is the result of the law of order. Moreover, even the miserable can be momentarily free from anxiety and can reach some measure of adjustment to their surroundings and, hence, some tranquility of order and, therefore, some slender peace. However, the reason why they remain unhappy is that, although they *may* be momentarily free from worry and from pain, they are not in a condition where they *must* be free both from worry and pain. Their condition of misery is worse when such peace as they have is not in harmony with that law which governs the order of nature. Their peace can also be disturbed by pain and in proportion to their pain; yet, some peace will remain, so long as the pain is not too acute and their organism as a whole does not disintegrate.

Notice that there can be life without pain, but no pain without some kind of life. In the same way, there can be peace without any kind of war, but no war that does not suppose some kind of peace. This does not mean that war as war involves peace; but war, in so far as those who wage it or have it waged upon them are beings with organic natures, involves peace—for the simple reason that to be organic means to be ordered and, therefore, to be, in some sense, at peace.

Similarly, there can be a nature without any defect and, even, a nature in which there can be no kind of evil whatever, but there can be no nature completely devoid of good. Even the nature of the Devil, in so far as it is a nature, is not evil; it was perversity—not being true to itself—that made it bad. The Devil did not 'stand in the truth' and, therefore, did not escape the judgment of truth. He did not stand fast in the tranquility of order—nor did he, for all that, elude the power of the Ordainer. The goodness which God gave to his nature does not withdraw him from the justice of God by which that nature is subject to punishment. Yet, even in that punishment, God does not hound the good which He created, but only the evil which the Devil committed. So it is that God does not take back the whole of His original gift. He takes a part and leaves a part; He leaves a nature that can regret what God has taken back. Indeed, the very pain inflicted is evidence of both the good that is lost and the good that is left. For, if there were no good left, there would be no one to lament the good that has been lost.

A man who sins is just that much worse if he rejoices in the loss of holiness; but one who suffers pain, and does not benefit by it, laments, at least, the loss of his health. Holiness and health are both good things and, because the loss of any good is more a cause for grief than for gladness (unless there be some higher compensation—the soul's holiness, to be sure, is preferable to the body's health), it is more in accordance with nature that a sinner grieve over his punishment than that he rejoice over his offense. Consequently, just as a man's happiness in abandoning the good of wrong-doing betrays his bad will, so his sorrowing for the good he has lost when in pain bears witness to the good of his nature. For, anyone who grieves over the loss of peace to his nature does so out of some remnant of that peace wherewith his nature loves itself. This is what happens—deservedly, too—in eternal punishment. In the midst of their agonies the evil and the godless weep for the loss of their nature's goods, knowing, meanwhile, that God whose great generosity they contemned was perfectly just when He took these goods away.

God, the wise Creator and just Ordainer of all natures, has made the mortal race of man the loveliest of all lovely things on earth. He has given to men good gifts suited to their existence here below. Among these is temporal peace, according to the poor limits of mortal life, in health, security, and human fellowship; and other gifts, too, needed to preserve this peace or regain it, once lost—for instance, the blessings that lie all around us, so perfectly adapted to our senses: daylight, speech, air to breathe, water to drink, everything that goes to feed, clothe, cure, and beautify the body. These good gifts are granted, however, with the perfectly just understanding that whoever uses the goods which are meant for the mortal peace of mortal men, as these goods should be used, will receive more abundant and better goods—nothing less than immortal peace and all that goes with it, namely, the glory and honor of enjoying God and one's neighbor in God everlastingly; but that whoever misuses his gifts on earth will both lose what he has and never receive the better gifts of heaven.

CHAPTER 14

In the earthly city, then, temporal goods are to be used with a view to the enjoyment of earthly peace, whereas, in the heavenly City, they are used with a view to the enjoyment of eternal peace. Hence, if we were merely unthinking brutes, we would pursue nothing beyond the orderly interrelationship of our bodily part and the appeasing of our appetites, nothing, that is, beyond the comfort of the flesh and plenty of pleasures, so that the peace of body might contribute to peace of the soul. For, if order in the body be lacking, the peace of an irrational soul is checked, since it cannot attain the satisfaction of its appetites. Both of these forms of peace meanwhile subserve that other form of peace which the body and soul enjoy between them, the peace of life and health in good order.

For, just as brutes show that they love the peace or comfort of their bodies by shunning pain, and the peace of their souls by pursuing pleasure to satisfy their appetites, so, too, by running from death, they make clear enough how much they love the peace which keeps body and soul together.

Because, however, man has a rational soul, he makes everything he shares with brutes subserve the peace of his rational soul, so that he first measures things with his mind before he acts, in order to achieve that harmonious correspondence of conduct and conviction which I called the peace of the rational soul. His purpose in desiring not to be vexed with pain, nor disturbed with desire, nor disintegrated by death is that he may learn something profitable and so order his habits and way of life. However, if the infirmity of his human mind is not to bring him in his pursuit of knowledge to some deadly error, he needs divine authority to give secure guidance, and divine help so that he may be unhampered in following the guidance given.

And because, so long as man lives in his mortal body and is a pilgrim far from the Lord, he walks, not by vision, but by faith. Consequently, he refers all peace of body or soul, or their combination, to that higher peace which unites a mortal man with the immortal God and which I defined as 'ordered obedience guided by faith, under God's eternal law.'

Meanwhile, God teaches him two chief commandments, the love of God and the love of neighbor. In these precepts man finds three beings to love, namely, God, himself, and his fellow man, and knows that he is not wrong in loving himself so long as he loves God. As a result, he must help his neighbor (whom he is obliged to love as himself) to love God. Thus, he must help his wife, children, servants, and all others whom he can influence. He must wish, moreover, to be similarly helped by his fellow man, in case he himself needs such assistance. Out of all this love he will arrive at peace, as much as in him lies, with every man—at that human peace which is regulated fellowship. Right order here means, first, that he harm no one, and, second, that he help whomever he can. His fundamental duty is to look out for his own home, for both by natural and human law he has easier and readier access to their requirements.

St. Paul says: 'But if any does not take care of his own, and especially of his household, he has denied the faith and is worse than an unbeliever.' From this care arises that peace of the home which lies in the harmonious interplay of authority and obedience among those who live there. For, those who have the care of the others give the orders—a man to his wife, parents to their children, masters to their servants. And those who are cared for must obey—wives their husband, children their parents, servants their masters. In the home of a religious man, however, of a man living by faith and as yet a wayfarer from the heavenly City, those who command serve those whom they appear to rule—because, of course, they do not command out of lust to domineer, but out of a sense of duty—not out of pride like princes but out of solicitude like parents.

CHAPTER 15

This family arrangement is what nature prescribes, and what God intended in creating man: 'let them have dominion over the fish of the sea, the birds of the air, the cattle, over all the wild animals and every creature that crawls on the earth.' God wanted rational man, made to His image, to have no dominion except over irrational nature. He meant no man, therefore, to have dominion over man, but only man over beast. So it fell out that those who were holy in primitive times became shepherds over sheep rather than monarchs over men, because God wishes in this way to teach us that the normal hierarchy of creatures is different from that which punishment for sin has made imperative. For, when subjection came, it was merely a condition deservedly imposed on sinful man. So, in Scripture, there is no mention of the word 'servant' until holy Noe used it in connection with the curse on his son's wrong-doing. It is a designation that is not natural, but one that was deserved because of sin.

The Latin word for 'slave' is *servus* and it is said that this word is derived from the fact that those who, by right of conquest, could have been killed were sometimes kept and guarded, *servabantur,* by their captors and so became slaves and were called *servi.* Now, such a condition of servitude could only have arisen as a result of sin, since whenever a just war is waged the opposing side must be in the wrong, and every victory, even when won by wicked men, is a divine judgment to humble the conquered and to reform or punish their sin. To this truth Daniel, the great man of God, bore witness. When he was languishing in the Babylonian captivity he confessed to God his sins and those of his people and avowed, with pious repentance, that these sins were the cause of the captivity. It is clear, then, that sin is the primary cause of servitude, in the sense of a social status in which one man is compelled to be subjected to another man. Nor does this befall a man, save by the decree of God, who is never unjust and who knows how to impose appropriate punishments on different sinners.

Our heavenly Master says: 'everyone who commits sin is a slave of sin.' So it happens that holy people are sometimes enslaved to wicked masters who are, in turn, themselves slaves. For, 'by whatever a man is overcome, of this also he is a slave.' Surely it is better to be the slave of a man than the slave of passion as when, to take but one example, the lust for lordship raises such havoc in the hearts of men. Such, then, as men now are, is the order of peace. Some are in subjection to others, and, while humility helps those who serve, pride harms those in power. But, as men once were, when their nature was as God created it, no man was a slave either to man or to sin. However, slavery is now penal in character and planned by that law which commands the preservation of the natural order and forbids its disturbance. If no crime had ever been perpetrated against this law, there would be no crime to repress with the penalty of enslavement.

It is with this in mind that St. Paul goes so far as to admonish slaves to obey their masters and to serve them so sincerely and with such good will that, if there is no chance of manumission, they may make their slavery a kind of freedom by serving with love and loyalty, free from fear and feigning, until injustice becomes a thing of the past and every human sovereignty and power is done away with, so that God may be all in all.

CHAPTER 16

Our holy Fathers in the faith, to be sure, had slaves, but in the regulation of domestic peace it was only in matters of temporal importance that they distinguished the position of their children from the status of their servants. So far as concerns the worship of God—from whom all must hope for eternal blessings—they had like loving care for all the household without exception. This was what nature demanded, and it was from this kind of behavior that there grew the designation 'father of the family,' which is so widely accepted that even wicked and domineering men love to be so called.

Those who are true fathers are as solicitous for every one in their households as for their own children to worship and to be worthy of God. They hope and yearn for all to arrive in that heavenly home where there will be no further need of giving orders to other human beings, because there will be no longer any duty to help those who are happy in immortal life. In the meantime, fathers ought to look upon their duty to command as harder than the duty of slaves to obey.

Meanwhile, in case anyone in the home behaves contrary to its peace, he is disciplined by words or whipping or other kind of punishment lawful and licit in human society, and for his own good, to readjust him to the peace he has abandoned. For, there is no more benevolence and helpfulness in bringing about the loss of a greater good than there is innocence and compassion in allowing a culprit to go from bad to worse. It is the duty of a blameless person not just to do no wrong, but to keep others from wrong-doing and to punish it when done, so that the one punished may be improved by the experience and others be warned by the example.

Now, since every home should be a beginning or fragmentary constituent of a civil community, and every beginning related to some specific end, and every part to the whole of which it is a part, it ought to follow that domestic peace has a relation to political peace. In other words, the ordered harmony of authority and obedience between those who live together has a relation to the ordered harmony of authority and obedience between those who live in a city. This explains why a father must apply certain regulations of civil law to the governance of his home, so as to make it accord with the peace of the whole community.

CHAPTER 17

While the homes of unbelieving men are intent upon acquiring temporal peace out of the posssessions and comforts of this temporal life, the families which live according to faith look ahead to the good things of heaven promised as imperishable, and use material and temporal goods in the spirit of pilgrims, not as snares or obstructions to block their way to God, but simply as helps to ease and never to increase the burdens of this corruptible body which weighs down the soul. Both types of homes and their masters have this in common, that they must use things essential to this mortal life. But the respective purposes to which they put them are characteristic and very different.

So, too, the earthly city which does not live by faith seeks only an earthly peace, and limits the goal of its peace, of its harmony of authority and obedience among its citizens, to the voluntary and collective attainment of objectives necessary to mortal existence. The heavenly City, meanwhile—or, rather, that part that is on pilgrimage in mortal life and lives by faith—must use this earthly peace until such time as our mortality which needs such peace has passed away. As a consequence, so long as her life in the earthly city is that of a captive and an alien (although she has the promise of ultimate delivery and the gift of the Spirit as a pledge), she has no hesitation about keeping in step with the civil law which governs matters pertaining to our existence here below. For, as mortal life is the same for all, there ought to be common cause between the two cities in what concerns our purely human living.

Now comes the difficulty. The city of this world, to begin with, has had certain 'wise men' of its own mold, whom true religion must reject, because either out of their own daydreaming or out of demonic deception these wise men came to believe that a multiplicity of divinities was allied with human life, with different duties, in some strange arrangement, and different assignments: this one over the body, that one over the mind; in the body itself, one over the head, another over the neck, still others, one for each bodily part; in the mind, one over the intelligence, another over learning, another over temper, another over desire; in the realities, related to life, that lie about us, one over flocks and one over wheat, one over wine, one over oil, and another over forests, one over currency, another over navigation, and still another over warfare and victory, one over marriage, a different one over fecundity and childbirth, so on and so on.

The heavenly City, on the contrary, knows and, by religious faith, believes that it must adore one God alone and serve Him with that complete dedication which the Greeks call *latreía* and which belongs to Him alone. As a result, she has been unable to share with the earthly city a common religious legislation, and has had no choice but to dissent on this score and so to become a nuisance to those who think otherwise. Hence, she has had to feel the weight of their anger, hatred, and violence, save in those instances when, by sheer numbers and God's help, which never fails, she has been able to scare off her opponents.

So long, then, as the heavenly City is wayfaring on earth, she invites citizens from all nations and all tongues, and unites them into a single pilgrim band. She takes no issue with that diversity of customs, laws, and traditions whereby human peace is sought and maintained. Instead of nullifying or tearing down, she preserves and appropriates whatever in the diversities of divers races is aimed at one and the same objective of human peace, provided only that they do not stand in the way of the faith and worship of the one supreme and true God.

Thus, the heavenly City, so long as it is wayfaring on earth, not only makes use of earthly peace but fosters and actively pursues along with other human beings a common platform in regard to all that concerns our purely human life and does not interfere with faith and worship. Of course, though, the City of God subordinates this earthly peace to that of heaven. For this is not merely true peace, but, strictly speaking, for any rational creature, the only real peace, since it is, as I said, 'the perfectly ordered and harmonious communion of those who find their joy in God and in one another in God.'

When this peace is reached, man will be no longer haunted by death, but plainly and perpetually endowed with life, nor will his body, which now wastes away and weighs down the soul, be any longer animal, but spiritual, in need of nothing, and completely under the control of our will.

This peace the pilgrim City already possesses by faith and it lives holily and according to this faith so long as, to attain its heavenly completion, it refers every good act done for God or for his fellow man. I say 'fellow man' because, of course, any community life must emphasize social relationships.

St. Peter Chrysologus
400-450

Sermons are one of the most interesting vehicles for exploring the social mores and attitudes of a given period. They usually
reveal what were considered to be major problems within a
society and the disciplinary or theological solutions proposed
by the church's leaders and teachers. For this reason, several
sermons of St. Peter Chrysologus have been selected for this
volume.

Peter was born in the year 400 in Imola, Italy. Around the
year 433, he was appointed archbishop of Ravenna which, at
that time, was the political capital of the Roman Empire in the
west. He was known as an excellent pastor who dedicated himself totally to guiding and preaching to his people. His sermons
contained sound doctrine and were designed to encourage the
members of the diocese to lead virtuous daily lives. Peter retired
to Imola, his birthplace, around the year 450 and died shortly
thereafter. The title Chrysologus, i.e., the Golden Orator or Of
the Golden Word, appears to have been attached to his name
during the seventh century or later. Pope Benedict XIII declared
him a Doctor of the Church in 1729.

Peter lived during a period of upheaval and transition. The
Roman Empire in the West was collapsing and the migrations
of the nations were creating havoc everywhere. The Huns, the
Visigoths, the Vandals and the Sueves were moving through

the empire. All of this was happening just at the time that Christianity was apparently coming into its own as the official religion of the Roman Empire. Only twenty years before Peter's birth, Emperor Theodosius I had directed all of his subjects to embrace Christianity. The process of actually permeating society with its ideals and way of life still lay before Christianity.

There are 176 sermons of Peter Chrysologus extant. Those chosen for this collection include his sermons on the prodigal son, the parable of the pearl and the net cast into the sea, St. Paul's concept of slavery to the law and to grace, the story of the rich man and Lazarus, the unity of the faithful in prayer, the birth of Christ and the peace of Christians.

The sermons of Peter Chrysologus definitely reflect the tensions that arose in fifth century society due to greed, envy, fraud, injustice, infidelity, ignorance and divisiveness. Peter almost always used a passage from sacred scripture as his point of departure. His style was to explain the passage, verse by verse, while working in examples of problems from everyday life. The sermons conclude with a brief exhortation to virtue. They do not contain any sophisticated speculation. For example, the theme of the peace of Christians is presented by way of vivid images, without any reflection on the meaning of the word peace. His message is simple and clear. Peace is the Church in the port, in security, in the safe place, in abundance, in joy, in exultation. Christ the King of Peace has routed the enemy, gotten rid of all dissention, discord and conflict. No doubt, Peter's listeners in Ravenna, who were experiencing the difficulties of the time in which they lived, filled out the meaning of Peter's sermons by relating them to their contemporary social conditions.

HOMILIES

SERMON 1

The Prodigal Son and His Brother: The Prodigal's Departure

(On Luke 15.11-16)

T oday, the Lord has summoned a father with his two
sons and made them the center of our attention. By
this beautiful figure He has desired to open up for us
an unfathomable revelation of His own love, the fierce jealousy
of the Jewish race, and the penitent return of the Christian
people.

'A certain man had two sons. And the younger of them
said to his father, Father, give me the share of the property
that falls to me. And,' the text goes on, 'he divided his means
between them.' The son is as impatient as the father was kind.
He is weary of his father's being alive. Since he cannot shorten
his father's life, he strives to get possession of his property. He
was not content to possess his father's wealth in company with
his father; and he deserved to lose the privileges of a son.

But let us make some inquiries. What reason brought the
son to such attempts? What bold prospect raised his spirits to
make so startling a request? What reason? Clearly, the fact that
the Father in heaven cannot be bounded by any limit, or shut
in by any time, or destroyed by any power of death. The son
could not await his father's death to get his wealth. So he conceived the desire to get his pleasure from the generosity of his
father still alive. That was the insult which lay in his request,
as the father's very bounty proved.

'And he divided his means between them,' the text states.
At the request of the one son he soon divided all his means
between the two. He wanted both sons to know the fact that up
till then he had been holding on to his property because of love,
not miserliness; that foresight, not jealousy, was the reason he
had not given it away. He retained control of his property to

preserve it for his sons, not to refuse it to them. He did not want his fortune to perish, but to remain intact for his sons.

Oh, happy are the sons whose entire property rests in the love of their father! Happy are the sons whose whole wealth consists in showing allegiance and honor to a father! Material riches, by contrast, tear unity apart, break the bond of brotherly love, disrupt family relationships, and violently sunder the ties of love between the members of a family. All this grows perfectly clear from the words which follow. 'Father, give me the share of the property that falls to me. And,' the text continues, 'he divided his means between them. And not many days later the younger son gathered up all his wealth, and took his journey into a far country; there he squandered his fortune in loose living. And after he had spent all, there came a grievous famine over that country, and he began himself to suffer want. And he went and joined one of the citizens of that country who sent him to his farm to feed swine. And he longed to fill his belly with the pods which the swine were eating, but no one offered to give them to him.'

See what covetousness works in its headlong pursuit of wealth. See how, without the father, this wealth did not enrich the son; it stripped him. It took him away from his father's bosom, expelled him from his house, withdrew him from his country, despoiled him of his reputation, and robbed him of his chastity. Whatever there is of life, good morals, filial reverence, liberty, glory—of all these it left him nothing. Indeed, it changed a citizen into a wanderer, a son into a hired servant, a rich man into a beggar, a free man into a slave. It separated him from a devoted father, and made him the companion of the swine. Consequently, he who spurned obedience to his father's sacred love became the servant of the muddy herd.

'The younger son gathered up all his wealth,' the text goes on. Clearly, it was because of his mentality rather than his age that he was the younger. It was in mind rather than in regard to place that he gathered up his father's goods and went far away. And it was by paying a price rather than by receiving one that he wretchedly sold himself into slavery. That is the type of contract this trader came to—he who did not know how to pay his debt to his parents, or make a fit return to his father.

In his father's house is agreeable order, free service, perfect care, pleasant reverence, kindly correction, rich poverty, unworried possession. The work is done for the father, but the fruit redounds to the sons.

'He squandered his fortune,' it says. The spendthrift son dissipates the goods accumulated under the father's control; all too late does he realize that his father has been the manager of his wealth, not its miserly possessor. 'In loose living.' Such a life is destined to death, because its virtues are dying. If a man lives for vices, his reputation gets buried, his glory perishes. If he tarries for debauchery, his infamy grows.

'And after he had spent all, there came a grievous famine over that country.' Like a torturer, famine becomes the inseparable companion to debauched living, and to the stomach, and to gluttony, in order that avenging pain may be fierce where punishable guilt once flamed up. 'There came a grievous famine over that country.' Ravenous living always tends to an end like that; extravagance of pleasure which ought to be avoided always comes to just such an end.

'And he began himself to suffer want.' The wealth which was given to the son brought him to suffer want. If it had been refused to him, it would have kept him rich. Consequently, he who in his father's house had abounded in wealth while not controlling it fell into want out on his own because he did control it.

'And he went and joined one of the citizens of that country, who sent him to his farm to feed swine.' This is the experience which comes to one who refuses to entrust himself to his father, but consigns himself to a stranger: he flees from a most indulgent provider and endures a severe judge. A deserter from affection, a refugee from fatherly love, he is assigned to the swine, sentenced to them, and given over to their service. He stirs about in their muddy fodder. He is bruised and soiled by the rush of the restless herd, so that he perceives how wretched and bitter it is to have lost the happiness of peaceful life in his father's house.

'And he longed to fill his body with the pods which the swine were eating, but no one offered to give them to him.' What a thankless task is his! He who is living for the swine does not even eat with them! O wretched man, who yearns and hungers for the fattening fodder of the dirty herd! O wretched man, who desires even such sordid food and fails to get even that!

Taught by these matters, and instructed by others like them, let us stay in the house of our Father; let us remain in the bosom of our Mother; and may we be held fast in our relatives' embraces. May our Father's affection hold us back, to keep that pitiful recklessness of youth from drawing us into the evils mentioned above. May our Father's love surround us like a hedge, and may our Mother's affection put us at ease, and may our relatives' esteem to be a protection for ourselves. Under the eyes of these dear ones we cannot easily sin; their eyes are just so many lanterns. The glance of our Mother is the day; the sun is aglow in the countenance of our Father. Consequently, the darkness of crimes cannot draw nigh to one living amid so many lights of virtues. On the contrary, our Father's table nourishes us with the food of virtue, with the banquet of salvation, with the delights of uprightness and of glory.

The great length of the passage read compels us to say more about this parable. Who is the father so ready to forgive, and readier still to welcome back his son? Who is the brother grieving over his brother's return? Who is the younger brother, foolish in his departure but most wise in his return? As you all desire, we shall investigate these matters in a later sermon.

SERMON 2

The Son's Return to His Father

(On Luke 15.17-19)

In the preceding sermon, to the best of our ability we censured the extravagant son—that son who deserted his deeply devoted father. We recalled what evils beset him to such an extent that, reduced by hunger, he gave himself to the service of the swine. Now, with more joyful words, we take up something more in line with our desires: his return and repentance.

'When he came to himself,' the text reads, 'he said, How many hired men in my father's house have bread in abundance!'

144

Previously, when he departed from his father, he had ceased to be himself; now, he came to himself. He first returned to himself that he might return to his father. The man who is unmindful of his father's devotion, and forgetful of his parent's love, departs from himself, and changes his whole self from man to beast.

'How many hired men in my father's house have bread in abundance, while I am perishing here with hunger!' Hunger calls back him whom abundance had exiled. Hunger enabled the son to understand his father, whereas abundance had caused him to recognize only a sire.

If even involuntary hunger did all this, try by experiment how beneficial a voluntary fast can be. A burdened stomach drags down the heart toward vices, and depresses the mind to keep it unable to experience heavenly piety. Scripture tells us: 'The corruptible body is a load upon the soul, and the earthly habitation presseth down the mind that museth upon many things.' Hence, the Lord said, too: 'Take heed lest your hearts be overburdened with self-indulgence and drunkenness.' Wherefore, the stomach should be relieved by the tempering influence of a fast, that the mind can be unburdened and attend to higher things, rise to virtues, and like a winged bird fly in its entirety to the very Author of piety. The case of Elias proves this. Relieved of bodily weight by continuing that fast which the Lord arranged, he flew to heaven as victor over death.

'I will get up and go to my father.' He who said 'I will arise' was lying down. He had understood his fall, he was aware of his ruin, and gazed upon himself lying in the mire of disgraceful prodigality. That is why he cried out: 'I will get up and go to my father.' With what hope? With what confidence? With what assurance?

With what hope? With that by which [he reflects] : He is a father. I have squandered the marks of a son; he has not lost the characteristics of a father. It is not a stranger who intercedes with a father; rather, it is that affection inside his own breast which intervenes and pleads. The father's heart is moved to beget his son again through forgiveness. I shall go as a culprit to a father. But a father, on seeing his son, soon covers up the guilt. He conceals his role of judge, and is more eager to fulfil that of father. He wants his son to return, not to perish, and soon changes his condemnation into forgiveness.

'I will get up and go to my father, and will say to him, Father I have sinned against heaven and before thee.' His confession touches his father; his repentence addresses his sire. 'I have sinned against heaven and before thee.' He in heaven against whom he sinned is not merely an earthly father, but indeed a heavenly Father. That is why the son added: 'before thee.' All things which are done in heaven and on earth are before the eyes of God.

'I have sinned against heaven and before thee. I am no longer worthy to be called thy son.' The son set out abroad and fled into a far country; but he did not escape from those accusing witnesses, the eyes of the heavenly Father. David explains this more clearly by his words: 'Whither shall I go from thy spirit? or whither shall I flee from thy face? If I ascend into heaven thou art there; if I descend into hell thou art present. If I take my wings early in the morning, and dwell in the uttermost parts of the sea: Even there shall thy hand lead me: and thy right hand shall hold me.' David sees that throughout the world all transgressions stand exposed to the eyes of God. Neither the sky, nor the earth, nor the seas, nor a deep cavern, nor night itself can hide sins from Him. The Psalmist perceives how criminal and evil it is to sin in the sight of God. Therefore, he cries out: 'To thee only have I sinned, and have done evil before thee.'

In similar manner, therefore, the younger son, too, cries aloud, and exclaims: 'I have sinned against heaven and before thee. I am no longer worthy to be called thy son.' He does not say: 'I am not worthy to be thy son,' but: 'I am not worthy to be called thy son.' The reason is that to be called pertains to grace; to be pertains to nature. Listen to the Apostle saying: 'from him who called you to the grace of Christ.' Therefore, since this younger son had lost the characteristic of his nature as a son, he judged himself not to deserve that which pertains to grace.

'Make me as one of thy hired men.' Look! To what point of his power has the son come? Look! To what have wanton pleasure and youthful license promoted him? 'Make me as one of thy hired men,' he cries. He desires his servitude to be renewed by his leasing out his services every year. He desires to pay off the obligations of his contract gradually by his unceasing labor. He desires to be as one of the slaves born in his father's house, to sigh the whole day in work which brings but little pay, and never to be able to get out of his state of dependence. There is a reason why he asks for this. Under a foreign master he had experienced a freedom which was really slavery; and he believes that under his father he will have a slavery which is really freedom.

Brethren, at this point I would already be willing to explain the mystery in this passage, but greater profit can be gained from doing this later on, and this restrains me. I observe that as you listen you are not experiencing fitting compassion, nor deeming these matters our concern; rather, you are passing over them quickly with fleeting attention.

But, messages which Christ speaks are indeed our concern; they will always be profitable to every one of us. Moreover, for our instruction the Lord often uses symbolic examples. He has always desired to be the Father of His servants, and to be loved more than feared. He gave Himself as the Bread of life, and poured His Blood into the cup of salvation. By these comparisons of the past He improves the men of the present and the future, to keep us from deserting our good and loving Father and going off to the remote and utterly foreign parts of the world. He does not want us to live riotously there and squander the whole substance of our welfare and life. He does not want us to use up everything we have, suffer an extreme hunger for hope, and through it to surrender ourselves soon to the ruler of that region—that is, to the Devil, the author of despair. Our Father does not want him to send us to his own farm, that is, to the seductive valleys of this world; nor to send us to give food to the swine, namely, those creatures who are always prone to grovel on the earth, who live for their stomach, temper their hot passions in a wallowing-place of mud, depress themselves in the mire, and cool themselves in a whirlpool of vices.

The Devil's insatiable cruelty is what causes him to send his hirelings to the swine. Not content that men become criminal, he also makes them leaders in vice and teachers of crime. And once he has made them such, he does not let them get satisfied even with the food and fodder of the swine. Wanton men cannot find satiety; their passion cannot be satisfied; consequently, in their hunger they commit more vices still.

Therefore, let us be with our good Father; let us remain with this devoted Parent. In this way we can avoid the Devil's snares and always enjoy our Father's goods. We shall scrutinize the deeper matters later, because we have greater obligation to our congregation and our customs.

SERMON 3

The Father's Welcome to the Son

(On Luke 15.20-24)

In two sermons so far, we have run through the prodigal son's departure, return, guilt, and repentance. Now let us proceed to treat the father's meeting his son, his goodness, and his indescribable mercy. The text tells us: 'He arose and went to his father. But while he was yet a long way off, his father saw him and was moved with compassion, and ran and fell upon his neck and kissed him.'

'He arose and went to his father.' He arose from the wreckage of his conscience and body alike. He arose from the depths of hell and touched the heights of heaven. Before the heavenly Father, a child rises higher because of pardon than he fell low because of guilt.

'He arose and went to his father.' He went not by the motion of his feet, but by the progress of his thought. Being afar off, he had no need of an earthly journey, because he had found short cuts along the way of salvation. He who seeks the divine Father by faith soon finds Him present to Himself, and has no need to seek Him by traversing roads.

'He arose and went to his father. But when he was yet a long way off.' How is he who is coming a long way off? Because he has not yet arrived. He who is coming is coming to do penance, but he has not yet arrived at grace. He is coming to his Father's house, but he has not yet reached the glory of his former condition, appearance, and honor.

'But when he was yet a long way off, his father saw him.' That Father saw, He 'who dwelleth on high; and looketh down on the low things,' 'and the high he knoweth afar off.' 'His father saw him.' The father saw him, in such a way that the son could also behold his father. The father's countenance illumined the face of the approaching son in such a way that all the dark aspect was dispelled which his guilt had previously cast about it. The darkness of the night is not such as that which comes from shame over sins. Hear the Prophet's words: 'My iniquities have overtaken me, and I was not able to see.' Elsewhere, he says: 'My iniquities are become heavy upon me,' and afterwards: 'And the light of my eyes is not with me.' Night overwhelms the light of the day just past; sins ruin our power of perception; our members encumber our soul. Clearly, if the heavenly Father had not cast His rays upon the returning son's face, if He had not lifted the mist of his shame by the light streaming from His own glance, that son would never have seen God's brilliant face.

'He saw him from afar and was moved with compassion.' He who cannot be removed from his location is moved with compassion. He runs forward, not by a movement of his body, but by his affectionate devotion. 'He fell upon his neck,' not because his muscles failed, but because of his compassion. 'He fell upon his neck' that he might raise up the son who lay upon the earth. 'He fell upon his neck' to remove the burden of sins by a burden of love. 'Come to me,' Scripture says, 'All you who labor and are burdened. Take my burden upon you because it is light.' You see that the son is helped, not weighed down, by the burden of that father.

'He fell upon his neck and kissed him.' This is how the father judged and corrects his wayward son, and gives him not floggings but kisses. The power of love overlooked the transgressions. Therefore, the father redeemed the sins of his son by his kiss, and covered them by his embrace, in order not to expose the crimes or debase the son. The father so healed the son's wounds as not to leave a scar or blemish upon him.

'Blessed are they', says Scripture 'whose iniquities are forgiven, and whose sins are covered.'

If the deed of this young son displeases us, and his departure horrifies us, then let us by no means depart from such a Father. A father's glance puts sins to flight, banishes crime, and drives away all malice and temptations. Certainly, if we have gone away, if by living riotously we have squandered the whole substance of our Father, if we have committed any crime or transgression anywhere, if we have come to the whole rocky coast of impurity and to complete ruin, let us now at last get up. An example like that of the son is an invitation to us. Let us return to such a Father.

'But when his father saw him, he was moved with compassion, and ran and fell upon his neck and kissed him.' What place for despair, I ask, is here? What occasion to make excuses? What false display of fear? None—unless perhaps the father's meeting is feared, and his kiss strikes up terror, and his embrace is disturbing, and he is believed to be seizing the son for punishment rather than receiving him with forgiveness when he leads him by the hand, draws him into his bosom, and winds his arms about him.

But the words which follow completely sweep away such a thought which is destructive of life and opposed to salvation. 'But the father said to his servants, fetch quickly the best robe and put it on him, and give a ring of gold for his finger and sandals for his feet; and bring out the fattened calf and kill it, and let us eat and make merry; because this my son was dead, and has come to life again; he was lost, and is found.' After hearing this do we yet delay? Do we still fail to return to the Father?

'Fetch quickly the best robe and put it on him.' He put up with his son's transgressions, but not his nakedness. Consequently, he wanted his servants to clothe the son before he was seen, that his nakedness might be known to his father alone. It was only a father who could not bear to see the nakedness of a son.

'Fetch quickly the best robe.' Here the father who did not suffer the sinner to be poorly clothed wants to derive his joy from pardon rather than justice. 'Fetch quickly the best robe.'

He did not ask: 'Where are you coming from? Where have you been? Where are the goods you carried off? Why did you exchange such great honor for such disgrace?' No, his words were: 'Fetch quickly the best robe and put it on him.' You see that the power of love overlooks transgressions. The mercy which a father knows is not a tardy kind. He who discusses sins publicizes them.

'Give him a ring for his finger.' The father's devotion is not content to restore his innocence alone; it also brings back his former honor. 'And give him sandals for his feet.' He was rich when he departed; how poor he has returned! Of all his substance he brings back not even shoes on his feet! 'Give him sandals for his feet'—that nakedness may disgrace not even a foot, and surely that he may have shoes when he returns to his former course of life.

'And bring out the fattened calf.' An ordinary calf is not good enough; it must be one sleek and fattened. The stout calf is evidence that the father's charity is stout. 'And bring out the fattened calf and kill it, and let us eat and make merry; because this my son was dead, and has come to life again; he was lost, and is found.' We are still recounting the narrative, and we are already planning to explain the hidden symbolic mystery in it. Through the death of a calf a dead son is resuscitated, and one calf is sacrificed for the feasting of the entire family. However, we must postpone this mystery, to set forth in proper order the elder brother's deep rooted grief and even deeper rooted envy.

SERMON 4

The Elder Brother's Jealousy

(On Luke 15.25-32)

We have rejoiced over the younger son's return and safety; with tearful grief we now take up the elder son's envy. Through his excessive sin of envious jealousy he spoiled the great virtue of his thriftiness.

The text reads: 'Now his elder son was in the field; and as he came and drew near the house, he heard music and dancing. And calling one of the servants he inquired what this meant.

And he said to him, Thy brother has come, and thy father has killed the fattened calf, because he has got him back safe. But he was angered and would not go in.'

'His elder son was in the field.' He was in the field, cultivating the earth but leaving himself uncared for. He breaks up the tough sod, but hardens the affection in his heart. He uproots briers and plants, but does not pluck out temptations to envy. Thus, in the harvest field of covetousness he gathers crops of jealousy and envy.

'And as he came and drew near the house, he heard the music and dancing.' The music of devoted affection puts the envious brother in flight, the dance of affection keeps him outside. Natural affection prompts him to come to his brother and draw near to the house. But his jealousy does not let him arrive; his envy does not suffer him to enter.

Envy is an ancient evil, the first sin, an old venom, the poison of the ages, a cause of death. In the beginning, this vice expelled the Devil from heaven and cast him down. This vice shut the first parent of our race out of paradise. It kept this elder brother out of his father's house. It armed the children of Abraham, the holy people, to work the murder of their Creator, the death of their Saviour. Envy is an interior foe. It does not batter the walls of the flesh or break down the encompassing armor of the members, but it plies its blows against the very citadel of the heart. Before the organs are aware, like a pirate it captures the soul, the master of the body, and leads it off as a prisoner.

Therefore, if we wish to merit heavenly glory, or to possess the beatitude of paradise, if we wish to dwell in the house of our father and to escape the guilt of divine parricide, then let us by vigilant faith and the Spirit's light drive and keep away the foul tricks of envy. Let us suppress this envy with all the force of heavenly arms. For, just as charity unites us to God, so does envy cut us off from Him.

'His father, therefore, came out and began to entreat him.' The father's anxious heart is straitened by the diverse movements of his sons. In astonishment and love, he ponders their different fortunes, for he sees that one brother is soon driven away by the return of the other, and that through the safety of the one the other will perish. Because of the malice of envy, he perceives his long-felt grief, compensated by a short-lived joy, stirred up all over again.

O cancer of jealousy! A spacious house does not contain two brothers! And what is strange about this, brethren? Envy has wrought this. Envy has made the whole breadth of the world too narrow for two brothers. For it goaded Cain to kill his younger brother. Thus, the law of nature made Cain the first-born son, but envious jealousy made him an only son.

'But he answered and said to his father, Behold, these many years I have been serving you.' This is the view of one who dares to sit in judgment on the father's love. 'Behold, these many years I have been serving you.' See the service which this son pays back to the father in return for the gift of being born!

'I have never transgressed one of thy commands.' This is the result, not of your innocence, but of your father's forgiveness, because with deep love he preferred to cover up a son's transgressions rather than expose them.

'And yet thou hast never given me a kid that I might make merry with my friends.' An attitude of ill will to a brother cannot be pleasing to a father. And he who is oblivious of brotherly love cannot be mindful of a father's generosity. He says that no kid was given to him. Yet, at the time of the division, he received his complete portion of the property. For, at the time when the younger brother was asking that his share of the property be given him, the father soon divided the whole among the two brothers. The Evangelist's words are: 'He divided his means between them.' But an envious man is always pretending something, always lying.

'And yet thou hast never given me a kid, that I might make merry with my friends.' He does not regard his father's friends as his own. He sees some men esteeming himself to please his father, and he regards these as strangers, not friends.

'But when this thy son comes, who has devoured his means with harlots, thou hast killed for him the fatted calf.' He is grieving because his brother has returned, not because the estate has perished. He is complaining, not because of the loss, but because of his envy. He should have used his own means to improve his brother's appearance, and not have dishonored him thus because of what he lost. A father's whole estate is in his son. Hence, when the father recovered his son, he regarded nothing as lost. But the brother did believe it a loss when he saw his co-heir back home. When is an envious man anything but avaricious? He reckons whatever another possesses as his own loss.

'But he said to him, Son, thou art always with me, and all that is mine is thine; but we were bound to make merry and rejoice, for this thy brother was dead, and has come to life; he was lost, and is found.' O what the force of love accomplishes! To a son, however base, he knows not how to be, he cannot be, less than a father. He sees that the son has degenerated in spirit; that he possesses nothing of the father's devotion or character; yet he calls him son, he urges affection upon him, he reawakens his attention to the kindness or the hope of his generosity, by saying: 'Son, thou art always with me, and all I have is thine. That is tantamount to saying: Bear with your brother's return to his father, bear with your father's welcome to his son. He did not seek anything else than his father. For he came with the request to be put in the place of a hired man, not of a son. 'Father, I have sinned against heaven and before thee. I am no longer worthy to be called thy son; make me as one of thy hired men.'

Keep all your possessions; his father is enough for him. Moreover, to keep you from thinking that any of your present or former possessions has been diminished, I shall search for new ones for him in the future. Assuredly, if you observe your father's counsel and command, share your present goods with your brother, that the future possessions may belong to you as well as to him. So be glad and rejoice that he has been found, that he, too, may rejoice that you have not been lost.

But let us now conclude our narrative sermon, that afterwards, through the revelation of Christ, we may unfold the matters that are symbolic and profound.

SERMON 5

The Two Sons as Types of the Gentiles and the Jews:
The Allegorical Interpretation.

Not to pay his obligations is often a trait of a clever and shameless debtor. By long and artful caviling he taxes his creditor's patience.

This is our fifth sermon on the departure and return of the Prodigal Son. In it we shall try, as we have promised, to raise its historical sense to a mystical and extraordinary sense which God gave it. In the case of so great a loan entrusted to me, I am, through my own power, a rather unsuitable debtor. Therefore, pray that through God's power I may be found a payer acceptable to yourselves.

'A certain man had two sons,' the passage says. Since the time when Christ took upon Himself the burden of our flesh, and, being God, clothed Himself with human vesture, God with truth calls Himself man. The Lord [i.e., God the Father] truly calls Himself the father of two sons, because the Deity mixed into the humanity, as also the human tenderness joined to the Deity, has mingled man and God, and it united the Lord to a Father.

Therefore, this man [in the parable], this father, had two sons. He had them through the bounty of the Creator, not because he was under any necessity to beget them, and he commanded their existence, rather than merited it. . . . For Christ was a man before our eyes in such a way that He always remained God in the mystery of His Godhead.

'He had two sons,' namely, two peoples: the Jews and the Gentiles. Prudent knowledge of the Law made the Jewish people His elder son, and the folly of paganism made the Gentile world His younger son. For, just as truly as wisdom brings venerable gray hairs, so does folly take away the traits of an adult. So morals, not age, made the Gentiles the younger son; and not years, but understanding [of the Law], made the Jews the elder son.

'And the younger of them said to his father, Father, give me the share of the property which falls to me.' The younger son [representing the Gentile world] addressed this petition to the Knower of hearts by his desire rather than his voice. For, with us, it is our own will which gets us good things from God or bad. See the result. He who in company with his father possessed the whole property became through this use of his own will the possessor of only a fraction of it. That is what he got by his request: 'Give me the share of the property that falls to me.'

And what is that share? What? Conduct, speech, knowledge, reason, judgment—all those characteristics which in this earthly habitat belong to a man above other living beings; in other words, according to the Apostle, the law of nature.

But he carried out the division in this way. To the younger He gave those five gifts of nature which we have mentioned. For the elder He divinely wrote the five Books of the Law. Through these arrangements the divided property was to have unequal value, but a numerical parity. The one share of property was to hold together through human arrangement, the other was to stand firm by divine ordination. But each of these two laws was intended to lead the two sons to the knowledge of their Father. Each law was to bring reverence to its Author.

'And not many days later, the younger son gathered up all his wealth, and took his journey into a far country; and there he squandered his fortune in loose living.' We stated that not age, but morals, had made him the younger son. That is why the text said: 'Not many days later.' And rightly, because in the very beginning of the world the Gentile race hastened off to the Fatherland of idols. It sojourned into the foreign country of the Devil more in spirit than in place. Through its vain thoughts it roamed through all the elements, and it was not by bodily motion that it was hurled from land after land. For, this younger son was in his Father's presence, yet he lacked this Father; although he was in his own house, he did not feel at home.

Hence it is that these Gentile peoples—this loose-living son—through their desire of worldly eloquence, through the brothels of the schools, through senseless disputation at the meeting places of the philosophical sects, dissipated the property of God the Father. By their conjectures they exhausted everything there was in the line of speech, knowledge, reason, and judgment. But, even after that, these poor wretches still suffered the greatest need and intensest hunger to know the truth. Philosophy enjoined the task of seeking God, but of that truth to be learned it gathered no fruit.

Consequently, these Gentile peoples kept on adhering to the chieftain of that country. He kept on banishing them into that world of his; that is, into his one country house of multitudinous superstitions. He did this that they might feed swine, that is, the devils who say to the Lord: 'If thou cast us out, send us into the herd of swine.' Yes, he sent them that they might feed the devils with incense, sacrificial victims, blood— and then get false replies from the oracles as the reward for all this labor. They killed many an animal in order to enable a creature which had no intelligence while alive to prophesy after being killed; to empower that which had never uttered speech with its mouth to speak with its entrails after death.

But in all this these Gentile peoples found nothing divine, nothing of salutary value. So they despaired of God, of His providence, of His judgment, and of all the future, and they betook themselves from the school down to the gluttony of the belly, eager to fill themselves with the pods which the swine were wont to eat.

The Epicureans knew this. When they were frequenting the Platonic and Aristotelian schools, and found there no elucidation of the divinity or of knowledge, they offered themselves to Epicurus, the most recent promoter of despair and pleasure. And they ate pods. In other words, they opened their mouths wide to the sinfully sweet pleasures of the body, and they themselves gave food to the devils who continually grow fat on the vices and filth of bodies. For, just as he who unites himself to God 'is one spirit with Him,' so he who associates himself with the Devil becomes one devil with him.

Despite his desire, this younger son did not satisfy his belly with those pods. Why? Because no one was giving to him. Assuredly, the Devil was eager to use this hunger for knowledge and distress of pleasure, in order to make the Gentile son the more eager to get forbidden goods and to commit sins. But God, the Father, allowed the Gentile son to hunger for another reason: that the confutation of his error might become an occasion of salvation. He abandoned the Jewish son in just such a way as not to let him perish utterly, and He suffered the Gentile son to endure hunger that he might come back.

He does come back now to his Father and cries: 'Father, I have sinned against heaven and before thee.' Every day in her prayer the Church testifies that the younger son has returned to his Father's house, and is calling God his Father, for she prays: 'Our Father, who art in heaven,' 'I have sinned against heaven and before thee.' He sinned against heaven when he said in blasphemy that the sun in the sky and the moon and the stars are gods, and when he profaned these same beings by adoring them.

'I am no longer worthy to be called thy son; make me as one of thy hired men.' This is to say: because I am no longer worthy of the glory of a son, or of pardon, I hope to earn the wages of a laborer's toil. May he who has lost the honor of being a son retain at least the sustenance of life in his daily bread.

But the father runs out, he runs out from afar. 'When as yet we were sinners, Christ died for us.' The Father runs out, He runs out in His Son, when through Him He descends from heaven and comes down upon earth. 'With me,' the Son says, 'is he who sent me, the Father.'

He 'fell upon his neck.' He fell, when through Christ the whole Divinity came down as ours and reposed in human nature. 'And he kissed him.' When? When 'mercy and truth have met each other: justice and peace have kissed.' 'He gave the best robe,' that which Adam lost, the everlasting glory of immortality. 'He put a ring upon his finger.' The ring of honor, the title of liberty, the outstanding pledge of the spirit, the seal of the faith, the dowry of the heavenly marriage. Hear the Apostle: 'I betrothed you to one spouse, that I might present you a chaste virgin to Christ.' 'And sandals upon his feet.' That his feet might be shod when he preached the Gospel, 'that the feet of those who preach the gospel of peace might be beautiful.'

'And he killed for him the fattened calf.' About that David sang: 'And it shall please God better than a young calf, that bringeth forth horns and hoofs.' The calf was slain at this command of the Father, because the Christ, God as the Son of God, could not be slain without the command of His Father. Listen to the Apostle: 'He who has not spared even His own son but has delivered Him for us all.' He is the calf who is daily and continually immolated for our food.

But the elder brother—the elder son coming from the field, the people of the Law—'The harvest indeed is abundant, but the laborers are few'—hears the music in the Father's house, and he hears the dancing, yet he does not wish to enter. Every day we gaze upon this same occurrence with our own eyes. For the Jewish people comes to the house of its Father, that is, to the Church. Because of its jealousy it stands outside. It hears the cithara of David resounding, and the music from the singing of the psalms, and the dancing carried on by so many assembled races. Yet it does not wish to enter. Through jealousy it remains without. In horror it judges its Gentile brother by its own ancient customs, and meanwhile it is depriving itself of its Father's goods, and excluding itself from His joys.

'Behold, these many years I have been serving thee, and have never transgressed one of thy commands; and yet thou hast never given me a kid.' As we already mentioned, this remark should be passed over rather than mentioned. For the Jewish son is speaking, and the words are not those of a doer, but of a man venting his anger.

The Father steps outside and says to his son: 'Son, thou art always with me.' How? In the person of Abel, and of Henoch, of Sem, Noe, Abraham, Isaac, Jacob, Moses, and all the holy men from whom stems Christ's Jewish lineage read in the Gospel when it says: 'Abraham begot Isaac, Isaac begot Jacob,' and the rest.

'And all that is mine is thine.' How? Because for you is the law, for you is prophecy, for you the temple, for you the priesthood, for you the sacrifices, for you the kingdom, for you the gifts, for you—and this is the greatest gift of all—Christ was born. But because you through your jealousy wish to destroy your Brother, you are no longer worthy to possess your Father's banquets and joys.

Within the narrow confines of this sermon we could not expound matters so extensive as fully as we desired. But the points which seem brief in our sermon form an ample field for you to exercise the power of perception which your own knowledge gives you. May this simple yet hidden comparison not be unpleasant. It has forced us to unfold and explain these allegorical and lofty matters, rather than to tell or declaim them.

SERMON 47

The Parables of the Pearl and the Net Cast into the Sea
(On Matt. 13.45-50)

By the fact that Christ our Lord created the sky, earth, sea, and the great, many, and varied creatures in them, He gave wonderful evidence of His power. By the fact that He assumes human nature, acts the part of man, enters into the centuries, passes through the periods of life, teaches by word, works cures by His power, tells parables, gives examples, and manifests in Himself the burden of our emotions—by all this He reveals that he has an indescribable affection of human love.

For this reason, He makes heavenly goods appear attractive through earthly examples. He uses beings of the present world to make us relish those of the future world. He represents invisible benefits by visible evidence. The parables which we hear from the Gospel today give forceful proof of all this.

'The kingdom of heaven is like a merchant in search of fine pearls. When he finds a single pearl of great price, he goes and sells all that he has and buys it.' Let no one who hears this take offense from the name merchant. Here Christ is speaking of a merchant who shows mercy, not of one who is always investing the profit from capital. He means one who provides the beauty of virtues, not the irritations of vices; one who brings forth seriousness of morals, not great weights of precious stones; one who has on a necklace of righteousness, not wantonness; one who wears the insignia of disciplinary control, not the trappings of pleasure.

Wherefore, that merchant displays these pearls of heart and body, not in human trading, but in heavenly commerce. He shows them, not to trade for a present advantage but for a future one—to trade in order to gain not earthly but heavenly glory; in order to be able to get the kingdom of heaven as the reward of his virtues, and to buy at the price of innumerable other goods, the one pearl of everlasting life.

The Lord added another parable in these words: 'Again, the kingdom of heaven is like a net cast into the sea and gathering in fish of every kind. When it was filled, they hauled it out and sitting down on the beach, they gathered the good fish into the vessels, but threw away the bad.' 'The kingdom of heaven is like a net cast into the sea.' This parable reveals why Christ chose fishermen to be His Apostles, and changed catchers of fish into fishers of men, that fishermen's practice might be recognized as a type of God's judgment.

The catch itself brings together fish of every sort, but the separation puts the chosen ones into vessels. Similarly, the vocation to the Christian faith brings together just and unjust, bad and good, but the divine election separates the good and the bad.

'The kingdom of heaven is like a net cast into the sea.' Christ sent His fishermen—Peter, Andrew, James, and John, all of them approved for their skill—to the sea of this world. It was a sea swelling with its vain display, proud of its confusion, stormy because of factions, fluctuating through uncertainty, noisy with grievances, roaring with anger, shipwrecked by sins, and sunk into impiety. 'Come, follow me,' He told them, 'and I will make you fishers of men.'

Hence, He sent His fishers forth with nets woven of the precepts of the Law and of the Gospel, hemmed with counsels, expanded with gifts of virtues and with grace, fit to gather an unceasing catch into the shelter of the Gospel. Now, brethren, right now is the time of this catch. Christ's nets are being drawn through the tribes and nations now. Throughout the whole world they are bringing in teeming catches, without discrimination of persons.

However, because the end of the world is near, the nets are bringing to the beach the fish of our capture (that is, the men who wander about free and untrammeled while immersed in worldly concerns), they are disturbed by the dryness of the shore (that is, the nearness of the end), and they dash against one another because of the whole arrangement of things. They see wicked nations wax prosperous through triumph after triumph, Christian peoples distressed in captivity all over the world. They see wicked men rejoice in success and prosperity, and pious men harrassed unceasingly by one evil after another. They see masters reduced to slavery, slaves gaining the upper hand over their masters, sons rebellious against their parents, aged men held up in contempt by youths. They see every condition of nature, every arrangement of order as something utterly perished.

However, although these facts are true, and perturb the weak [in faith], they do not unsettle the strong. They cannot perturb the strong because the strong increase their strength through parable, and build up their fortitude through aid from the figure.

The fish taken out of the deep toss about in their confusion for a little while on the shore, but the quick selection, while it discards the bad ones, separates the good. That brief confusion soon to pass makes them the good ones, rather than perturbs them. That heavenly selection consigns the evil to their penalties and quickly gathers the good to their honors. It leads the wicked below and places the faithful in the kingdom. It consoles them all—fathers, the aged, the just, the elect—with everlasting glory in return for the short-lived insults they bore. The parable itself demonstrates this when it says: 'At the end of the world the angels of God will go out and separate the wicked from the just.'

'At the end of the world.' He who believes in the end of the world and discusses its deterioration, and has hope that the lasting possessions will be his later on—why does he seek to possess the perishable ones?

Brethren, the world takes a beginning from its very terminations. A creature is renewed by its end, not destroyed. It withdraws itself not from its Creator, but from sin. Not for the just, but for the sinners, do the elements come to an end [of their usefulness]. 'At the end of the world, the angels will go out to separate the just apart.' Let no one doubt that the angels will appear to the saints. Even Christ promises His service to the saints. His maxim is: 'I shall gird myself and minister to you.'

'The angels of God will go out and separate the wicked from among the just.' Bear up, O just ones, endure for a while.

Yea, more, even grant a truce to your opponents. This short-lived mingling with the unjust will be compensated by a long separation.

'They will separate the wicked from among the just and will cast them into the furnace of fire.' See what sort of abode those prepare for themselves who expel their neighbors and drive away their guests! See how great a fire those men kindle for themselves from their short-lived pleasure, who in this world prepare delights for themselves out of the hunger of the poor and the pain they inflict on others!

'There will be weeping and gnashing of teeth.' How woefully will that man gnash his teeth there who smiles in evil here! And he who has joy now from the misfortunes of the poor will then weep over their good fortune, because he had it within his power to rejoice with the poor, but would not. But you, my faithful ones, rejoice forever in the Lord.

SERMON 114

Slaves to the Law and to Grace

(On Rom. 6.15-21)

A traveler always finds it sweet and pleasant to return to his own home. The courtyards of his ancestral house are attractive to him after an absence. Similarly, after these intervals, I find it sweeter to return to my series of passages from the Apostle. Some necessity of religion often compels us to depart from the order of discourses which we had intended, and from the straight path which our discourse was to follow. For, we must so control the sequence of our instruction that one matter does not hinder another.

Wherefore, let us hear what the holy Apostle has told us today. What does he say? 'Have we sinned because we are not under the Law but under grace? By no means.' Brethren, this question reveals the inexperience of those who, captivated by their custom of living according to the Law, cannot perceive the powers we get from the gift of grace. They were an unyielding people, as we learn from the long series of the precepts of the Law, and the benefits they gained from their sacrificial gifts and the splendor of their festivals made and kept them obstinate in vain observances. When the passage of time will bring the Law to its end, what will one do who has cultivated the Law and been wrenched away from it?

O Hebrew, what is there that you have not lost? And if you have lost it, why do you glory as if you had not lost it? Where is your temple? your priest? your sacrifice? your incense? your purifications? the devout celebration of your festivals, which you thought should never be omitted?

Rightly are you circumcized that you may be a Jew, because you have been cut away from all those goods mentioned above. For it is written: 'Cursed be he that abideth not in all the precepts which have been written in the books of the Law.' If the man who offends against one precept is cursed, how often will he be cursed who will stand convicted of having observed none of them?

'Have we sinned,' he says, 'because we are not under the Law but under grace?' As if he were asking, brethren: 'Have we sinned because, already cured, we have not kept ourselves under the treatment? Have we sinned because, already healed, we have abandoned cauterization, the iron, and the medicants?' The sick man is indeed unfortunate who after a cure is unwilling to trouble himself about the painful instruments.

Why should I say more, brethren? He who seeks and awaits a sick man's desires never effects a cure. A cold humor always produces a veritable fire in the body. Excessive firmness irritates and strikes the members, makes and begets a sharper burning sensation. Consequently, when the sick man impatiently requests that cold water be given him, the effect is an increase of the fire which is ever seething and panting in his veins. He is unaware that at such a time feverheat is extinguished by heat; and that the fire is nourished by what is cold.

Therefore, when the Law anticipates and restrains man's inclination, and when man, impeded by his load of sin, is not strong enough to obey the precepts of the Law, the Law does not free its devotee from the bond of sin. Rather, it binds him the more by bringing a charge of transgression upon him. That is why the Apostle added: 'Do you not know that to whom you offer yourselves as slaves for obedience, to him who you obey you are the slaves, whether to sin unto death or to obedience unto justice?'

How is it, brethren, that the very fact of our speaking about the Law has revealed that man was the slave of sin? 'Whether to sin unto death,' the text says, 'or unto justice?' A little earlier the Apostle had said that sin was not to have dominion over you, since you are not under the Law but under grace. Clearly, therefore, those who are under the Law of sin are weighed down and bent by its domination; wretched men that they are, they cannot be liberated from this base slavery to sin unless grace sets them free.

The Apostle continues: 'But thanks be to God that you were the slaves of sin.' Is he giving thanks as one who rejoices because man was the slave of sin? Far from it. He is giving thanks not because we were previously slaves of such a cruel master, but because we are slaves no longer. He expressly makes that point clear by his next words: 'but you have now obeyed from the heart that form of doctrine into which you have been delivered, and having been set free from sin, you have become the slaves of justice.' We have become obedient, brethren, through the gift of Him who calls us, not through our own will, for we were being held as captives by it.

'You have now obeyed from the heart that form of doctrine.' What form? Beyond question, that of the Gospel, where the slavery has not been abolished by a new kind of freedom, but changed, because a devoted service is better than a capricious and headstrong freedom.

'You have become the slaves of justice.' Brethren, this slavery does not restrain, it liberates. It does not burden, it honors. It does not brand a man with the stain of slavery, but removes it. Here, where one form of slavery expels the other form, where one state drives out another state, where death dies because of a death, where loss is healed by a loss, and—to say it properly and briefly—where all adversity is laid low by a sword of adversity, what is there here, I ask, that is not divine? The Apostle expresses this: 'I speak in a human way because of the weakness of your flesh; for as you yielded your members as slaves of uncleanness and iniquity unto iniquity, so now yield your members as slaves of justice unto sanctification.'

165

He shows the greatness of his love when he reduces the doctrine of the Gospel to such humble and almost shameful examples, so that he recommends that you now devote yourselves as much to holiness as you once did to uncleanness, as much to justice as formerly to iniquity. Consequently, he gains control over slavery.

Brethren, that comparison seems absurd and unbecoming. It would have man subject only as much to glory as to depravity. And would that he were subject only as much, and no more! Yet, when does human frailty give as much service to God as to the world? as much to heaven as to the earth? as much to virtue as to vices? Wretched man is so entirely given over to the flesh, so occupied with present affairs, that he relinquishes nothing in him which might be of service to his future life, to supernatural well-being.

In one phrase the Apostle fittingly described the force of temporal allurement upon the human conscience. He properly stated that the human members should yield themselves as eagerly to justice, purity and cleanness as they had once yielded themselves over with vehemence and madness to depravity and vices. The man who wishes to withdraw from his property after losing his right of ownership demands little or perhaps nothing. Likewise, he takes away your excuse who enjoins upon you only insignificant and ordinary payments which you ought to pay back in return for great benefits.

Therefore, O man, give to God as much as you once gave to your flesh and vices. Why do you keep yourself bound to vices rather than to God, since it is only because of His love for you that God asks so much of you?

The text continues: 'For when you were the slaves of sin, you were free as regards justice. . . . But now set free from sin, you have become the slave of justice.' Previously you were slaves of sin, now you are slaves of justice. Behold, according to the Apostle one kind of slavery follows upon another. O obstinate man, now show the time of your liberty! Sin previously told the lie that you, the unhappy man whom it was holding captive, were free. Now, grace calls you its slave; and that it might make you truly free it has made you the adopted son of God Himself. Therefore, Christ's statement has been fulfilled:

St. Peter Chrysologus

'Whoever wishes to become the master, let him be the servant.' Blessed is this slavery! It begets an everlasting reign. For, that former liberty brought upon us a penalty as its fruit, and unbearable confusion, as the Apostle says: 'For what fruit had you then from these things of which you are now ashamed? For the end of these things is death.'

Behold how the Devil does his liberating! See the reward with which he honors that slavery! He wants death simultaneously to end your life and begin your punishment.

But those who serve Christ, brethren, contemn death and its wages; and they are transferred into an everlasting life of holiness. For death in Christ does not admit a termination, because it does not kill a man, but brings him to his perfection.

SERMON 122

The Rich Man and Lazarus

(On Luke 16.23-24)

Today, brethren, our sermon ought to treat adequately the virtues of St. Andrew. However, we promised to go back and treat the remainder of the subject of the rich man and Lazarus, the poor man of the Gospel. Furthermore, the prerogative of St. Andrew's apostolate and martyrdom suffice—yes, more than suffice—for his glory. Therefore, if it is agreeable to you, we shall, with the aid of the Lord, give you what we promised and owe.

Aware that weariness begets aversion in both the hearers and the speaker, in our previous treatise we postponed [treatment of] the greatest part of the passage which is set forth. This was to enable us to refresh the strength of our mental faculties and then, with full vigor and proper attention, grasp the remainder of the salutary word.

After the words we spoke come these: 'And lifting up his eyes, being in torments, the rich man saw Abraham afar off, and Lazarus in his bosom.' 'And lifting up his eyes.' Late does the rich man lift up his eyes toward heaven; he has always kept them intent upon the earth. O rich man, those very eyes you lift up are your accusers. Those eyes you lift up do not placate your Judge, but enkindle Him to anger. They gain you, not forgiveness, but a feeling of guilt. They call for the full measure of penalties, not solace. Whither do you raise your eyes? Why do you still cry out, O rich man? Whither do you cast your glance again and again, O rich man? There is Lazarus, there is the betrayer of your impiety, the witness of your crimes, the herald of your cruelty.

'And he cried out,' the text says, 'Father Abraham, have pity on me.' Now you recognize him as a father. But in the person of Lazarus you spurned Abraham as a father, and you cannot now know him as a father toward you. Now you see him as a just man who then, to be kindly to you, long allowed Lazarus to be tormented. Unhappy is he whom his own ancestor thus accuses, whom the one responsible for his seeing the light of day thus condemns. Unhappy is he whose crimes were so great that in the judgment his ancestor could not show mercy to him, or his father forgive him, or his father's affection help him.

Why do you still cry out, O rich man? You are still rich, but in crime, not in wealth; not in possessions, but in guilt. Why do you cry out? What do you ask for? Here we see no more petitioning, but a controversy in which the one who suffered is one of the opponents. The participants are in separated places. The one speaks from nearby; the other, from afar. The one carries on from a bosom; the other, from hell. The one pleads from a place of repose; the other complains from amid his torments.

What does the rich man say? 'Father Abraham, have pity on me.' Well would you be speaking, O rich man, if Lazarus, reposing in Abraham's bosom, were not holding the very heart of the judge. Well would you be speaking if Lazarus did not possess all the secrets of this perfectly just reviewer. He whom an innocent Confessor thus accuses petitions the judge to no purpose. He believes in vain that the judge can help him when the very man who endured so much is talking through the judge's mouth.

'Have pity on me, and send Lazarus.' Are you still so cruel to Lazarus? 'Send Lazarus.' Whither? From Abraham's bosom to hell, from his lofty throne to the deepest abyss, from the holy repose and deep silence of the blessed to the din of the tortures? 'And send Lazarus.' As I see the matter the rich man's actions spring not from new pain, but from ancient envy. This is enkindled not so much by hell as by Lazarus' possession of heaven. Men find it a grace evil and an unbearable fire to see in happiness those whom they once held in contempt. The rich man's malice does not leave him, even though he already endures its punishment. He does not ask to be led to Lazarus, but wants Lazarus to be led to him. O rich man, the loving Abraham cannot send to the bed of your tortures Lazarus whom you did not condescend to admit to your table. Your respective fortunes have now been reversed. You look upon the glory of him whose misery you once spurned. He gazes upon your tortures who then wondered at you in your glory.

Let us see, brethren, why he thus begs in tears to have Lazarus sent to him. 'Send Lazarus to dip the tip of his finger in water and cool my tongue.' You are in error, O rich man. This fire is not so much in your tongue as in your mind; not so much of the tongue as of the heart. That heat is still one of the conscience, not that extreme flame which waits in readiness for you. For, if the full fire of the Last Judgment were already surrounding you, if the sentence of that hopeless condemnation already held you, you would never be lifting your eyes. You would never be presuming to speak with your father, or to ask for yourself, or to intercede for your brothers. Surely, if all the fire of hell already holds you, and the flame of Gehenna enwraps you, why do you want help only for the burning in your tongue?—unless it is because, when your breast is heaving with the flame of your crime and guilt, your tongue which insulted the poor man and refused mercy to him is burnt the more, and catches fire, and violently burns. The tongue precedes to the Judgment. It first tastes and suffers tortures. It is the first member of all the body to sense heat. For, when it was the first member to taste here on earth various delicious foods and to sample the perfumed cups, it refused to order generosity. It did not command mercy to be shown, but, when others were showing it, the tongue complained.

This is he who used to clothe himself in purple and fine linen. What is the matter, rich man? Does the fine linen fail to protect you from the heat? Does the purple fail to resist hell? Those goods remained behind. They deserted you, and yourself, who once mocked at the heat while clothed with garments ingeniously light, you are now naked and sweat and burn.

'And send Lazarus to dip the tip of his finger in water and cool my tongue.' Why this, rich man? Where are the torrents from your wine presses? Where are your barns, expanded not less by your greediness than by your supplies, as far as the poor man's hunger is concerned? As far as his need is concerned, where are those wines preserved so long because of their age and oblivion of their dates? Where are all the prodigalities, bustlings, and pourings of your servants? All this exists no more for you; it is no more an occasion of sin. Now you have thirst for the drop on a finger tip. If you had given only this to the poor man, you would not have this thirst. A drop made you unmerciful, and a crumb made you inhuman. Drops and crumbs make up the whole sustenance and life of a poor man.

I should like to know, O rich man, if you in your suffering excuse even your own self. You would not have come to these evils if on earth you had given a crumb from your huge barns and a drop from your great wine presses. What the flesh needs, and nature demands, and suffices for life, is little. Avarice is the reason why a man stores up many great possessions, not for himself but for others, and that clearly to his present or future suffering.

But, you object, O rich man: 'Even if I did refuse to give wine, what I ask for is water, which the Creator Himself of all beings and nature gave as something common to all human beings.' I think, O rich man, that you refused even water to the poor man. You exposed him to as many dogs as you could to keep him from entering your door and coming to your well.

'Send Lazarus to dip the tip of his finger in water.' What is the meaning of this which you say if he is not to bring the water? Evidently, that water is nearby, to you. And if it is near, why do you not take it from nearby? Why? Because your hands are rightly bound, O rich man. Because you spurned to give help to Lazarus' hands when they had lost their strength through weakness. Man should certainly share his members with the weak. When Job was not so much giving them as giving them back, he spoke as follows: 'I was an eye of the blind, and a foot of the lame. I was the father of the weak.' O man, if you do not have a coin, give a poor man your hand, because he shows greater mercy who by his own hand, leads a poor man who is weak to his table. He gives his very self to the poor man who devotes himself to his service, makes himself the poor man's servant.

Again, brethren, let us postpone the completion of the present discourse, in order to expound in a third sermon what sentence the rich man endured from holy Abraham.

SERMON 132

The Unity of the Faithful in Prayer

(On Matt. 18.19, 20)

If nature begot and brought forth all things as fully developed, hardy, and in want of nothing, all love would perish. Natural inclinations would fail, and skill would pass away.

Gold would remain in the earth, unpolished; the sparkle of the gem would be left hidden in the uncut stone. However, the craftsman finds them both through his skill. He cleanses, enhances, and polishes them. He artfully works on them to evoke all the beauty and charm of a perfect necklace. Similarly, what the earth sprouts forth from nature's bounteous supply either gets bruised by brambles or grows like a wild grapevine with the luxuriance of virgin country, unless the farmer by skillful work brings it under the control of his cultivation. That I may not wander longer, let us bring out our labored point by one household example. When a newborn infant lies in the cradle, a man is in that human nature, but he is not yet fully apparent. There is a body, yet there is not. The members are seen, yet they are practically nonexistent. They are alive, yet not alive with sensation. Then, love turns itself upon the infant. It applies its industry to the point of perspiration, and exercises its skill. To speak more fully, as many arts of instruction are put to work to make him a developed man as he has members. And why should I say more? Love nourishes, industry develops,

171

and ingenuity embellishes everything which nature generates or produces.

Then why should we be astonished, brethren, if God, who willed to suffer for man's sake, willed that man's nature, too, should be weak in regard to what we are considering today? He wanted to bring honor to human industry.

Hence, too, arises the fact that the meaning lies hid in the letter; that a divine mystery is concealed in human speech. The future things which are already clear to believers are to be made obscure to heretics and unbelievers—just as if the penal blindness of the unbelievers redounded to glory of the faithful. For, it is quite trying not to comprehend the things seen, not to understand those heard, to reject as harmful those which are salutary, to shun virtues as if they were vices. Christ Himself has said: I speak in parables, 'That seeing they may not perceive, and hearing they may not understand.' To the faithful He said: 'To you it is given to know the mystery of God.'

Wherefore, brethren, let no one in his simplicity deem the Gospel text common or cheap, especially in that verse where the resounding trumpet of its reading predicts that nothing is to be refused to those who ask well and desire piously. The verse states 'that if two of you shall agree on earth about anything at all for which they ask, it shall be done for them by my Father in heaven.' You have heard what power and efficacy arises from group agreement in a holy petition. Christ did not mention one thing or another, but He promised to give everything—whatever the united request desires. His words are: 'about anything at all for which they ask, it shall be done for them.' Of course, that reverent caution should not be disregarded: that we should ask of God things worthy of God. He who asks evil things of God judges and supposes that God is the author of evil. And he who asks for cheap and unworthy things is an ignoble petitioner and ignores the power and might of the Giver. Consequently, we should always ask from such a Giver not unholy gifts, but holy ones; not earthly, but heavenly ones; gifts compatible with virtues, not dangerous attractions; not things likely to stir up hatreds, but those consonant with virtue.

St. Peter Chrysologus

Christ promises that He will be in the midst of two or three who are gathered, and that He will give everything they request of Him. If this is so, where are those who presume that the congregation of the Church can be disregarded, and assert that private prayers should be preferred to those of an honorable assembly? If He denies nothing to so small a group, will He refuse anything to those who ask for it in the assemblies and congregation of the Church? This is what the Prophet believed, and what he exults over having obtained when he states: 'I will praise thee, O Lord, with my whole heart, in the council of the just, and in the congregation.' The man who hears that everything he will ask for in the council of the saints will be granted praises with his whole heart.

Some, however, endeavor to excuse under an appearance of faith the idleness which prompts their contempt [for assemblies]. They omit participation in the fervor of the assembled congregation, and pretend that they have devoted to prayer the time they have expended upon their household cares. While they give themselves up to their own desires, they contemn and despise divine arrangements. These are men of the sort who tear apart the [Mystical] Body of Christ and scatter its members. They do not suffer the form of its Christlike appearance to develop to its full beauty—that form which the Prophet saw and then sang about: 'Thou are beautiful in form above the sons of men.'

It is true that the individual members have, each one, their own function to perform. But they will fulfill these respective functions best if they are joined together and compacted and attain to the full beauty of the fully developed Body. This, therefore, is the difference between the glorious richness of a congregation and the presumptious vanity of separation which springs either from ignorance or negligence: that from the health and praiseworthiness of the entire body a beautiful unity arises, while from the separation of its members there springs base, deadly, and hideous ruin.

O man, consider either the separation of the joints in your own body or the joining together of the separate members. Has it taught you anything else than this, that you should live both as one man compounded of many parts and as one man in many members? The eye is precious for the healthy functioning of the members—but only if it remains in the body. Otherwise, when it fails the body it also fails itself. All the other members are indebted to the eye for the service of light which it furnishes. But the eye itself perceives, too, that it owes to the body the fact that it is a light. When united with the members it provides a service for them; plucked out of the body, it itself does not see.

Whoever he is who thinks that he is something, let him be instructed by such an example and remain in the Church, that he may be something. Otherwise, when he fails the Church, he soon terminates his own importance. If anyone desires a more extensive understanding of this, let him read the Apostle's treatise in which he speaks about the [Mystical] Body of Christ. The desirable brevity of our sermon does not permit us to run through it. The Law was given not for one, but for all. So, too, Christ came not for one or to one, but to all and for all. He desired to bring all things together into a unity which alone is good and pleasant. The Prophet, aware of the future, assures us: 'Behold how good and pleasant it is for brethren to dwell together in unity.' For, not singularity, but unity, is acceptable to God. The Holy Spirit descended upon the Apostles with all His welling fountain when they were assembled together. This occurred after the Apostles had been instructed by the Lord's own commandment to wait in a group for the Spirit's coming.

Brethren, suppose that a man is evil to himself, and because of his shortcomings foolishly self-sufficient. Suppose that thus he seeks life outside the Church. He loses divine gifts, he spoils the outpouring of grace, he cheats himself of the benefits of charity. The blessing of that unity will not await him. The Prophet testifies that that life is only in the Church: 'Behold how good and pleasant it is for brethren to dwell together in unity . . . For there the Lord hath commanded blessing, and life forevermore.'

174

St. Peter Chrysologus

SERMON 149

The Birth of Christ and the Peace of Christians

(On Luke 2.8-14)

When our Lord and Saviour came to earth and made Himself bodily present, the angels appeared in chorus and gave the good news to the shepherds: 'I bring you good news of great joy which shall be to all the people.' We, too, borrow this hymn from these holy angels and announce great joy to you.

For, today, the Church is in peace, and the heretics in anger. Today, the ship of the Church is in port, and the fury of the heretics is tossed about on the waves. Today, brethren, the pastors of the Church are in security, and the heretics in consternation. Today, the sheep of the Lord are in a safe place, and the wolves rave in anger. Today, the vineyard of the Lord has abundance, and the workers of iniquity are indigent. Today, very dearly beloved, the people of Christ has been exalted, and the enemies of truth have been humbled. Today, dearly beloved, Christ is in joy, and the Devil in grief. Today, the angels are in exultation, and the demons in confusion.

Why should I say more? Today, Christ, who is the King of peace, has come forth with His peace and routes all discord, banished dissensions, and dissipated conflicts. As the brilliance of the sun lights up the sky, so He illumines the Church with the splendor of peace. 'For,' the text says, 'there has been born to you today a Savior of the world.' O how desirable is the very name of peace! How firm a foundation peace is for the Christian religion, and what a heavenly ornament for the altar of the Lord!

What can we utter worthy of peace? Peace is a name of Christ Himself, as even the Apostle says: 'For Christ is our peace, He it is who has made both one.' The two were at variance, not over conflicting opinions or faith, but because of the Devil's envy. But, just as the streets are cleansed when the king comes forth, and the whole city decked with myriad flowers and banners to keep out of sight anything less worthy of the king's countenance, so also now, when Christ the King of peace comes forth, let everything depressing be removed

175

from our midst. While truth is shining, let falsehood be banished, and discord flee, and concord be resplendent. We often see that when the pictures of kings or of brothers are painted, the skillful painter, to produce symbols of unity between them, portrays Concord attired in feminine dress behind the back of the two. Embracing them both with her arms, she is meant to indicate that these who seem separated in body are in agreement of opinion and will. Just so, at present, the Peace of the Lord standing in our midst, and with palpitating bosom joining both of us together, teaches separated persons to come to agreement in spirit by linking elbows. In all this is fulfilled, no doubt, the prophetical statement which says: 'And the counsel of peace shall be between them both.'

Yesterday, indeed, our common father uttered a preliminary prayer in the Gospel language of peace. Today, to be sure, we make our declarations by means of a message of peace. With upturned hands he received us yesterday. So, with expanded heart and outstretched arms we today hasten to him bearing gifts of peace. Wars have now been destroyed. The beauty of peace holds everything. The Devil is in mourning, and all his cohort of demons in lamentation. But the heavenly beings now have joy, and the angels who hold peace especially dear are in exultation. An unfailing spring of peace is found among the heavenly powers, and they admire peace. And the dwellers of earth are refreshed by at least some drops falling from this spring. For this reason, even if peace is praised by the saints on earth, the splendor of that praise has an effect of overflow into heaven. The angels of heaven praise that peace and say: 'Glory to God in the highest, and peace on earth among men of good will.'

You see, brethren, how the dwellers of heaven and of earth mutually send gifts of peace. The angels of heaven announce peace to the earth. The saints on earth praise Christ our peace, again restored among the dwellers of heaven, and in mystical choirs they exclaim: 'Glory in the highest.' So let us also say with the angels: 'Glory in the highest to God,' who humbled the Devil and exalted His Christ. 'Glory in the highest to God,' who has banished discord and established peace. You perceive, brethren, that the angelic hymn is sonorously vibrant. 'Glory to God in the highest, and peace on earth.'

To be sure, I mention the Devil's cunning. You are not unaware how clear he is. Satan observed the solidity and stability of the faith. He saw it hedged about with God's kind gift of doctrine, and abounding in fruits of good works. Therefore, in the sight of all he fell into madness, and burned in a rage of fury, in order to shatter concord, uproot charity, and tear peace asunder. But may peace be always with us.

St. Francis of Assisi
1182-1226

Few personalities in the history of Christianity have had the attractiveness and magnetism of St. Francis of Assisi. His name evokes images of peacefulness and joy, of poverty, of oneness with nature. His impact on the centuries that have passed since his death in 1226 extends far beyond the religious orders that consider themselves his spiritual sons and daughters. Laypersons, Catholic and Protestant alike, easily identify with him, feel that they know him. He has captured the attention and imagination of countless writers, artists and poets and has been a source of inspiration for them.

Why? What was it about this ordinary man from Assisi who lived only 45 years or so? He was born into a comfortable family, lived the beautiful life and then went through a conversion process. Followers quickly gathered around the "new" Francis, who demanded of them only that they live the gospel of Jesus Christ. Perhaps it was the simplicity with which he understood and lived the gospel that made of him a man most rare. The message was in no way complicated; yet the living called for more than most humans are willing to give.

Poverty—a deliberate, responsible, symbolic renunciation of all possessions both material and immaterial; Joy—the endurance of rejection and abuse, and the acceptance of all suffering with love and gladness; Fraternal Love—the willing of the good of one's brothers and sisters (and all humans are brothers and sisters); Peace—the capacity to be totally at home with oneself, all creatures, the universe—such were the evangelical insights on which Francis built his life. Most all humans dream of such a life. Francis is proof that these basic teachings of Jesus can be realized in time.

Of course, as is often the case with great persons, Francis's life is more easily admired than imitated. For he purchased his poverty, joy, love and peace at no small cost. It required a lifetime of prayer, of negation, of renewal of spirit, of detachment.

The Mirror of Perfection *appeared around the year 1300. It is more likely the work of several authors rather than of any single person. As with many other writings related to St. Francis of Assisi, it is the written version of early reliable oral Franciscan tradition. The following selection from* The Mirror of Perfection *is a series of simple anecdotes on the themes of poverty, charity and compassion toward one's neighbor. The modern reader may find the passages rather quaint. Their significance can be grasped only within the context of Francis's life. He lived at a point in history when the life style of the holy man had an impact on society. Francis understood the power of exemplary action as a social mover. Thus, rather than complicate life with lengthy treatises on poverty and charity, he made the public, responsible choice to live poverty and charity. In this way, Francis established a tradition by means of a visible community whose lifestyle became a question mark in society. Faced with the Franciscan way of life, people were gently rebuked and challenged to reflect on their value systems, their attachment to material goods, treatment of their neighbor, and the sincerity of their commitment to Christianity.*

THE MIRROR OF PERFECTION

PART I

ON THE PERFECTION OF POVERTY

Firstly, how blessed Francis made known his will and intention (which he maintained from beginning to end) with regard to the observance of poverty.

F riar Richard of the March was a man of noble birth, but even more noble in his holiness, and blessed Francis loved him dearly. One day he visited blessed Francis in the palace of the Bishop of Assisi, and among other matters that they discussed relating to the Order and the observance of the Rule, he asked him particularly on the following, saying, 'Tell me, Father, what was your original intention when you began to have brethren? And what is it to-day? And do you intend to maintain it to the day of your death? If I know this, I shall be able to testify to your intention and will from first to last. For example, may we friars who are clergy and possess many books keep them, provided that we regard them as the property of the Order?'

Blessed Francis said to him, 'I assure you, brother, that it has been and remains my first and last intention and desire—had the brethren only believed me—that no friar should possess anything but a habit, a cord, and an undergarment, as our Rule allows.'

But if any friar should be inclined to ask, 'Why did not blessed Francis insist that poverty was observed by the friars in his own day, as he told Brother Richard? And why did he not enforce its observance?', we who were with him can answer this question as we have heard it from his own mouth, for he himself spoke to the friars on this and on many other matters. For the guidance of the Order he also caused many things which he had learned from God by constant prayer and meditation, to be written in the Rule, declaring them to be in accordance with

God's will. But after he had revealed these things to the friars, they thought them harsh and unbearable, for they did not know what was to happen in the Order after his death.

And because he feared dissension between himself and the friars, he was not willing to argue with them, but reluctantly yielded to their wishes, and asked pardon of God. But in order that the words which the Lord had put into his mouth for the guidance of the friars should not pass unheeded, he resolved to observe them himself, and by so doing to obtain his reward from God. At length he found contentment in this, and his soul received comfort.

Saint Francis's reply to a Minister who asked his permission to have books; and how the Ministers removed the chapter containing the Gospel prohibitions from the Rule without his knowledge.

Once, when blessed Francis had returned from overseas, one of the Ministers was discussing the chapter on poverty with him, wishing in particular to learn his own will and interpretation of it; especially since at that time the Rule contained a chapter on the prohibitions of the Gospel, namely, *Take nothing with you on the journey, etc.*

And blessed Francis answered him, 'My intention is that the friars should possess nothing but a habit, with a cord and undergarment, as the Rule requires. And anyone who is compelled by necessity may wear sandals.'

The Minister said, 'What shall I do, for I have books worth more than fifty pounds?' He said this because he wished to have them with a clear conscience, and knowing how strictly blessed Francis interpreted the chapter on poverty, it troubled him to possess so many books.

Blessed Francis said to him, 'I will not, should not, and cannot go against my own conscience and the perfection of the holy Gospel which we have vowed to observe.' Hearing this, the Minister was grieved; but seeing him so disturbed, blessed Francis said to him with great fervour of spirit in the presence of all the friars, 'You wish people to recognize you as Friars Minor, and to regard you as men who observe the holy Gospel; yet you want to have chests for your books!'

But although the Ministers knew that the friars were obliged to observe the holy Gospel according to the Rule, they removed from the Rule the chapter where it is said, *Take nothing for your journey*, and thought that by so doing they would not be bound to observe the perfection of the Gospel. This was revealed to blessed Francis by the Holy Spirit, and he said in the presence of certain friars, 'The Friar Ministers think they can deceive God and me. On the contrary, in order that all friars shall know themselves bound to observe the perfection of the Gospel, I wish it to be written at the beginning and at the end of the Rule that friars are bound to the strict observance of the Holy Gospel of our Lord Jesus Christ. And in order that the brethren may never have any excuse to set aside the things that I have proclaimed and still proclaim, which the Lord has placed in my mouth for their salvation and my own, I intend to demonstrate these things before God by my own actions, and by His help, I will observe them for ever.'

So, from the early days when he began to have brethren to the day of his death, blessed Francis observed the whole of the Gospel to the letter.

On the novice who sought his permission to own a psalter.

At another time a friar novice who knew how to recite the psalter, although not fluently, obtained leave from the Minister General to have his own copy. But having heard that blessed Francis did not wish his friars to hanker after learning and books, he was not happy about having it without his permission. So when blessed Francis was visiting the friary to which this novice belonged, the novice said to him, 'Father, it would give me great pleasure to have a psalter. But although the Minister General has granted permission, I would like to have it with your approval.' To which blessed Francis replied, 'The Emperor Charles Roland, Oliver, and all the paladins and men of valour were mighty in battle, fought the Infidels until death with great sweat and toil, and they gained a famous victory. And the holy martyrs themselves gave their lives in battle for the Faith of Christ. But in these days there are many who wish to win honour and praise from men by merely telling of their deeds. In the same way, there are many among us who want to win honour and praise by merely proclaiming and reciting the deeds of the Saints.' As though to say, 'Our concern is not with books and learning, but with holy deeds; for learning brings pride, but charity edifies.'

Some days later, as blessed Francis was sitting by the fire, the novice spoke to him again about the psalter. And blessed Francis said to him, 'Once you have a psalter, you will want a breviary. And when you have a breviary, you will sit in a high chair like a great prelate, and say to your brother, "Bring me my breviary!" ' As he spoke, blessed Francis in great fervour of spirit took up a handful of ashes and placed them on his head, and rubbing his hand around his head as though he was washing it, he exclaimed, 'I, a breviary! I, a breviary!' And he repeated this many times, passing his hand over his head. And the friar was amazed and ashamed.

Later, blessed Francis said to him, 'Brother, I was tempted in the same way to have books, but in order to learn the will of our Lord in this matter, I took the Gospels and prayed the Lord to reveal His will to me at the first opening of the book. And when my prayer was ended, at the first opening of the book I came upon the words of the holy Gospel, *It is granted to you to understand the secret of God's kingdom; the rest must learn of it by parables.*' And he said, 'There are so many who are eager to acquire learning, that blessed is the man who is content to be without it for love of the Lord God.'

Many months later, when blessed Francis was at S. Mary of the Porziuncula, this friar spoke to him yet again about the psalter as he stood on the road near his cell beyond the house. And blessed Francis told him, 'Go and do as your Minister says on this matter.' When he heard this, the friar turned back along the road, while blessed Francis stood thinking over what he had said to the friar. Suddenly he called after him, saying, 'Wait for me, brother, wait for me!' Overtaking him, he said, 'Come back and show me the place where I told you to do as your Minister directs about the psalter.' So when they had arrived at the place, blessed Francis knelt down before the friar and said, *'Mea culpa,* brother, *mea culpa*; for whoever wishes to be a Friar Minor should possess nothing but a habit with a cord and undergarment, as the Rule allows him. And those whom need obliges to do so may have sandals.' And whenever friars came to him to ask his advice on this matter, he used to give them the same reply. He often used to say, 'A man's knowledge is revealed by his actions, and the words of a Religious must be supported by his own deeds; for *the test of the tree is in its fruit.'*

On observing poverty in books and beds, buildings and appointments.

The most blessed Father used to teach the friars to value books for their witness to God and not for their costliness, for their edification and not their elegance. He wished books to be few and held in common, and suitable to the needs of penniless friars. They were so badly provided with beds and blankets that whoever had some threadbare rags spread over straw regarded it as a fine bed.

He also told the friars to build their houses small and their cells of wood, not of stone, and he wanted them built in a humble style. He abhorred pretentious buildings, and disliked superfluous or elaborate appointments. He wished nothing about their tables or appointments to appear worldly or to remind them of the world, so that everything should proclaim their poverty and remind them that they were pilgrims and exiles.

How Saint Francis compelled all the friars to leave a house which had been called 'the house of the friars.'

While he was passing through Bologna, he heard that a house had recently been built there for the friars. Directly he learned that it was known as 'the house of the friars,' he turned on his heel and left the city, giving strict orders that all the friars were to leave it at once and live in it no longer.

So they all abandoned it, and even the sick were not allowed to remain, but were turned out with the rest, until the Lord Ugolino, Bishop of Ostia and Legate in Lombardy, publicly proclaimed that the house belonged to him. One of these friars, who was sick and obliged to leave the house, is still living today, and has written this account.

*How Saint Francis wished to destroy a house which the people
of Assisi had built at S. Mary of the Porziuncula.*

At this period the friars had only a single poor cell thatched
with straw, with walls of wattle and daub. So when the time
drew near for the General Chapter, which was held each year at
S. Mary of the Porziuncula, the people of Assisi, realizing that
the friars were increasing in number daily, and that all of them
assembled there each year, held a meeting. And within a few
days, with great haste and zeal, they erected a large building of
stone and mortar while blessed Francis was absent and knew
nothing of it.

When he returned from one of the Provinces and arrived
for the Chapter, he was astonished at the house built there. And
he was afraid that the sight of this house might make other friars
build similar large houses in the places where they lived or were
to live, and he desired this place to remain the example and
pattern for all other houses of the Order. So before the Chapter
ended he climbed onto the roof of the house and told other
friars to climb up with him. And with their help he began to
throw to the ground the tiles with which the house was roofed,
intending to destroy it to the very foundations. But some men-at-
arms of Assisi were present to protect the place from the great
crowd of sightseers who had gathered to watch the Chapter of
the Friars. And when they saw that blessed Francis and other
friars intended to destroy the house, they went up to him at
once and said, 'Brother, this house belongs to the Commune of
Assisi, and we are here to represent the Commune. We forbid
you to destroy our house.' When he heard this, blessed Francis
said to them, 'If the house is yours, I will not touch it.' And
forthwith he and the other friars came down.

As a result of this incident, the people of the City of Assisi
decreed that thenceforward whoever held the office of Mayor
should be responsible for the repair of the house. And each year
for a long time this decree was carried out.

How he rebuked his Vicar because he was having a small house built for the recitation of the Office.

On another occasion the Vicar of blessed Francis began to have a small house built at S. Mary's, where the friars could be quiet and recite the Hours, because so many friars visited the place that they had nowhere in which to say the Office. For all the friars of the Order used to come there, because no one was received into the Order except in S. Mary's.

When the building was nearly completed, blessed Francis returned to the friary, and while in his cell he heard the noise made by the workmen. Calling his companion, he inquired what the friars were doing, and his companion told him all that was happening.

Blessed Francis immediately sent for his Vicar, and said to him, 'Brother, this place is the example and pattern of the whole Order. I would rather have the friars living here put up with trouble and discomfort for the love of the Lord God, so that other friars who come here carry away to their own houses a good example of poverty, rather than that they should enjoy every convenience and that these others should carry back to their own houses an example of building, saying, "At the friary of Saint Mary of the Porziuncula, which is the chief house of the Order, there are such and such great buildings, so we may rightly build in our own places as well." '

How he was not willing to remain in a well-built cell, or one that was called his own.

One of the friars, a deeply spiritual man, who was very intimate with blessed Francis, had a cell built standing a little distance from the hermitage where he lived, so that blessed Francis could remain at prayer there whenever he visited the place. So when blessed Francis came there, this friar conducted him to the cell; but although it was built only of wood, rough-hewn with axe and hatchet, the Father said, 'This cell is too fine. If you wish me to stay here, have a cell made with branches and ferns as its only covering inside and out.' For the poorer and smaller the house or cell, the readier he was to live in it. And when the friar had done this, blessed Francis remained there for some days.

One day, however, when he had left the cell, one of the friars went to look at it, and afterwards came to the place where blessed Francis was. Seeing him, the holy Father said to him, 'Where have you come from, brother?' 'I have come from your cell,' he replied. Then blessed Francis said, 'Because you have called it mine, some one else shall use it henceforward, and not I.' For we who were with him have often heard him quote the saying, *Foxes have holes, and the birds of the air their resting-places; the Son of Man has nowhere to lay His head.* He also used to say, 'When the Lord remained in the desert, where He prayed and fasted forty days and forty nights, He did not have a cell or house built for Him there, but sheltered beneath the rocks in the mountains.' So, after His example, he would not have any house or cell that could be called his own, nor did he ever have one built. Indeed, if ever he chanced to say to the friars, 'Go and make that cell ready,' he would not afterwards live in it, because of that saying in the holy Gospel, *Be not anxious, etc.* For even at the time of his death he had it written in his Testament that all cells and houses of the friars were to be built only of wood and clay, the better to safeguard poverty and humility.

The Saint's purpose and methods of choosing building sites in towns.

Once when blessed Francis was in Siena for treatment of his disease of the eyes, Master Bonaventura (*not the Saint*), who had given the friars the land on which the friary was built, said to him, 'Father, how do you like this place?' And blessed Francis said to him, 'Do you wish me to explain how the houses of the friars should be built?' 'Please do, Father,' he replied. And blessed Francis said, 'When the friars come to any city where they have no house, and meet anyone there who is willing to give them sufficient land to build a house, have a garden, and all that is necessary, they should first reckon how much land is sufficient for them, always bearing in mind holy poverty and the good example that we are obliged to show in all things.'

This he said because he did not want the friars to transgress against poverty in any way, either in their house, churches, gardens, or anything else that they used. He did not wish them to possess places by right of ownership, but to live in them *as strangers and exiles.* This was why he did not wish the friars to live together in large numbers in their houses, because he thought it difficult to observe poverty in a large community. And from the beginning of his conversion until his death it was his intention that absolute poverty should be observed in all things.

'When the friars have examined the land necessary for a house,' he said, 'they should go to the Bishop of that city and say to him, "My Lord, so-and-so is willing to give us so much land for the love of God and for the salvation of his soul, so that we may build a house there. We are therefore coming to you first of all, because you are the father and lord of the souls of all the flock entrusted to you, as well as of ourselves and of all the brethren who will dwell in this place. So, with God's blessing and your own, we would like to build there." '

He spoke thus because the harvest of souls which the friars desire to gather is more readily obtained by working in harmony with the clergy, thereby helping both them and the people, than by antagonizing them, even though they may win the people. And he said, 'The Lord has called us to maintain His Faith, and support the Bishops and clergy of Holy Church. So we are bound always to love, honour and respect them to the best of our ability. For, as their name implies, the Friars are called Minors because they ought to be more humble than all other men in this world, both in example and in action. At the beginning of my conversion the Lord put His word into the mouth of the Bishop of Assisi so that he might counsel me rightly and strengthen me in the service of Christ; because of this and many other excellent virtues that I see in prelates, I wish to love and respect not only the Bishops but the poor priests as well, and to regard them as my masters.

'When the friars have received the blessing of the Bishop, let them go and mark out the boundaries of the land which they have accepted for their house, and as a sign of holy poverty and humility, let them plant a hedge instead of building a wall. Afterwards let them erect simple little huts of clay and wood, and a number of cells where the friars can pray or work from time to time in order to increase their merit and avoid idleness. Their churches are to be small; they are not to build great churches in order to preach to the people, or for any other reason, for they show greater humility and a better example when they visit other churches to preach. And should prelates or clergy, whether Religious or secular, visit their houses, their humble little dwellings, cells, and tiny churches will speak for themselves, and these things will edify them more than any words.'

He said also, 'Friars often raise large buildings, and violate our holy poverty, and by so doing provoke criticism and set a bad example. And sometimes, in order to obtain a better or holier place, or a larger congregation, they abandon their own houses out of covetousness and greed; or they pull them down and build others that are large and pretentious. Consequently those who have contributed to their cost, and others who see it, are greatly offended and distressed. So it is better for friars to erect humble little buildings, remaining loyal to their profession and setting a good example to their neighbours, rather than to act contrary to their profession and set a bad example to others. But should the friars ever leave a poor little house for one in a more suitable place, the offence caused would be less.'

How friars, especially those who had been prelates and scholars, opposed Saint Francis's desire to erect humble friaries and buildings.

As a sign of holy poverty, and humility blessed Francis decreed that the churches of the friars were to be small and their houses built only of wood and clay. For he wanted the friary of Saint Mary of the Porziuncula to be a pattern especially for buildings constructed of wood and clay, so that it might be a permanent memorial for all friars, present and to come, since it was the first and chief house of the whole Order. But some of the friars opposed him in this matter, saying that in some Provinces timber was more costly than stone, so that it did not seem sensible to them that their houses should be built of wood and clay.

But blessed Francis refused to argue with them, especially since he was nearing death and seriously ill. So he caused it to be written in his Testament: *Friars are to beware of accepting churches, houses, and all other places built for them unless they conform to holy poverty; and they are always to lodge in them as strangers and pilgrims.*

But we, who were with him when he wrote the Rule and most of his other writings, testify that he had many things written in the Rule and in his other writings to which many friars were opposed, especially the prelates and scholars among us; and to-day these things would have been very beneficial and valuable to the whole Order. But he had a great fear of scandal, and yielded, although with reluctance, to the wishes of the brethren. But he often said: 'Woe to those friars who oppose me in this matter, which I am firmly convinced to be the will of God for the greater usefulness and needs of the whole Order, although I unwillingly submit to their wish.' So he often used to say to his companions, 'It causes me great grief and distress that in these matters, which I learn from God with great effort in prayer and meditation, and which I know to be in accordance with His will, certain brethren who rely on their own experience and false prudence, oppose me and render them ineffective, saying, "These things are to be held and observed, and not those." '

How he regarded it as theft to obtain alms beyond one's needs.

Blessed Francis used to say to his friars, 'I have never been a thief in the matter of alms, and obtained or used more than I needed. I have always accepted less than my needs, lest other poor folk should be cheated of their share; for to act otherwise would be theft.'

How Christ told blessed Francis that He did not wish friars to possess anything, either in common or individually.

When the Friar Ministers urged him to allow the friars to possess something, at least, in common, so that so great a company might have some resources, blessed Francis called upon Christ in prayer, and took counsel with Him on the matter.

And Christ at once answered him, saying, 'It is My will to withhold all things from them, both in general and in particular. I will always be ready to provide for this family, however great it may become, and I will always cherish it so long as it shall trust in Me.'

Saint Francis's hatred of money, and how he punished a friar who touched money.

Francis, the true friend and imitator of Christ, utterly despised all things belonging to this world, and hated money above all else. He always urged his brethren both by word and example to avoid it as they would the devil. And he told the friars to have as little love and use for money as for dung.

One day, a layman happened to enter Saint Mary of the Porziuncula to pray, and laid some money near the cross as an offering. When he had left, one of the friars unthinkingly picked it up and placed it on a window ledge. But when this was reported to blessed Francis, this friar, realizing himself detected, at once hastened to ask forgiveness; and, falling to the ground, offered himself for punishment.

The holy Father reproved him, and took him severely to task for touching the money; and he ordered him to take the money from the window in his mouth, carry it outside the friary, and lay it on a heap of ass's dung.

When this friar readily obeyed this order, all who saw or heard was filled with the greatest fear, and thenceforward despised money as ass's dung. And further examples moved them to despise it altogether.

On avoiding luxury and many changes of clothing; and on being patient in privations.

Blessed Francis, endowed with virtue from on high, was warmed by divine fire within rather than by outward clothing. He strongly disapproved of those in the Order who wore three garments and used finer clothing than necessary. He used to say that any need revealed by a love of pleasure and not by reason was the sign of a dead spirit, for 'when the spirit becomes lukewarm and inward grace grows cold, it follows that flesh and blood seek their own pleasures.' He also used to say, 'When the soul lacks any desire for spiritual joys, the flesh is bound to turn to its own. Then the lower desires plead the excuse of necessity, and the desires of the flesh influence the conscience. But if a genuine need besets any Brother and he immediately hastens to satisfy it, what reward can he expect? For an opportunity has arisen to win merit, but he has already shown clearly that he has no desire for it. For to refuse to endure these wants patiently is nothing but a return to Egypt' (*Exod.* xvi. 2).

Lastly, he desired that friars should on no account possess more than two habits, although he allowed these to be lined with patches stitched together. He used to say that choice materials were abhorrent, and sharply rebuked those who acted contrary to this; and in order to shame such people by his own example, he always repaired his own habit with rough sacking. For this reason, even in death he directed that his burial habit was to be covered with sacking. But if any friars were troubled by sickness, or had other needs, he would allow them another soft garment next the skin, provided that austerity and roughness was always maintained in their outer garment. For he used to say with the greatest sorrow, 'Henceforward strictness will be so greatly relaxed and lukewarmness rule, that the sons of a poor Father will not be ashamed to wear scarlet cloth, only the colour being changed.'

How he refused to comfort his own body with things that he thought other friars might lack.

While blessed Francis was staying in the hermitage of Saint Eleutherius near Rieti, he lined his own habit and those of his companions with some pieces of cloth because of the intense cold—for, as was his custom, he had only one habit—and as a result his body began to derive a little comfort. A short while afterwards, when he returned from prayer, he said with great joy to his companion, 'It is my duty to be the pattern and example to all the brethren; so although it is necessary for my body to have a lined habit, I must consider my other brethren who have the same needs, and who perhaps do not and cannot possess it. I must therefore have sympathy with them in this matter, and endure the same privations as they, so that when they see me doing so, they may have the strength to bear theirs patiently.'

But we who were with him cannot express either in words or writing how many great necessities he denied his body in order to give a good example to the friars, and help them to bear their poverty patiently. For once the friars began to increase in numbers, he made it his chief and particular concern to teach the brethren what they should do or avoid by his own actions rather than by words.

How he was ashamed to see anyone poorer than himself.

Once, when he had met a poor man and considered his poverty, he said to his companion, 'This man's poverty brings great shame on us, and is a stern rebuke to our own. For since I have chosen holy poverty as my lady, my delight, and my spiritual and bodily treasure, I feel the greatest shame when I find someone poorer than myself. And the story has gone round the whole world that I am vowed to poverty before God and men.'

How, when the first friars were ashamed, he encouraged and taught them to go out and seek alms.

When blessed Francis began to have friars he was full of joy at their conversion, and that God had given him a goodly company. And he had such love and respect for them that he did not insist that they went out for alms, because it was clear to him that they were ashamed to go. So, in order to spare them the shame, he used to go out every day to collect alms alone. But he had been accustomed to comfort in the world, was frail by nature, and was further weakened by overmuch fasting and hardship. And when he became exhausted by his efforts, he realized that he could not continue this work single-handed. He knew, also, that his brethren were called to the same way of life, although they were ashamed to follow it; for as yet they did not fully realize this, nor were they discerning enough to say, 'We also will go out for alms.'

So he said to them, 'My dearest brothers, little children, do not be ashamed to go out for alms, for our Lord made Himself poor in this world for our sakes, and we have chosen to follow His example on the road of true poverty. This is our heritage, which our Lord Jesus Christ has won and bequeathed to us and to all who desire to live after His example in most holy poverty. I solemnly assure you that many of the noblest and wisest men of this age will join our company and regard it as a great honour to go out begging. So go out for alms confidently and gladly with the blessing of God. You should be more willing and happy to go for alms than a man who brings back an hundred coins in exchange for one, because you are offering the love of God to those from whom you ask alms when you say, "Give us alms for the love of the Lord God," for in comparison with Him heaven and earth are as nothing.'

But because the friars were as yet few in number, he could not send them out two by two, but he sent them singly through the towns and villages. So when they returned with the alms they had obtained, each of them showed blessed Francis the alms that he had received. And one would say to another, 'I have received more alms than you.' And blessed Francis was glad when he saw them so happy and cheerful. And thenceforward each of them readily asked permission to go out begging.

How he did not wish the friars to be provident and anxious for to-morrow.

While blessed Francis was with the first friars, he lived with them in such poverty that they observed the holy Gospel to the the letter in all things and through all things, from the very day when our Lord revealed to him that he and his friars were to live according to the pattern of the holy Gospel. He therefore forbade the friar who cooked for the brethren to put dried beans into warm water in the evening, as is usual, when he intended to to give them to the friars to eat on the following day. This was in order to observe the saying of the holy Gospel, *Do not fret over to-morrow.* So the friar delayed putting them to soften until after Matins on the day when they were to be eaten. Many friars, especially in towns, continued to observe this custom for a long time, and would not seek or accept more alms than were necessary to support them for a single day.

How by word and example he reproved friars who had prepared
a lavish meal on Christmas Day because a Minister was present.

When one of the Friar-Ministers had visited blessed Francis
in order to keep the Feast of Christmas with him in the friary at
Rieti, the friars prepared the tables rather elaborately and carefully on Christmas Day in honour of the Minister, putting on
fair white linen and glass vessels. But when the Father came
down from his cell to eat, and saw the tables raised up from the
ground and prepared with such great care, he went back secretly
and took the hat and staff of a poor beggar who arrived that
day. And calling in a low voice to one of his companions, he
went out of the door of the friary unseen by the brethren in the
house, while his companion remained inside near the door. Meanwhile the friars came in to dine, for blessed Francis had ordered
that, whenever he did not come at once at mealtime, the friars
were not to wait for him.

When he had stood outside for a while, he knocked on the
door, and his companion immediately opened to him. And entering with his hat on his back and his staff in his hand, he came
like a stranger or beggar to the door of the room where the
friars were eating, and called out, 'For the love of God, give alms
to this poor sick stranger!' But the Minister and the other friars
recognized him at once. And the Minister replied, 'Brother, we
are poor as well, and because we are so many, the alms that we
have only meet our needs. But for the love of God which you
have invoked, come in and we will share with you the alms which
the Lord has given us.'

When he had entered and stood before the friars' table, the
Minister handed to him the plate from which he was eating, and
also some bread. And taking it, he humbly sat down on the floor
beside the fire in the sight of the friars sitting at table. Then he
sighed and said to the brethren, 'When I saw the table elaborately
laid, I felt that this was not the table of poor religious who go
around for alms from door to door each day. Dearest brothers,
we are under a greater obligation than other Religious to follow
the example of Christ's humility and poverty, for it is to this
end that we have been called and professed before God and men.
So it seems to me that I am sitting like a Friar Minor, because

196

the feasts of our Lord and the Saints are better honoured in the want and poverty by which these Saints won heaven than in the luxury and excess by which a soul is estranged from heaven.'

The friars were ashamed at his words, realizing that he was speaking no more than the truth. And seeing him seated on the ground, wishing to correct and teach them in such a holy and simple way, some of them began to weep aloud. For he warned the brethren to eat humbly and simply, so as to edify lay folk. And if any poor man should visit them or be invited by the friars, he was to sit with them as an equal, and not the poor man on the floor and the friars on high.

How the Lord Bishop of Ostia wept and was edified by the poverty of the friars at the time of the Chapter.

When the Lord Bishop of Ostia, who later became Pope Gregory (IX), attended the Chapter of the friars at Saint Mary of the Porziuncula, he entered the house with many knights and clergy to see the friars' dormitory. And seeing how the friars lay on the ground and had nothing beneath them but a little straw, and a few poor broken-down pallets, and no pillows, he began to weep freely before them all, saying, 'Look how the friars sleep here! But we, wretched creatures, enjoy so many luxuries! What will become of us?' So he and all the others were much edified. He did not even find a table in the place, because the friars used to eat on the ground; for as long as blessed Francis lived, all the friars in that house used to eat on the ground.

How, at blessed Francis's advice, the soldiers obtained their needs by asking alms from door to door.

When blessed Francis was in the friary at Bagni near the city of Nocera, his feet began to swell badly because of the disease of dropsy, and he became seriously ill. When the people of Assisi heard of this, they hurriedly sent soldiers to the friary to escort him to Assisi, fearing that if he remained there, others would obtain his most holy body. But while they were bringing him, they stopped in a fortress-town belonging to the Commune of Assisi in order to eat; and blessed Francis rested in the house of a poor man who welcomed him willingly and gladly. Meanwhile the soldiers went through the town to buy themselves what they needed, and found nothing. So they came back to the holy Father and told him jokingly, 'Brother, you will have to let us share your alms, for we cannot buy anything to eat!' Then blessed Francis said to them with great fervour, 'You have not found anything because you trusted in your flies (*meaning, your money*), and not in God. Go back to the houses where you went trying to buy food; put aside your shame, and ask alms for the love of the Lord God. The Holy Spirit will move them to give generously.' So they went away and asked alms as blessed Francis had told them; and those from whom they asked alms gave them whatever they had with great gladness and generosity. And recognizing that a miracle had happened to them, they returned to blessed Francis praising God with great joy.

The holy Father used to regard it as an act of great nobility and dignity before God and the world to ask alms for love of the Lord God, for all things which our heavenly Father has created for the use of men are granted freely despite their sin both to the worthy and to the unworthy through the love of His beloved Son. He used to say that the servant of God ought to ask alms for the love of God more willingly and gladly than one who, out of his own generosity and sympathy, might go and say, 'If anyone will give me a penny, I will give him a thousand pieces of gold.' For, by asking alms, the servant of God offers the love of God to those of whom he begs, and in comparison with this all things in heaven and earth are nothing.

So before the friars increased in numbers, and even after they had became numerous, whenever a friar went through the world preaching, and was invited by anyone, however noble or wealthy, to eat and lodge with him, he would always go for alms at mealtime before he came to his host's house, in order to uphold the good example of the friars and the dignity of Lady Poverty. Blessed Francis often used to say to his host, 'I will not resign my royal dignity and heritage, and my profession and that of my brethren (that is, to beg bread from door to door).' And sometimes his host would go with him and carry the alms which blessed Francis had collected, and preserve them like relics out of devotion to him.

The writer has seen this happen many times, and testifies to these things.

St. Francis of Assisi

How he went out for alms before he would go in to
the Cardinal's table.

Once when blessed Francis was visiting the Lord Bishop of
Ostia, who later became Pope Gregory (IX), he went out un-
observed at dinner-time in order to ask alms from door to door.
And when he returned, the Lord of Ostia had already gone in to
table with many knights and nobles. But when the holy Father
entered, he laid the alms that he had collected on the table before the Cardinal, and sat down beside him, for the Cardinal
always wished that blessed Francis should sit next him at table.
The Cardinal was somewhat embarrassed to find that blessed
Francis had gone out for alms and laid them on the table; but
he said nothing at the time because of his guests.

When blessed Francis had eaten a little, he took up his alms
and in the name of the Lord God distributed a little to each of
the knights and chaplains of the Lord Cardinal. And they all
accepted them with great reverence and devotion, reaching out
their hoods and sleeves; and some ate the alms, while others kept
them out of devotion to him.

After dinner the Cardinal entered his own apartment, taking
blessed Francis with him. And stretching out his arms, he embraced him with great joy and gladness, saying, 'My simple
brother, why have you shamed me to-day by going out for alms
when you visit my house, which is a home for your friars?' 'On
the contrary, my lord,' replied blessed Francis, 'I have shown
you the greatest honour; for when a servant does his duty and
fulfils his obedience to his lord, he does honour to his lord.'
And he said, 'It is my duty to be the pattern and example of
our poor friars, especially as I know that in this Order of friars
there are, and will be, friars who are Minors in name and deed,
who, for love of the Lord God and by the anointing of the Holy
Spirit Who will guide them in all things, will be humble and
obedient, and the servants of their brethren. There are also, and
will be, some among them who are held back by shame or bad
custom, and who scorn to humble themselves and stoop to going
for alms and doing other servile work. Because of this I must by
my own actions teach those who belong, and will belong, to the
Order, that they are inexcusable in the eyes of God both in this

life and in the life to come. So while I am with you, who are our Lord and Apostolic Protector, or with other great and wealthy men of this world who for love of God not only receive me into your houses but even press me to eat at your table, I will not be ashamed to go out for alms. Indeed, I intend to regard and retain this practice as the highest nobility and royal dignity, and to do it in honour of Him Who, though He was Lord of all, willed for our sakes to become the servant of all. And when He was rich and glorious in His majesty, He came as one poor and despised in our humility. So I want all present or future friars to know that I regard it as a greater consolation of soul and body to sit at the poor little table of the brethren, and to see in front of me the meagre alms that they beg from door to door for love of the Lord God, than to sit at your table and that of other lords, abundantly provided with different dishes. For the bread of charity is holy bread, hallowed by the praise and love of God, and when a friar goes out for alms he should first say, "Praised and blessed be the Lord God!" And afterwards he should say, "Give us alms for the love of the Lord God." '

The Cardinal was much edified by the holy Father's words, and said, 'My son, do whatever seems good to you, for God is with you, and you with Him.' For, as blessed Francis often said, it was his wish that no friar should remain long without going out to beg alms, both because of its great merit, and lest he should become ashamed to go. Indeed, the nobler and greater a friar had been in the world, the more pleased and edified he was when he went for alms and did other humble work as the friars were then accustomed to do.

On the friar who neither prayed nor worked, but ate well.

In the early days of the Order, when the friars were living at Rivo Torto near Assisi, there was one friar among them who prayed little and did no work; he refused to go out for alms, but used to eat heartily. Thinking the matter over, blessed Francis knew by the Holy Spirit that the man was a lover of the flesh, and said to him, "Be off with you, Brother Fly, since you want to eat up the labours of your brethren, and be idle in the work of God. You are like a barren and idle drone, who gathers nothing and does no work, but consumes the toil and gain of the good bees!'

200

So he went his way, and because he was a lover of the flesh, he neither asked mercy nor found it.

How he went out with fervour to meet a beggar who was walking along with his alms and praising God.

On another occasion, when blessed Francis was at S. Mary of the Porziuncula, a friar of true spiritual poverty was coming along the street on his way back from Assisi with alms, and as he walked he was cheerfully singing God's praises in a loud voice. As he drew near the church of S. Mary, blessed Francis heard him, and at once went out to meet him with the greatest fervour and joy. He ran up to him in the road, and joyfully kissed the shoulder on which he was carrying a bag with alms. Then he took the bag from his shoulder, laid it on his own shoulder, and thus bore it into the friary. And he told the brethren, 'This is how I want a friar of mine to go out and return with alms, happy, joyful, and praising God.'

How the Lord revealed to him that the friars were to be called Minors, and were to proclaim peace and salvation.

One day blessed Francis said, 'The Order and life of the Friars Minor is a little flock which the Son of God has asked of His heavenly Father in these latter days, saying, "Father, I would that Thou shouldest form and give Me a new and humble people in these latter days, who will be unlike all others who have preceded them in humility and poverty, and content to possess Me alone." And the Father said to His beloved Son, "My Son, it is done as Thou hast asked." '

So blessed Francis used to say that God willed and revealed to him that they should be called Friars Minor, because they were to be the poor and humble people whom the Son of God had asked of His Father. Of this people the Son of God Himself speaks in the Gospel: *Do not be afraid, My little flock. Your Father has determined to give you His kingdom.* And again: *Believe Me, when you did it to one of the least of My brethren here, you did it to Me.* And although the Lord was speaking of all poor and spiritual people, He was referring more particularly to the Order of Friars Minor which was to arise in His Church.

201

Therefore, since it was revealed to blessed Francis that it should be called the Order of Friars Minor, he caused it to be written in his first Rule, which he took before the Lord Pope Innocent III; who approved and granted it, and later proclaimed it publicly in Consistory.

The Lord also revealed to him the greeting which the friars were to use, and he caused this to be written in his Testament, saying: *The Lord revealed to me that I should say as a greeting, 'The Lord give you peace.'*

In the early days of the Order, while he was travelling with a friar who was one of the first twelve, he used to greet men and women along the road and in the fields, saying, 'The Lord give you peace.' And because people had never heard such a greeting from any Religious, they were very startled. Indeed, some said indignantly, 'What do you mean by this greeting of yours?' As a result the friar became embarrassed, and said to blessed Francis, 'Allow me to use some other greeting.' But the holy Father said, 'Let them chatter, for they do not understand the ways of God. Don't feel ashamed because of this, for one day the nobles and princes of this world will respect you and the other friars for this greeting. For it is no marvel if the Lord should desire to have a new little flock, whose speech and way of life are unlike those of all its predecessors, and which is content to possess Him alone, the Most High and most glorious.'

PART II

ON CHARITY AND COMPASSION TOWARDS ONE'S NEIGHBOUR

Firstly, how blessed Francis made concessions to a friar who was dying of hunger by eating with him, and how he warned the friars to use discretion in their penance.

During the period when blessed Francis began to have brethren, and was living with them at Rivo Torto near Assisi, one night while all the brethren were asleep one of the friars cried out, saying, 'I am dying! I am dying!' Startled and frightened, all the friars awoke. Blessed Francis got up and said, 'Rise, brothers, and light a lamp.' And when it was lit, he said, 'Who was it who said, "I am dying"?' The friar answered, 'It is I.' And he said, 'What is the matter, brother? How are you dying?' And he said, 'I am dying of hunger.'

The holy Father at once ordered food to be brought, and having great charity and discretion, he ate with him lest he should be ashamed to eat alone; and, at his wish, all the other friars joined them. For that friar and all the others were newly converted to the Lord, and used to discipline their bodies without restraint. After they had eaten blessed Francis said to the other friars, 'My brothers, everyone must consider his own constitution, for although one of you may be able to sustain his body on less food, I do not want another who needs more food to try and imitate him in this matter. Each brother must consider his own constitution and allow his body its needs, so that it has the strength to serve the spirit. For while we are bound to avoid over-indulgence in food, which injures both body and soul, we must also avoid excessive abstinence, especially as the Lord *desires mercy, and not sacrifice.*' And he added, 'Dearest brothers, necessity and charity for my brother have moved me to act as I have done, and we have eaten with him lest he be ashamed to to eat alone. But I do not wish to do so again, for it would be neither regular nor fitting. It is my wish and command that each of you is to satisfy his body as need demands and so far as our poverty allows.'

For the first friars, and those who followed them for a long while, afflicted their bodies beyond measure by abstinence from food and drink, by vigils, by cold, by coarse clothing, and by manual labour. They wore iron bands and breast-plates, and the roughest of hair shirts. So the holy Father, considering that the friars might fall ill as a result of this—as had already happened in a short time—gave orders in Chapter that no friar should wear anything but the habit next his skin.

But we who were with him bear witness that although he was discreet and moderate towards the brethren throughout his life, this was in order that they should never fall away from poverty and the spirit of our Order. Nevertheless, from the beginning of his conversion until the end of his life, the most holy Father was severe towards his own body, although he was frail by nature and while in the world could not have lived without comfort. At one time, therefore, considering that the friars were exceeding

203

THE CATHOLIC TRADITION: Social Thought

the bounds of poverty and sincerity in food and other matters, he said to a number of friars as representing all the brethren, 'Do not let the brethren imagine that any concession is necessary to my own body. For since it is my duty to be a pattern and example to all the friars, I wish to have, and to be content with, scanty and very poor food, and to make use of all other things in the spirit of poverty, and to shun delicate food altogether.'

How he made a concession to a sick friar by eating grapes with him.

On another occasion, while blessed Francis was living in the same place, one of the friars, who was a spiritual man and an early member of the Order, was ill and very weak. As he looked at him, the holy Father felt great compassion for him. But because at that time the friars, both healthy and sick, were cheerfully regarding their poverty as plenty, and would not use or ask for medicines in sickness, but willingly accepted bodily privations, blessed Francis said to himself, 'If only this brother could eat some ripe grapes first thing in the morning, I think they would do him good.'

And he acted on this idea, for he rose very early one day, and calling the friar to him privately, led him into a vineyard near the friary. Choosing a vine where the grapes were good to eat, he sat down beside the vine with the friar, and began to eat the grapes lest the brother should be ashamed to eat alone. And as they ate the friar was cured, and they praised God together. This friar remembered the compassion and kindness of the most holy Father for the rest of his life, and often used to tell the brethren about it with devotion and tears.

How he stripped himself and his companion to provide clothing for a poor old woman.

At Celano, one winter, blessed Francis had a length of cloth folded to form a cloak, which a friend of the friars had lent him. When an old woman came to him asking alms, he immediately took the cloth from his shoulders, and although it did not belong to him, he gave it to the poor old woman, saying, 'Go and make a garment for yourself, for you need it badly enough!'

The old woman laughed and was astonished—whether from fear or joy I cannot say—and took the cloth from his hands. Fearing that if she delayed he might take it back, she hurried away and cut up the cloth with shears. But when she discovered that the cloth was not sufficient for a garment, she put her trust in the kindness already shown by the holy Father, and told him that the cloth was not sufficient for a garment.

The Saint looked at his companion, who was wearing a similar piece of cloth on his shoulders, and said, 'Do you hear what this poor woman says? Let us put up with the cold for the love of God, and give the cloth to this poor woman so that her garment can be completed.' And at once his companion gave her his own, just as blessed Francis had done. So both of them remained without a cloak in order that the poor woman might be clothed.

How he regarded it as robbery not to give a cloak to one who had greater need.

Once when he was returning from Siena, he met a poor man on the road, and said to his companion, 'We ought to return this cloak to the poor man, whose it is; for we have accepted it as a loan until we should find someone poorer than ourselves.' But knowing how badly the generous Father needed it, his companion protested strongly that he should not neglect himself to provide for someone else. But the Saint said to him, 'I refuse to be a thief, for we should be guilty of theft if we refused to give it to one more poor than ourselves.' So the kindly Father gave away the cloak to the poor man.

How he gave a cloak to a poor man on a certain condition.

At Celle di Cortona blessed Francis was wearing a new cloak which the friars had taken great trouble to obtain for him. But when a poor man came to the friary, weeping for his dead wife and poverty-stricken, bereaved family, the compassionate Saint said to him, 'I give you this cloak on condition that you part with it to no one unless he buys it from you and pays a good price.' Hearing this, the friars ran to take the cloak away from the poor man; but taking courage from the face of the holy Father, he clung to it with both hands. And at length the friars bought back the cloak, and paid a fair price for it to the poor man.

How, through the alms of blessed Francis, a poor man forgave his injuries and abandoned his hatred for his master.

At Celle, in the lordship of Perugia, blessed Francis met a poor man whom he had formerly known in the world, and asked him, 'Brother, how are things with you?' But the man began to utter angry curses on his master, saying, 'Thanks to my master—God curse him!—I have had nothing but misfortune, for he has stripped me of all that I possess.'

Seeing him persist in mortal hatred, blessed Francis was filled with pity for his soul, and said, 'Brother, pardon your master for the love of God, and free your own soul; it is possible that he will restore to you whatever he has taken away. Otherwise, you have lost your goods and will lose your soul as well.' And the man said, 'I cannot fully forgive him unless he first restores to me what he has taken away.' Then blessed Francis said to him, 'Look, I will give you this cloak; I beg you to forgive your master for the love of the Lord God.' And at once his heart was melted and touched by this act of kindness, and he forgave his master his wrongs.

How he sent a cloak to a poor woman who, like himself, suffered from her eyes.

A poor woman of Machilone came to Riete to be treated for a disease of the eyes. And when the doctor visited blessed Francis, he said to him, 'Brother, a woman has come to me with a disease of the eyes, and she is so poor that I have to pay her expenses myself.' As soon as he heard this he was moved with pity for her, and calling one of the friars who was his Guardian, he said to him, 'Brother Guardian, we have to repay a loan.' 'What is this loan?' asked the Guardian. And he said, 'This cloak, which we have borrowed from a poor, sick woman, and which we must return to her.' And the Guardian said, 'Do whatever seems best to you, Brother.'

Then blessed Francis, with great merriment, called a friend of his who was a spiritual man, and told him, 'Take this cloak, and twelve loaves with it, and go to this poor woman with a disease of the eyes whom the doctor will point out to you. And say to her, "The poor man to whom you lent this cloak thanks you for the loan of it; take back what belongs to you." ' So he went and said to the woman all that blessed Francis had told him. But thinking that he was making a fool of her, she was nervous and embarrassed, saying, 'Leave me in peace; I don't know what you are talking about.' But he laid the cloak and the twelve loaves in her hands. Then, realizing that he was speaking in earnest, she accepted them with fear and reverence, rejoicing and praising the Lord. And afraid that they might be taken from her, she rose secretly by night and returned home with joy. But blessed Francis had arranged with the Guardian to pay her expenses daily as long as she remained there.

We who lived with him testify to the greatness of his charity and compassion towards sick and healthy alike, both to his own friars and to other poor folk. For after persuading us not to be upset, he used to give away to the poor with great inward and outward joy even his own bodily necessities, which the friars had sometimes obtained with great trouble and difficulty, thus depriving himself even of things that he badly needed. Because of this the Minister General and his Guardian told him not to give away his habit to any friar without their permission. For in their devotion to him the friars used sometimes to ask him for his habit, and at once he would give it; but sometimes he divided it and gave away a portion, retaining part for himself, for he wore only a single habit.

How he gave away his habit to friars who asked it for the love of God.

When he was travelling through one of the Provinces preaching, two French friars met him. And having received great consolation from him, they finally begged his habit for the love of God. And as soon as he heard 'for the love of God,' he took off his habit and gave it to them, remaining unclothed for a good while. For when anyone invoked the love of God he would never refuse his cord, or habit, or anything that they asked. But he was very displeased, and often rebuked the friars, when he heard them use the words 'for the love of God' without good cause. For he used to say, 'The love of God is so sublime and precious that it should only be mentioned on rare occasions and in great need, and then with great reverence.'

But one of these friars removed his own habit, and gave it to him in exchange. Whenever he gave away his own habit, or part of it to anyone, he suffered great want and distress, because he could not obtain another or have it made quickly, especially as he always wished to have a shabby habit, patched up with pieces of cloth, sometimes both inside and out. Indeed, he would seldom or never wear a new habit, but obtained an old habit from another friar. And sometimes he would obtain part of his habit from one friar, and part from another. But at times he used to line it inside with new cloth, because of his frequent illnesses and chills of the stomach and spleen. He observed this absolute poverty in clothing up to the very year in which he departed to the Lord. For, a few days before his death, since he was suffering dropsy and almost dried up by his many ailments, the friars made him several habits, so that his habit could be changed night or day whenever necessary.

How he wished to give some cloth to a poor man secretly.

On another occasion a poor man came to the friary where blessed Francis was staying, and begged a piece of cloth from the friars for the love of God. When he heard of this, the holy Father said to one of the friars, 'Search through the house, and see if you can find any length or piece of cloth, and give it to this poor man.' But having gone around the whole house, the friar told him that he could find nothing.

So in order that the poor man should not go away empty-handed, blessed Francis stole away quietly—lest the Guardian should forbid him—and took a knife. Then he sat down in a remote place and began to cut away part of his habit which was sewed on the inside, intending to give it to the poor man secretly. But the Guardian noticed him, and at once forbade him to give it away, especially as there was a hard frost at the time, and he was very frail and cold. So the holy Father said to him, 'If you do not want me to give the man this piece, you must make sure that some other piece is given to our poor brother.' And at the insistence of blessed Francis, the friars gave the poor man some cloth from their own garments.

Whenever he travelled about the world preaching, if any brother lent him a cloak, he would not accept it unless he was allowed to give it to any poor man whom he met or who came to him, if the voice of his own conscience told him that it was necessary to that person. He always went on foot, and only rode a donkey after he became ill. Only in the most pressing need would he use a horse; normally he refused to ride at all, and only did so a short while before his death.

How he told Brother Giles, before he was received into the Order, to give his cloak to a poor man.

At the beginning of the Order, when he was living at Rivo Torto with only two friars, a man named Giles, who became the third friar, came to him from the world in order to share his way of life. And when he had remained there for some days, still wearing his secular clothes, a poor man came to the place asking alms of blessed Francis. Turning to Giles, blessed Francis said to him, 'Give this poor brother your cloak.' At once Giles gladly removed it from his back and gave it to the poor man. Then it became clear to him that God had imparted a new grace to his heart, since he had given his cloak to the poor man with great cheerfulness. So he was received into the Order by blessed Francis, and constantly advanced in virtue to the greatest perfection.

On the penance that he imposed on a friar who had wrongfully criticized a certain poor man.

When blessed Francis had gone to preach at a house of the friars near Rocca Brizzi, it happened that on the day he was due to preach, a poor, sick man came to him. Full of compassion for him, he began to speak about the man's poverty and sickness to his companion. And his companion said to him, 'Brother, it is true that this man seems poor enough, but it may be that no one in the whole Province has a greater desire for riches.' He was at once severely rebuked by blessed Francis, and confessed his fault. Then the Father said to him, 'Are you ready to perform

THE CATHOLIC TRADITION: Social Thought

the penance that I give you?' 'I will do it willingly,' he replied. And he said to him, 'Go and remove your habit, and throw yourself naked at the poor man's feet, and tell him how you have sinned in speaking ill of him, and ask him to pray for you.' So the friar went and did all tht blessed Francis had told him. Then he rose and resumed his habit, and returned to blessed Francis. And the Father said to him, 'Do you want to know how you sinned against him, and against Christ Himself? Whenever you see a poor man, remember Christ in Whose Name he comes, and how He took upon Himself our poverty and weakness. For this man's poverty serves us as a mirror, in which we should view and consider with pity the weakness and poverty of our Lord Jesus Christ, which He endured in His own body for our salvation.'

How he ordered a New Testament to be given to a poor woman, the mother of two friars.

Another time, while he was staying at S. Mary of the Porziuncula, a poor old woman, who had two sons in the Order, came to the friary asking alms of blessed Francis. He immediately asked Brother Peter Catanii, who was then Minister General, 'Have we anything to give our mother?' For he used to say that the mother of any friar was mother to himself and to all the friars. Brother Peter said to him, 'There is nothing in the house that we can give her, for she wants the kind of alms that can sustain her bodily needs. But in the church we have a single New Testament, from which we read the lessons at Matins.' (For at that time the friars had no breviaries and few psalters.) So blessed Francis said to him, 'Give the New Testament to our mother, so that she can sell it for her needs. I am sure that this will please our Lord and the Blessed Virgin better than if we were to read from it.' So he gave it to her. For it can be said and written of him as is read of blessed Job: *Loving care has borne me company as I grew up from childhood, ever since I left my mother's womb.*

To us who lived with him it would be a long and very difficult task to write or describe not only what we have learned from others about his charity and kindness toward the friars and other poor folk, but what we have seen with our own eyes.

St. Thomas Aquinas
1225-1274

*Among the great thinkers and writers of the Christian
theological tradition, St. Thomas Aquinas is one of the very
few whose influence is too vast to measure. His philosophy
and theology have been central to Catholic teaching for seven
centuries. He was born in Italy in 1225. He was schooled as a
child in the Benedictine Monastery of Montecassino, studied at
the University of Naples and continued his studies in Paris and
Cologne. From 1252 through to the end of his life, he was dedicated to teaching, though he also found time to preach. He was
a member of the Dominican Order. He died at the age of 49.*

*Thomas lived during a period of tremendous intellectual
ferment. The philosophies of Plato and Aristotle were being explored vigorously by the theologians of the thirteenth century.
Thomas contributed his abilities generously. The result was
the creation of a philosophico-theological structure which
incorporated not only the best in Plato and Aristotle but the
major elements of the Christian theological tradition as well.*

No doubt, Thomas is best known for his Summa Theologica,
though he wrote much more than that. The Summa *is an exhaus-
tive and systematic treatment of all the significant themes of
theology, such as, God, creation, man—his nature, purpose,
knowledge, actions, habits, law, and grace.*

Thomas recognized that man, by his very nature, is a social being, that he necessarily dwells in a set of relationships. Insofar as he is also a rational being, man must establish his social existence on the laws of reason. Thomas contended that, by using his intellect correctly, man could know what is true and good for mankind, and thereby construct a social order that would lead man to his fulfillment. Virtue, for him, is the permanent disposition which enables one to act in conformity with knowledge of the true and good. Justice, temperance, courage and prudence are the virtues basic to sound morality. Thomas analyzed each of these carefully and minutely in order to provide a solid foundation for social conduct.

Too often, when facing social problems, people use a naive "fix it" approach which may resolve a given situation for a brief period of time but usually creates more serious problems for the future. Thomas's methodology of clarifying precisely what is the meaning of the basic terms involved in a given issue is not only a corrective to the problem solving approach, but is essential to the health of a society as well.

In the selection below, the concepts of right and justice are analyzed. Justice is the virtue which directs man in his relations with others. The special proper object of justice is called the just, or right, that by which things are adjusted to persons according to some kind of equality. He considers natural and positive rights, the right of nations, and paternal right. Thomas sees justice as foremost among all the moral virtues, thus making it the foundation virtue for his treatment of the human as social being.

SUMMA THEOLOGICA
ON RIGHT

QUESTION LVII

OF RIGHT

(In Four Articles.)

A fter considering prudence we must in due sequence consider justice, the consideration of which will be fourfold: (1) Of justice: (2) Of its parts: (3) Of the corresponding gift: (4) Of the precepts relating to justice.

Four points will have to be considered about justice: (1) Right: (2) Justice itself: (3) Injustice: (4) Judgment.

Under the first head there are four points of inquiry: (1) Whether right is the object of justice? (2) Whether right is fittingly divided into natural and positive right? (3) Whether the right of nations is the same as natural right? (4) Whether right of dominion and paternal right are distinct species?

FIRST ARTICLE

WHETHER RIGHT IS THE OBJECT OF JUSTICE?

We proceed thus to the First Article:—

Objection 1. It would seem that right is not the object of justice. For the jurist Celsus says that *right is the art of goodness and equality.* Now art is not the object of justice, but is by itself an intellectual virtue. Therefore right is not the object of justice.

Obj. 2. Further, *Law,* according to Isidore (*Etym.* v. 3), *is a kind of right.* Now law is the object not of justice but of prudence, wherefore the Philosopher reckons *legislative* as one of the parts of prudence. Therefore right is not the object of justice.

Obj. 3. Further, Justice, before all, subjects man to God: for Augustine says (*De Moribus Eccl.* xv.) that *justice is love serving God alone, and consequently governing aright all things subject to man.* Now right (*jus*) does not pertain to Divine things, but only to human affairs, for Isidore says (*Etym.* v. 2) that *'fas' is the Divine law, and 'jus,' the human law.* Therefore right is not the object of justice.

On the contrary, Isidore says (*ibid.*) that *jus (right) is so called because it is just.* Now the *just* is the object of justice, for the Philosopher declares (*Ethic.* v. 1) that *all are agreed in giving the name of justice to the habit which makes men capable of doing just actions.*

I answer that, It is proper to justice, as compared with the other virtues, to direct man in his relations with others: because it denotes a kind of equality, as its very name implies; indeed we are wont to say that things are adjusted when they are made equal, for equality is in reference of one thing to some other. On the other hand the other virtues perfect man in those matters only which befit him in relation to himself. Accordingly that which is right in the works of the other virtues, and to which the intention of the virtue tends as to its proper object, depends on its relation to the agent only, whereas the right in a work of justice, besides its relation to the agent, is set up by its relation to others. Because a man's work is said to be just when it is related to some other by way of some kind of equality, for instance the payment of the wage due for a service rendered. And so a thing is said to be just, as having the rectitude of justice, when it is the term of an act of justice, without taking into account the way in which it is done by the agent: whereas in the other virtues nothing is declared to be right unless it is done in a certain way by the agent. For this reason justice has its own special proper object over and above the other virtues, and this object is called the just, which is the same as *right.* Hence it is evident that right is the object of justice.

Reply Obj. 1. It is usual for words to be distorted from their original signification so as to mean something else: thus the word *medicine* was first employed to signify a remedy used for curing a sick person, and then it was drawn to signify the art by which this is done. In like manner the word *jus* (right) was first of all used to denote the just thing itself, but afterwards it was transferred to designate the art whereby it is known what is just, and further to denote the place where justice is administered, thus a man is said to appear *in jure,* and yet further, we say even that a man, who has the office of exercising justice, administers the *jus* even if his sentence be unjust.

Reply Obj. 2. Just as there pre-exists in the mind of the craftsman an expression of the things to be made externally by his craft, which expression is called the rule of his craft, so' too there pre-exists in the mind an expression of the particular just work which the reason determines, and which is a kind of rule of prudence. If this rule be expressed in writing, it is called a *law,* which according to Isidore (*Etym.* v. 1) is *a written decree:* and so law is not the same as right, but an expression of right.

Reply Obj. 3. Since justice implies equality, and since we cannot offer God an equal return, it follows that we cannot make Him a perfectly just repayment. For this reason the Divine law is not properly called *jus* but *fas,* because, to wit, God is satisfied if we accomplish what we can. Nevertheless justice tends to make man repay God as much as he can, by subjecting his mind to Him entirely.

SECOND ARTICLE

WHETHER RIGHT IS FITTINGLY DIVIDED INTO NATURAL RIGHT AND POSITIVE RIGHT?

We proceed thus to the Second Article:—

Objection 1. It would seem that right is not fittingly divided into natural right and positive right. For that which is natural is unchangeable, and is the same for all. Now nothing of the kind is to be found in human affairs, since all the rules of human right fail in certain cases, nor do they obtain force everywhere. Therefore there is no such thing as natural right.

Obj. 2. Further, A thing is called *positive* when it proceeds from the human will. But a thing is not just, simply because it proceeds from the human will, else a man's will could not be unjust. Since then the *just* and the *right* are the same, it seems that there is no positive right.

Obj. 3. Further, Divine right is not natural right, since it transcends human nature. In like manner, neither is it positive right, since it is based not on human, but on Divine authority. Therefore right is unfittingly divided into natural and positive.

On the contrary, The Philosopher says (*Ethic.* v. 7) that *political justice is partly natural and partly legal,* i.e. established by law.

I answer that, As stated above (A. 1) the *right* or the *just* is a work that is adjusted to another person according to some kind of equality. Now a thing can be adjusted to a man in two ways: first by its very nature, as when a man gives so much that he may receive equal value in return, and this is called *natural right.* In another way a thing is adjusted or commensurated to another person, by agreement, or by common consent, when, to wit, a man deems himself satisfied, if he receive so much. This can be done in two ways: first by private agreement, as that which is confirmed by an agreement between private individuals; secondly, by public agreement, as when the whole community agrees that something should be deemed as though it were adjusted and commensurated to another person, or when this is decreed by the prince who is placed over the people, and acts in its stead, and this is called *positive right.*

Reply Obj. 1. That which is natural to one whose nature is unchangeable, must needs be such always and everywhere. But man's nature is changeable, wherefore that which is natural to man may sometimes fail. Thus the restitution of a deposit to the depositor is in accordance with natural equality, and if human nature were always right, this would always have to be observed; but since it happens sometimes that man's will is unrighteous, there are cases in which a deposit should not be restored, lest a man of unrighteous will make evil use of the thing deposited: as when a madman or an enemy of the common weal demands the return of his weapons.

Reply Obj. 2. The human will can, by common agreement, make a thing to be just provided it be not, of itself, contrary to natural justice, and it is in such matters that positive right has its place. Hence the Philosopher says (*Ethic.* v. 7) that *in the case of the legal just, it does not matter in the first instance whether it takes one form or another, it only matters when once it is laid down.* If, however, a thing is, of itself, contrary to natural right, the human will cannot make it just, for instance by decreeing that it is lawful to steal or to commit adultery. Hence it is written (Isa. x. 1): *Woe to them that make wicked laws.*

Reply Obj. 3. The Divine right is that which is promulgated by God. Such things are partly those that are naturally just, yet their justice is hidden to man, and partly are made just by God's decree. Hence also Divine right may be divided in respect of these two things, even as human right is. For the Divine law commands certain things because they are good, and forbids others, because they are evil, while others are good because they are prescribed, and others evil because they are forbidden.

THIRD ARTICLE

WHETHER THE RIGHT OF NATIONS IS THE SAME AS THE NATURAL RIGHT?

We proceed thus to the Third Article:—

Objection 1. It would seem that the right of nations is the same as the natural right. For all men do not agree save in that which is natural to them. Now all men agree in the right of nations; since the jurist says that *the right of nations is that which is in use among all nations.* Therefore the right of nations is the natural right.

Obj. 2. Further, Slavery among men is natural, for some are naturally slaves according to the Philosopher (*Polit.* i. 2). Now *slavery belongs to the right of nations,* as Isidore states (*Etym.* v. 4). Therefore the right of nations is a natural right.

Obj. 3. Further, Right as stated above (A. 2) is divided into natural and positive. Now the right of nations is not a positive right, since all nations never agreed to decree anything by common agreement. Therefore the right of nations is a natural right.

On the contrary, Isidore says (*Etym.* v. 4) that *right is either natural, or civil, or right of nations,* and consequently the right of nations is distinct from natural right.

I answer that, As stated above (A. 2), the natural right or just is that which by its very nature is adjusted to or commensurate with another person. Now this may happen in two ways; first, according as it is considered absolutely: thus a male by its very nature is commensurate with the female to beget offspring by her, and a parent is commensurate with the offspring to nourish it. Secondly a thing is naturally commensurate with another person, not according as it is considered absolutely, but according to something resultant from it, for instance the possession of property. For if a particular piece of land be considered absolutely, it contains no reason why it should belong to one man more than to another, but if it be considered in respect of its adaptability to cultivation, and the unmolested use of the land, it has a certain commensuration to be the property of one and not of another man, as the Philosopher shows (*Polit.* ii. 2).

Now it belongs not only to man but also to other animals to apprehend a thing absolutely: wherefore the right which we call natural, is common to us and other animals according to the first kind of commensuration. But the right of nations falls short of natural right in this sense, as the jurist says because *the latter is common to all animals, while the former is common to men only.* On the other hand to consider a thing by comparing it with what results from it, is proper to reason, wherefore this same is natural to man in respect of natural reason which dictates it. Hence the jurist Gaius says (*ibid.* 9): *Whatever natural reason decrees among all men, is observed by all equally, and is called the right of nations.* This suffices for the *Reply* to the *First Objection.*

Reply Obj. 2. Considered absolutely, the fact that this particular man should be a slave rather than another man, is based, not on natural reason, but on some resultant utility, in that it is useful to this man to be ruled by a wiser man, and to the latter to be helped by the former, as the Philosopher states (*Polit.* i. 2). Wherefore slavery which belongs to the right of nations is natural in the second way, but not in the first.

Reply Obj. 3. Since natural reason dictates matters which are according to the right of nations, as implying a proximate equality, it follows that they need no special institution, for they are instituted by natural reason itself, as stated by the authority quoted above.

WHETHER PATERNAL RIGHT AND RIGHT OF DOMINION SHOULD BE DISTINGUISHED AS SPECIAL SPECIES?

We proceed thus to the Fourth Article:—

Objection 1. It would seem that *paternal right* and *right of dominion* should not be distinguished as special species. For it belongs to justice to render to each one what is his, as Ambrose states (*De Offic.* i. 24). Now right is the object of justice, as stated above (A. 1). Therefore right belongs to each one equally; and we ought not to distinguish the rights of fathers and masters as distinct species.

Obj. 2. Further, The law is an expression of what is just, as stated above (A. 1, *ad* 2). Now a law looks to the common good of a city or kingdom, as stated above (I.-II., Q. XC., A. 2), but not to the private good of an individual or even of one household. Therfore there is no need for a special right of dominion or paternal right, since the master and the father pertain to a household, as stated in *Polit.* i. 2.

Obj. 3. Further, There are many other differences of degrees among men, for instance some are soldiers, some are priests, some are princes. Therefore some special kind of right should be allotted to them.

On the contrary, The Philosopher (*Ethic.* v. 6) distinguishes right of dominion, paternal right and so on as species distinct from civil right.

I answer that, Right or just depends on commensuration with another person. Now *another* has a twofold signification. First, it may denote something that is other simply, as that which is altogether distinct; as, for example, two men neither of whom is subject to the other, and both of whom are subjects of the ruler of the state; and between these according to the Philosopher (*Ethic.* v. 6) there is the *just* simply. Secondly a thing is said to be other from something else, not simply, but as belonging in some way to that something else: and in this way, as regards human affairs, a son belongs to his father, since he is part of him somewhat, as stated in *Ethic.* viii. 12, and a slave belongs to his master, because he is his instrument, as stated in *Polit.* i. 2. Hence a father is not compared to his son as to another simply, and so between them there is not the just simply, but a kind of just, called *paternal.* In like manner neither is there the just simply, between master and servant, but that which is called *dominative.* A wife, though she is something belonging to the husband, since she stands related to him as to her own body, as the Apostle declares (Eph. v. 28), is nevertheless more distinct from her husband, than a son from his father, or a slave from his master: for she is received into a kind of social life, that of matrimony, wherefore according to the Philosopher (*Ethic.* v. 6) there is more scope for justice between husband and wife than between father and son, or master and slave, because, as husband and wife have an immediate relation to the community of the household, as stated in *Polit.* i. 2, 5, it follows that between them there is *domestic justice* rather than *civic.*

Reply Obj. 1. It belongs to justice to render to each one his right, the distinction between individuals being presupposed: for if a man gives himself his due, this is not strictly called *just.* And since what belongs to the son is his father's, and what belongs to the slave is his master's, it follows that properly speaking there is not justice of father to son, or of master to slave.

Reply Obj. 2. A son, as such, belongs to his father, and a slave, as such, belongs to his master; yet each, considered as a man, is something having separate existence and distinct from others. Hence in so far as each of them is a man, there is justice towards them in a way: and for this reason too there are certain laws regulating the relations of a father to his son, and of a master to his slave; but in so far as each is something belonging to another, the perfect idea of *right* or *just* is wanting to them.

Reply Obj. 3. All other differences between one person and another in a state, have an immediate relation to the community of the state and to its ruler, wherefore there is just towards them in the perfect sense of justice. This *just* however is distinguished according to various offices, hence when we speak of *military,* or *magisterial,* or *priestly* right, it is not as though such rights fell short of the simply right, as when we speak of *paternal* right, or right of *dominion,* but for the reason that something proper is due to each class of person in respect of his particular office.

QUESTION LVIII

OF JUSTICE

(In Twelve Articles.)

We must now consider justice. Under this head there are twelve points of inquiry: (1) What is justice? (2) Whether justice is always towards another? (3) Whether it is a virtue? (4) Whether it is in the will as its subject? (5) Whether it is a general virtue? (6) Whether, as a general virtue, it is essentially the same as every virtue? (7) Whether there is a particular justice? (8) Whether particular justice has a matter of its own? (9) Whether it is about passions, or about operations only? (10) Whether the mean of justice is the real mean? (11) Whether the act of justice is to render to everyone his own? (12) Whether justice is the chief of the moral virtues?

FIRST ARTICLE

WHETHER JUSTICE IS FITTINGLY DEFINED AS BEING THE PERPETUAL AND CONSTANT WILL TO RENDER TO EACH ONE HIS RIGHT?

We proceed thus to the First Article:—

Objection 1. It would seem that lawyers have unfittingly defined justice as being *the perpetual and constant will to render to each one his right.* For, according to the Philosopher (*Ethic.* v. 1), justice is a habit which makes a man *capable of doing what is just, and of being just in action and in intention.* Now *will* denotes a power, or also an act. Therefore justice is unfittingly defined as being a will.

Obj. 2. Further, Rectitude of the will is not the will; else if the will were its own rectitude, it would follow that no will is unrighteous. Yet, according to Anselm (*De Veritate* xii.), justice is rectitude. Therefore justice is not the will.

Obj. 3. Further, No will is perpetual save God's. If therefore justice is a perpetual will, in God alone will there be justice.

Obj. 4. Further, Whatever is perpetual is constant, since it is unchangeable. Therefore it is needless in defining justice, to say that it is both *perpetual* and *constant*.

Obj. 5. Further, It belongs to the sovereign to give each one his right. Therefore, if justice gives each one his right, it follows that it is in none but the sovereign: which is absurd.

Obj. 6. Further, Augustine says (*De Moribus Eccl.* xv.) that *justice is love serving God alone*. Therefore it does not render to each one his right.

I answer that, The aforesaid definition of justice is fitting if understood aright. For since every virtue is a habit that is the principle of a good act, a virtue must needs be defined by means of the good act bearing on the matter proper to that virtue. Now the proper matter of justice consists of those things that belong to our intercourse with other men, as shall be shown further on (A. 2). Hence the act of justice in relation to its proper matter and object is indicated in the words, *Rendering to each one his right*, since, as Isidore says (*Etym.* x.), *a man is said to be just because he respects the rights* (jus) *of others.*

Now in order that an act bearing upon any matter whatever be virtuous, it requires to be voluntary, stable, and firm, because the Philosopher says (*Ethic.* ii. 4) that in order for an act to be virtuous it needs first of all to be done *knowingly,* secondly to be done *by choice,* and *for a due end,* thirdly to be done *immovably.* Now the first of these is included in the second, since *what is done through ignorance is involuntary* (*Ethic.* iii. 1). Hence the definition of justice mentions first the *will,* in order to show that the act of justice must be voluntary; and mention is made afterwards of its *constancy* and *perpetuity* in order to indicate the firmness of the act.

Accordingly, this is a complete definition of justice; save that the act is mentioned instead of the habit, which takes its species from that act, because habit implies relation to act. And if anyone would reduce it to the proper form of a definition, he might say that *justice is a habit whereby a man ren-*

ders *to each one his due by a constant and perpetual will:* and this is about the same definition as that given by the Philosopher (*Ethic.* v. 5) who says that *justice is a habit whereby a man is said to be capable of doing just actions in accordance with his choice.*

Reply Obj. 1. Will here denotes the act, not the power: and it is customary among writers to define habits by their acts: thus Augustine says (*Tract. in Joan.* xl.) that *faith is to believe what one sees not.*

Reply Obj. 2. Justice is the same as rectitude, not essentially but causally; for it is a habit which rectifies the deed and the will.

Reply Obj. 3. The will may be called perpetual in two ways. First on the part of the will's act which endures for ever, and thus God's will alone is perpetual. Secondly on the part of the subject, because, to wit, a man wills to do a certain thing always, and this is a necessary condition of justice. For it does not satisfy the conditions of justice that one wish to observe justice in some particular matter for the time being, because one could scarcely find a man willing to act unjustly in every case; and it is requisite that one should have the will to observe justice at all times and in all cases.

Reply Obj. 4. Since *perpetual* does not imply perpetuity of the act of the will, it is not superfluous to add *constant*: for while the *perpetual will* denotes the purpose of observing justice always, *constant* signifies a firm perseverance in this purpose.

Reply Obj. 5. A judge renders to each one what belongs to him, by way of command and direction, because a judge is the *personification of justice,* and *the sovereign is its guardian* (*Ethic.* v. 4). On the other hand, the subjects render to each one what belongs to him, by way of execution.

Reply Obj. 6. Just as love of God includes love of our neighbour, as stated above (Q. XXV., A. 1), so too the service of God includes rendering to each one his due.

SECOND ARTICLE

WHETHER JUSTICE IS ALWAYS TOWARDS ANOTHER?

We proceed thus to the Second Article:—

Objection 1. It would seem that justice is not always towards another. For the Apostle says (Rom. iii. 22) that *the justice of God is by faith of Jesus Christ.* Now faith does not concern the dealings of one man with another. Neither therefore does justice.

Obj. 2. Further, According to Augustine (*De Moribus Eccl.* xv.), *it belongs to justice that man should direct to the service of God his authority over the things that are subject to him.* Now the sensitive appetite is subject to man, according to Gen. iv. 7, where it is written: *The lust thereof,* viz. of sin, *shall be under thee, and thou shalt have dominion over it.* Therefore it belongs to justice to have dominion over one's own appetite: so that justice is towards oneself.

Obj. 3. Further, The justice of God is eternal. But nothing else is co-eternal with God. Therefore justice is not essentially towards another.

Obj. 4. Further, Man's dealings with himself need to be rectified no less than his dealings with another. Now man's dealings are rectified by justice, according to Prov. xi. 5, *The justice of the upright shall make his way prosperous.* Therefore justice is about our dealings not only with others, but also with ourselves.

On the contrary, Tully says (*De Officiis* i. 7) that *the object of justice is to keep men together in society and mutual intercourse.* Now this implies relationship of one man to another. Therefore justice is concerned only about our dealings with others.

I answer that, As stated above (Q. LVII., A. 1) since justice by its name implies equality, it denotes essentially relation to another, for a thing is equal, not to itself, but to another. And forasmuch as it belongs to justice to rectify human acts, as stated above (Q. LVII., A. 1: I.-II., Q. CXIII., A. 1) this otherness which justice demands must needs be between beings capable of action. Now actions belong to supposits and wholes and, properly speaking, not to parts and forms or powers, for we do not say properly that the hand strikes, but a man with his hand, nor that heat makes a thing hot, but fire by heat, although such expressions may be employed metaphorically. Hence, justice properly speaking demands a distinction of supposits, and consequently is only in one man towards another. Nevertheless in one and the same man we may speak metaphorically of his various principles of action such as the reason, the irascible, and the concupiscible, as though they were so many agents: so that metaphorically in one and the same man there is said to be justice in so far as the reason commands the irascible and concupiscible, and these obey reason; and in general in so far as to each part of man is ascribed what is becoming to it. Hence the Philosopher (*Ethic.* v. 11) calls this *metaphorical justice.*

Reply Obj. 1. The justice which faith works in us, is that whereby the ungodly is justified: it consists in the due co-ordination of the parts of the soul, as stated above (I.-II., Q. CXIII., A. 1) where we were treating of the justification of the ungodly. Now this belongs to metaphorical justice, which may be found even in a man who lives all by himself.

This suffices for the *Reply* to the *Second Objection.*

Reply Obj. 3. God's justice is from eternity in respect of the eternal will and purpose (and it is chiefly in this that justice consists); although it is not eternal as regards its effect, since nothing is co-eternal with God.

Reply Obj. 4. Man's dealings with himself are sufficiently rectified by the rectification of the passions by the other moral virtues. But his dealings with others need a special rectification, not only in relation to the agent, but also in relation to the person to whom they are directed. Hence about such dealings there is a special virtue, and this is justice.

THIRD ARTICLE

WHETHER JUSTICE IS A VIRTUE?

We proceed thus to the Third Article:—

Objection 1. It would seem that justice is not a virtue. For it is written (Luke xvii. 10): *When you shall have done all these things that are commanded you, say: We are unprofitable servants; we have done that which we ought to do.* Now it is not unprofitable to do a virtuous deed: for Ambrose says *(De Offic.* ii. 6): *We look to a profit that is estimated not by pecuniary gain but by the acquisition of godliness.* Therefore to do what one ought to do, is not a virtuous deed. And yet it is an act of justice. Therefore justice is not a virtue.

Obj. 2. Further, That which is done of necessity, is not meritorious. But to render to a man what belongs to him, as justice requires, is of necessity. Therefore it is not meritorious. Yet it is by virtuous actions that we gain merit. Therefore justice is not a virtue.

Obj. 3. Further, Every moral virtue is about matters of action. Now those things which are wrought externally are not things concerning behaviour but concerning handicraft, according to the Philosopher *(Metaph.* ix.). Therefore since it belongs to justice to produce externally a deed that is just in itself, it seems that justice is not a moral virtue.

On the contrary, Gregory says *(Moral.* ii. 49) that *the entire structure of good works is built on four virtues,* viz. temperance, prudence, fortitude and justice.

I answer that, A human virtue is one *which renders a human act and man himself good:* and this can be applied to justice. For a man's act is made good through attaining the rule of reason, which is the rule whereby human acts are regulated. Hence, since justice regulates human operations, it is evident that it renders man's operations good, and, as Tully declares *(De Officiis* i. 7), good men are so called chiefly from their justice, wherefore, as he says again *(ibid.) the lustre of virtue appears above all in justice.*

Reply Obj. 1. When a man does what he ought, he brings no gain to the person to whom he does what he ought, but only abstains from doing him a harm. He does however profit himself, in so far as he does what he ought, spontaneously and readily, and this is to act virtuously. Hence it is written (Wis. viii. 7) that Divine wisdom *teacheth temperance, and prudence, and justice, and fortitude, which are such things as men* (i.e. virtuous men) *can have nothing more profitable in life.*

Reply Obj. 2. Necessity is twofold. One arises from *constraint,* and this removes merit, since it runs counter to the will. The other arises from the obligation of a *command,* or from the necessity of obtaining an end, when, to wit, a man is unable to achieve the end of virtue without doing some particular thing. The latter necessity does not remove merit, when a man does voluntarily that which is necessary in this way. It does however exclude the credit of supererogation, according to 1 Cor. ix. 16, *If I preach the Gospel, it is no glory to me, for a necessity lieth upon me.*

Reply Obj. 3. Justice is concerned about external things, not by making them, which pertains to art, but by using them in our dealings with other men.

FOURTH ARTICLE

WHETHER JUSTICE IS IN THE WILL AS ITS SUBJECT?

We proceed thus to the Fourth Article:—

Objection 1. It would seem that justice is not in the will as its subject. For justice is sometimes called truth. But truth is not in the will, but in the intellect. Therefore justice is not in the will as its subject.

Obj. 2. Further, Justice is about our dealings with others. Now it belongs to the reason to direct one thing in relation to another. Therefore justice is not in the will as its subject but in the reason.

Obj. 3. Further, Justice is not an intellectual virtue, since it is not directed to knowledge; wherefore it follows that it is a moral virtue. Now the subject of moral virtue is the faculty which is *rational by participation,* viz. the irascible and the concupiscible, as the Philosopher declares (*Ethic.* i. 13). Therefore justice is not in the will as its subject, but in the irascible and concupiscible.

On the contrary, Anselm says (*De Verit.* xii.) that *justice is rectitude of the will observed for its own sake.*

I answer that, The subject of a virtue is the power whose act that virtue aims at rectifying. Now justice does not aim at directing an act of the cognitive power, for we are not said to be just through knowing something aright. Hence the subject of justice is not the intellect or reason which is a cognitive power. But since we are said to be just through doing something aright, and because the proximate principle of action is the appetitive power, justice must needs be in some appetitive power as its subject.

Now the appetite is twofold; namely, the will which is in the reason, and the sensitive appetite which follows on sensitive apprehension, and is divided into the irascible and the concupiscible, as stated in the First Part (Q. LXXXI., A. 2). Again the act of rendering his due to each man cannot proceed from the sensitive appetite, because sensitive apprehension does not go so far as to be able to consider the relation of one thing to another; but this is proper to the reason. Therefore justice cannot be in the irascible or concupiscible as its subject, but only in the will: hence the Philosopher (*Ethic.* v. 1) defines justice by an act of the will, as may be seen above (A. 1).

Reply Obj. 1. Since the will is the rational appetite, when the rectitude of the reason which is called truth is imprinted on the will on account of its nighness to the reason, this imprint retains the name of truth; and hence it is that justice sometimes goes by the name of truth.

Reply Obj. 2. The will is borne towards its object consequently on the apprehension of reason: Wherefore, since the reason directs one thing in relation to another, the will can will one thing in relation to another, and this belongs to justice.

Reply Obj. 3. Not only the irascible and concupiscible parts are *rational by participation,* but the entire *appetitive* faculty, as stated in *Ethic.* i. 13, because all appetite is subject to reason. Now the will is contained in the appetitive faculty, wherefore it can be the subject of moral virtue.

FIFTH ARTICLE

WHETHER JUSTICE IS A GENERAL VIRTUE?

We proceed thus to the Fifth Article:—
Objection 1. It would seem that justice is not a general virtue. For justice is specified with the other virtues, according

to Wis. viii. 7, *She teacheth temperance and prudence, and justice, and fortitude.* Now the *general* is not specified or reckoned together with the species contained under the same *general.* Therefore justice is not a general virtue.

Obj. 2. Further, As justice is accounted a cardinal virtue, so are temperance and fortitude. Now neither temperance nor fortitude is reckoned to be a general virtue. Therefore neither should justice in any way be reckoned a general virtue.

Obj. 3. Further, Justice is always towards others, as stated above (A. 2). But a sin committed against one's neighbour cannot be a general sin, because it is condivided with sin committed against oneself. Therefore neither is justice a general virtue.

On the contrary, The Philosopher says (*Ethic.* v. 1) that *justice is every virtue.*

I answer that, Justice, as stated above (A. 2) directs man in his relations with other men. Now this may happen in two ways: first as regards his relations with individuals, secondly as regards his relations with others in general, in so far as a man who serves a community, serves all those who are included in that community. Accordingly justice in its proper acceptation can be directed to another in both these senses. Now it is evident that all who are included in a community, stand in relation to that community as parts to a whole; while a part, as such, belongs to a whole, so that whatever is the good of a part can be directed to the good of the whole. It follows therefore that the good of any virtue, whether such virtue direct man in relation to himself, or in relation to certain other individual persons, is referable to the common good, to which justice directs: so that all acts of virtue can pertain to justice, in so far as it directs man to the common good. It is in this sense that justice is called a general virtue. And since it belongs to the law to direct to the common good, as stated above (I.-II. Q. XC., A. 2), it follows that the justice which is in this way styled general, is called *legal justice,* because thereby man is in harmony with the law which directs the acts of all the virtues to the common good.

Reply Obj. 1. Justice is specified or enumerated with the other virtues, not as a general but as a special virtue, as we shall state further on (AA. 7, 12).

Reply Obj. 2. Temperance and fortitude are in the sensitive appetite, viz. in the concupiscible and irascible. Now these powers are appetitive of certain particular goods, even as the senses are cognitive of particulars. On the other hand justice is in the intellective appetite as its subject, which can have the universal good as its object, knowledge whereof belongs to the intellect. Hence justice can be a general virtue rather than temperance or fortitude.

Reply Obj. 3. Things referable to oneself are referable to another, especially in regard to the common good. Wherefore legal justice, in so far as it directs to the common good, may be called a general virtue: and in like manner injustice may be called a general sin; hence it is written (1 Jo. iii. 4) that all *sin is iniquity.*

SIXTH ARTICLE

WHETHER JUSTICE, AS A GENERAL VIRTUE, IS ESSENTIALLY
THE SAME AS ALL VIRTUE?

We proceed thus to the Sixth Article:—

Objection 1. It would seem that justice, as a general virtue, is essentially the same as all virtue. For the Philosopher says (*Ethic.* v. 1) that *virtue and legal justice are the same as all virtue, but differ in their mode of being.* Now things that differ merely in their mode of being or logically do not differ essentially. Therefore justice is essentially the same as every virtue.

Obj. 2. Further, Every virtue that is not essentially the same as all virtue is a part of virtue. Now the aforesaid justice, according to the Philosopher *(ibid.)* *is not a part but the whole of virtue.* Therefore the aforesaid justice is essentially the same as all virtue.

Obj. 3. Further, The essence of a virtue does not change through that virtue directing its act to some higher end even as the habit of temperance remains essentially the same even though its act be directed to a Divine good. Now it belongs to

230

legal justice that the acts of all the virtues are directed to a higher end, namely the common good of the multitude, which transcends the good of one single individual. Therefore it seems that legal justice is essentially all virtue.

Obj. 4. Further, Every good of a part can be directed to the good of the whole, so that if it be not thus directed it would seem without use or purpose. But that which is in accordance with virtue cannot be so. Therefore it seems that there can be no act of any virtue, that does not belong to general justice, which directs to the common good; and so it seems that general justice is essentially the same as all virtue.

On the contrary, The Philosopher says (*Ethic.* v. 1) that *many are able to be virtuous in matters affecting themselves, but are unable to be virtuous in matters relating to others,* and (*Pol.* iii. 2) that *the virtue of the good man is not strictly the same as the virtue of the good citizen.* Now the virtue of a good citizen is general justice, whereby a man is directed to the common good. Therefore general justice is not the same as virtue in general, and it is possible to have one without the other.

I answer that, A thing is said to be *general* in two ways. First, by *predication:* thus *animal* is general in relation to man and horse and the like: and in this sense that which is general must needs be essentially the same as the things in relation to which it is general, for the reason that the genus belongs to the essence of the species, and forms part of its definition. Secondly a thing is said to be general *virtually;* thus a universal cause is general in relation to all its effects, the sun, for instance, in relation to all bodies that are illumined, or transmuted by its power; and in this sense there is no need for that which is *general* to be essentially the same as those things in relation to which it is general, since cause and effect are not essentially the same. Now it is in the latter sense that, according to what has been said (A. 5), legal justice is said to be a general virtue, in as much, to wit, as it directs the acts of the other virtues to its own end, and this is to move all the other virtues by its command; for just as charity may be called a general virtue in so far as it directs the acts of all the virtues to the Divine good, so too is legal justice, in so far as it directs the acts of all the virtues to the common good. Accordingly, just as charity which regards the Divine good as its proper object, is a special virtue in respect of its essence, so too legal justice is a special virtue in respect of its essence, in so far as it regards the common good as its proper object. And thus it is in the sovereign principally and by way of a master craft, while it is secondarily and administratively in his subjects.

However the name of legal justice can be given to every virtue, in so far as every virtue is directed to the common good by the aforesaid legal justice, which though special essentially is nevertheless virtually general. Speaking in this way, legal justice is essentially the same as all virtue, but differs therefrom logically: and it is in this sense that the Philosopher speaks.

Wherefore the *Replies* to the *First* and *Second Objections* are manifest.

Reply Obj. 3. This argument again takes legal justice for the virtue commanded by legal justice.

Reply Obj. 4. Every virtue strictly speaking directs its act to that virtue's proper end: that it should happen to be directed to a further end either always or sometimes, does not belong to that virtue considered strictly, for it needs some higher virtue to direct it to that end. Consequently there must be one supreme virtue essentially distinct from every other virtue, which directs all the virtues to the common good; and this virtue is legal justice.

SEVENTH ARTICLE

WHETHER THERE IS A PARTICULAR BESIDES A GENERAL JUSTICE?

We proceed thus to the Seventh Article:—

Objection 1. It would seem that there is not a particular besides a general justice. For there is nothing superfluous in the virtues, as neither is there in nature. Now general justice directs man sufficiently in all his relations with other men. Therefore there is no need for a particular justice.

Obj. 2. Further, The species of a virtue does not vary according to *one* and *many*. But legal justice directs one man to another in matters relating to the multitude, as shown above (AA. 5, 6). Therefore there is not another species of justice directing one man to another in matters relating to the individual.

Obj. 3. Further, Between the individual and the general public stands the household community. Consequently, if in addition to general justice there is a particular justice corresponding to the individual, for the same reason there should be a domestic justice directing man to the common good of a household: and yet this is not the case. Therefore neither should there be a particular besides a legal justice.

On the contrary, Chrysostom in his commentary on Matth. v. 6, *Blessed are they that hunger and thirst after justice,* says (*Hom.* xv. *in Matth.*): *By justice He signifies either the general virtue, or the particular virtue which is opposed to covetousness.*

I answer that, As stated above (A. 6), legal justice is not essentially the same as every virtue, and besides legal justice which directs man immediately to the common good, there is a need for other virtues to direct him immediately in matters relating to particular goods: and these virtues may be relative to himself or to another individual person. Accordingly, just as in addition to legal justice there is a need for particular virtues to direct man in relation to himself, such as temperance and fortitude, so too besides legal justice there is need for particular justice to direct man in his relations to other individuals.

Reply Obj. 1. Legal justice does indeed direct man sufficiently in his relations towards others. As regards the common good it does so immediately, but as to the good of the individual, it does so mediately. Wherefore there is need for particular justice to direct a man immediately to the good of another individual.

Reply Obj. 2. The common good of the realm and the particular good of the individual differ not only in respect of the *many* and the *few,* but also under a formal aspect, For the aspect of the *common* good differs from the aspect of the *individual* good, even as the aspect of *whole* differs from that of *part.* Wherefore the Philosopher says (*Polit.* i. 1) that *they are wrong who maintain that the State and the home and the like differ only as many and few and not specifically.*

Reply Obj. 3. The household community, according to the Philosopher (*Polit.* i. 2), differs in respect of a threefold fellowship; namely *of husband and wife, father and son, master and slave*, in each of which one person is, as it were, part of the other. Wherefore between such persons there is not justice simply, but a species of justice, viz. *domestic* justice, as stated in *Ethic.* v. 6.

EIGHTH ARTICLE

WHETHER PARTICULAR JUSTICE HAS A SPECIAL MATTER?

We proceed thus to the Eighth Article:—

Objection 1. It would seem that particular justice has no special matter. Because a gloss on Gen. ii. 14, *The fourth river is Euphrates*, says: *Euphrates signifies 'fruitful'; nor is it stated through what country it flows, because justice pertains to all the parts of the soul.* Now this would not be the case, if justice had a special matter, since every special matter belongs to a special power. Therefore particular justice has no special matter.

Obj. 2. Further, Augustine says (*QQ.* lxxxiii., qu. 61) that *the soul has four virtues whereby, in this life, it lives spiritually, viz. temperance, prudence, fortitude and justice;* and he says that *the fourth is justice, which pervades all the virtues.* Therefore particular justice, which is one of the four cardinal virtues, has no special matter.

Obj. 3. Further, Justice directs man sufficiently in matters relating to others. Now a man can be directed to others in all matters relating to this life. Therefore the matter of justice is general and not special.

On the contrary, The Philosopher reckons (*Ethic.* v. 2) particular justice to be specially about those things which belong to social life.

I answer that, Whatever can be rectified by reason is the matter of moral virtue, for this is defined in reference to right reason, according to the Philosopher (*Ethic.* ii. 6). Now the reason can rectify not only the internal passions of the soul, but also external actions, and also those external things of which man can make use. And yet it is in respect of external actions and external things by means of which men can communicate with one another, that the relation of one man to another is to be considered; whereas it is in respect of internal passions that we consider man's rectitude in himself. Consequently, since justice is directed to others, it is not about the entire matter of moral virtue, but only about external actions and things, under a certain special aspect of the object, in so far as one man is related to another through them.

Reply Obj. 1. It is true that justice belongs essentially to one part of the soul, where it resides as in its subject; and this is the will which moves by its command all the other parts of the soul; and accordingly justice belongs to all the parts of the soul, not directly but by a kind of diffusion.

Reply Obj. 2. As stated above (I.-II., Q. LXI., AA. 3, 4), the cardinal virtues may be taken in two ways: first as special virtues, each having a determinate matter; secondly, as certain general modes of virtue. In this latter sense Augustine speaks in the passage quoted: for he says that *prudence is knowledge of what we should seek and avoid, temperance is the curb on the lust for fleeting pleasures, fortitude is strength of mind in bearing with passing trials, justice is the love of God and our neighbour which pervades the other virtues, that is to say, is the common principle of the entire order between one man and another.*

Reply Obj. 3. A man's internal passions which are a part of moral matter, are not in themselves directed to another man, which belongs to the specific nature of justice; yet their effects, i.e. external actions, are capable of being directed to another man. Consequently it does not follow that the matter of justice is general.

NINTH ARTICLE

WHETHER JUSTICE IS ABOUT THE PASSIONS?

We proceed thus to the Ninth Article:—

Objection 1. It would seem that justice is about the passions. For the Philosopher says (*Ethic.* ii. 3) that *moral virtue is about pleasure and pain.* Now pleasure or delight, and pain are passions, as stated above when we were treating of the passions. Therefore justice, being a moral virtue, is about the passions.

Obj. 2. Further, Justice is the means of rectifying a man's operations in relation to another man. Now suchlike operations cannot be rectified unless the passions be rectified, because it is owing to disorder of the passions that there is disorder in the aforesaid operations: thus sexual lust leads to adultery, and overmuch love of money leads to theft. Therefore justice must needs be about the passions.

Obj. 3. Further, Even as particular justice is towards another person so is legal justice. Now legal justice is about the passions, else it would not extend to all the virtues, some of which are evidently about the passions. Therefore justice is about the passions.

On the contrary, The Philosopher says (*Ethic.* v. 1) that justice is about operations.

I answer that, The true answer to this question may be gathered from a twofold source. First from the subject of justice i.e. from the will, whose movements or acts are not passions, as stated above (I.-II., Q. XXII., A. 3: Q. LIX., A. 4), for it is only the sensitive appetite whose movements are called passions. Hence justice is not about the passions, as are temperance and fortitude, which are in the irascible and concupiscible parts. Secondly, on the part of the matter, because justice is about a man's relations with another, and we are not directed immediately to another by the internal passions. Therefore justice is not about the passions.

Reply Obj. 1. Not every moral virtue is about pleasure and pain as its proper matter, since fortitude is about fear and daring: but every moral virtue is directed to pleasure and pain, as to ends to be acquired, for, as the Philospher says (*Ethic.* vii. 11), *pleasure and pain are the principal end in respect of which we say that this is an evil, and that a good:* and in this way too they belong to justice, since *a man is not just unless he rejoice in just actions* (*Ethic.* i. 8).

Reply Obj. 2. External operations are as it were between external things, which are their matter, and internal passions, which are their origin. Now it happens sometimes that there is a defect in one of these, without there being a defect in the other. Thus a man may steal another's property, not through the desire to have the thing, but through the will to hurt the man; or vice versa, a man may covet another's property without wishing to steal it. Accordingly the directing of operations in so far as they tend towards external things, belongs to justice, but in so far as they arise from the passions, it belongs to the other moral virtues which are about the passions. Hence justice hinders theft of another's property, in so far as stealing is contrary to the equality that should be maintained in external things, while liberality hinders it as resulting from an immoderate desire for wealth. Since, however, external operations take their species, not from the internal passions but from external things as being their objects, it follows that, external operations are essentially the matter of justice rather than of the other moral virtues.

Reply Obj. 3. The common good is the end of each individual member of a community, just as the good of the whole is the end of each part. On the other hand the good of one individual is not the end of another individual: wherefore legal justice which is directed to the common good, is more capable of extending to the internal passions whereby man is disposed in some way or other in himself, than particular justice which is directed to the good of another individual: although legal justice extends chiefly to other virtues in the point of their external operations, in so far, to wit, as *the law commands us to perform the actions of a courageous person . . . the actions of a temperate person . . . and the actions of a gentle person (Ethic.* v. 5).

TENTH ARTICLE

WHETHER THE MEAN OF JUSTICE IS THE REAL MEAN?

We proceed thus to the Tenth Article:—

Objection 1. It would seem that the mean of justice is not the real mean. For the generic nature remains entire in each species. Now moral virtue is defined (*Ethic.* ii. 6) to be *an elective habit which observes the mean fixed, in our regard, by reason.* Therefore justice observes the rational and not the real mean.

Obj. 2. Further, In things that are good simply, there is neither excess nor defect, and consequently neither is there a mean; as is clearly the case with the virtues, according to *Ethic.* ii. 6. Now justice is about things that are good simply, as stated in *Ethic.* v. Therefore justice does not observe the real mean.

Obj. 3. Further, The reason why the other virtues are said to observe the rational and not the real mean, is because in their case the mean varies according to different persons, since what is too much for one is too little for another (*Ethic.* ii. 6). Now this is also the case in justice: for one who strikes a prince does not receive the same punishment as one who strikes a private individual. Therefore justice also observes, not the real, but the rational mean.

On the contrary, The Philosopher says (*Ethic.* ii. 6, v. 4) that the mean of justice is to be taken according to *arithmetical* proportion, so that it is the real mean.

I answer that, As stated above (A. 9: I.-II., Q. LIX., A. 4), the other moral virtues are chiefly concerned with the passions, the regulation of which is gauged entirely by a comparison with the very man who is the subject of those passions, in so far as his anger and desire are vested with their various due circumstances. Hence the mean in suchlike virtues is measured not by the proportion of one thing to another, but merely by comparison with the virtuous man himself, so that with them the mean is only that which is fixed by reason in our regard.

On the other hand the matter of justice is external operation, in so far as an operation or the thing used in that operation is duly proportionate to another person, wherefore the mean of justice consists in a certain proportion of equality between the external thing and the external person. Now equality is the real mean between greater and less, as stated in *Metaph.* x.: wherefore justice observes the real mean.

Reply Obj. 1. This real mean is also the rational mean, wherefore justice satisfies the conditions of a moral virtue.

Reply Obj. 2. We may speak of a thing being good simply in two ways. First a thing may be good in every way: thus the virtues are good; and there is neither mean nor extremes in things that are good simply in this sense. Secondly a thing is said to be good simply through being good absolutely i.e. in its nature, although it may become evil through being abused. Such are riches and honours; and in the like it is possible to find excess, deficiency and mean, as regards men who can use them well or ill: and it is in this sense that justice is about things that are good simply.

Reply Obj. 3. The injury inflicted bears a different proportion to a prince from that which it bears to a private person: wherefore each injury requires to be equalized by vengeance in a different way: and this implies a real and not merely a rational diversity.

ELEVENTH ARTICLE

WHETHER THE ACT OF JUSTICE IS TO RENDER TO EACH ONE HIS OWN?

We proceed thus to the Eleventh Article:—

Objection 1. It would seem that the act of justice is not to render to each one his own. For Augustine (*De Trin.* xiv. 9) ascribes to justice the act of succouring the needy. Now in succouring the needy we give them what is not theirs but ours. Therefore the act of justice does not consist in rendering to each one his own.

Obj. 2. Further, Tully says (*De Offic.* i. 7) that *beneficence which we may call kindness or liberality, belongs to justice.* Now it pertains to liberality to give to another of one's own, not of what is his. Therefore the act of justice does not consist in rendering to each one his own.

Obj. 3. Further, It belongs to justice not only to distribute things duly, but also to repress injurious actions, such as murder, adultery and so forth. But the rendering to each one of what is his seems to belong solely to the distribution of things. Therefore the act of justice is not sufficiently described by saying that it consists in rendering to each one his own.

On the contrary, Ambrose says (*De Offic.* i. 24): *It is justice that renders to each one what is his, and claims not another's property; it disregards its own profit in order to preserve the common equity.*

THE CATHOLIC TRADITION: Social Thought

I answer that, As stated above (AA. 8, 10), the matter of justice is an external operation, in so far as either it or the thing we use by it is made proportionate to some other person to whom we are related by justice. Now each man's own is that which is due to him according to equality of proportion. Therefore the proper act of justice is nothing else than to render to each one his own.

Reply Obj. 1. Since justice is a cardinal virtue, other secondary virtues, such as mercy, liberality and the like are connected with it, as we shall state further on (Q. LXXX., A. 1). Wherefore to succour the needy, which belongs to mercy or pity, and to be liberally beneficent, which pertains to liberality, are by a kind of reduction ascribed to justice as to their principal virtue.

This suffices for the *Reply* to the *Second Objection.*

Reply Obj. 3. As the Philosopher states (*Ethic.* v. 4), in matters of justice, the name of *profit* is extended to whatever is excessive, and whatever is deficient is called *loss.* The reason for this is that justice is first of all and more commonly exercised in voluntary interchanges of things, such as buying and selling, wherein those expressions are properly employed; and yet they are transferred to all other matters of justice. The same applies to the rendering to each one of what is his own.

TWELFTH ARTICLE

WHETHER JUSTICE STANDS FOREMOST AMONG ALL MORAL VIRTUES?

We proceed thus to the Twelfth Article:—

Objection 1. It would seem that justice does not stand foremost among all the moral virtues. Because it belongs to justice to render to each one what is his, whereas it belongs to liberality to give of one's own, and this is more virtuous. Therefore liberality is a greater virtue than justice.

Obj. 2. Further, Nothing is adorned by a less excellent thing than itself. Now magnanimity is the ornament both of justice and of all the virtues, according to *Ethic.* iv. 3. Therefore magnanimity is more excellent than justice.

Obj. 3. Further, Virtue is about that which is *difficult* and *good,* as stated in *Ethic.* ii. 3. But fortitude is about more difficult things than justice is, since it is about dangers of death, according to *Ethic*. iii. 6. Therefore fortitude is more excellent than justice.

On the contrary, Tully says (*De Offic*. i. 7): *Justice is the most resplendent of the virtues, and gives its name to a good man.*

I answer that, If we speak of legal justice, it is evident that it stands foremost among all the moral virtues, for as much as the common good transcends the individual good of one person. In this sense the Philosopher declares (*Ethic*. v. 1) that *the most excellent of the virtues would seem to be justice, and more glorious than either the evening or the morning star.* But, even if we speak of particular justice, it excels the other moral virtues for two reasons. The first reason may be taken from the subject, because justice is in the more excellent part of the soul, viz. the rational appetite or will, whereas the other moral virtues are in the sensitive appetite, whereunto appertain the passions which are the matter of the other moral virtues. The second reason is taken from the object, because the other virtues are commendable in respect of the sole good of the virtuous person himself, whereas justice is praiseworthy in respect of the virtuous person being well disposed towards another, so that justice is somewhat the good of another person, as stated in *Ethic*. v. 1. Hence the Philosopher says (*Rhet*. i. 9): *The greatest virtues must needs be those which are most profitable to other persons, because virtue is a faculty of doing good to others. For this reason the greatest honours are accorded the brave and the just, since bravery is useful to others in warfare, and justice is useful to others both in warfare and in time of peace.*

Reply Obj. 1. Although the liberal man gives of his own, yet he does so in so far as he takes into consideration the good of his own virtue, while the just man gives to another what is his, through consideration fo the common good. Moreover justice is observed towards all, whereas liberality cannot extend to all. Again liberality which gives of a man's own is based on justice, whereby one renders to each man what is his.

Reply Obj. 2. When magnanimity is added to justice it increases the latter's goodness; and yet without justice it would not even be a virtue.

Reply Obj. 3. Although fortitude is about the most difficult things, it is not about the best, for it is only useful in warfare, whereas justice is useful both in war and in peace, as stated above.

Dante Alighieri
1265-1321

Peace — Justice — Order — Love. These are the ideals that sustain mankind in the face of war, injustice, disarray and hatred. Humans live and die for them, burn out lives searching for them. Modern man, wearied by the search, is toying with the temptation to give up hope. Yet, in spite of the tragedy that the twentieth century has known, there continue to be voices that speak up in behalf of peace and its companion ideals. Perhaps a world community could achieve what nationalism could not. But first, the majority of humans must anchor their lives on concepts such as international unity and relationships, a single world government, and a politic established on human reason and freedom, not power and force.

It is not surprising that the great Dante is alive and well today. He dared to dream the incredible; he saw what human existence could and would be at its best; he tried to raise mankind up above the unnecessary tragedy of war, division and slavery. The concept of peace established on a single world government comes from his Monarchy.

A dreamer no longer in touch with the harsh realities of life? Not quite. Dante knew suffering, loss, rejection, deceit, and exile firsthand. He was born in Florence in 1265. He was immersed in literature, knew philosophy and theology, and was intensely involved in the politics of his beloved city Florence.

Dante was a victim of political intrigue and party factions. In 1302, while absent from the city, he was sentenced to death. Thus began the period of exile which ended when he died in Ravenna in 1321.

The Divine Comedy *is the most famous of all his writings. As one journeys with him through the circles of Hell, Purgatory and Heaven, it becomes obvious why he is considered one of the greatest poets of all time and all languages. Because he is thought of as the poet, it may seem surprising to meet him in a volume on social thought. Central to his poetic genius is his awareness of the social nature of mankind.*

The Monarchy *is Dante's statement of this awareness in a political setting. He divided the work into three books, each with a specific thesis. Book I, which is the book presented below, argues that monarchy is necessary for the well-being of the world. Dante states that the task proper to mankind is to fulfill the total capacity of the possible intellect (the human as the knowing being not yet perfected) all the time. The necessary condition to do this is peace, which can be only when justice is at its best and when rightly ordered love is most intense. This is possible only if all mankind is gathered together in a single world wide government. Book II discusses the Roman Empire and Book III, the relationship of the empire to the papacy.*

The book was interpreted by its readers as more than a dream. Its probable date of authorship is 1309-1313. In 1329 it was burned as heretical in Bologna. Various rulers as late as the sixteenth century used it as they saw fit, for their advantage. In 1554 it was placed on the Index and then removed from the Index during the nineteenth century. In 1921, Dante's works were praised by a papal encyclical.

Dante's ideas cannot be put aside as mere dreams. Admittedly the world has changed since the fourteenth century. But the basic insight of the radical unity of mankind, on which a world community can be established, thus rendering possible peace, justice, order, and love, is essential to the survival of the modern world.

MONARCHY

BOOK ONE

I

All men whom the higher Nature has imbued with a love of truth should feel impelled to work for the benefit of future generations, whom they will thereby enrich just as they themselves have been enriched by the labours of their ancestors. Let there be no doubt in the mind of the man who has benefited from the common heritage but does not trouble to contribute to the common good that he is failing sadly in his duty. For he is not 'a tree beside the running waters bearing fruit in due season' but rather a vicious whirlpool, for ever swallowing things but never throwing them up again. Since I have often reflected much on this matter and have been afraid that I might one day be held guilty of burying my talents, I desire not simply to blossom but to bear fruit for the public good, by demonstrating truths that no-one else has considered. For what fruit would a man bear if he were merely to prove once again some theorem of Euclid, or to demonstrate for the second time the nature of happiness, which Aristotle has already done? Or to undertake an apologia for old age of the sort that Cicero has produced? None whatever. Such a wearisome and superfluous undertaking would simply provoke disgust.

Now since the truth about temporal monarchy is the most beneficial yet most neglected of all these other beneficial but obscure truths, and yet has been neglected by all because it leads to no immediate reward, I intend to draw it out of the shadows into the light. There I shall be able to examine it for the benefit of the world, and to my own glory gain the palm of so great an enterprise. This is an arduous task, and one beyond my strength, yet in addressing myself to it I am trusting not in my own talents, but in the illumination of the Giver 'who gives to all liberally and upbraids none'.

II

Therefore we must first consider the meaning of 'temporal monarchy', what its essence is and what its end. The temporal monarchy that is called the Empire is a single Command exercised over all persons in time, or at least in those matters which are subject to time. Doubts about temporal monarchy give rise to three principal questions. The first is the question whether it is necessary for the well-being of the world. The second is whether it was by right that the Roman people took upon itself the office of the Monarch. And thirdly, there is the question whether the Monarch's authority is derived directly from God or from some vicar or minister of God.

Now every truth that is not itself a first principle must be demonstrated by means of some truth that is a first principle. Therefore in any inquiry it is a prerequisite to have a full understanding of that principle which under analysis we see to guarantee the certainty of all the other propositions which are deduced from it. So the present treatise being a sort of speculative inquiry, we must begin by examining that principle which will be the basis for all our subsequent reasoning. Now it is to be noted that there are some subjects that are completely outside human control, about which we can only speculate, being unable to affect them by our actions; such are mathematics, physics and revealed truth. There are others, however, that fall within our control; not only can we speculate about them, but also we can do something about them. In these, action is not subordinate to speculation but speculation is for the sake of action, because the aim in such matters is action. Since the present subject is political—indeed, the source and principle of all just governments—and anything political lies within our power, it is obvious that the matter in hand is not primarily directed towards speculation but towards action. Again, since in practical affairs the ultimate end is the principle and cause of all that is done (the end being the original motive of the agent), it follows that the formulation of means is derived from the end in view: thus wood is shaped in one way to build a house and in another way to build a ship. Similarly if the whole process of human society has an end, then this end can serve as the principle by which to demonstrate the validity of our subsequent argument. It would be absurd to suppose that this or that society has an end without acknowledging that there is one end common to them all.

III

Therefore let us see what is the ultimate end of human society as a whole; once that is grasped our task is more than half accomplished, as the Philosopher says in the *Nicomachean Ethics*.

In order to clarify the issue it may be noted that nature forms the thumb for one end and the whole hand for another, and the arm for yet another, whilst each of these ends is different from that to which the whole man is destined. Similarly the end towards which the individual's life is directed is different from that of the family community; the village has one end, the city another and the kingdom yet another; and last of all there is the end that the eternal God has established for the whole human race by means of nature, which is the mode of his art. It is this last-mentioned end that we are looking for and that will be the building principle in our inquiry.

The first point to realize is that 'God and nature never do anything in vain', for whatever is brought into existence has some purpose to serve. Yet it is not the being of any creature but its proper function that is the ultimate end of the Creator in creating, and so the proper function is not instituted for the sake of the creature but the latter is created to serve its proper function. From this it follows that there must be some particular function proper to the human species as whole and for which the whole species in its multitudinous variety was created; this function is beyond the capacity of any one man or household or village, or even of any one city or kingdom. What this function is will become clear once the specific capacity of mankind as a whole is evident.

I say therefore that no property that is common to beings of different species represents the specific capacity of any one of them; because, since its ultimate capacity is what constitutes

THE CATHOLIC TRADITION: Social Thought

each species, it would follow that one being would be specifically constituted by several specifying factors—which is impossible. And so the specific capacity of man does not consist simply in *being*, since the very elements also share in being: nor does it consist in *compound being*, for this is also found in the minerals; nor in *animate being*, which the plants also enjoy; nor in the capacity to apprehend things, for this is shared by brute animals, but it consists in the capacity to apprehend by means of the *possible intellect*, and it is this that sets man apart both from inferior and from superior beings. For although there are other beings endowed with intellect, their intellect is not *possible* like that of man, since such beings are completely intellectual; in them intellect and being coincide, and their very *raison d'être* is to perform intellectual operations without pause, otherwise they would not be eternal. From which it is evident that the specific capacity of mankind is an intellectual capacity or potentiality. And because that potentiality cannot wholly and at once be translated into action by one man, or by any one of the particular communities listed above, mankind has to be composed of a multitude through which this entire potentiality can be actualized. Similarly there needs to be a multitude of things which can be generated from prime matter if the entire potency of that matter is to be brought into action all the time. The alternative is for potentiality to exist separately; this is impossible. Averroes agrees with this opinion in his commentary on the *De Anima*.

This intellectual power of which I am speaking not only deals with universal forms or species but also extends to particulars. Hence it is commonly said that the speculative intellect becomes practical by extension, and is thereby directed towards action and making things. I am referring to action as governed by the virtue of political prudence, and to the making of things as governed by art. But both are subordinate to speculation as the highest function for the sake of which the Supreme Goodness brought mankind into being.

From all this one begins to appreciate what is meant in the *Politics* by the sentence: 'Men of superior intellect naturally rule over others.'

IV

Thus it is quite clear that the task proper to mankind considered as a whole is to fulfil the total capacity of the possible intellect all the time, primarily by speculation and secondarily, as a function and extension of speculation, by action. Now since what applies to the part applies also to the whole, and since the individual man becomes perfect in wisdom and prudence through sitting in quietude, so it is in the quietude or tranquillity of peace that mankind finds the best conditions for fulfilling its proper task (almost a divine task, as we learn from the statement: 'Thou hast made him a little lower than the angels.') Hence it is clear that universal peace is the most excellent means of securing our happiness. This is why the message from on high to the shepherds announced neither wealth, nor pleasure, nor honour, nor long life, nor health, nor strength, nor beauty, but peace. The heavenly host, indeed, proclaims: 'Glory to God on high, and on earth peace to men of good will.' 'Peace be with you' was also the salutation given by the Saviour of men, because it was fitting that the supreme Saviour should utter the supreme salutation—a custom which, as everyone knows, his disciples and Paul sought to preserve in their own greetings.

This argument shows us what is the better, indeed the very best means available to mankind for fulfilling its proper role; and also what is the most direct means of reaching that goal to which all our doings are directed—universal peace. This will serve as the basis for our subsequent argument. Such is the common ground which we declared to be essential so as to have something axiomatic to which all our proofs and demonstrations can refer.

V

Let us now return to what was said at the beginning; that there are three main problems to be solved concerning temporal monarchy, or, as it is more commonly called, the Empire. As we promised, we intend to investigate them in the order signified and on the basis of the axiom that we have established.

Thus the first question is whether temporal monarchy is necessary for the well-being of the world. Now no substantial objection either from reason or authority can be urged against it, and its truth can be demonstrated by the clearest and most cogent arguments, the first of which is derived from the authority of the Philosopher in his *Politics*. There the acknowledged authority states that when several things are directed towards a single end it is necessary for one of them to act as director or ruler and for the others to be directed or ruled. This statement is supported not only by the glorious renown of its author but also by inductive reason. Again, if we consider an individual man we see the same principle verified: since all his faculties are directed towards happiness, his intellectual faculty is the director and ruler of all the others—otherwise he cannot attain happiness. If we consider a home, the purpose of which is to train its members to live well, we see that there has to be one member who directs and rules, either the 'pater familias' or the person occupying his position, for, as the Philosopher says, 'every home is ruled by the eldest'. And his function, as Homer says, is to rule the others and lay down laws for them; hence the proverbial curse, 'May you have an equal in your home.' If we consider a village, whose purpose is mutual help in questions of persons and goods, it is essential for one person to be supreme over all others, whether he is appointed from outside or raised to office by the consent of the others; otherwise, not only would the community fail to provide mutual sustenance, but in some cases the community itself would be utterly destroyed through some members' scheming to take control. Similarly if we examine a city, whose purpose is to be sufficient unto itself in everything needed for the good life, we see that there must be one governing authority—and this applies not only to just but even to degenerate forms of government. If this were not so, the purpose of civil life would be frustrated and the city, as such, would cease to exist. Lastly, every kingdom (and the end of a kingdom is the same as that of a city but with a stronger bond of peace) needs to have a king to rule over and govern it; otherwise its inhabitants will not only fail to achieve their end as citizens but the kingdom itself will crumble, as is affirmed by the infallible Word: 'Every kingdom divided against itself shall be laid waste.'

If this is true of all communities and individuals who have a goal towards which they are directed, then our previous supposition is also valid. For, if it is agreed that mankind as a whole has a goal (and this we have shown to be so), then it needs one person to govern or rule over it, and the title appropriate to this person is Monarch, or Emperor.

Thus it has been demonstrated that a Monarch or Emperor is necessary for the well-being of the world.

VI

Furthermore, the order of a part stands in the same relation to the order of the whole as the part does to the whole; therefore the order within a part has as its end the order of the whole, which brings it to perfection. Hence the goodness of the order amongst the parts does not surpass the goodness of the total order; in fact the reverse is true. Now in all things this twofold order is to be found: that is, the relation of the parts towards each other; and the relation of the parts to that unity which is not itself a part (in the same way that the parts of an army are related towards each other yet are all subordinated to their commander). Hence the relation of the parts to that unity is the superior of the two orders; and the other relation is simply a function of the superior order, not vice versa. Now if this pattern of relationship is found in individual groups of human beings it must apply all the more to mankind as a group or whole, in virtue of the previous syllogism concerning the superior pattern of relationship. But it has been adequately proved in the previous chapter that this pattern is in fact found in all human groups: therefore it should also be found in the whole.

Consequently all those parts below the level of a kingdom, as well as kingdoms themselves, must be subordinate to one ruler or rule, that is, to the Monarch or to Monarchy.

VII

Furthermore, mankind in one sense is a whole (that is, in relation to its component parts), but in another sense it is itself a part. It is a whole in relation to particular kingdoms and peoples, as we have previously shown; but in relation to the whole universe it is, of course, a part. Therefore just as its component parts are brought to harmony in mankind, so mankind itself has to be brought into the harmony of its appropriate whole. The component parts of mankind are brought into harmony by a single principle (as may easily be gathered from the preceding argument); and mankind itself is similarly related to 'the whole universe, or to its principle (that is, God, the Monarch); this harmony is achieved by one principle only, the one Prince.

It follows that Monarchy is necessary for the well-being of the world.

VIII

And everything is at its best and most perfect when in the condition intended for it by the first cause, which is God; this is self-evident—except to those who deny that the divine goodness achieves supreme perfection. It is God's intention that every created thing, in so far as its natural capacity allows, should reflect the divine likeness. This explains why it is said: 'Let us make man after our image and likeness.' Although the phrase 'after our image' cannot be applied to anything inferior to man, 'likeness' can be applied to anything whatsoever, since the whole universe is simply a sort of shadow of the divine goodness. Therefore the human race is at its best and most perfect when, so far as its capacity allows, it is most like to God. But mankind is most like to God when it enjoys the highest degree of unity, since He alone is the true ground of unity— hence it is written: 'Hear, O Israel, the Lord thy God is one.' But mankind is most one when the whole human race is drawn together into complete unity, which can only happen when it is subordinate to one Prince, as is self-evident.

Therefore when mankind is subject to one Prince it is most like to God and this implies conformity to the divine intention, which is the condition of perfection, as was proved at the beginning of this chapter.

IX

Again, a son's condition is most perfect when the son, as far as his nature allows, reproduces the perfection of the father. Mankind is the son of the heavens, which is perfect in all its works; but man is begotten by man and the sun (according to the second book of the *Physics*). Therefore mankind's condition is most perfect when it reproduces the perfection of the heavens, so far as human nature allows. And just as the heavens are governed and directed in every movement by a single mover, which is God (as human reasoning in philosophy amply demonstrates), so, if our argument has been correct, mankind is at its best when all its movements and intentions are governed by one Prince as its sole mover and with one law for its direction.

Hence it is obvious that the world's well-being demands a Monarch or single government known as the Empire.

This is the argument that led Boethius to sigh:

'How happy you would be, O mankind, if your minds were ruled by the love that rules the heavens.'

X

And wherever there is a possibility of dispute there has to be a judgment to settle it; otherwise there would be imperfection without a remedy to heal it, which is impossible, since God and nature never fail in essentials.

It is clear that a dispute may arise between two princes, neither of whom is subject to the other, and that this may be their fault or their subjects'; therefore a judgment between them is indispensable. However, since neither can take cognizance over the other (neither being subject to the other—and equals do not rule over equals), there needs to be a third person enjoying wider jurisdiction who by right rules over both of them. This person must be either the monarch (in which case our argument is complete) or not the monarch, in which case he himself will have an equal outside his own jurisdiction, and it will again be necessary to have recourse to a third person. Either this process will go on to infinity (which is impossible) or eventually it will lead us back to a first and supreme judge whose judgment will either directly or indirectly solve all disputes: he will be the Monarch, or Emperor.

Therefore monarchy is necessary to the world. And the Philosopher appreciated this truth when he wrote: 'Things resent being badly ordered; but to have different rulers is bad; therefore, one Prince.'

XI

Besides, the world is best ordered when justice is at its strongest. Hence Virgil, wishing to praise the new order that seemed to be emerging in his day, said: 'Now the Virgin is again returning; and the Saturnian reign begins once more.' By 'Virgin' he meant Justice, which is also called Astrea; by 'Saturn's rule' he referred to the finest ages, which are also described as 'golden'. Justice is at its strongest only under a Monarch; therefore Monarchy or Empire is essential if the world is to attain a perfect order.

If we are to understand the minor premiss fully, it is essential to appreciate that justice, in itself and strictly considered, is rectitude, a rule permitting no deviation; consequently it is not subject to shades of more or less, any more, for instance, than *whiteness* considered in the abstract. For such forms, though realized in particular circumstances, are simple and unchangeable in essence, as the Master of the Six Principles rightly says. In actuality, however, these qualities vary in intensity according to the degree in which the subjects of them are subject also to their contraries. But where the contrary of justice is at its faintest (whether actively or potentially), there justice is at its strongest; and then one may truly say—as, indeed, the philosopher does— 'Neither Lucifer nor Hesperus is so wonderful.' For then she is like Phoebe in the rosy serenity of the dawn gazing across at her brother on the opposite horizon.

Considered in its potentiality the contrary of justice sometimes lies in the will; for even when justice is present, if the will is not entirely purified of all cupidity, justice is not present in all the splendour of its purity; because such a subject offers a certain resistance to it, however slight; hence those who try to arouse a judge's passions deserve to be censured. In regard to acts, the contrary of justice is to be found in limitations on power; for since justice is a virtue governing relations, between people, how can it operate in practice without the power of rendering to each his due? Hence the stronger the just man is in practice, the greater will be his justice.

On the basis of this exposition we reason as follows: justice is most powerful in the world when located in a subject with a perfect will and most power; such is the Monarch alone; therefore justice is at its most potent in this world when located in the Monarch alone.

This preparatory syllogism is of the second figure, with intrinsic negation, and takes the following form: all B is A; only C is A; therefore only C is B. That is: all B is A; nothing except C is B. The first proposition clearly holds, for the reasons already given; the other follows by reference first to the will and then to power.

To see the first clearly we must recognize, as Aristotle affirms in the fifth book of his *Nicomachean Ethics*, that the greatest obstacle to justice is cupidity. When cupidity is entirely eliminated there remains nothing opposed to justice: hence the Philosopher's maxim that 'nothing which can be judged by the law should ever be left to the judge's discretion'; and he gave this salutary warning because he feared that cupidity which all too easily distorts men's minds. But when there is nothing to be desired there can be no cupidity, because the passions cannot remain when their objects have been eliminated. But the Monarch has nothing to desire, since the ocean alone is the limit of his jurisdiction—unlike other princes, such as the Kings of Castile and Aragon, whose jurisdictions are limited by one another's frontiers. It follows that of all mortals the Monarch can be the purest incarnation of justice. Moreover, just as cupidity invariably clouds the vision of justice no matter how slightly, so charity, or rightly ordered love, illuminates and sharpens it. Therefore justice finds its strongest bastion in the place where rightly ordered love is most intense; such is the Monarch, and so justice is at its most powerful, or at least can be, when there is a Monarch. That rightly ordered love does have this effect can be shown as follows: cupidity, scorning man's intrinsic nature, aims at other things; but charity scorns

255

those other things, is directed towards God and man, and so towards the good of man. And since to live in peace, as we previously demonstrated, is the chief of human blessings, and since justice is the most powerful means towards it, charity gives force to justice, so that the more powerful it is the more force justice will have. That rightly ordered love should be found most of all in the Monarch is shown thus: an object is the more loved the nearer it is to the lover; but men are nearer to the Monarch than to other princes; therefore they are more greatly loved by him, or ought to be.

The first proposition becomes evident if we consider the general nature of agents and patients; the second is demonstrated by the fact that it is only as belonging to different parts that men are drawn to other princes, whereas it is through belonging to the whole that they are related to the Monarch. Again, they are brought into contact with other princes through the Monarchs, and not vice versa. So prior and immediate tutelage over them all belongs to the Monarch, and to other princes through the Monarch, which means that their tutelage is derived from his. Again, the more universal a cause is, the more perfect a cause it is, because the subordinate cause is only such in virtue of the superior, as is shown in the *De Causis*; and the more perfect the cause, the more it loves its proper effect, because this love is a function of the cause as such. Since, therefore, the Monarch is of all mortals the most universal cause of human well-being (because other princes, as we have seen, are only effective in virtue of him), it follows that the good of man is most keenly desired by him.

And who but a person ignorant of the world's meaning would doubt that justice is most powerfully served by the Monarch? For if there is a Monarch then he cannot have any enemies.

The minor premiss having been proved, the conclusion is certain: that Monarchy is necessary for perfect world-order.

XII

And the human race is at its best when most free.

This statement will become clear if we explain the principle of freedom, for then it will be seen that the fundamental principle of our freedom is free choice; and though many pay service to this truth with their lips, few do with their understanding. They do indeed go so far as to say that free choice is a free judgment exercised upon the will; and they speak the truth—but are far from understanding the meaning of the words. They are like our logicians who produce certain propositions mechanically, as examples in logic, such as: 'A triangle has three angles equal to two right angles.' Therefore I say that a judgment is the middle term connecting apprehension and appetite. First of all, something is apprehended; then it is judged to be either good or bad; and finally the person judging either seeks or rejects it. If the judgment completely directs the appetite and is in no way deflected by it, then it is free; but if the judgment is in any way deflected or influenced by the appetite it cannot be free, because it is not independent but is dragged along captive in the wake of another. And this is why the brute beasts cannot enjoy free judgment; because their judgments always follow their appetites. It also explains how intellectual substances, whose wills are immutable, and disembodied souls who depart this life in a state of grace, do not lose their free choice on account of their wills being immutable but rather enjoy it in its highest perfection.

Once this is realized, it becomes equally clear that this liberty, or this principle of all our liberty, is God's most precious gift to human nature, for by it we are made happy here as men, and happy as gods in the beyond. In which case who would not agree that mankind is at its best when it is able to make fullest use of this principle? But this plenitude of freedom it enjoys only under a Monarchy.

Hence it must be recognized that to be free means 'self-dependence, and not dependence on another', as the Philosopher maintains in the *Metaphysics*. For whatever is dependent on another is conditioned by it even as the means is conditioned by the end it serves. But only under a Monarchy is mankind self-dependent and not dependent on another; then only are perverted forms of government rectified, such as democracies, oligarchies and tyrannies (which force mankind into slavery, as is obvious to anyone who considers the matter); their government is conducted by kings, aristocrats (known as *optimates*) and zealots for the people's freedom, because, as we have already shown, the Monarch in his supreme love for men wishes all of them to be good. This is impossible for the perverted forms of government. Hence the Philosopher says that 'in the perverted forms a good man is a bad citizen, whereas in the true form to be a good citizen is the same as being a good man'. And these true forms of government aim at liberty; they intend men to go on living for their own sakes. Here the citizens do not exist for the sake of the consuls, nor the people for the sake of the king; on the contrary, the king is for the sake of the people, and the consuls for the citizen. Because just as the laws are made for the sake of the body politic rather than the body politic for the laws, likewise those living under the law do not exist for the sake of the legislator but he for them (as the Philosopher asserts in the writings which he has left to us on this issue). From which it is evident that although the consul or the king are lords over others in regard to means, they are themselves ministers towards others in regard to ends. And this is particularly true of the Monarch, who is to be considered the minister of everyone. Thus one can already recognize how the very purpose of law-making postulates the necessity of Monarchy.

Therefore mankind is in its best condition under a Monarch; from which it follows that monarchy is necessary for the well-being of the world.

XIII

Again, the person best suited for governing is the one who brings the best out of others; for in every action the agent (whether acting from choice or from the exigencies of its nature) seeks primarily to reproduce its own likeness. Hence every agent delights in its own action; for since everything that is desires its own being, and since the being of any agent is increased through its actions, joy is the necessary consequence, because joy always accompanies the desired object. Therefore nothing can act unless it has the quality that is to be transferred to the patient, on which account the Philosopher in the *Metaphysics* writes: 'The movement from potentiality to act takes place by means of something already in act.' Any attempt to act in another manner would prove vain.

And this argument refutes the error of those who believe that they can mould the lives and morals of others by speaking well and doing evil, who do not realize that it was the hands of Jacob rather than his words that proved persuasive, the former speaking truth and the latter falsehood. Hence the Philosopher says in the *Nicomachean Ethics*: 'In regard to passions and actions words carry less conviction than deeds.' Similarly the voice from heaven questioned the sinner David: 'Why do you tell of my righteousness?' as if to say; 'Your speech is in vain so long as what you are belies your speech.'

From which it can be seen that the person wishing to bring the best out of others must himself be in the best condition. But the one in the best condition for governing is none other than the Monarch. This is demonstrated as follows: any thing is in a better and more suitable condition to acquire a particular quality or perform a particular act the less it contains of any contrary tendency. Thus persons who have never been taught anything are in a better condition for acquiring philosophical truth than those who have long been imbued with false opinions; on which Galen wisely comments: 'Such people need double the time to acquire knowledge.' Since the Monarch, then, can have no cause for cupidity (or, of all men, has the least cause for it, as we have already shown), and in this differs from other princes, and since cupidity alone perverts the judgment and compels justice, it follows that the Monarch is in a perfect—or at least the best possible—condition for governing, because he surpasses all others in the power of his judgment and justice. And these two qualities are those supremely fitting for the person who makes and carries out the law, as was maintained by that most holy king when he implored God to grant the things most essential for a king and his son: 'God,' he said, 'give to the king your judgment, and to the king's son your justice.'

Therefore what was said in the minor premiss was right, that the Monarch alone is completely equipped to rule; therefore the Monarch alone is able to bring the best out of others. From which it follows that Monarchy is necessary for the perfect ordering of the world.

XIV

And it is better, wherever possible, for something to be performed by one single means rather than by several.

This is demonstrated as follows. Let A be the means by which a certain thing can be accomplished, and let A and B be several means by which the same thing can be accomplished. But if A alone is adequate for doing what A and B together can do, the introduction of B is unnecessary; because no consequence follows from making the assumption B, for the consequence desired has already been achieved by A alone. And since all similar assumptions are idle or superfluous, and superfluity is displeasing both to God and nature, and everything displeasing to God and nature is evil (as is self-evident), then not only is it better for something that can be accomplished by a single means to be done by that single means rather than by several, it is good in itself to use the single means and plain evil to employ several. Moreover, a thing is considered better the nearer it is to the best; and the best is found in the end envisaged; but to use a single means is to shorten the distance towards the end: therefore it is the better. That it is nearer is obvious: let C be the end; let it be reached by a single means A; let it be reached by several, A and B; clearly the distance from A through B to C is greater than from A straight to C.

But mankind is capable of being governed by a single supreme prince, who is the Monarch.

Of course, when we say 'mankind can be governed by one supreme prince' we do not mean to say that minute decisions concerning every township can proceed directly from him (though even municipal laws sometimes prove wanting and need supplementing from outside, as we see from the Philosopher's remarks in the fifth book of the *Ethics*, where he commends the principle of equity). For nations, kingdoms and cities have different characteristics which demand different laws for their government, law being intended as a concrete rule of life. The Scythians, for instance, live outside the seventh circle, experience extreme inequalities of day and night and endure an almost intolerably piercing frost; they require a different rule from the Garamantes who live in the equinoctial zone, where the days and nights are of equal duration and where the excessive heat makes it unbearable to wear clothes. But our meaning is that mankind should be ruled by one supreme prince and directed towards peace by a common law issuing from him and applied to those characteristics which are common to all men. This common rule, or law, should be accepted from him by particular princes, in the same way as the practical reason preparing for action accepts its major proposition from the speculative intellect and then derives from it the minor proposition appropriate to the particular case, and finally proceeds to action. It is not only possible for one movement to issue from a single source, it is necessary for it to do so in order to eliminate confusion about universal principles. Indeed this was precisely what Moses says he did in writing the Law: having called together the chiefs of the tribes of Israel he left minor judgments to them whilst reserving to himself the major decisions that affected everyone; these were then applied by the chiefs of the tribes according to the particular needs of each tribe.

Therefore it is better for mankind to be ruled by one person than by several (that is, by the Monarch who is the sole prince) and if better, then more acceptable to God; for God always wills the better. And since when only two things are being compared the better is the same as the best, then not only is rule by 'one' more acceptable to God than rule by 'several', it is the *most* acceptable. It follows that mankind is at its best when under a single ruler; and so Monarchy is essential to the well-being of the world.

XV

Again, I say that priority is attributed to 'being', 'unity' and 'goodness', in that order, according to the fifth sense of the word 'priority'. For being naturally comes before unity, and unity before goodness: the perfect being is perfect unity and the perfect unity is perfect goodness, and the further anything is removed from perfect being the further it is from being one and being good. Therefore within each kind of being the best is that which is most one, as the Philosopher maintains in the *Metaphysics*. Hence unity seems to be the ground of goodness and multiplicity the ground of evil; for this reason Pythagoras in his Correlations places unity on the side of goodness and multiplicity on the side of evil, as we are told in the first book of the *Metaphysics*. Hence we can see that to sin is to despise and abandon unity for the sake of multiplicity. The Psalmist perceived this when he said: 'They are multiplied in the fruit of corn and wine and oil.'

It is clear, then, that every good thing is good in virtue of being one. And since concord, as such, is a good, it is obviously rooted in unity. The root of concord is discovered if we examine its definition and nature. Concord is a harmonious movement of several wills. This definition shows that the unity of wills connoted by 'harmonious movement' is the root of concord or is itself concord. For just as we should describe several clods which all fell towards the same centre as concordant and say that several flames shooting out towards the same circumference were concordant (if they did so voluntarily), similarly we describe several men as being in concord when their wills are simultaneously directed towards the same formal object (which is present in their wills as the quality of gravity is present in the clods and levity in the flames). But the capacity for willing represents a potentiality and the good it apprehends is its form. This form, though one in itself, like other forms, becomes multiplied through the multiplicity of the matter on which it is impressed—just like soul and number, and other composite forms.

These premisses having been stated we can now develop the argument for the proposition we wish to maintain: all concord depends upon the unity of wills; mankind is at its best in a state of concord; for as a man is at his best in body and soul when he is in a state of concord, the same is true of a house, a city and a kingdom, and of mankind as a whole. Therefore mankind at its best depends upon unity in the wills of its members. But this is impossible unless there is one will which dominates all others and holds them in unity, for the wills of mortals, influenced by their adolescent and seductive delights, are in need of a director, as the Philosopher teaches at the end of the *Nicomachean Ethics*. Nor can there be such a single will unless there is a prince over all, whose will guides and rules those of all others.

Dante Alighieri

Now if the preceding conclusions are all true—as they are—then Monarchy is necessary for the perfect order of mankind in this world. Consequently a Monarch is essential to the well-being of the world.

XVI

The preceding arguments are confirmed by a noteworthy historical fact, that is, by the state of humanity which the Son of God either awaited or himself brought about when He was to become man for the salvation of men. For if we survey the ages and condition of men since the fall of our first parents (the false step from which all our errors have proceeded) at no time do we see universal peace throughout the world except during the perfect monarchy of the immortal Augustus. The fact that mankind at that time was resting happily in universal peace is attested by all the historians and the illustrious poets. Even the recorder of Christ's gentleness has deigned to bear witness to it. Finally Paul, also, described that blissful state as 'the fulness of time'. The times were indeed full, and temporal desires fulfilled because nothing that ministers to our happiness was without its minister. But what state the world has been in since that seamless garment was rent on the nail of cupidity we may easily read—would that we could not behold it!

O humanity, in how many storms must you be tossed, how many shipwrecks must you endure, so long as you turn yourself into a many-headed beast lusting after a multiplicity of things! You are ailing in both your intellectual powers, as well as in heart: you pay no heed to the unshakeable principles of your higher intellect, nor illumine your lower intellect with experience, nor tune your heart to the sweetness of divine counsel when it is breathed into you through the trumpet of the Holy Spirit: 'Behold how good and pleasant it is for brethren to dwell together in unity.'

St. Thomas More
1477-1535

Utopia—the land of nowhere, yet the land that could be, if only mankind would allow it. Utopia haunts every human being who looks at the problems of the world, its poverty, suffering, political and religious corruption, wars, ignorance, family collapse, waste of the goods of the earth, and feels that things could or should be better. Utopia stirs the human mind to rethink a present situation and construct ideal models that could improve life. Utopia is part of the human social condition.

In modern times Utopian thinking was given a central role in the shaping of western society through the writing of Thomas More, English humanist, lawyer, saint and martyr. His book, Utopia, *became the model for countless utopias from the seventeenth century through to our own day.*

More himself lived from 1477 to 1535. He was born in London, became a highly successful lawyer with a reputation for unusual fairness and honesty, entered the royal service of King Henry VIII, was knighted and, in 1529, became the Lord Chancellor of England. Few men have been more faithful to their country than was Sir Thomas More. Following his conscience and his religious convictions, More refused to be party to the King's decision to divorce Catherine of Aragon in order to marry Anne Boleyn. Because of this, he was eventually condemned of treason. He was executed on July 6, 1535. It is recorded that he went cheerfully to his death, declaring him-self "The King's good servant, but God's first." His death was mourned throughout Europe, for his learning, his fairness and his holiness were internationally known and respected. Pope Pius XI canonized him in 1935. Saint Thomas More is the patron of Catholic lawyers and university students.

The times in which Thomas More lived were a mixture of decadence and renewal, of commitment and rebellion, of unification and division. The Americas were discovered, the printing press was coming into its own, Martin Luther declared a new day for Christianity, England established its own church. More is one of the persons who was at the very center of the life of Europe and England, by way of his professional work and because of his involvement with the great intellectual personalities of the day. He was attuned to the problems of his times and was convinced that life could be lived out much more joyously than most humans will allow.

His Utopia *is essential reading for any person who is concerned about the way society is going.* Utopia *is a dialogue between the human as searching and groping, and the human as responding. It raises the questions of human injustice, greed, pride, and meanness, and though it provides no solution (for there is none) points in the direction that mankind must go if our human lot is to be improved. All of this is done in story form.* Utopia *is a country with a specific political and social structure, with very distinct educational and religious outlooks, and with its own way of handling wars, work, economics and related issues.*

The purpose and meaning of the book has been debated for four centuries and is still open to interpretation. This, in itself, is a sign of the greatness of the work. Utopia, *one of the few authentic dialogues of modern literature, naturally evokes a response from everyone who dares read it.*

UTOPIA

BOOK TWO

The island of Utopia contains in breadth in the middle part of it (for there it is broadest) two hundred miles. Which breadth continues through the most part of the land, save that little by little it comes in and waxes narrow towards both ends, which forming a circuit or compass of five hundred miles fashions the whole island like to the new moon. Between these two corners the sea runs in, dividing them asunder by a distance of eleven miles or thereabouts, and there spreads out into a large and wide sea, which by reason that the land on every side compasses it about, and shelters it from the winds, is not rough, nor mounts with great waves, but flows almost quietly, not much unlike a great standing pool; and makes almost all the space within the heart of the land like a haven, and to the great convenience of the inhabitants receives ships bound towards every part of the land. The forefronts or frontiers of the two corners, what with shallows and reefs and what with rocks, are very jeopardous and dangerous.

In the middle between them both stands up above the water a great rock, which is not perilous because it is in sight. Upon the top of this rock is a fair and strong tower built, which they hold with a garrison of men. Other rocks there are that lie hid under the water, and therefore are dangerous. The channels are known only to themselves. And therefore it seldom chances that any stranger, unless he be guided by a Utopian, can come into this haven. Insomuch that they themselves could scarcely enter without danger if their way were not directed and ruled by certain landmarks standing on the shore. By turning, transferring, and removing these marks into other places they may destroy their enemies' navies, be they never so many. The outer side of the land is also full of havens, but the landing is so surely defended, both by nature and by workmanship of man's hand, that a few defenders may drive back many armies. Howbeit, as they say, and as the fashion of the place does partly show, it was ever the sea that compassed it about. But King Utopus, whose name as conqueror the island bears (for before that time it was called Abraxa), who also brought the rude and wild people to that excellent perfection in all good fashions, humanity, and civil gentleness, wherein they now surpass all the people of the world,—even at his first arriving and entering upon the land, forthwith obtaining the victory, caused fifteen miles of upland ground, where the sea had no passage, to be cut and dug up, and so brought the sea round to the land. He set to this work not only the inhabitants of the island, that they should not think it done in contumely and despite, but also all of his own soldiers. Thus the work, being divided among so great a number of workmen, was with exceeding, marvelous speed despatched. Insomuch that the neighboring people who at the first began to mock, and to jest at this vain enterprise, then turned their laughter to marvel at the success, and to fear.

There are in the island fifty-four large and fair cities, or shire towns, agreeing all together in one tongue, like manners, institutions, and laws. They are all set and situate alike, and in all points fashioned alike, as far as the place or plot permits. Of these cities they that are nearest together are twenty-four miles apart. Again, there is none of them distant from the next more than one day's journey afoot. There come yearly to Amaurote out of every city three old men, wise and well experienced, there to treat and debate of the common matters of the land. For this city (because it stands just in the midst of the island, and is therefore most meet for the ambassadors of all parts of the realm) is taken for the chief and head city. The precincts and bounds of the shires are so conveniently appointed and marked out for the cities that never a one of them all has less than twenty miles of ground on every side, and in places also much more, as in that part where the cities are farthest.

None of the cities desires to enlarge the bounds and limits of its shires, for they count themselves rather the good farmers than the owners of their lands. They have built in the country, in all parts of the shire, houses or farms well appointed and furnished with all sorts of farming implements and tools. These houses are inhabited by the citizens, who come thither to dwell in turn. No household or farm in the country has fewer than forty persons, men and women, besides two bondmen, who are all under the rule and order of the goodman and goodwife of the house, both very sage and discreet persons. And every thirty farms or families have one head ruler, who is called a *philarch*, being as it were a head bailiff. Out of every one of these families or farms come every year into the city twenty persons who have been two years in the country. In their place so many fresh are sent thither out of the city, to be instructed and taught by those who have been there a year already, and are therefore expert and skilled in the care and cultivation of the land. And they the next year shall teach the others. This order is kept for fear that either scarceness of victuals, or some other like misfortune should result from lack of knowledge, if they were altogether new, and fresh, and unexpert in farming.

This manner and fashion of yearly changing and renewing those engaged in farming, though it be customary and regularly followed, to the intent that no man shall be constrained against his will to continue long in that hard and sharp kind of life, yet many of them take such pleasure and delight in the work on the land that they remain a longer space of years. These farmers plow and till the ground, and breed cattle, and make ready wood, which they carry to the city either by land, or by water, as they may most conveniently. They bring up a multitude of poultry, and that by a marvelous device. For the hens do not sit upon the eggs, but the farmers by keeping them in a certain even heat bring life into them, and hatch them. The chickens, as soon as they come out of the shell, follow men and women instead of the hens. They raise very few horses; and none but very fierce ones, and for no other use or purpose but only to exercise their youth in riding and feats of arms. For oxen are put to all the labor of plowing and drawing, which they grant are not so good as horses at a sudden spurt, and, as we say, at lifting a dead weight. Yet they hold the opinion that they will endure and suffer much more labor and pain than horses will. And they think that oxen are not in danger and subject to so many diseases, and that they are kept and maintained with much less cost and charge; and finally that they are good for meat, when they are past labor.

They sow corn only for bread. For their drink is either wine made of grapes, or else of apples or of pears; or else it is clean water. And many times mead is made of honey or liquorice boiled in water, for thereof they have great store. And though they know certainly—for they know it perfectly indeed—how much victuals the city with the whole country or shire round about it uses, yet they sow much more corn, and breed up much more cattle than serves for their own use, and the overplus they divide among their neighbors. Whatsoever necessary things are lacking in the country, all such stuff they fetch out of the city; where without any exchange they easily obtain it from the magistrates of the city. For every month many of them go into the city on the holy day. When their harvest day draws near and is at hand, then the philarchs, who are the head officers and bailiffs on the farms, send word to the magistrates of the city what number of harvest men is needful to be sent to them out of the city. And this company of harvest men are there ready at the day appointed, and almost in one fair day despatch all the harvest work.

Of the cities, and namely, of Amaurote

As for their cities, he that knows one of them knows them all, for all are as like one to another, as the nature of the place permits. I will describe therefore to you one or another of them, for it matters not greatly which; but what one is better than Amaurote? Of them all this is the worthiest and of most dignity. For the rest acknowledge it as the head city, because there is the council house. Nor is any of them all better beloved by me, as I lived therein five whole years together. The city of Amaurote stands upon the side of a low hill, in fashion almost foursquare. For the breadth of it begins a little beneath the top of the hill, and still continues for the space of two miles, until it comes to the river of Anyder. The length of it, which lies by the river's side, is somewhat more. The river of Anyder rises twenty-four miles above Amaurote out of a little spring. But being increased by other small floods and brooks that run into it—among others, two somewhat big ones—opposite the city it is a half mile broad, and farther broader. And sixty miles beyond the city it falls into the Ocean sea. Through all that space that lies between the sea and the city, and a good number of miles also above the city, the water ebbs and flows six hours together with a swift tide. When the sea flows in, for the length of thirty miles it fills all the Anyder with salt water, and drives back the fresh water of the river. And somewhat further it taints the sweetness of the fresh water with saltness. But a little beyond that the river waxes sweet, and runs past the city fresh and pleasant. And when the sea ebbs, and goes back again, the fresh water follows it almost even to the very fall into the sea.

There goes a bridge over the river, made not of piles of timber but of stonework, with gorgeous and substantial arches at that part of the city that is fathest from the sea, to the intent that ships may pass along all the side of the city without hindrance. They have also another river which indeed is not very great, but it runs gently and pleasantly. For it rises even out of the same hill that the city stands upon, and runs down a slope through the midst of the city into Anyder. And because it rises a little outside the city, the Amaurotians have enclosed the head spring of it with strong fences and bulwarks, and so have joined it to the city. This is done to the intent that the water should not be stopped, or turned away, or poisoned, if their enemies should chance to come upon them. From thence the water is diverted in all directions and brought down in canals of brick divers ways into the lower parts of the city. Where that cannot be done, because the place will not allow it, there they gather the rain water in great cisterns, which does them as good service.

The city is compassed about with a high and thick wall full of turrets and bulwarks. A dry ditch, but deep and broad, and overgrown with bushes, briers, and thorns, surrounds three sides or quarters of the city. To the fourth side the river itself serves for a ditch. The streets are laid out very conveniently and handsomely, both for transport, and also against the winds. The houses are of fair and gorgeous building, and on the street side they stand joined together in a long row through the whole street, without any partition or separation. The streets are twenty feet broad. On the back side of the houses through the

271

whole length of the street lie large gardens which are closed in round about by the back part of the streets. Every house has two doors, one into the street, and a postern door on the back side into the garden. These doors are made with two leaves, never locked or bolted, so easy to be opened that they will follow the least drawing of a finger, and shut again by themselves. Every man that wills may go in, for there is nothing within the houses that is private or any man's own. And every tenth year they change their houses by lot.

They set great store by their gardens. In them they have vineyards, all manner of fruit, herbs, and flowers, so pleasant, so well planted and so finely kept that I never saw anything more fruitful or better trimmed in any place. Their study and diligence herein comes not only from pleasure, but also from a certain strife and rivalry that is between street and street, concerning the trimming, tilling, and furnishing of their gardens, every man for his own part. And verily you shall not lightly find in all the city anything that is better arranged, either for the profit of the citizens, or for pleasure. And therefore it may seem that the first founder of the city cared for nothing so much as he did for these gardens. For they say that King Utopus himself, even at the first beginning, appointed and drew the ground plan of the city in the fashion and figure that it has now, but the handsome garnishing, and the beautiful setting forth of it, for which he saw that one man's age would not suffice, that he left to his posterity.

For their chronicles, which they keep written with all diligent circumspection, containing the history of 1760 years, even from the first conquest of the island, record and witness that the houses in the beginning were very low, and like homely cottages or poor shepherd houses built in haphazard fashion of every rude piece of wood that came first to hand, with mud walls and ridged roofs, thatched over with straw. But now the houses are elaborately built, in a gorgeous and ornate style, with three stories one over another. The outsides of the walls are made either of hard flint, or of plaster, or else of brick, and the inner sides are well strengthened with timber work. The roofs are plain and flat, covered with a certain kind of plaster that is of no cost, and yet so tempered that no fire can hurt or destroy it, and it withstands the violence of the weather better than any lead. They keep the wind out of their windows with glass, for it is there much used, or in some places with fine linen cloth dipped in oil or resin of amber, a convenience in two ways; for by this means more light comes in, and the wind is better kept out.

Of the magistrates

Every thirty families or farms choose yearly an officer, who in their old language is called the *syphogrant*, and by a newer name, the *philarch*. Every ten syphogrants, with their 300 families are under an officer who was once called the *tranibore*, now the chief philarch. Moreover, as concerning the election of the prince, all the syphogrants, who are in number 200, first are sworn to choose him whom they think most fitting and expedient. Then by a secret election they name prince one of those four whom the people before named unto them. For out of the four quarters of the city there are four chosen, out of every quarter one, to stand for the election, which is put up to the council. The prince's office continues all his lifetime, unless he is deposed or put down for suspicion of tyranny. They choose the tranibores yearly, but do not lightly change them. All the other offices are but for one year. The tranibores every third day, and sometimes, if need be, oftener, come into the council house with the prince. Their council is concerning the commonwealth. If there are any controversies among the commoners, which are very few, they despatch and end them speedily. They take always two syphogrants with them in counsel, and every day a new couple. And it is provided that nothing touching the commonwealth shall be confirmed and ratified unless it has been reasoned and debated three days in the council before it is decreed. To have any consultation for the commonwealth outside the council, or the place of the common election, is punishable by death. This statute, they say, was made to the intent that the prince and tranibores might not easily conspire together to oppress the people by tyranny, and to change the state of the commonwealth.

Therefore matters of great weight and importance are brought to the election house of the syphogrants, who explain the matter to their families. And afterward, when they have consulted among themselves, they report their plan to the council. Sometimes the matter is brought before the council of the whole island. Furthermore this custom also the council observes: to dispute or reason of no matter the same day that it is first proposed or put forth, but to defer it to the next sitting of the council, in order that no man, when he has rashly there spoken what came first to his tongue's end, shall then afterward study rather for reasons wherewith to defend and confirm his first foolish sentence than for the good of the commonwealth: as one more willing to suffer harm or hindrance to the commonwealth than any loss or diminution of his own reputation; and as one that would not for shame (which is a very foolish shame) appear to have been misled in the matter at the first, when at the first he ought to have spoken rather wisely, than hastily, or rashly.

Of sciences, crafts, and occupations

Agriculture is a science common to them all in general, both men and women, wherein they are all expert and cunning. In this they are all instructed, even from their youth, partly in schools with traditions and precepts, and partly in the country nigh the city, brought up as it were in playing, not only to behold the use of it, but for the sake of exercising their bodies to practice it also. Besides farming which, as I said, is common to them all, every one of them learns one or another distinct and particular skill, as his own proper craft. That is most commonly either clothworking in wool or flax, or masonry, or the smith's craft, or the carpenter's craft. For there is no other occupation that any number to speak of follows there. For their garments, which throughout all the island are of one fashion (save that there is a difference between the man's garment and the woman's, between the married and the unmarried) continue forevermore unchanged. They are seemly and comely to the eye, permitting free movement and exercise of the body, and are also fit both for winter and summer. As for these garments, I say, every family makes their own. But of the other aforesaid crafts every man learns one. And not only the men, but also the women. But the women, as the weaker sort, are put to the easier crafts; they work wool and flax. The other more labor-some skills are committed to the men. For the most part every man is brought up in his father's craft. For most commonly they are naturally thereto bent and inclined. But if a man's mind turn to any other, he is by adoption put into a family of that occupation which he does most fancy; and not only his father, but also the magistrates do diligently look to him, that he be put with a discreet and an honest householder. Yea, and if any person, when he has learned one craft, is desirous to learn another also, he is likewise permitted. When he has learned both, he follows whichever he will, unless the city has more need of the one than of the other.

The chief and almost the only office of the syphogrants is to see and take heed that no man sit idle, but that everyone ply his own craft with earnest diligence. And yet for all that, not to be wearied from early in the morning to late in the evening with continual work, like laboring and toiling beasts. For this is worse than the miserable and wretched condition of bondmen, but it is nevertheless almost everywhere the life of workmen and artisans, save in Utopia. For they, dividing the day and the night into twenty-four equal hours, appoint and assign only six of those hours to work, three before noon, after which they go straight to dinner; and after dinner, when they have rested two hours, then they work three, and upon that they go to supper. After eight of the clock in the evening, counting one of the clock as the first hour after noon, they go to bed; eight hours they give to sleep. All the spare time, that is, between the hours of work, sleep, and meat, they are permitted to spend every man as he likes best himself. Not to the intent that they should misspend this time in riot or slothfulness, but that being then freed from the labor of their own occupations, they should bestow the time well and thriftily upon some other good science, as shall please them. For it is a regular custom there, to have lectures daily, early in the morning, where only those are constrained to be present that are chosen and appointed to learning. Howbeit a great multitude of every sort of people, both men and women, go to hear lectures, some to one and some to another, as every man's nature is inclined. Yet, this notwithstanding, if any man had rather bestow this time upon his own occupation, as it chances with many, whose minds rise not to the contemplation of any liberal science, he is not prevented or prohibited, but is also praised and commended, as being profitable to the commonwealth. After supper they spend one hour in play, in summer in their gardens, in winter in their common halls, where they dine and sup. There they exercise themselves in music, or else in honest and wholesome conversation. Diceplay, and such other foolish and pernicious games, they know not.

But they play two games not unlike chess. The one is the battle of numbers, wherein one number steals away another. The other is one wherein vices fight with virtues, as it were in battle array, or a set field. In this game is very properly shown both the strife and discord that vices have among themselves, and again their unity and concord against virtues. And also what vices are repugnant to what virtues, with what power and strength they assail them openly, by what wiles and subtlety they assault them secretly, with what help and aid the virtues resist and overcome the power of the vices, by what craft they frustrate their purpose, and finally by what cunning or means the one gets the victory.

But here, lest you be deceived, one thing you must look more narrowly upon. For seeing they bestow but six hours in work, perchance you may think that a lack of some necessary things may ensue therefrom. But this is not so. For that short time is not only enough but even too much for the store and abundance of all things that are requisite, either for the necessity or the comfort of life. And this you also shall perceive, if you weigh and consider with yourselves how great a part of the people in other countries live idle. First, almost all women, who are half of the whole number; or else if the women be anywhere occupied, there most commonly in their stead the men are idle. Besides this how great and how idle a company is there of priests and religious men, as they call them. Add thereto all rich men, especially all landed men, who are commonly called gentlemen and noblemen. Take into this number also their servants: I mean all that flock of stout bragging swashbucklers. Join to them also the sturdy and lusty beggars, cloaking their idle life under the color of some disease or sickness. And truly you shall find them much fewer than you thought, by whose labor all things are gotten that men use and live by. Next consider with yourself, of these few that do work, how few are occupied in necessary works. For where money is everything, there must needs be many vain and superfluous occupations, to serve only for riotous superfluity and unhonest pleasure. For the same multitude that now is occupied in work, if they were divided into as few occupations as the necessary use of nature requires, so great plenty of things of necessity would be produced that doubtless the prices would be too little for the workers to maintain their livings. But if all these that are now busied about unprofitable occupations, with all the whole flock of them that now live idly and slothfully, who consume and waste every one of them more of the things that come by other men's labor than two of the workmen themselves do; if all these, I say, were set to profitable occupations, you easily perceive how little time would be enough, yea and too much, to supply us with all things that may be requisite either for necessity, or for comfort, yea or for pleasure, so long as that pleasure is genuine and natural.

And in Utopia the condition makes this manifest and plain. For there, in all the city, with the whole country or shire adjoining to it, scarcely 500 persons of the whole number of men and women, who are neither too old nor too weak to work, are freed from labor. Among them are the syphogrants who (though they are by the laws exempt and privileged from labor) yet exempt not themselves, to the intent they may the rather by their example incite others to work. The same vacation from labor is also enjoyed by those to whom the people, persuaded by the commendation of the priests and the secret election of the syphogrants, have given a perpetual freedom from labor for learning. But if any one of them prove not equal to the expectation and hope conceived of him, he is forthwith plucked back into the company of artisans. And contrariwise, often it chances that a handicraftsman does so earnestly bestow his vacant and spare hours in learning, and through diligence so profits therein that he is taken from his manual occupation, and promoted to the company of the learned. Out of this order of the learned are chosen ambassadors, priests, tranibores, and finally the prince himself, whom they in their old tongue call Barzanes, and by a newer name, Adamus. The residue of the people being neither idle nor occupied about unprofitable exercises, it may easily be judged in how few hours how much good work can be done by them towards those things that I have spoken of. This advantage they have also above others, that in most of the necessary occupations they need not do as much work as other nations do.

For first of all the building or repairing of houses demands everywhere else so many men's continual labor, because the unthrifty heir suffers the houses that his father built to fall in time in decay; so that which he might have maintained with little cost, his successor is constrained to build again anew, to his great charge. Yea, many times also a house cost one man much money, but another is of so nice and so delicate a mind that he thinks nothing of it; and it being neglected, and therefore shortly falling into ruin, he builds up another in another place with no less cost and charge. But among the Utopians, where all things are set up in good order, and where the commonwealth is on a good foundation, it very seldom chances that they choose a new plot to build a house upon. And they do not only make speedy and quick repairs of present weaknesses, but also preserve them that are like to fall. And by this means their houses endure and last very long with little labor and small repairs; insomuch that this kind of workmen sometimes have almost nothing to do. But they are commanded to hew timber at home, and to square and trim up stones, to the intent that if any work arise, it may the speedier be taken care of.

Now, sir, for their apparel, mark, I pray you, how few workmen they need. First of all, while they are at work they are plainly clad in leather or skins that will last seven years. When they go forth abroad they cast over them a cloak which hides the other plain apparel. These cloaks throughout the whole island are all of one color, and that is the natural color of the wool. They therefore do not only use much less woolen cloth than is used in other countries, but also the same stands them in much less cost. But linen cloth is made with less labor, and is therefore more in use. But in linen cloth only whiteness, in woolen only cleanliness is regarded. As for the thinness or fineness of the thread, that is not considered important. Yet this is the cause why in other places four or five cloth gowns of divers colors, and as many silk coats, are not enough for one man. Yea, and if he be of a particular and nice sort, ten are too few; whereas there one garment will serve a man most commonly two years. For why should he desire more? Seeing if he had them, he would not be the better wrapped or covered from the cold, nor in his apparel any whit handsomer. Wherefore, seeing they are all exercised in profitable occupations, and that a few workers in the same crafts are sufficient, and for this cause plenty of everything being among them, they do sometimes bring out an innumerable company of people to mend the highways, if any are broken. Many times also, when they have no such work to be occupied about, a public proclamation is made, that they shall spend fewer hours in work. For the magistrates do not exercise their citizens against their wills in unnecessary labors. And why? In the institution of that commonwealth, this end only is aimed at the minded, that whatever time may possibly be spared from the necessary occupations and affairs of the commonwealth, all that, the citizens should withdraw from manual labor and apply to the free liberty of the mind, and to cultivating the same. For herein they suppose the felicity of this life to consist.

Of their living and mutual intercourse together

But now will I declare how the citizens bear themselves one towards another, what familiar intercourse there is among the people, and what fashion they employ in distributing everything. First, the city consists of families, the families most commonly composed of kindred. For the women, when they are married at a lawful age, go into their husbands' houses. But the male children with all the whole male offspring continue still in their own family and are governed by the eldest and ancientest father, unless he becomes a dotard; for then the next to him in age is put in his place. But to the intent the prescribed number of citizens should neither decrease, nor above measure increase, it is ordained that no city, including its outskirts, shall have more than six thousand families, and that no family shall include fewer than ten or more than sixteen grown children, that is, of the age of fourteen or above. There is no rule for children under this age. This measure or number is easily observed and kept, by putting those that in too full families are above the number into families of smaller increase. But if it chance that in the whole city the population increase above the just number, they fill up therewith the lack of other cities. But if it happen that the multitude throughout the whole island pass and exceed the due number, then they choose out of every city certain citizens, and build up a town under their own laws in the next land where the inhabitants have much waste and unoccupied ground, also some of the inhabitants among them, if they will join and dwell with them. Thus joining and dwelling together, they do easily agree on one fashion of living, and that to the great wealth of both peoples. For they so bring the matter about by their laws, that the ground which before was neither good nor profitable for the one or for the other, is now sufficient and fruitful enough for them both.

But if the inhabitants of that land will not dwell with them, to be ordered by their laws, then they drive them out of those bounds which they have limited and defined for themselves. And if they resist and rebel, then they make war against them. For they count this the most just cause of war, when any people holds a piece of ground void and vacant, to no good or profitable use, keeping others from the use and possession of it, who, notwithstanding the law of nature, ought to be nourished and supported thereon. If any chance do so much diminish the numbers in any of their cities that it cannot be filled up again, without the diminishing of the just number in the other cities (which they say chanced but twice since the beginning of the land through a great pestilent plague), then they make up the number with citizens fetched out of their own foreign towns, for they had rather suffer their foreign towns to decay and perish than any city of their own island to be diminished.

But now again to the intercourse of the citizens among themselves. The eldest, as I said, rules the family. The wives are ministers to their husbands, the children to their parents, and, to be short, the younger to their elders. Every city is divided into four equal parts. In the midst of every quarter there is a market place for all manner of things. Thither the produce of every family is brought into certain houses. And every kind of thing is laid up in the several barns or store houses. From hence the father of every family, or every householder, takes whatsoever he and his have need of, and carries it away with him without money, without exchange, without any security. For why should anything be denied him? Seeing there is abundance of all things, and that it is not to be feared that any man will ask for more than he needs. For why should it be thought that a man would ask for more than enough, who is sure never to lack? Certainly in all kinds of living creatures, fear of lack causes covetousness and greed; in man also pride, which counts it a glorious thing to surpass and excel others in the superfluous and vain ostentation of things. But this kind of vice among the Utopians can have no place.

Next to the market places that I spoke of, stand the food markets, whither are brought not only all sorts of herbs, and fruits of trees, with bread, but also fish, and all manner of four-footed beasts, and wild fowl that are man's meat. But first the filthiness and ordure thereof are clean washed away in the running river outside the city in places appointed for the same purpose. From thence the beasts are brought in killed, and clean washed by the hands of the bondmen. For they permit not their free citizens to accustom themselves to the killing of beasts, through which practice they think that clemency, the gentlest affection of our nature, little by little decays and perishes. Neither do they permit anything that is filthy, loathsome, or uncleanly to be brought into the city, lest the air by the stench thereof, infected and corrupt, should cause pestilent diseases.

Moreover every street has certain great large halls set an equal distance one from another, every one known by its own name. In these halls dwell the syphogrants. And to every one of the same halls are appointed thirty families, fifteen on either side. The stewards of every hall at a certain hour come into the meat markets, where they receive meat according to the number of their halls.

But first and chiefly of all, respect is paid to the sick, that are in the hospitals. For in the circuit of the city, a little beyond the walls, they have four hospitals, so big, so wide, so ample, and so large that they may seem four little towns, which were planned of that size partly to the intent that the sick, be they never so many in number, should not lie too crowded, and therefore uneasily and uncomfortably; and partly in order that they who are taken and suffering with contagious diseases, such as are wont by infection to creep from one to another, might be laid apart from the company of the rest. These hospitals are so well appointed, and so furnished with all things necessary to health, and moreover such diligent attention is given through the continual presence of skilful physicians, that though no man is sent thither against his will, yet still there is no sick person in all the city who had not rather lie there than at home in his own house.

When the steward of the sick has received such meats as the physicians have prescribed, then the best is equally divided among the halls, according to the company in every one, save that there respect is paid to the prince, the bishop, the trani- bores, and to ambassadors and all strangers, if there are any, which is seldom. But they also when they are there have certain houses appointed and prepared for them. To these halls at the set hours of dinner and supper come all the whole syphogranty or ward, called by the noise of a brazen trumpet, except such as are sick in the hospitals, or else in their own houses. Howbeit, no man is prohibited or forbidden, after the halls are served, to fetch home meat out of the market to his own house, for they know that no man will do it without a reasonable cause. For though no man is prohibited to dine at home, yet no man does it willingly, because it is counted an act of small honor. And also it were folly to take the pains to prepare a bad dinner at home, when they may be welcome to good and fine fare so nigh at hand in the hall.

In this hall all menial service, all slavery, and drudgery, with all laborsome toil and business, are done by bondmen. But the women of every family in turn have the office and charge of cookery for boiling and dressing the meat, and ordering all things belonging thereto. They sit at three tables or more, according to the number of their company. The men sit upon the bench next the wall, and the women opposite them on the other side of the table, so that if any sudden evil should chance to them, as many times happens to women with child, they may rise without trouble or disturbance of anybody, and go thence to the nursery. The nurses sit separately alone with their young sucklings in a certain parlor appointed and deputed to the same purpose, never without fire and clean water, nor yet without cradles, that when they will they may lay down the young infants, or at their pleasure take them out of their swathing clothes, and hold them to the fire, and refresh them with play. Every mother is nurse to her own child, unless either death or sickness prevent her. When that chances, the wives of the syphogrants quickly provide a nurse. And that is not hard to be done. For they that can do it, do offer themselves to no service so gladly as to that, because this kind of pity is much praised there, and the child that is nourished ever after takes his nurse for his own natural mother. Also among the nurses sit all the children that are under the age of five years. All the other children of both kinds, boys as well as girls, that are under the age of marriage, do either serve at the tables, or else if they are too young for that, stand by with marvelous silence. That which is given them from the table they eat, and a separate dinner-time they have none.

The syphogrant and his wife sit at the middle of the high table, forasmuch as that is counted the honorablest place, and because from thence all the whole company is in their sight. For that table stands across the upper end of the hall. To them are joined two of the ancientest and eldest. For at every table they sit four at a meal. But if there is a church in that syphogranty or ward, then the priest and his wife sit with the syphogrant, as chief of the company. On both sides of them sit young men, and next unto them again old men. And thus throughout all the house those of equal age are set together, and yet are mixed with unequal ages. This, they say, was ordained to the intent that the sage gravity and reverence of the elders should keep the younger from wanton license of words and behavior: forasmuch as nothing can be so secretly spoken or done at the table but that they who sit on the one side or on the other must needs perceive it. The dishes are not set down in order from the first place, but all the old men (whose places are marked with some special token to be known) are first served with their meat, and then the rest equally. The old men divide their dainties as they think best with the younger that sit on each side of them.

Thus the elders are not defrauded of their due honor, and nevertheless equal comfort comes to everyone. They begin every dinner and supper by reading something that pertains to good manners and virtue. But it is short, because no man shall be wearied thereby. Thereupon the elders take occasion for honest conversation, but neither sad nor unpleasant. Howbeit, they do not spend the whole dinner-time themselves in long and tedious talks, but they gladly hear also the young men; yea, and do purposely provoke them to talk, to the intent that they may have a proof of every man's wit, and inclination or disposition to virtue, which commonly in the liberty of feasting does show and utter itself.

Their dinners are very short, but their suppers are somewhat longer, because after dinner follows labor, after supper sleep and natural rest, which they think to be of more strength and efficacy to wholesome and healthful digestion. No supper goes by without music. Their banquets lack no dainties or delicacies. They burn sweet gums and spices for perfumes and pleasant smells, and sprinkle about sweet ointments and waters; yea, they leave nothing undone that makes for the cheering of the company. For they are much inclined to this opinion: to think no kind of pleasure forbidden wherefrom comes no harm. Thus therefore and after this sort they live together in the city, but in the country they that dwell alone far from any neighbors dine and sup at home in their own houses. For no family there lacks any kind of victuals, since from them comes all that the citizens eat and live by.

* * * * *

Of the religions in Utopia

There are divers kinds of religion not only in sundry parts of the island, but also in divers places in every city. Some worship the sun as God; some, the moon; some, others of the planets. There are those who worship a man, who was once of excellent virtue and famous glory, not only as God, but also as the chiefest and highest God. But the most and wisest number, rejecting all these, believe that there is a certain divine power, unknown, everlasting, incomprehensible, inexplicable, far above the capacity and reach of man's wisdom, dispersed throughout the world, not in size, but in virtue and power. Him they call the Father of All. To him alone they attribute the beginnings, the increasings, the proceedings, the changes and the ends of all things. They give no divine honors to any other but to him. Yea, all the others also, though they are of divers opinions, yet on this point agree all together with the wisest, in believing that there is one chief and principal God, the maker and ruler of the whole world, whom they all commonly in their country call Mithra. But on this point they disagree, so that among some he is counted one thing, and among some another. For every one of them, whatever it is which he takes for the chief God, thinks it to be the very same nature; to whose only divine might and majesty the sum and sovereignty of all things by the consent of all people is attributed and given.

Howbeit, they all begin now little by little to forsake and abandon this variety of superstitions, and to agree together in that religion which seems by reason to surpass and excel the rest. And it is not to be doubted that all the others would long ago have been abolished, except that whatever unfortunate thing happened to any of them, as he was considering a change in his religion, the fearfulness of the people took it not as a thing coming by chance, but as sent from God out of heaven; as though the God whose honor he was forsaking would avenge that wicked purpose against him. But after they heard us speak of the name of Christ, of his doctrine, laws, miracles, and of the no less wonderful constancy of so many martyrs, whose blood willingly shed brought a great number of nations throughout all parts of the world into their sect, you will not believe with what glad minds they agreed to the same, whether it were by the secret inspiration of God, or else because they thought it nearest that opinion which among them is counted chief. Howbeit, I think this was no small help and furtherance in the matter that they heard us say that Christ approved among his followers that all things be held in common; and that the same community of ownership does yet remain amongst the rightest Christian companies.

Verily, howsoever it came to pass, may of them consented to accept our religion, and were washed in the holy water of baptism. But because among us four (for no more of us were left alive, two of our company being dead) there was no priest, which I am right sorry for, they, though initiated and instructed in all other points of our religion, lack those sacraments which here none but priests administer. Howbeit, they understand and recognize them and are very desirous of the same. Yea, they reason and dispute the matter earnestly among themselves, whether without the sending of a Christian bishop, one chosen out of their own people may receive the order of priesthood. And truly they were minded to choose one. But at my departure from them they had chosen none. They also who do not agree to Christ's religion frighten no man from it, nor speak against any man who has received it, save one of our company who in my presence was sharply punished. He, as soon as he was baptized, began against our wills, with more zeal than wisdom, to reason on Christ's religion; and began to wax so hot on his subject that he not only praised our religion above all others, but also utterly despised and condemned all others, calling them profane, and the followers of them wicked and devilish and children of everlasting damnation. When he had thus long discoursed on the subject, they laid hold of him, accused him and condemned him to exile, not as a despiser of religion, but as a seditious person and an inciter of dissension among the people. For this is one of the most ancient laws among them, that no man shall be blamed for reasoning in the support of his own religion.

For King Utopus, even at the first beginning, hearing that the inhabitants of the land were, before his coming thither, in continual dissension and strife among themselves over their religions; perceiving also that this general dissension (since every separate sect took a different side in fighting for their country) was the only cause of his conquest of them all; as soon as he had gotten the victory, first of all made a decree that it should be lawful for every man to favor and follow whatever religion he would, and that he might do the best he could to lead others to his opinion, so long as he did it peaceably, gently, quietly, and soberly, without haste and contentious rebuking and denouncing others. If he could not by fair and gentle speech induce them to accept his opinion, still he should use no kind of violence and should refrain from unpleasant, seditious words. For him who would vehemently and fervently strive and contend for this cause was decreed banishment or bondage.

This law did King Utopus make, not only for the maintenance of peace, which he saw through continual contention and mortal hatred would be utterly extinguished, but also because he thought this decree would make for the furtherance of religion. On which he dared define and ordain nothing unadvisedly, as doubting whether God, desiring manifold and divers sorts of honour, might not inspire sundry men with sundry kinds of religion. And this he thought surely a very improper and foolish thing, and a sign of arrogant presumption, to compel all others by violence and threatenings to agree to the same that he believed to be true. Furthermore, though there is one religion which alone is true, and all others vain and superstitious, yet did he well foresee, that if the matter were handled with reason and sober modesty, the truth of its own power would at the last issue forth and come to light. But if contention and debate on that question should continue, as the worst men are most obstinate and stubborn, and in their evil opinion most constant, he perceived that the best and holiest religion would be trodden underfoot and destroyed by vain superstitions, even as good corn is by thorns and weeds overgrown and choked.

Therefore, all this matter he left undiscussed and gave to every man free liberty and choice to believe what he would. Saving that he earnestly and strictly charged them that no man should conceive so vile and base an opinion of the dignity of man's nature as to think that souls die and perish with the body, or that the world runs by chance, governed by no divine providence. And they believe that after this life vices are extremely punished and virtue bountifully rewarded. Him that is of a contrary opinion they count not in the number of mankind, but as one who has abased the high nature of his soul to the vileness of brute beasts' bodies; much less in the number of their citizens, whose laws and ordinances, if it were not for fear, he would not at all respect. For you may be sure he would study either with craft secretly to mock, or else violently to break the common laws of his country, in whom there remains no further fear but of the laws, nor any further hope beyond the body. Wherefore he that is thus minded is deprived of all honors, excluded from all offices and rejected from all public administration in the commonwealth. And he is despised by all sorts of people as of an unprofitable and base and vile nature. Howbeit, they give him no punishment, because they are persuaded that it is in no man's power to believe whatever he wishes. No, and they force him not by threatenings to dissemble his opinion and show a countenance contrary to his thought. For deceit and falsehood and all manner of lies, as next to fraud, they marvelously detest and abhor. But they suffer him not to discuss his opinions among the common people. But among the priests and men of gravity they do not only permit but also exhort him to dispute and argue, hoping that at last his madness will give place to reason.

There are also others, and of them no small number, who are not forbidden to speak their minds, since they ground their opinion upon some reason, and in their living are neither evil nor vicious. Their heresy is quite contrary to the other, for they believe that the souls of brute beasts are immortal and everlasting, but not to be compared to ours in dignity, nor ordained and predestined to a like felicity. For they all believe certainly and surely that man's bliss shall be so great that they mourn and lament everyone's sickness but no one's death, unless it is one whom they see depart his life reluctantly and against his will. For this they take as a very evil token, as though the soul were in despair and vexed in conscience, through some private and secret foreboding of punishment now at hand, and were afraid to depart. And they think he will not be welcome to God, if, when he is called, he runs not to him gladly, but is dragged by force and sore against his will. They, therefore, who see this kind of death abhor it, and bury with sorrow and silence those who do so die. And when they have prayed God to be merciful to the soul and mercifully to pardon the infirmities thereof, they cover the dead corpse with earth. Contrariwise, for all who depart merrily and full of good hope, no man mourns, but follows the hearse with joyful singing, commending the soul to God with great affection. And at the last, not with a mourning sorrow but with a great reverence, they burn the body. And in the same place they set up a pillar of stone, with the dead man's titles thereon engraved. When they come home they relate his virtuous manners and his good deeds. But no part of his life is so oft or so gladly talked of as his merry death.

They think that this remembrance of his virtue and goodness vehemently encourages and strengthens the living to virtue, and that nothing can be more pleasant and acceptable to the dead, whom they suppose to be present among them when they talk of them, though to the dull and feeble eyesight of mortal men they are invisible. For it were a hardship if the blessed were not at liberty to go whither they would. And it were a mark of great unkindness in them to utterly cast away the desire of visiting and seeing their friends, to whom they were in their lifetime joined by mutual love and charity. For this in good men after their death they count as increased rather than diminished. They believe therefore that the dead are personally present among the living, as beholders and witnesses of all their words and deeds. Therefore, they go more courageously to their business, having a trust and confidence in such overseers. And this same belief in the presence of their forefathers and ancestors among them makes them shrink from all secret dishonesty.

They utterly despise and mock at soothsayings and divinations of things to come by the flight or the voices of birds, and all other divinations of vain superstition, which in other countries are given much attention. But they highly esteem and worship miracles that come outside the regular course of nature, as works and witnesses of the present power of God. And these they say happen very often. And sometimes in great and doubtful matters, by common intercession and prayers, they procure and obtain them with a sure hope and confidence and steadfast belief.

They think that the contemplation of nature and the praise which grows out of it are to God a very acceptable honor. Yet there are many so earnestly bent and devoted to religion that they care nothing for learning, nor give their minds to any knowledge of secular things. But idleness they utterly shun and avoid, thinking felicity after this life is won and obtained by busy labors and good exercises. Some of them, therefore, tend the sick, some mend highways, clean ditches, repair bridges, dig turfs, gravel and stones, fell and cleave wood, bring wood, corn, and other things into the cities in carts, and serve not only in public works but also in private labors as servants, yea, more than bondmen. For whatsoever unpleasant, hard, and vile work is anywhere being done, the labor, loathsomeness, and desperation of which frighten others, all that they take on themselves willingly and gladly, securing the quiet and rest of others, but remaining in continual work and labor themselves, and not upbraiding others therefor. They neither reprove other men's lives, nor glory in their own. The more like servants these men behave themselves, the more they are honored of all men.

They are divided into two sects, the one that lives single and chaste, abstaining not only from the company of women, but also from the eating of flesh, and some of them from all manner of beasts. They utterly reject the pleasures of this present life as hurtful, and are wholly set upon desire of the life to come, hoping by watching and sweating shortly to obtain it, and being in the meantime merry and lusty. The other sect is no less desirous of labor, but they embrace matrimony, not despising the solace thereof, and thinking they cannot be relieved of their bounden duties towards nature without labor and toil, nor towards their native country without procreation of children. They abstain from no pleasure that does not hinder them from labor. They love the flesh of four-footed beasts, because they believe that by that meat they are made hardier and stronger to work. The Utopians count this sect the wiser, but the other the holier. If their preference for a single life before matrimony, and a sharp life before an easier life, were grounded upon reason, they would mock them. But now, inasmuch as they say they are led to it by religion, they honor and worship them. And they call them by a peculiar name, Buthrescas, which word by interpretation signifies to us men of religion or religious men.

They have priests of exceeding holiness, and therefore very few. For there are but thirteen in every city according to the number of their churches, save when they go forth to battle. For then seven of them go forth with the army; in whose stead as many new are created at home. But the others at their return home again re-enter every one his own place, those that are above the number, until such time as they succeed to the places of the others at their dying, are in the meantime continually in the company of the bishop. For he is the chief head of them all. They are chosen by the people, as the other magistrates are, by secret voting, for the avoiding of strife. After their election they are consecrated by their own company. They are overseers of all divine matters, orderers of religious ceremonies, and, as it were, judges and masters of manners. And it is a great dishonor and shame to be rebuked or spoken to by any of them for dissolute and incontinent living. But whereas it is their office to give good exhortations and counsel, it is the duty of the prince and the other magistrates to correct and punish offenders, except that the priests excommunicate from having any part in divine matters those whom they find exceedingly vicious livers. And there is almost no punishment more feared among them. For they fall into very great infamy, and are inwardly tormented with a secret fear of religion, and do not long escape free with their bodies. For unless by quick repentance they prove the amendment of their lives to the priests, they are taken and punished by the council, as wicked and irreligious.

Both childhood and youth are instructed and taught by them. Nor are they more diligent to instruct them in learning than in virtue and good manners. For they use very great endeavor and diligence to put into the heads of their children while they are yet tender and pliant, good opinions, profitable for the conservation of their public weal, which when they are once rooted in children, remain with them all their life after, and are wondrous profitable for the defense and maintenance of the state of the commonwealth, which never decays but through vices arising from evil opinions. The priests, unless they are women (for they are not excluded from priesthood, howbeit few are chosen, and none but widows and old women), the men priests, I say, take for their wives the chiefest women in all their country. For to no office among the Utopians is more honor and pre-eminence given. Insomuch that if priests commit any offense, they come under no public judgment, but are left only to God and themselves. For they think it not lawful to touch with a man's hand one who though never so vicious was so specially dedicated and consecrated to God, as a holy offering.

This custom they may easily observe, because they have so few priests, and choose them with such circumspection. For it scarcely ever chances that the most virtuous among a virtuous people, who by reason only of his virtue was advanced to so high a dignity, can fall to vice and wickedness. And if it should chance indeed—as man's nature is mutable and frail—yet because they are so few and promoted to no might or power but only honor, it is not to be feared that any great damage should happen and ensue from them to the commonwealth. They have such rare and few priests, lest if the honor were communicated to many, the dignity of the order, which among them now is so highly esteemed, should fall into contempt. Especially because they think it hard to find many persons so good as to be fit for that dignity, to the execution and discharge whereof it is not sufficient to be endowed with mediocre virtues.

Furthermore, these priests are not more esteemed by their own countrymen than they are by foreign and strange countries. Which thing may hereby plainly appear. And I think also that this is the cause of it. While the armies are fighting together in open field, the priests a little to one side kneel upon their knees in their hallowed vestments, holding up their hands to heaven and praying first of all for peace, next for victory for their own side, but for neither side a bloody victory. If their host get the upper hand, they run into the thick of the fight and restrain their own men from slaying and cruelly pursuing their vanquished enemies. If these enemies do but see and speak to them, it is enough for the safeguard of their lives. And the touching of their clothes defends and saves all their goods from plunder and spoil. This thing has raised them to such great worship and true majesty among all nations that many times they have safely preserved their own citizens from the cruel force of their enemies, or else their enemies from the furious rage of their own men. For it is well known that when their own army has recoiled and in despair turned back and run away, while their enemies fiercely pursued with slaughter and spoil, then the priests coming between have stayed the murder, and parted both the hosts. So that peace has been made and concluded between both sides upon equal and impartial terms. For there was never any nation so fierce, so cruel and rude, but held them in such reverence that they counted their bodies hallowed and sanctified, and therefore not to be violently and unreverently touched.

The Utopians keep holy the first and the last day of every month and year, dividing the year into months, which they measure by the course of the moon, as they do the year by the course of the sun. The first days they call in their language Cynemernes and the last Trapemernes, which words may be interpreted, primifest and finifest, or else in our speech, first feast and last feast. Their churches are very gorgeous and not only of fine and elaborate workmanship, but also—which in view of the fewness of them was necessary—very wide and large, and able to receive a great company of people. But they are all somewhat dark. Howbeit, that was not the effect of ignorance in building, but as they say, by the counsel of the priests, because they thought that overmuch light disperses men's cogitations, whereas in dim and doubtful light they are collected and more earnestly fixed upon religion and devotion. Although religion is not there the same among all men, yet all the kinds and fashions of it, though they are sundry and manifold, agree together in honor of the divine nature, going divers ways to one end. Therefore nothing is seen or heard in the churches, which seems not to agree impartially with them all. If there is a distinct kind of sacrament peculiar to any one sect, that they perform at home in their own houses. The public sacraments are so ordered that they are no derogation or prejudice to any of the private rites and religions. Therefore, no image of any god is seen in the church, to the intent it may be free for every man to conceive God by his religion after what likeness and similitude he will.

They call upon no peculiar name of God, but only Mithra, in which word they all agree on one nature of the divine majesty, whatsoever it may be. No prayers are used but such as every man may boldly pronounce without offending any sect. They come to the church the last day of every month and year, in the evening still fasting, there to give thanks to God for having prosperously passed over the year or month, of which that holy day is the last day. The next day they come to the church early in the morning, to pray to God that they may have good fortune and success all the new year or month which they begin on that same holy day. But on the holy days that are the last days of the months and years, before they come to the church, the wives fall down prostrate before their husbands' feet at home and the children before the feet of their parents, confessing and acknowledging that they have offended either by some actual deed, or by the omission of their duty, and desire pardon for their offense. Thus, if any cloud of secret ill-feeling was risen at home, by this satisfaction it is blown away, that they may be present at the rites with pure and charitable minds. For they are afraid to come there with troubled consciences. Therefore, if they know themselves to bear any hatred or grudge toward any man, they presume not to come to the sacrament, before they have reconciled themselves and purged their consciences, for fear of great vengeance and punishment for their offense.

When they come thither, the men go to the right side of the church and the women to the left side. There they place themselves in such order that all those of the male kind in every household sit before the goodman of the house, and those of the female kind before the goodwife. Thus it is provided that all their gestures and behavior are marked and observed abroad by those by whose authority and discipline they are governed at home. This also they diligently see to, that the younger evermore is coupled with his elder, lest if children are joined together, they pass the time in childish wantonness, wherein they ought principally to conceive a religious and devout fear towards God, which is the chief and almost the only incitement to virtue.

They kill no living beast in sacrifice, nor do they think that the merciful clemency of God delights in blood and slaughter, which has given life to beasts to the intent they should live. They burn frankincense and other sweet savors, and light also a great number of wax candles and tapers, not supposing these things to be anything necessary to the divine nature, any more than the prayers of men are. But this unhurtful and harmless kind of worship pleases them. And by these sweet savors and lights and other such ceremonies men feel themselves secretly lifted up and encouraged to devotion with more willing and fervent hearts.

The people in church wear white apparel. The priest is clothed in changeable colors, which in workmanship are excellent but in stuff not very precious. For their vestments are neither embroidered with gold nor set with precious stones, but are wrought so finely and cunningly with divers feathers of birds, no costly stuff can equal the price of the work. Furthermore, in these birds' feathers and in the due order of them, which is observed in their setting, is contained, they say, certain divine mysteries. The interpretation whereof is diligently taught by the priests that they may be put in remembrance of the bountiful benefits of God to them, and of the love and honor which on their behalf is due to God; and also of their duties one to another.

When the priest first comes out of the vestry thus appareled, they fall down straightway every one reverently to the ground, with such still silence on every one's part that the very manner of the thing strikes into them a certain fear of God, as though he were personally present. When they have lain a little space on the ground, the priest gives them a sign to rise. Then they sing praises unto God, which they intermix with instruments of music, for the most part unlike those which we use in this part of the world. And as some of ours are much sweeter than theirs, so some of theirs far surpass ours. But in one thing doubtless they go exceedingly far beyond us. For all their music, both what they play upon instruments, and what they sing with man's voice, does so resemble and express natural emotions, the sound and tune are so applied and made harmonious to the words, that whether it be a prayer, or a ditty of gladness, of patience, of trouble, of mourning, or of anger, the fashion of the melody does so represent the meaning of the thing that it does wonderfully move, stir, pierce, and inflame the hearers' minds. At the end the people and the priest together repeat solemn prayers in words, pronounced in set phrases, so made that every man may privately apply to himself that which is publicly spoken by all.

In these prayers every man recognizes and acknowledges God to be his maker, his governor, and the principal cause of all other goodness, thanking him for so many benefits received at his hand, but chiefly that through the favor of God he has chanced to be in that commonwealth which is most happy and well ordered, and has chosen that religion which he hopes to be most true. In which respect if he errs, or if there is any other better than either of them and more acceptable to God, he desires him that he will of his goodness let him have knowledge thereof, as one who is ready to follow what way soever he will lead him. But if this form and fashion of commonwealth is best, and his own religion most true and perfect, then he desires God to give him a constant steadfastness in the same, and to bring all other people to the same order of living and to the same opinion of God, unless there is something in this diversity of religions that delights his inscrutable pleasure. In brief, he prays him that after death he may come to him, but how soon or late he dares not assign or determine. Howbeit, if it might agree with his majesty's pleasure, he would be much gladder to die a painful death and so go to God, than by long living in worldly prosperity to stay away from him. When this prayer is said, they fall down to the ground again and a little after rise up and go to dinner. And the rest of the day they pass in play and military exercise.

Now I have declared and described unto you, as truly as I could, the form and order of that commonwealth, which verily in my judgment is not only the best, but also that which alone of good right may claim and take upon itself the name of commonwealth or public weal. For in other places they speak still of the commonwealth, but every man procures his own private wealth. Here, where nothing is private, the common interests are earnestly looked to. And truly on both accounts they have good cause to do as they do. For in other countries, who knows that he will not starve for hunger, unless he make some private provision for himself, even though the commonwealth flourish never so much in riches? And, therefore, he is compelled even of very necessity to pay regard to himself rather than to the people, that is to say, to others. Contrariwise, where all things are common to every man, it is not doubted that no man shall lack anything necessary for his private use, so long as the common storehouses and barns are sufficiently stored. For there nothing is distributed in a niggardly fashion, nor is there any poor man or beggar. And though no man owns anything, yet every man is rich. For what can be more rich than to live joyfully and merrily, without grief and worry, not concerned for his own living, nor vexed and troubled with his wife's importunate complaints, nor dreading poverty for his son, nor sorrowing for his daughter's dowry? Yea, they take no care at all for the living and wealth of themselves and all theirs, their wives, their children, their nephews, their children's children, and all the succession that ever shall follow in their posterity.

And, besides this, there is no less provision for those who were at once laborers and are now weak and impotent than for those who now labor and bear the burden. Here now I would see, if any man dare be so bold as to compare with this equity the justice of other nations; among whom, may I perish utterly, if I can find any sign or token of equity and justice! For what justice is this, that a rich goldsmith, or usurer, or to be brief, any one of those who either do nothing at all, or else something that is not very necessary to the commonwealth, should have a pleasant and wealthy living, either in idleness, or in unnecessary business, when meanwhile poor laborers, carters, ironsmiths, carpenters, and plowmen, by such great and continual toil, as beasts of burden are scarce able to sustain, and again such necessary toil that without it no commonwealth would be able to continue and endure one year, yet get so hard and poor a living and live so wretched and miserable a life that the state and condition of the laboring beasts may seem much better and more comfortable? For they are not put to such continual labor, nor is their living much worse; yea, for them it is much pleasanter, for they take no thought in the meantime for the future. But these ignorant, poor wretches are now tormented with barren and unfruitful labor, and the remembrance of their poor, indigent, and beggarly old age kills them off. For their daily wage is so little that it will not suffice for the same day, much less yield any overplus that may daily be laid up for the relief of old age.

Is not this an unjust and an unkind commonwealth, which gives great fees and rewards to gentlemen, as they call them, and to goldsmiths, and to others who are either idle persons, or else only flatterers, and devisers of vain pleasures; and on the other hand, makes no considerate provision for poor plowmen, colliers, laborers, carters, ironsmiths, and carpenters, without whom no commonwealth can continue? But when it has misused the labors of their lusty and flowering age, at the last when they are oppressed with old age, sickness, needy, poor, and indigent of all things, then forgetting their many painful watchings, nor remembering their many and great benefits, it recompenses and requites them most unkindly with a miserable death.

And yet, in addition to this, the rich not only by private fraud, but also by public laws, every day pluck and snatch away from the poor some part of their daily living. So whereas it seemed previously unjust to recompense with unkindness the toils that have been beneficial to the public weal, the rich have now to this their wrong and unjust dealing—which is a much worse act—given the name of justice, yea, and that by force of law. Therefore, when I consider and weigh in my mind all these commonwealths, which nowadays flourish everywhere, so God help me, I can perceive nothing but a certain conspiracy of rich men procuring their own comforts under the name and title of the commonwealth. They invent and devise all means and schemes, first how to keep safely, without fear of losing what they have unjustly gathered together, and next, how to hire and misuse the work and labor of the poor for as little money as may be. When the rich men decreed these devices to be kept and observed for the commonwealth's sake, that is to say, for the wealth also of the poor, then they are made laws.

Yet these most wicked and vicious men, when they have by their insatiable covetousness divided among themselves all the things which would have sufficed everyone, still how far are they from the wealth and felicity of the Utopian commonwealth! From which, in that all desire of money and use thereof are utterly excluded and banished, how great a heap of cares is cut away! How great a cause of wickedness and mischief is plucked up by the roots! For who does not know that fraud, theft, rapine, brawling, quarreling, brabling, strife, chiding, contention, murder, treason, poisoning, which by daily punishments are rather avenged than restrained, die when money dies? And also that fear, grief, care, labors and watchings perish even the very moment that money perishes? Yes, poverty itself, which only seemed to lack money, if money were gone, would also decrease and vanish away.

And that you may perceive this more plainly, consider yourselves some barren and unfruitful year, wherein many thousands of people have starved for hunger. I dare be bold to say that at the end of that penury so much corn and grain would have been found in the rich men's barns, if they had been searched, that if it had been divided among those whom famine and pestilence killed, no man at all would have felt that plague and penury. So easily might men get their living, if that same worthy princess, Lady Money, did not alone stop up the way between us and our livelihood, though she in God's name was excellently devised and invented, in order that by her the way thereto should be opened. I am sure the rich perceive this, nor are they ignorant how much better it would be to lack no necessary thing than to abound with overmuch superfluity; to be rid of innumerable cares and troubles than to be beseiged with great riches.

And I doubt not that either respect for every man's private comfort, or else the authority of our saviour Christ (which for his great wisdom could not but know what was best, and for his inestimable goodness could not but counsel that which he knew to be best) would have brought all the world long ago unto the laws of this commonwealth, if it were not that one single beast, the princess and mother of all mischief, Pride, resists and hinders it. She measures not wealth and prosperity by her own well being, but by the miseries and discomforts of others; she would not of her own will be made a goddess, if there were no wretches left whom she might be lady over to mock and scorn, over whose miseries her felicity might shine, and whose poverty she might vex, torment, and increase by gorgeously vaunting her riches. This hell-hound creeps into men's hearts, and plucks them back from entering the right path of life, and is so deeply rooted in men's breasts that she cannot be plucked out.

This form and fashion of a commonwealth, which I would gladly wish for all nations, I am glad at least that it has chanced to the Utopians, who have followed those institutions of life whereby they have laid such foundations for their state as shall continue and last not only happily, but also, as far as man's wit may judge and conjecture, endure forever. For seeing that the chief causes of ambition and sedition with other vices are plucked up by the roots and abandoned at home, there can be no danger of civil strife, which alone has cast underfoot and brought to nought the well-fortified and strongly defended wealth and riches of many cities. And forasmuch as perfect concord remains, and wholesome laws are executed at home, the envy of all foreign princes is not able to shake or move the empire, though they have many times long ago gone about to do it, being evermore driven back.

When Raphael had thus made and end of his tale, many things came to my mind, which in the manners and laws of that people seemed to be instituted and founded on no good reason, not only the fashion of their military arts, their rites and religions, and others of their laws, but also, yea and chiefly, that which is the principal foundation of all their ordinances, that is to say, the community of their life and living, without any use of money, by which practice alone all the nobility, magnificence, worship, honor and majesty, the true ornaments and honors, as the common opinion is, of a commonwealth, are utterly overthrown and destroyed. Yet because I knew that he was weary of talking, and was not sure whether he could bear that anything should be said against his opinion; and especially because I remembered that he had blamed this fault in others, who are afraid lest they seem not wise enough, unless they can find some fault in other men's inventions; therefore, I praising both their institutions and his account of them took him by the hand and led him in to supper, saying that we would choose another time to weigh and examine the same matters, and talk with him more at length thereon: which would to God it may some day come to pass. In the meantime, as I cannot agree and consent to all the things that he said, though he is without doubt a man singularly well learned, and in all worldly matters exactly and profoundly experienced, so must I needs confess and grant that there are many things in the Utopian commonwealth which in our cities I may rather wish than hope for.

Thus ended the afternoon's talk of Raphael Hythloday concerning the laws and institutions of the Island of Utopia.

Bartolomé de Las Casas
1474-1566

Why is it that the magnificent experience of discovery is so often demeaned by greed and cruelty? Why do humans, at the very moment that the opportunity to create a new and radically joyous situation for mankind, opt for tragedy and destruction? The questions cannot be answered, simply pondered. Yet they are questions that lie in the very heart of the human as social being, questions that reflect the human condition and serve as some kind of judge for human action, questions that remind the human of its failures and encourage the human to rebuild.

One of the greatest opportunities to expand human horizons and establish a new world came with the discovery of the Americas. What actually happened is now history. As Europe realized what had been found, the lust for power and profit drove individuals and nations mad. Fortunes were made at the expense of the lives of millions of innocent Indians who had received the European as some kind of god.

Bartolomé de Las Casas, who was born in Seville in 1474, came from a family that had very early contact with the New World. His father and uncles travelled with Columbus on his second voyage. In 1502 he himself journeyed to the Indies and was successful as a landowner and farmer. Like other Spanish settlers he owned Indians; but unlike the majority of his countrymen, he considered the Indians as human beings. The cruelty and abuse of the Indians that he witnessed eventually turned Las Casas into the defender of the Indians. In 1514, two years after being ordained a priest (the first in the New World), he preached a sermon in which he denounced the Spaniards for their mistreatment of the natives. Thus began more than fifty years of fighting for the rights of his beloved Indian people. He crossed the Atlantic Ocean at least ten times in his efforts to correct an inhuman situation. His enemies and opponents far outnumbered his supporters and he knew many defeats. Hatred for him and what he was trying to do was not veiled. Even as a bishop he met with defiant opposition to his efforts to humanize the treatment of Indians. But several of his victories were significant. Obviously the original life and dignity of the Indians would never be restored; he at least succeeded in bringing about some concrete legislation to protect the natives from too much abuse.

For the final fifteen years of his life, Las Casas stayed in Spain and hounded the royal court in behalf of the Indians. From Seville he published seven treatises on the New World and his theories for developing it. Needless to say, his writings were not popular in Spain. It is tragic to think that there was such injustice and inhumanity prevalent among the conquerors of the Americas. Given that there was, it is consoling to know that a man such as Bartolomé de Las Casas rose up to speak in behalf of the Indians and to do battle for their human right to freedom and justice.

The reading below, A Very Brief Account of the Destruction of the Indies, *is a straightforward condemnation of the conquistadores for their cruelty and total lack of Christian principle. Perhaps it was even too severe. It does reveal the conditions in the New World within a decade after Columbus's discovery as well as introduce the reader to one of the most unusual and exciting personalities in the history of the Americas.*

A VERY BRIEF ACCOUNT OF THE DESTRUCTION OF THE INDIES

A s divine Providence has ordained that in his world, for its government, and for the common utility of the human race, Kingdoms and Countries should be constituted in which are Kings almost fathers and pastors (as Homer calls them), they being consequently the most noble, and most generous members of the Republics, there neither is nor can be reasonable doubt as to the rectitude of their royal hearts. If any defect, wrong, and evil is suffered, there can be no other cause than that the Kings are ignorant of it; for if such were manifested to them, they would extirpate them with supreme industry and watchful diligence.

It is seemingly this that the divine Scriptures mean in the Proverbs of Solomon, *qui sedet in solio iudicii, dissipat omne malum intuitu suo*: because it is thus assumed from the innate and peculiar virtue of the King namely, that the knowledge alone of evil in his Kingdom is absolutely sufficient that he should destroy it; and that not for one moment, as far as in him lies, can he tolerate it.

As I have fifty, or more, years of experience in those countries, I have therfore been considering the evils I have seen committed, the injuries, losses, and misfortunes, such as it would not have been thought could be done by man; such kingdoms, so many, and so large, or to speak better, that most vast and new world of the Indies, conceded and confided by God and his Church to the Kings of Castile, that they should rule and govern it; that they should convert it, and should prosper it temporally, and spiritually.

When some of their particular actions are made known to Your Highness, it will not be possible to forbear supplicating His Majesty with importunate insistence, that he should not concede nor permit that which the tyrants have invented, pursued, and put into execution, calling it Conquests; which if permitted, will be repeated; because these acts in themselves, done against those pacific, humble, and mild Indian people, who offend none, are iniquitous, tyrannous, condemned and cursed by every natural, divine, and human law.

So as not to keep criminal silence concerning the ruin of numberless souls and bodies that these persons cause, I have decided to print some, though very few, of the innumerable instances I have collected in the past and can relate with truth, in order that Your Highness may read them with greater facility.

Although the Archbishop of Toledo, Your Highness' Preceptor, when Bishop of Cartagena, asked me for them and presented them to Your Highness, nevertheless, because of the long journeys by sea and land Your Highness has made, and of the continual royal occupations it may be that Your Highness either has not read them or has already forgotten them.

The daring and unreasonable cupidity of those who count it as nothing to unjustly shed such an immense quantity of human blood, and to deprive those enormous countries of their natural inhabitants and possessors, by slaying millions of people and stealing incomparable treasures, increase every day; and they insist by various means and under various feigned pretexts, that the said Conquests are permitted, without violation of the natural and divine law, and, in consequence, without most grievous mortal sin, worthy of terrible and eternal punishment. I therefore esteemed it right to furnish Your Highness with this very brief summary of a very long history that could and ought to be composed, of the massacres and devastation that have taken place.

I supplicate Your Highness to receive and read it with the clemency, and royal benignity he usually shows to his creatures, and servants, who desire to serve solely for the public good and for the prosperity of the State.

Having seen and understood the monstrous injustice done to these innocent people in destroying and outraging them, without cause or just motive, but out of avarice alone, and the ambition of those who design such villainous operations, may Your Highness be pleased to supplicate and efficaciously persuade His Majesty to forbid such harmful and detestable practices to those who seek license for them: may he silence this infernal demand for ever, with so much terror, that from this time forward there shall be no one so audacious as to dare but to name it.

This—Most High Lord—is most fitting and necessary to do, that God may prosper, preserve and render blessed, both temporally and spiritually, all the State of the royal crown of Castile. Amen.

The Indies were discovered in the year fourteen hundred and ninety-two. The year following, Spanish Christians went to inhabit them, so that it is since forty-nine years that numbers of Spaniards have gone there; and the first land, that they invaded to inhabit, was the large and most delightful Isle of Hispaniola, which has a circumference of six hundred leagues.

There are numberless other islands, and very large ones, all around on every side, that were all—and we have seen it—as inhabited and full of their native Indian peoples as any country in the world.

Of the continent, the nearest part of which is more than two hundred and fifty leagues distant from this Island, more than ten thousand leagues of maritime coast have been discovered, and more is discovered every day; all that has been discovered up to the year forty-nine is full of people, like a hive of bees, so that it seems as though God had placed all, or the greater part of the entire human race in these countries.

God has created all these numberless people to be quite the simplest, without malice or duplicity, most obedient, most faithful to their natural Lords, and to the Christians, whom they serve; the most humble, most patient, most peaceful, and calm, without strife nor tumults; not wrangling, nor querulous, as free from uproar, hate and desire of revenge, as any in the world.

They are likewise the most delicate people, weak and of feeble constitution, and less than any other can they bear fatigue, and they very easily die of whatsoever infirmity; so much so, that not even the sons of our Princes and of nobles, brought up in royal and gentle life, are more delicate than they; although there are among them such as are of the peasant class. They are also a very poor people, who of worldly goods possess little, nor wish to possess: and they are therefore neither proud, nor ambitious, nor avaricious.

Their food is so poor, that it would seem that of the Holy Fathers in the desert was not scantier nor less pleasing. Their way of dressing is usually to go naked, covering the private parts; and at most they cover themselves with a cotton cover, which would be about equal to one and a half or two ells square of cloth. Their beds are of matting, and they mostly sleep in certain things like hanging nets, called in the language of Hispaniola *Hamacas*.

They are likewise of a clean unspoiled, and vivacious intellect, very capable, and receptive to every good doctrine; most prompt to accept our Holy Catholic Faith, to be endowed with virtuous customs; and they have as little difficulty with such things as any people created by God in the world.

Once they have begun to learn of matters pertaining to faith, they are so importunate to know them, and in frequenting the sacraments and divine service of the Church, that to tell the truth, the clergy have need to be endowed of God with the gift of preeminent patience to bear with them: and finally, I have heard many lay Spaniards frequently say many years ago (unable to deny the goodness of those they saw), certainly these people were the most blessed of the earth, had they only knowledge of God.

Among these gentle sheep, gifted by their Maker with the above qualities, the Spaniards entered as soon as they knew them like wolves, tigers, and lions which had been starving for many days, and since forty years they have done nothing else; nor do they otherwise at the present day, than outrage, slay, afflict, torment, and destroy them with strange and new, and divers kinds of cruelty, never before seen, nor heard of, nor read of, of which some few will be told below: to such extremes has this gone that, whereas there were more than three million souls, whom we saw in Hispaniola, there are today, not two hundred of the native population left.

The island of Cuba is almost as long as the distance from Valladolid to Rome; it is now almost entirely deserted. The islands of San Juan (Porto Rico) and Jamaica, very large and happy and pleasing islands, are both desolate. The Lucaya Isles lie near Hispaniola and Cuba to the north and number more than sixty, including those that are called the Giants, and other large and small Islands; the poorest of these, which is more fertile, and pleasing than the King's garden in Seville, is the healthiest country in the world, and contained more than five hundred thousand souls, but today there remains not even a single creature. All were killed in transporting them, to Hispaniola, because it was seen that the native population there was disappearing.

A ship went three years later to look for the people that had been left after the gathering in, because a good Christian was moved by compassion to convert and win those that were found to Christ; only eleven persons, whom I saw, were found.

More than thirty other islands, about the Isle of San Juan, are destroyed and depopulated, for the same reason. All these islands cover more than two thousand leagues of land, entirely depopulated and deserted.

We are assured that our Spaniards, with their cruelty and execrable works, have depopulated and made desolate the great continent, and that more than ten Kingdoms, larger than all Spain, counting Aragon and Portugal, and twice as much territory as from Seville, to Jerusalem (which is more than two thousand leagues), although formerly full of people, are now deserted.

We give as a real and true reckoning, that in the said forty years, more than twelve million persons, men, and women, and children, have perished unjustly and through tyranny, by the infernal deeds and tyranny of the Christians; and I truly believe, nor think I am deceived, that it is more than fifteen.

Two ordinary and principal methods have the self-styled Christians, who have gone there, employed in extirpating these miserable nations and removing them from the face of the earth. The one, by unjust, cruel and tyrannous wars. The other, by slaying all those, who might aspire to, or sigh for, or think of liberty, or to escape from the torments that they suffer, such as all the native Lords, and adult men; for generally, they leave none alive in the wars, except the young men and the women, whom they oppress with the hardest, most horrible, and roughest servitude, to which either man or beast, can ever be put. To these two ways of infernal tyranny, all the many and divers other ways, which are numberless, of exterminating these people, are reduced, resolved, or subordered according to kind.

The reason why the Christians have killed and destroyed such infinite numbers of souls, is solely because they have made gold their ultimate aim, seeking to load themselves with riches in the shortest time and to mount by high steps, disproportioned to their condition: namely by their insatiable avarice and ambition, the greatest, that could be on the earth. These lands, being so happy and so rich, and the people so humble, so patient, and so easily subjugated, they have had no more respect, nor consideration nor have they taken more account of them (I speak with truth of what I have seen during all the aforementioned time) than,—I will not say of animals, for would to God they had considered and treated them as animals,—but as even less than the dung in the streets.

In this way have they cared for their lives—and for their souls: and therefore, all the millions above mentioned have died without faith, and without sacraments. And it is a publicly known truth, admitted, and confessed by all, even by the tyrants and homicides themselves, that the Indians throughout the Indies never did any harm to the Christians: they even esteemed them as coming from heaven, until they and their neighbors had suffered the same many evils, thefts, death, violence and visitations at their hands. . . .

I was induced to write this work I, Fray Bartolomeus de las Casas, or Casaus, friar of Saint Dominic, who by God's mercy do go about this Court of Spain, trying to drive the hell out of the Indies, and to bring about that all those numberless multitudes of souls, redeemed with the blood of Jesus Christ, shall not hopelessly perish for ever; moved also by the compassion I feel for my fatherland, Castile, that God may not destroy it for such great sins, committed against His faith and honor and against fellow creatures. A few persons of quality who reside at this Court and are jealous of God's honor and compassionate towards the afflictions and calamities of others, urged me to this work although it was my own intention which my continual occupations had never allowed me to put into effect.

I brought it to a close at Valencia the 8th of December 1542, when all the violence was more terrible, and the oppression, tyranny, massacres, robberies, destructions, slaughter, depopulation, anguish, and calamity aforesaid, are actually at their height in all the regions where the Christians of the Indies are; although in some places they are fiercer, and more abominable than in others.

Mexico and its neighborhood are a little less badly off; there, at least, such things dare not be done publicly, because there is somewhat more justice than elsewhere, although very little, for they still kill the people with infernal burdens.

I have great hope, for the Emperor and King of Spain our Lord Don Carlos, Fifth of this name is getting to understand the wickedness and treachery that, contrary to the will of God, and of himself, is and has been done to those people and in those countries; heretofore the truth has been studiously hidden from him, that it is his duty to extirpate so many evils and bring succour to that new world, given him by God, as to one who is a lover and observer of justice, whose glorious, and happy life and Imperial state may God Almighty long prosper, to the relief of all his universal Church, and for the final salvation of his own Royal soul. Amen.

Since the above was written, some laws and edicts have been published by His Majesty, who was then in the town of Barcelona, in the month of November, 1542, and in the town of Madrid the following year; these contain such provisions as now seem suitable to bring about the cessation of the great wickedness and sin committed against God and our fellow creatures, to the total ruin and destruction of that world.

After many conferences and debates amongst conscientious and learned authorities, who were assembled in the town of Valladolid, His Majesty made the said laws; acting finally on the decision and opinion of the greater part of all those who gave their votes in writing, and who drew nearer to the law of Jesus Christ, as true Christians. They were likewise free from the corruption and foulness of the treasures stolen from the Indies that soiled the hands, and still more the souls of many in authority who, in their blindness, had committed unscrupulous destruction.

When these laws were published, the agents of the tyrants, then at Court, made many copies of them; they displeased all these men who considered that they shut the doors to their participation in what was robbed and taken by tyranny: and they sent the copies to divers parts of the Indies.

None of these who there had charge of robbing the Indians, and of finishing their destruction by their tyranny, had ever observed any order, but such disorder as might have been made by Lucifer; when they saw the copies, before the arrival of the new judges who were to execute them, it is said and believed that they had been warned of what was coming by those in Spain, who have till now encouraged their sins and violence. They were so agitated, that when the good judges who were to carry out the laws arrived, they resolved to set aside shame and obedience to the King, just as they had already lost all love and fear of God.

They thus determined to let themselves be called traitors, for they are cruel and unbridled tyrants, particularly in the kingdoms of Peru, where at present, in this year of 1546, such horrible, frightful, and execrable deeds are committed, as have never been done, either in the Indies or in the world; not only do such things happen among the Indians whom they have already all or nearly all killed, but among themselves. In the absence of the King's justice to punish them, God's justice has come from heaven to bring dissension amongst them and to make one to be the executioner of the other.

Shielded by the rebellion of these tyrants, those in all the other regions, would not obey the laws and, under pretext of appealing against them, have also revolted; they resent having to abdicate the dignities and power they have usurped, and to losing the Indians whom they hold in perpetual slavery.

Where they have ceased to kill quickly by the sword, they kill slowly by personal servitude and other unjust and intolerable vexations. And till now the King has not succeeded in preventing them because all, small and great, go there to pilfer, some more, some less, some publicly and openly, others secretly and under disguise; and with the pretext that they are serving the king, they dishonor God, and rob and destroy the King.

Francois René de Chateaubriand

1768-1848

Francois René de Chateaubriand is one of the great French literary figures of the nineteenth century. His powerful imagination and his brilliant writing style made him a major contributor to the romantic movement. But Chateaubriand was a political personality as well. The blend of his literary abilities and his political interests accounts for a fascinating nineteenth century statement on social thought.

Chateaubriand was born at Saint-Malo in 1768. After his schooling in Brittany, he retained a military commission for a few years. In 1791 he travelled to the United States; then, in 1792, he settled in England for eight years. Upon his return to France in 1800, Chateaubriand's double career, that of writer and politician, started to take shape. His famous work, The Genius of Christianity, *was published in 1802 and resulted in his being sent to Rome as secretary to the French ambassador. Napoleon had intended to make good use of Chateaubriand's abilities for his own purposes, but the execution of the Duke of Enghien severed their developing relationship. Chateaubriand wrote* The Martyrs, *a prose poem on Roman decadence, as a polemic against Napoleon. The remainder of his life was filled with journeys, political activity and writing. He died on July 4, 1848, in Paris.*

The writings of Chateaubriand revealed a vision of history that is steeped in Christian faith as it was perceived in his time. He was confident that divine Providence was active in history and that mankind was progressing toward its fulfillment under the guidance of Christianity.

The Genius of Christianity was an effort to draw a parallel between the revolutions of antiquity and the French revolution that occurred during Chateaubriand's lifetime. The first part of the book, "Dogmas and Doctrines," explores the mysteries of faith, the sacraments, the Mosaic tradition, and the proofs for the existence of God drawn from the wonders of nature. Parts two and three, "The Poetry of Christianity" and "Arts and Literature," treat various aspects of the Christian tradition, such as its poetry, music, art and architecture. All of these, for Chateaubriand, give witness to the truth of Christianity. The final part of the book, "Worship," extols the beauty of Christian liturgy and argues that human society is all the better for the existence of the Christian religion.

The passage below is the book's concluding chapter. Chateaubriand asks what would be the present state of the human society if Christianity had not appeared. By selectively reviewing the most deplorable aspects of the pre-Christian era, he establishes the argument that the coming of Jesus Christ as Savior was the most important event that ever occurred among men, since the regeneration of society commenced only with the proclamation of the gospel. Through Christianity, mankind took an immense step toward perfection.

Chateaubriand's confidence in Christianity as the means to perfect the human society rests upon his conviction that Christianity stands the test of reason, explains man and nature, and replaces the cruelty of the ancients with its own law of charity. Though men are imperfect, Christianity is perfect.

The reader will sense the poetic optimism that sustained Chateaubriand's world view. Could the human society have been shaped according to his vision, all would indeed be beautiful. Little did he realize that the century following his death would bring revolutions and wars that would throw into question even the imperturbable truths of Christianity.

THE GENIUS OF CHRISTIANITY

CHAPTER XIII

WHAT WOULD THE PRESENT STATE OF SOCIETY BE IF CHRISTIANITY HAD
NOT APPEARED IN THE WORLD?–CONJECTURES–CONCLUSION.

We shall conclude this work with a discussion of the important question which forms the title of this last chapter. By endeavoring to discover what we should probably be at present if Christianity had not existed, we shall learn to appreciate more fully the advantages which we owe to it.

Augustus attained imperial power by the commission of crime, and reigned under the garb of virtue. He succeeded a conqueror, and to distinguish himself he cultivated peace. Incapable of being a great man, he determined to acquire the character of a fortunate prince. He gave a long repose to his subjects. An immense focus of corruption became stagnant, and the prevailing calm was called prosperity. Augustus possessed the genius of circumstances, which knew how to gather the fruits which true genius had produced. It follows true genius, but does not always accompany it.

Tiberius had too great a contempt for mankind, and but too plainly manifested this contempt. The only sentiment which he frankly displayed was the only one that he ought to have dissembled; but he could not repress a burst of joy on finding the Roman people and senate sunk even below the baseness of his own heart.

When we behold this sovereign people falling prostrate before Claudius and adoring the son of Ænobarbus, we may naturally suppose that it had been honored with some marks of indulgence. Rome loved Nero. Long after the death of that tyrant, his phantoms thrilled the empire with joy and hope. Here we must pause to contemplate the manners of the Romans. Neither Titus, nor Antoninus, nor Marcus Aurelius, could change the groundwork of them; by nothing less than a God could this be accomplished.

The Roman people was always an odious people; it is impossible to fall into the vices which it displayed under its imperial rulers, without a certain natural perverseness and some innate defect in the heart. Corrupted Athens never was an object of execration; when in chains, she thought only of enjoying herself. She found that her conquerors had not deprived her of every thing, since they had left her the temple of the Muses.

When Rome had virtues, they were of an unnatural kind. The first Brutus butchered his sons, and the second assassinated his father. There are virtues of situation, which are too easily mistaken for general virtues, and which are but mere local results. Rome, while free, was at first frugal, because she was poor; courageous, because her institutions put the sword into her hand, and because she sprang from a cavern of banditti. She was, besides, ferocious, unjust, avaricious, luxurious; she had nothing admirable but her genius; her character was detestable.

The decemvirs trampled her under foot. Marius spilt at pleasure the blood of the nobles, and Sylla that of the people; as the height of insult, he publicly abdicated the dictatorship. Catiline's accomplices engaged to murder their own fathers, and made a sport of overthrowing that majesty of Rome which Jugurtha proposed to purchase. Next come the triumvirs and their proscriptions. Augustus commands a father and son to kill each other, and the father and son obey. The senate proves itself too debased even for Tiberius. The god Nero has his temples. Without mentioning those informers belonging to the most distinguished patrician families; without showing the leaders of one and the same conspiracy denouncing and butchering one another; without pointing to philosophers discoursing on virtue amid the debaucheries of Nero, Seneca excusing a parricide, Burrhus at once praising and deploring it; without seeking under Galba, Vitellius, Domitian, and Commodus, for those acts of meanness which, though you have read them a hundred times, will never cease to astonish,—one single fact will fully portray Roman infamy. Plautian, the minister of

Severus, on the marriage of his daughter with the eldest son of the emperor, caused one hundred freemen of Rome, some of whom were husbands and fathers of families, to be mutilated, "in order," says the historian, "that his daughter might have a retinue of eunuchs worthy of an Eastern queen.

To this baseness of character must be added a frightful corruption of manners. The grave Cato made no scruple to assist at the prostitutions of the Floral games. He resigns his wife Marcia, pregnant as she was, to Hortensius; some time afterward Hortensius dies, and, having left Marcia heir to all his fortune, Cato takes her back again, to the prejudice of the son of Hortensius. Cicero repudiates Terentia for the purpose of marrying Publia, his ward. Seneca informs us that there were women who no longer counted their years by consuls, but by the number of their husbands; Tiberius invents the *scellarii* and the *spintriæ;* Nero publicly weds his freedman Pythagoras, and Heliogabalus celebrates his marriage with Hierocles.

It was this same Nero, already so often mentioned, that instituted the Juvenalian feasts. Knights, senators, and ladies of the highest rank, were obliged to appear on the stage, after the example of the emperor, and to sing obscene songs, at the same time imitating the gestures of the clowns. For the banquet of Tigellinus, on the lake of Agrippa, houses were erected on the shore, where the most illustrious females of Rome were placed opposite to courtesans perfectly naked! At the approach of night all was illuminated, that, the veil of darkness being removed, the debauchees might gratify an additional sense.

Death formed an essential part of these festivities of the ancients. It was introduced as a contrast, and for the purpose of giving a zest to the pleasures of life. Gladiators, courtesans, and musicians, were all introduced to enliven the entertainment. A Roman, on quitting the arms of a strumpet, went to enjoy the spectacle of a wild beast quaffing human blood; after witnessing a prostitution, he amused himself with the convulsions of an expiring fellow-creature. What sort of a people must that have been who stationed disgrace both at the entrance and at the exit of life, and exhibited upon a stage the two great mysteries of nature, to dishonor at once the whole work of God?

315

The slaves who cultivated the earth were constantly chained by the foot, and the only nourishment allowed them consisted of a little bread, with salt and water. At night they were confined in subterraneous dungeons, which had no air but what they received through an aperture in the roof. There was a law that prohibited the killing of African lions, which were reserved for the Roman shows. A peasant who would have defended his life against one of those animals would have been severely punished. When an unfortunate wretch perished in the arena, torn by a panther or gored by the horns of a stag, persons afflicted with certain diseases ran to bathe themselves in his blood and to lick it with their eager lips. Caligula wished that the whole Roman people had but one head, that he might strike it off with a single blow. The same emperor fed the lions intended for the games of the circus with human flesh; and Nero was on the point of compelling an Egyptian remarkable for his voracity to devour living people. Titus, by way of celebrating his father's birthday, delivered up three thousand Jews to be devoured by wild beasts. Tiberius was advised to put to death one of his old friends who was languishing in prison. "I am not yet reconciled to him," replied the tyrant,—an expression which breathes the true spirit of Rome. It was a common thing to slaughter five, six, ten, twenty thousand persons of all ranks, of both sexes, of every age, on the mere suspicion of the emperor; and the relatives of the victims adorned their houses with garlands, kissed the hands of the *god,* and assisted at his entertainments. The daughter of Sejanus, only nine years old, who said that she would do so no more, and who requested to be scourged, when on her way to prison was violated by the executioner before he strangled her—so great was the respect paid by these virtuous Romans to the laws. During the reign of Claudius was exhibited the spectacle (and Tacitus mentions it as a fine sight) of nineteen thousand men slaughtering one another on the lake Fucinus for the amusement of the Roman populace. The combatants, before engaging in the bloody work saluted the emperor with these words, *Ave imperator, morituri te salutant!* "Hail, Cæsar! those who are about to die salute thee!"—an expression not less base than impressive.

316

Francois René de Chateaubriand

It was the total extinction of all moral feeling which inspired the Romans with that indifference in regard to death which has been so foolishly admired. Suicide is always common among a people of corrupt morals. Man, reduced to the instinct of the brute, dies with the same unconcern. We shall say nothing of the other vices of the Romans: of infanticide, authorized by a law of Romulus and confirmed by the Twelve Tables, or of the sordid avarice of that renowned people. Scaptius lent a sum of money to the senate of Salamis, which being unable to repay it at the stipulated time, he kept the assembly besieged by armed men till several of the members dies with hunger. Brutus, the Stoic, being connected in some way with this extortioner, interested himself in his behalf with Cicero, who could not restrain his indignation at the circumstance.

If therefore the Romans sank into slavery, their morals were the cause of it. It is baseness that first produces tyranny, and by a natural reaction tyranny afterward prolongs that baseness. Let us no more complain of the present state of society; the most corrupt people of modern times is a people of sages in comparison with the pagan nations.

If we could for a moment suppose that the political order of the ancients was more excellent than ours, still their *moral* order could not be compared to that which Christianity has produced among us; and, as morality is after all the basis of every social institution, never while we are Christians shall we sink into such depths of depravity as the ancients.

When at Rome and in Greece the political ties were broken, what restraint was left for men? Could the worship of so many infamous divinities preserve those morals which were no longer supported by the laws? So far from checking the corruption, this worship became one of its most powerful agents. By an excess of evil which makes us shudder, the idea of the existence of the Deity, which tends to the maintenance of virtue among men, encouraged vice among the pagans, and seemed to eternize guilt by imparting to it a principle of everlasting duration.

We have traditions of the wickedness of men and of the dreadful catastrophes which have never failed to follow the corruption of manners. May we not suppose that God has so

317

combined the physical and moral order of the universe that a subversion of the latter necessarily occasions a change in the former, and that great crimes naturally produce great revolutions? The mind acts upon the body in an inexplicable manner, and man is perhaps the mind of the great body of the universe. How much this would simplify nature, and how prodigiously it would enlarge the sphere of man! It would also be a key to the explanation of miracles, which would then fall into the ordinary course of things. Let deluges, conflagrations, the overthrow of states, have their secret causes in the vices and virtues of man; let guilt and its punishment be the weights placed in the two scales of the moral and physical balance of the world: the correspondence would be admirable, and would make but one whole of a creation which at the first view appears to be double.

It may be, then, that the corruption of the Roman empire drew forth from the recesses of their deserts the barbarians, who, unconscious of the secret commission that was given them to destroy, instinctively denominated themselves *the scourge of God.* What would have become of the world if the great ark of Christianity had not saved the remnant of the human race from this new deluge? What chance would have been left for posterity? Where would the light of knowledge have been preserved?

The priests of polytheism did not form a body of learned men, except in Persia and Egypt; but the magi and the Egyptian priests, who, be it remarked, never communicated their knowledge to the vulgar, no longer existed as bodies at the time of the invasion of the barbarians. As for the philosophic sects of Athens and Alexandria, they were confined almost entirely to those two cities, and consisted at the utmost of a few hundred rhetoricians who might have been massacred with the rest of the inhabitants.

Among the ancients we find no zeal for making converts, no ardor for diffusing instruction, no retirement to the desert, there to live with God and to cultivate and preserve the sciences. What priest of Jupiter would have gone forth to arrest Attila in his way? What pagan pontiff would have persuaded an Alaric to withdraw his troops from Rome? The barbarians who overran the empire were already half-christianized; but, marching as they were under the bloody banner of the Scandinavian or Tartar god,—meeting in their way no force of religious sentiment which would compel them to respect existing institutions, nor any solidly-established morals, which had only begun to be formed among the Romans under the influence of Christianity,—it cannot be doubted that they would have destroyed all before them. Such, indeed, was the design of Alaric. "I feel within me," says that barbarous monarch, "something that impels me to burn the city of Rome." We behold here a man elevated upon ruins and exhibiting the proportions of a giant.

Of the different nations that invaded the empire, the Goths seem to have been the least tinctured with the spirit of devastation. Theodoric, the conqueror of Odoacer, was a great prince, but then he was a Christian. Boetius, his prime minister, was also a Christian and a scholar. This baffles all conjectures. What would the Goths have done had they been *idolaters?* They would doubtless have overthrown every thing, like the other barbarians. They indeed sank very rapidly into a state of corruption; and if, instead of adoring Christ, they had worshipped Flora, Venus, and Bacchus, what a horrid medley would have resulted from the sanguinary religion of Odin and the obscure fables of Greece!

Polytheism was so little calculated for the work of conservation that it could not sustain itself, and, on falling into ruins on every side, Maximinus wished to invest it with the Christian forms by way of propping up the tottering fabric. He placed in each province a priest who corresponded to the bishop, a high-pontiff who represented the metropolitan. Julian founded pagan convents, and made the ministers of Baal preach in their temples. This arrangement, copied from Christianity, soon disappeared, because it was not upheld by the spirit of virtue nor founded on morality.

The only class amid the conquered nations whom the barbarians respected was that of the priests and monks. The monasteries became so many asylums where the sacred flame of science was preserved together with the Greek and Latin languages. The most illustrious citizens of Rome and Athens, having sought a refuge in the Christian priesthood, thus escaped death or slavery, to which they would have been doomed with the rest of the people.

We may form some conception of the abyss into which we should at this day be plunged, if the barbarians had overrun the world during the prevalence of polytheism, by the present state of those nations in which Christianity is extinguished. We should all be Turkish slaves, or something still worse; for Mohammedanism has at least a tincture of morality borrowed from the Christian religion, of which it is, after all, but a very wretched excrescence. But, as the first Ismael was an enemy of Jacob of old, so the second is the persecutor of the modern Israel.

It is, therefore, highly probable that, but for Christianity, the wreck of society and of learning would have been complete. It is impossible to calculate how many ages would have been necessary for mankind to emerge from the ignorance and gross barbarism in which they would have been ingulfed. Nothing less than an immense body of recluses scattered over three quarters of the globe, and laboring in concert for the promotion of the same object, was requisite to preserve those sparks which have rekindled the torch of science among the moderns. Once more, we repeat it, no order of paganism, either political, philosophical, or religious, could have rendered this inestimable service in the absence of Christianity. The writings of the ancients, by being dispersed in the monasteries, partly escaped the ravages of the Goths. Finally, polytheism was not, like Christianity, a kind of *lettered* religion, if we may be allowed the expression; because it did not, like the latter, combine metaphysics and ethics with religious dogmas. The necessity which the Christian clergy were under of publishing books themselves, either to propagate the faith or to confute heresy, powerfully contributed to the preservation and the revival of learning.

Under every imaginable hypothesis we shall invariably find that the gospel has been a barrier to the destruction of society; for, supposing that it had never appeared upon earth, and, on the other hand, that the barbarians had continued in their forests, the Roman world, sinking more and more in its corruption, would have been menaced with a frightful dissolution.

Francois René de Chateaubriand

Would the slaves have revolted? The slaves were as depraved as their masters; they shared the same pleasures and the same disgrace; they had the same religion,—a religion of the passions,—which destroyed every hope of a change in the principles of morality. Science made no further progress; its movement was retrograde; the arts declined. Philosophy served but to propagate a species of impiety, which, without leading to a destruction of the idols, produced the crimes and calamities of atheism among the great, while it left to the vulgar those of superstition. Did mankind improve because Nero ceased to believe in the deities of the Capitol and contemptuously defiled the statues of the gods?

Tacitus asserts that a regard for morality still existed in the remote provinces; but these provinces were beginning to be indoctrinated in the Christian faith, and we are reasoning in the supposition that Christianity was not known, and that the barbarians had not quitted their deserts. As for the Roman armies, which would probably have dismembered the empire, the soldiers were as corrupt as the rest of the citizens, and would have been much more depraved had they not been recruited by Goths and Germans. All that we can possibly conjecture is that, after protracted civil wars and a general commotion which might have lasted several centuries, the human race would have been reduced to a few individuals wandering among ruins. But what a length of time would have been requisite for this new stock to put forth its branches! What a series of ages must have revolved before the sciences, lost or forgotten, could have revived, and in what an infant state would society be at the present day!

As Christianity preserved society from total destruction by converting the barbarians and by collecting the wrecks of civilization and the arts, so it would have saved the Roman world from its own corruption, had not the latter fallen beneath foreign arms. Religion alone can renew the original energy of a nation. That of the Saviour had already laid the moral foundation. The ancients permitted infanticide, and the dissolution of the marriage tie, which is, in fact, the first bond of society; their probity and justice were relative things; they extended not beyond the limits of their native land; the people collectively had different principles from the individual citizen; modesty and humanity were not ranked among the virtues; the most numerous class of the community was composed of slaves; and the state was incessantly fluctuating between popular anarchy and despotism. Such were the mischiefs to which Christianity applied an infallible remedy, as she has proved, by delivering modern societies from the same evils. The very excess of Christian austerity in the first ages was necessary. It was requisite that there should be martyrs of chastity when there were public prostitutions,—penitents covered with sackcloth and ashes when the law authorized the grossest violations of morality,—heroes of charity when there were monsters of barbarity; finally, to wean a whole degenerate people from the disgraceful combats of the circus and the arena, it was requisite that religion should have her champions and her exhibitions, if we may so express it, in the deserts of Thebais.

Jesus Christ may therefore, with strict truth, be denominated, in a material sense, that *Saviour of the World* which he is in a spiritual sense. His career on earth was, even humanly speaking, the most important event that ever occurred among men, since the regeneration of society commenced only with the proclamation of the gospel. The precise time of his advent is truly remarkable. A little earlier, his morality would not have been absolutely necessary, for the nations were still upheld by their ancient laws; a little later, that divine Messiah would have appeared after the general wreck of society. We boast of our philosophy at the present day; but, most assuredly, the levity with which we treat the institutions of Christianity is any thing but philosophical. The gospel has changed mankind in every respect and enabled it to take an immense step toward perfection. If you consider it as a grand religious institution, which has regenerated the human race, then all the petty objections, all the cavils of impiety, fall to the ground. It is certain that the pagan nations were in a kind of moral infancy in comparison to what we are at the present day. A few striking acts of justice, exhibited by a few of the ancients, are not sufficient to shake this truth or to change the general aspect of the case.

Christianity has unquestionably shed a new light upon mankind. It is the religion that is adapted to a nation matured

322

by time. It is, if we may venture to use the expression, the religion congenial to the present age of the world, as the reign of types and emblems was suited to the cradle of Israel. In heaven it has placed one only God; on earth it has abolished slavery. On the other hand, if you consider its mysteries (as we have done) as the archetype of the laws of nature, you will find nothing in them revolting to a great mind. The truths of Christianity, so far from requiring the submission of reason, command, on the contrary, the most sublime exercise of that faculty.

This remark is so just, and Christianity, which has been characterized as the religion of barbarians, is so truly the religion of philosophers, that Plato may be said to have almost anticipated it. Not only the morality, but also the doctrine, of the disciple of Socrates bears a striking resemblance to that of the gospel. Dacier, his translator, sums them up in the following manner:—

"Plato proves that the *Word* arranged this universe and rendered it visible; that the knowledge of this Word leads to a happy life here below and procures felicity after death; that the soul is immortal; that the dead will rise again; that there will be a last judgment of the righteous and the wicked, where each will appear only with his virtues or his vices, which will be the cause of everlasting happiness or misery.

"Finally," says the learned translator, "Plato had so grand and so true a conception of supreme justice, and was so thoroughly acquainted with the depravity of men, that, according to him, if a man supremely just were to appear upon earth, he would be imprisoned, calumniated, scourged, and at length, *crucified,* by those who, though fraught with injustice, would nevertheless pass for righteous.

The detractors of Christianity place themselves in a false position, which it is scarcely possible for them not to perceive. If they assert that this religion originated among the Goths and Vandals, it is an easy matter to prove that the schools of Greece had very clear notions of the Christian tenets. If they maintain, on the contrary, that the doctrine of the gospel is but the *philosophical* teaching of the ancients, why then do our *philosophers* reject it? Even they who discover in Christianity nothing more than ancient allegories of the heavens, the planets, and the signs of the zodiac, by no means divest that religion of all its grandeur. It would still appear profound and magnificent in its mysteries, ancient and sacred in its traditions, which in this way would be traceable to the infancy of the world. How extraordinary that all the researches of infidels cannot discover in Christianity any thing stamped with the character of littleness or mediocrity!

With respect to the *morality* of the gospel, its beauty is universally admitted: the more it is known and practised, the more will the eyes of men be opened to their real happiness and their true interest. Political science is extremely circumscribed. The highest degree of perfection which it can attain is the representative system,—the offspring, as we have shown, of Christianity. But a religion whose precepts form a code of morality and virtue is an institution capable of supplying every want, and of becoming, in the hands of saints and sages, a universal means of felicity. The time may perhaps come when the mere form of government, excepting despotism, will be a matter of indifference among men, who will attach themselves more particularly to those simple, moral, and religious laws which constitute the permanent basis of society and of all good government.

Those who reason about the excellence of antiquity, and would fain persuade us to revive its institutions, forget that social order is not, neither can it be, what it formerly was. In the absence of a great moral power, a great coercive power is at least necessary among men. In the ancient republics, the greater part of the population, as is well known, were slaves; the man who cultivated the earth belonged to another man: there were *people*, but there were no *nations*.

Polytheism, which is defective in every respect as a religious system, might therefore have been adapted to that imperfect state of society, because each master was a kind of absolute magistrate, whose rigid despotism kept the slave within the bounds of duty and compensated by chains for the deficiency of the moral religious force. Paganism, not possessing sufficient excellence to render the poor man virtuous, was obliged to let him be treated as a malefactor.

Francois René de Chateaubriand

But, in the present order of things, how could you restrain an immense multitude of free peasants, far removed from the vigilance of the magistrate? how could you prevent the crimes of an independent populace, congregated in the suburbs of an extensive capital, if they did not believe in a religion which enjoins the practice of duty and virtue upon all the conditions of life? Destroy the influence of the gospel, and you must give to every village its police, its prisons, its executioners. If, by an impossibility, the impure altars of paganism were ever re-established among modern nations,—if, in a society where slavery is abolished, the worship of *Mercury the robber* and *Venus the prostitute* were to be introduced,—there would soon be a total extinction of the human race.

Here lies the error of those who commend polytheism for having separated the moral from the religious force, and at the same time censure Christianity for having adopted a contrary system. They perceive not that paganism, having to deal with an immense nation of slaves, was consequently afraid of enlightening the human race; that it gave every encouragement to the sensual part of man, and entirely neglected the cultivation of the soul. Christianity, on the contrary, meditating the destruction of slavery, held up to man the dignity of his nature, and inculcated the precepts of reason and virtue. It may be affirmed that the doctrine of the gospel is the doctrine of a free people, from this single circumstance:—that it combines morality with religion.

It is high time to be alarmed at the state in which we have been living for some years past. Think of the generation now springing up in our towns and provinces; of all those children who, born during the revolution, have never heard any thing of God, nor of the immortality of their souls, nor of the punishments or rewards that await them in a future life: think what may one day become of such a generation if a remedy be not speedily applied to the evil. The most alarming symptoms already manifest themselves: we see the age of innocence sullied with many crimes. Let philosophy, which, after all, cannot penetrate among the poor, be content to dwell in the mansions of the rich, and leave the people in general to the care of religion; or, rather, let philosophy, with a more enlightened zeal and with a spirit more worthy of her name, remove those barriers which she proposed to place between man and his Creator.

Let us support our last conclusions with authorities which philosophy will not be inclined to suspect.

"A little philosophy," says Bacon, "withdraws us from religion, but a good deal of philosophy brings us back to it again: nobody denies the existence of God, excepting the man who has reason to wish that there were none."

"To say that religion is not a restraint," observes Montesquieu, "because it does not always restrain, is equally absurd as to say that the civil laws also are not a deterring agent. . . . The question is not to ascertain whether it would be better for a certain individual or a certain nation to have no religion than to abuse that which they have; but to know which is the least evil,—that religion should be sometimes abused, or that there should be none at all among mankind.

"The history of Sabbaco," says that eminent writer, whom we continue to quote, "is admirable. The god of Thebes appeared to him in a dream, and ordered him to put to death all the priests of Egypt. He conceived that it was not pleasing to the gods that he should reign any longer, since they enjoined things so contrary to their ordinary pleasures, and accordingly he retired into Ethiopia."

Finally, Rousseau exclaims, "Avoid those who, under the pretence of explaining nature, sow mischievous doctrines in the hearts of men, and whose apparent skepticism is a hundred times more positive and dogmatic than the decided tone of their adversaries. Under the arrogant pretext that they alone are enlightened, true, and sincere, they imperiously subject us to their peremptory decisions, and presume to give us, as the general principles of things, the unintelligible systems which they have erected in their imaginations. Overthrowing, destroying, trampling under foot all that is respected by men, they bereave the afflicted of the last consolation in their misery; they take from the rich and powerful the only curb of their passions; they eradicate from the heart the remorse consequent on guilt, the hopes inspired by virtue; and still they boast of

326

being the benefactors of the human race. Never, say they, can truth be hurtful to men. I think so too; and this, in my opinion, is a strong proof that what they teach is not the truth.

"One of the most common sophisms with the philosophic party is to contrast a supposed nation of good philosophers with one of bad Christians; as if it were easier to form a people of genuine philosophers than a people of genuine Christians. I know not if, among individuals, one of these characters is more easy to be found than the other; but this I know, that when we come to talk of nations, we must suppose such as will make a bad use of philosophy without religion, just as ours abuses religion without philosophy; and this seems to me to make a material alteration in the state of the question.

"It is an easy matter to make a parade of fine maxims in books; but the question is whether they agree with, and necessarily flow from, the principles of the writer. So far, this has not been the case. It also remians to be seen whether philosophy, at its ease and upon the throne, would be capable of controlling the love of glory, the selfishness, the ambition, the little passions of men, and *whether it would practise that engaging humanity which, with pen in hand, it so highly commends.*

"*According to principles, philosophy can do no good which religion would not far surpass; and religion does much that philosophy cannot accomplish.*

"Our modern governments are unquestionably indebted to Christianity for a better-established authority and for less frequent revolutions. It has made them less sanguinary, as is proved by comparing them with the governments of antiquity. Religion, becoming better known and discarding fanaticism, imparted a greater mildness to Christian manners. This change was not the effect of letters; for the spirit of humanity has not been the more respected in those countries which could boast of their superior knowledge. The cruelties of the Athenians, the Egyptians, the Roman emperors, the Chinese, attest this truth. What numberless works of mercy have been produced by the gospel!"

As for us, we are convinced that Christianity will rise triumphant from the dreadful trial by which it has just been purified. What gives us this assurance is that it stands the test of reason perfectly, and the more we examine it the more we discover its profound truth. Its mysteries explain man and nature; its works corroborate its precepts; its charity in a thousand forms has replaced the cruelty of the ancients. Without losing any thing of the pomp of antiquity, its ceremonies give greater satisfaction to the heart and the imagination. We are indebted to it for every thing,—letters, sciences, agriculture, and the fine arts; it connects morality with religion, and man with God; Jesus Christ, the saviour of moral man, is also the saviour of physical man. His coming may be considered as an advent the most important and most felicitous, designed to counterbalance the deluge of barbarism and the total corruption of manners. Did we even reject the supernatural evidences of Christianity, there would still remain in its sublime morality, in the immensity of its benefits, and in the beauty of its worship, sufficient proof of its being the most divine and the purest religion ever practised by men.

"With those who have an aversion for religion," says *Pascal*, "you must begin with demonstrating that it is not contradictory to reason; next show that it is venerable, and inspire them with respect for it; afterward exhibit it in an amiable light, and excite a wish that it were true; then let it appear by incontestable proofs that it is true; and, lastly, prove its antiquity and holiness by its grandeur and sublimity."

Such is the plan which that great man marked out, and which we have endeavored to pursue. Though we have not employed the arguments usually advanced by the apologists of Christianity, we have arrived by a different chain of reasoning at the same conclusion, which we present as the result of this work.

Christianity is perfect; men are imperfect.

Now, a perfect consequence cannot spring from an imperfect principle.

Christianity, therefore, is not the work of men.

If Christianity is not the work of men, it can have come from none but God.

If it came from God, men cannot have acquired a knowledge of it but by revelation.

Therefore, Christianity is a revealed religion.

Orestes Augustus Brownson
1803-1876

Orestes Augustus Brownson was born in Stockton, Vermont in 1803. At the age of nineteen he joined the Presbyterian Church, thus beginning a religious journey that led him successively into the Universalist, the Unitarian and finally the Catholic Church. Between his Unitarian and Catholic stages, Brownson tried to establish his own "Church of the Future." He was active within each group as a preacher and writer. As a Catholic (he entered the Church in 1864 and remained a member until his death in 1876), Brownson is best known for his journalism. He sought to interpret the major issues of his time in the light of the Catholic intellectual tradition and was particularly interested in exploring the role that Christianity plays in shaping a civilization. Brownson tried to find the best expression of the middle way between what so often appear as irreconcilable opposites, such as church and state, authority and freedom, conservatism and liberalism. His own intellectual history is, in many ways, an example of the human dialectical journey in search of a synthesis.

The American Republic: Its Constitution, Tendencies, and Destiny, *appeared in 1866, one year after the close of the War Between the States. The chapter that we have selected for the reading below, entitled* Political Tendencies, *contains a very interesting interpretation of the War Between the States. One might assume that Brownson, being a Northerner, would natu-*

rally stress the victory theme and fault the South for its tradition of slavery. Brownson saw much more than two armies fighting a war. He had the unusual ability to get beyond the winner-loser mentality and to perceive two unhealthy philosophies of democracy which were locked in struggle. The one, which he called personal or popular democracy, was the vision of the southern states; the other, the socialist or humanitarian democracy, was the force behind the northern states. The former, while protecting the rights of the individual, denied the solidarity of mankind. The latter forgot the rights of the individual in its effort to insist on human solidarity. For Brownson, there was no winner, no loser; in a sense, both sides lost and won something. If the war did anything, it clarified that neither pure socialism nor pure individualism is compatible with true American democracy, and that the slaveholder and the abolitionist are equally barbaric.

It is easy to understand how Brownson's writing must have evoked controversy during his lifetime. He had the ability to get behind catchwords and slogans and to expose the dangers that lie in the naive problem-solving approach to human questions. He challenged his readers to use their intelligence vigorously in search of the richest possible resolution of an issue and to avoid the laziness that allows one simply to take sides. Brownson insisted, above all, that a people should establish its convictions on solid, well-critiqued principles.

As the twentieth century enters its final years, it is obvious that the American society has not yet worked out a healthy balance between the extremes of individualism and socialism. Both extremes have their strong advocates in America; individualism seems to be the more dominant of the two. Though each serves at least to keep the other in check, both stand as obstacles to the flowering of democracy. Brownson recognized this as early as 1866. His insights on the tension between individualism and socialism can be of service in trying to understand the process that America is presently experiencing.

THE AMERICAN REPUBLIC

T he most marked political tendency of the American people has been, since 1825, to interpret their government as a pure and simple democracy, and to shift it from a territorial to a purely popular basis, or from the people as the state, inseparably united to the national territory or domain, to the people as simply population, either as individuals or as the race. Their tendency has unconsciously, therefore, been to change their constitution from a republican to a despotic, or from a civilized to a barbaric constitution.

The American constitution is democratic, in the sense that the people are sovereign; that all laws and public acts run in their name; that the rulers are elected by them, and are responsible to them; but they are the people territorially constituted and fixed to the soil, constituting what Mr. Disraeli, with more propriety perhaps than he thinks, calls a "territorial democracy." To this territorial democracy, the real American democracy, stand opposed two other democracies—the one personal and the other humanitarian—each alike hostile to civilization, and tending to destroy the state, and capable of sustaining government only on principles common to all despotisms.

In every man there is a natural craving for personal freedom and unrestrained action—a strong desire to be himself, not another—to be his own master, to go when and where he pleases, to do what he chooses, to take what he wants, wherever he can find it, and to keep what he takes. It is strong in all nomadic tribes, who are at once pastoral and predatory, and is seldom weak in our bold frontier-men, too often real "border ruffians." It takes different forms in different stages of social development, but it everywhere identifies liberty with power.

Restricted in its enjoyment to one man, it makes him chief, chief of the family, the tribe, or the nation; extended in its enjoyment to the few, it founds an aristocracy, creates a nobility—for nobleman meant originally only freeman, as it does still with the Magyars; extended to the many, it founds personal democracy, a simple association of individuals, in which all are equally free and independent, and no restraint is imposed on any one's action, will, or inclination, without his own consent, express or constructive. This is the so-called Jeffersonian democracy, in which government has no powers but such as it derives from the consent of the governed, and is personal democracy or pure individualism—philosophically considered, pure egoism, which says, "I am God." Under this sort of democracy, based on popular, or rather individual sovereignty, expressed by politicians when they call the electoral people, half seriously, half mockingly, "the sovereigns," there obviously can be no state, no social rights or civil authority; there can be only a voluntary association, league, alliance, or confederation, in which individuals may freely act together as long as they find it pleasant, convenient, or useful, but from which they may separate or secede whenever they find it for their interest or their pleasure to do so. State sovereignty and secession are based on the same democratic principle applied to the several States of the Union instead of individuals.

The tendency to this sort of democracy has been strong in large sections of the American people from the first, and has been greatly strengthened by the general acceptance of the theory that government originates in compact. The full realization of this tendency, which, happily, is impracticable save in theory, would be to render every man independent alike of every other man and of society, with full right and power to make his own will prevail. This tendency was strongest in the slaveholding States, and especially, in those States, in the slaveholding class, the American imitation of the feudal nobility of mediæval Europe; and on this side the war just ended was, in its most general expression, a war in defence of personal democracy, or the sovereignty of the people individually, against the humanitarian democracy, represented by the abolitionists, and the territorial democracy, represented by the Government.

This personal democracy has been signally defeated in the defeat of the late confederacy, and can hardly again become strong enough to be dangerous.

But the humanitarian democracy, which scorns all geographical lines, effaces all in individualities, and professes to plant itself on humanity alone, has acquired by the war new strength, and is not without menace to our future. The solidarity of the race, which is the condition of all human life, founds, as we have seen, society, and creates what are called social rights, the rights alike of society in regard to individuals, and of individuals in regard to society. Territorial divisions or circumscriptions found particular societies, states, or nations; yet as the race is one, and all its members live by communion with God through it and by communion one with another, these particular states or nations are never absolutely independent of each other, but bound together by the solidarity of the race, so that there is a real solidarity of nations as well as of individuals—the truth underlying Kossuth's famous declaration of "the solidarity of peoples."

The solidarity of nations is the basis of international law, binding on every particular nation, and which every civilized nation recognizes, and enforces on its own subjects or citizens, through its own courts, as an integral part of its own municipal or national law. The personal or individual right is therefore restricted by the rights of society, and the rights of the particular society or nation are limited by international law, or the rights of universal society—the truth the ex-governor of Hungary overlooked. The grand error of Gentilism was in denying the unity and therefore the solidarity of the race, involved in its denial or misconception of the unity of God. It therefore was never able to assign any solid basis to international law, and gave it only a conventional or customary authority, thus leaving the *jus gentium*, which it recognized indeed, without any real foundation in the constitution of things, or authority in the real world. Its real basis is in the solidarity of the race, which has its basis in the unity of God, not the dead or abstract unity asserted by the old Eleatics, the Neo-Platonists, or the modern Unitarians, but the living unity consisting in the threefold relation in the Divine Essence, of Father, Son, and Holy Ghost, as asserted by Christian revelation, and believed, more or less intelligently, by all Christendom.

The tendency in the Southern States has been to overlook the social basis of the state, or the rights of society founded on the solidarity of the race, and to make all rights and powers personal, or individual; and as only the white race has been able to assert and maintain its personal freedom, only men of that race are held to have the right to be free. Hence the people of those States felt no scruple in holding the black or colored race as slaves. Liberty, said they, is the right only of those who have the ability to assert and maintain it. Let the negro prove that he has this ability by asserting and maintaining his freedom and he will prove his right to be free, and that it is a gross outrage, a manifest injustice, to enslave him; but, till then, let him be my servant, which is best for him and for me. Why ask me to free him? I shall by doing so only change the form of his servitude. Why appeal to *me*? Am I my brother's keeper? Nay, is he my brother? Is this negro, more like an ape or a baboon than a human being, of the same race with myself? I believe it not. But in some instances, at least, my dear slaveholder, your slave is literally your brother, and sometimes even your son, born of your own daughter. The tendency of the Southern democrat was to deny the unity of the race, as well as all obligations of society to protect the weak and helpless, and therefore all true civil society.

At the North there has been, and is even yet, an opposite tendency—a tendency to exaggerate the social element, to overlook the territorial basis of the state, and to disregard the rights of individuals. This tendency has been and is strong in the people called abolitionists. The American abolitionist is so engrossed with the unity that he loses the solidarity of the race, which supposes unity of race and multiplicity of individuals; and fails to see any thing legitimate and authoritative in geographical divisions or territorial circumscriptions. Back of these, back of individuals, he sees humanity, superior to individuals, superior to states, governments, and laws, and holds that he may trample on them all or give them to the winds at the call of humanity or "the higher law." The principle on which he acts is as indefensible as the personal or egoistical democracy of the slaveholders and their sympathizers. Were his socialistic tendency to become exclusive and realized, it would found in the name of humanity a complete social despotism, which, proving impracticable from its very generality, would break up in anarchy, in which might makes right, as in the slaveholder's democracy.

The abolitionists, in supporting themselves on humanity in its generality, regardless of individual and territorial rights, can recognize no state, no civil authority, and therefore are as much out of the order of civilization, and as much in that of barbarism, as is the slaveholder himself. Wendell Phillips is as far removed from true Christian civilization as was John D. Calhoun, and William Lloyd Garrison is as much of a barbarian and despot in principle and tendency as Jefferson Davis. Hence the great body of the people in the non-slaveholding States, wedded to American democracy as they were and are, could never, as much as they detested slavery, be induced to make common cause with the abolitionists, and their apparent union in the late civil war was accidental, simply owing to the fact that for the time the social democracy and the territorial coincided, or had the same enemy. The great body of the loyal people instinctively felt that pure socialism is as incompatible with American democracy as pure individualism; and the abolitionists are well aware that slavery has been abolished, not for humanitarian or socialistic reasons, but really for reasons of state, in order to save the territorial democracy. The territorial democracy would not unite to eliminate even so barbaric an element as slavery, till the rebellion gave them the constitutional right to abolish it; and even then so scrupulous were they, that they demanded a constitutional amendment, so as to be able to make clean work of it, without any blow to individual or State rights.

The abolitionists were right in opposing slavery, but not in demanding its abolition on humanitarian or socialistic grounds. Slavery is really a barbaric element, and is in direct antagonism to American civilization. The whole force of the national life opposes it, and must finally eliminate it, or become itself extinct; and it is no mean proof of their utter want of sympathy with all the living forces of modern civilization, that the leading

335

men of the South and their prominent friends at the North really persuaded themselves that with cotton, rice, and tobacco, they could effectually resist the anti-slavery movement, and perpetuate their barbaric democracy. They studied the classics, they admired Greece and Rome, and imagined that those nations became great by slavery, instead of being great even in spite of slavery. They failed to take into the account the fact that when Greece and Rome were in the zenith of their glory, all contemporary nations were also slaveholding nations, and that if they were the greatest and most highly civilized nations of their times, they were not fitted to be the greatest and most highly civilized nations of all times. They failed also to perceive that, if the Græco-Roman republic did not include the whole territorial people in the political people it yet recognized both the social and the territorial foundation of the state, and never attempted to rest it on pure individualism; they forgot, too, that Greece and Rome both fell, and fell precisely through internal weakness caused by the barbarism within, not through the force of the barbarism beyond their frontiers. The world has changed since the time when ten thousand of his slaves were sacrificed as a religious offering to the manes of a single Roman master. The infusion of the Christian dogma of the unity and solidarity of the race into the belief, the life, the laws, the jurisprudence of all civilized nations, has doomed slavery and every species of barbarism; but this our slaveholding countrymen saw not.

It rarely happens that in any controversy, individual or national, the real issue is distinctly presented, or the precise question in debate is clearly and distinctly understood by either party. Slavery was only incidentally involved in the late war. The war was occasioned by the collision of two extreme parties; but it was itself a war between civilization and barbarism, primarily between the territorial democracy and the personal democracy, and in reality, on the part of the nation, as much a war against the socialism of the abolitionist as against the individualism of the slaveholder. Yet the victory, though complete over the former, is only half won over the latter, for it has left the humanitarian democracy standing, and perhaps for the moment stronger than ever. The socialistic democracy was enlisted by the territorial, not to strengthen the government at home, as it imagines, for that it did not do, and could not do, since the national instinct was even more opposed to it than to the personal democracy; but under its anti-slavery aspect, to soften the hostility of foreign powers, and ward off foreign intervention, which was seriously threatened. The populations of Europe, especially of France and England, were decidedly anti-slavery, and if the war here appeared to them a war, not solely for the unity of the nation and the integrity of its domain, as it really was, in which they took and could take no interest, but a war for the abolition of slavery, their governments would not venture to intervene. This was the only consideration that weighed with Mr. Lincoln, as he himself assured the author, and induced him to issue his Emancipation Proclamation; and Europe rejoices in our victory over the rebellion only so far as it has liberated the slaves, and honors the late President only as their supposed liberator, not as the preserver of the unity and integrity of the nation. This is natural enough abroad, and proves the wisdom of the anti-slavery policy of the government, which had become absolutely necessary to save the Republic long before it was adopted; yet it is not as the emancipator of some two or three millions of slaves that the American patriot cherishes the memory of Abraham Lincoln, but, aided by the loyal people, generals of rare merit, and troops of unsurpassed bravery and endurance, as the saviour of the American state, and the protector of modern civilization. His anti-slavery policy served this end, and therefore was wise, but he adopted it with the greatest possible reluctance.

There were greater issues in the late war than negro slavery or negro freedom. That was only an incidental issue, as the really great men of the Confederacy felt, who to save their cause were willing themselves at last to free and arm their own negroes, and perhaps were willing to do it even at first. This fact alone proves that they had, or believed they had, a far more important cause than the preservation of negro slavery. They fought for personal democracy, under the form of State sovereignty, against social democracy; for personal freedom and independence against social or humanitarian despotism; and so far their cause was as good as that against which they took up arms; and if they had or could have fought against that, without fighting at the same time against the territorial, the real American, the only civilized democracy, they would have succeeded. It is not socialism nor abolitionism that has won; nor is it the North that has conquered. The Union itself has won no victories over the South, and it is both historically and legally false to say that the South has been subjugated. The Union has preserved itself and American civilization, alike for North and South, East and West. The armies that so often met in the shock of battle were not drawn up respectively by the North and the South, but by two rival democracies, to decide which of the two should rule the future. They were the armies of two mutually antagonistic systems, and neither army was clearly and distinctly conscious of the cause for which it was shedding its blood; each obeyed instinctively a power stronger than itself, and which at best it but dimly discerned. On both sides the cause was broader and deeper than negro slavery, and neither the pro-slavery men nor the abolitionists have won. The territorial democracy alone has won, and won what will prove to be a final victory over the purely personal democracy, which had its chief seat in the Southern States, though by no means confined to them. The danger to American democracy from that quarter is forever removed, and democracy *à la* Rousseau has received a terrible defeat throughout the world, though as yet it is far from being aware of it.

But in this world victories are never complete. The socialistic democracy claims the victory which has been really won by the territorial democracy, as if it had been socialism, not patriotism, that fired the hearts and nerved the arms of the brave men led by McClellan, Grant, and Sherman. The humanitarians are more dangerous in principle than the egoists, for they have the appearance of building on a broader and deeper foundation, of being more Christian, more philosophic, more generous and philanthropic; but Satan is never more successful than under the guise of an angel of light. His favorite guise in modern times is that of philanthropy. He is a genuine humanitarian, and aims to persuade the world that humanitarianism is Christianity, and that man is God; that the soft and charming sentiment of philanthropy is real Christian charity; and he dupes both individuals and nations, and makes them do his work, when they believe they are earnestly and most successfully doing the work of God. Your leading abolitionists are as much affected by satanophany as your leading confederates, nor are they one whit more philosophical or less sophistical. The one loses the race, the other the individual, and neither has learned to apply practically that fundamental truth that there is never the general without the particular, nor the particular without the general, the race without individuals, nor individuals without the race. The whole race was in Adam, and fell in him, as we are taught by the doctrine of original sin, or the sin of the race, and Adam was an individual, as we are taught in the fact that original sin was in him actual or personal sin.

The humanitarian is carried away by a vague generality, and loses men in humanity, sacrifices the rights of men in a vain endeavor to secure the rights of man, as your Calvinist or his brother Jansenist sacrifices the rights of nature in order to secure the freeedom of grace. Yesterday he agitated for the abolition of slavery, to-day he agitates for negro suffrage, negro equality, and announces that when he has secured that he will agitate for female suffrage and the equality of the sexes, forgetting or ignorant that the relation of equality subsists only between individuals of the same sex; that God made the man the head of the woman, and the woman for the man, not the man for the woman. Having obliterated all distinction of sex in politics, in social, industrial, and domestic arrangements, he must go farther, and agitate for equality of property. But since property, if recognized at all, will be unequally acquired and distributed, he must go farther still, and agitate for the total abolition of property, as an injustice, a grievous wrong, a theft, with M. Proudhon, or the Englishman Godwin. It is unjust that one should have what another wants, or even more than another. What right have you to ride in your coach or astride your spirited barb while I am forced to trudge on foot? Nor can our humanitarian stop there. Individuals are, and as long as there are individuals will be, unequal: some are handsomer and some are uglier, some wiser or sillier, more or less gifted, stronger or weaker, taller or shorter, stouter or thinner than others, and therefore some have natural advantages which others have not. There is inequality, therefore injustice, which can be remedied only by the abolition of all individualities, and the reduction of all individuals to the race, or humanity, man in general. He can find no limit to his agitation this side of vague generality, which is no reality, but a pure nullity, for he respects no territorial or individual circumscriptions, and must regard creation itself as a blunder. This is not fancy, for he has gone very nearly as far as it is here shown, if logical, he must go.

The danger now is that the Union victory will, at home and abroad, be interpreted as a victory won in the interest of social or humanitarian democracy. It was because they regarded the war waged on the side of the Union as waged in the interest of this terrible democracy, that our bishops and clergy sympathized so little with the Government in prosecuting it; not, as some imagined, because they were disloyal, hostile to American or territorial democracy, or not heartily in favor of freedom for all men, whatever their race or complexion. They had no wish to see slavery prolonged, the evils of which they, better than any other class of men, knew, and more deeply deplored; none would have regretted more than they to have seen the Union broken up; but they held the socialistic or humanitarian democracy represented by Northern abolitionists as hostile alike to the Church and to civilization. For the same reason that they were backward or reserved in their sympathy, all the humanitarian sects at home and abroad were forward and even ostentatious in theirs. The Catholics feared the war might result in encouraging *La République démocratique et sociale;* the humanitarian sects trusted that it would. If the victory of the Union should turn out to be a victory for the humanitarian democracy, the civilized world will have no reason to applaud it.

That there is some danger that for a time the victory will be taken as a victory for humanitarianism or socialism, it would be idle to deny. It is so taken now, and the humanitarian party throughout the world are in ecstasies over it. The party claim it. The European Socialists and Red Republicans applaud it, and the Mazzinis and the Garibaldis inflict on us the deep humiliation of their congratulations. A cause that can be approved by the revolutionary leaders of European Liberals must

340

be strangely misunderstood, or have in it some infamous element. It is no compliment to a nation to receive the congratulations of men who assert not only people-king, but people-God; and those Americans who are delighted with them are worse enemies to the American democracy than ever were Jefferson Davis and his fellow conspirators, and more contemptible, as the swindler is more contemptible than the highwayman.

But it is probable the humanitarians have reckoned without their host. Not they are the real victors. When the smoke of battle has cleared away, the victory, it will be seen, has been won by the Republic, and that that alone has triumphed. The abolitionists, in so far as they asserted the unity of the race and opposed slavery as a denial of that unity, have also won; but in so far as they denied the reality or authority of territorial and individual circumscriptions, followed a purely socialistic tendency, and sought to dissolve patriotism into a watery sentimentality called philanthropy, have in reality been crushingly defeated, as they will find when the late insurrectionary States are fully reconstructed. The Southern or egoistical democrats, so far as they denied the unity and solidarity of the race, the rights of society over individuals, and the equal rights of each and every individual in face of the state, or the obligations of society to protect the weak and help the helpless, have been also defeated; but so far as they asserted personal or individual rights which society neither gives nor can take away, and so far as they asserted, not State sovereignty, but State rights, held independently of the General government, and which limit its authority and sphere of action, they share in the victory, as the future will prove.

European Jacobins, revolutionists, conspiring openly or secretly against all legitimate authority, whether in Church or State, have no lot or part in the victory of the American people: not for them nor for men with their nefarious designs or mad dreams, have our brave soldiers fought, suffered, and bled for four years of the most terrible war in modern times, and against troops as brave and as well led as themselves; not for them has the country sacrificed a million of lives, and contracted a debt of four thousand millions of dollars, besides the waste and destruction that it will take years of peaceful industry to repair.

They and their barbaric democracy have been defeated, and civilization has won its most brilliant victory in all history. The American democracy has crushed, actually or potentially, every species of barbarism in the New World, asserted victoriously the state, and placed the government definitively on the side of legitimate authority, and made its natural association henceforth with all civilized governments—not with the revolutionary movements to overthrow them. The American people will always be progressive as well as conservative; but they have learned a lesson, which they much needed, against false democracy: civil war has taught them that "the sacred right of insurrection" is as much out of place in a democratic state as in an aristocratic or a monarchical state; and that the government should always be clothed with ample authority to arrest and punish whoever plots its destruction. They must never be delighted again to have their government send a national ship to bring hither a noted traitor to his own sovereign as the nation's guest. The people of the Northern States are hardly less responsible for the late rebellion than the people of the Southern States. Their press had taught them to call every government a tyranny that refused to remain quiet while the traitor was cutting its throat or assassinating the nation, and they had nothing but mad denunciations of the Papal, the Austrian, and the Neapolitan governments for their severity against conspirators and traitors. But their own government has found it necessary for the public safety to be equally arbitrary, prompt, and severe, and they will most likely require it hereafter to co-operate with the governments of the Old World in advancing civilization, instead of lending all its moral support, as heretofore, to the Jacobins, revolutionists, socialists, and humanitarians, to bring back the reign of barbarism.

The tendency to individualism has been sufficiently checked by the failure of the rebellion, and no danger from the disintegrating element, either in the particular State or in the United States, is henceforth to be apprehended. But the tendency in the opposite direction may give the American state some trouble. The tendency now is, as to the Union, consolidation, and as to the particular state, humanitarianism, socialism, or centralized democracy. Yet this tendency, though it may do much mischief, will hardly become exclusive. The States that seceded, when restored, will always, even in abandoning State sovereignty, resist it, and still assert State rights. When these States are restored to their normal position, they will always be able to protect themselves against any encroachments on their special rights by the General government. The constitution, in the distribution of the powers of government, provides the States severally with ample means to protect their individuality against the centralizing tendency of the General government, however strong it may be.

The war has, no doubt, had a tendency to strengthen the General government, and to cause the people, to a great extent, to look upon it as the supreme and exclusive national government, and to regard the several State governments as subordinate instead of co-ordinate governments. It is not improbable that the Executive, since the outbreak of the rebellion, has proceeded throughout on that supposition, and hence his extraordinary assumptions of power; but when once peace is fully re-established, and the States have all resumed their normal position in the Union, every State will be found prompt enough to resist any attempt to encroach on its constitutional rights. Its instinct of self-preservation will lead it to resist, and it will be protected by both its own judiciary and that of the United States.

The danger that the General government will usurp the rights of the States is far less than the danger that the Executive will usurp all the power of Congress and the judiciary. Congress, during the rebellion, clothed the President, as far as it could, with dictatorial powers, and these powers the Executive continues to exercise even after the rebellion is suppressed. They were given and held under the rights of war, and for war purposes only, and expired by natural limitation when the war ceased; but the Executive forgets this, and, instead of calling Congress together and submitting the work of reconstruction of the States that seceded to its wisdom and authority, undertakes to reconstruct them himself, as if he were an absolute sovereign; and the people seem to like it. He might and should, as commander-in-chief of the army and navy, govern them as military departments, by his lieutenants, till Congress could either create provisional civil governments for them or recognize them as self-governing States in the Union; but he has no right, under the constitution nor under the war power, to appoint civil governors, permanent or provisional; and every act he has done in regard to reconstruction is sheer usurpation, and done without authority and without the slightest plea of necessity. His acts in this respect, even if wise and just in themselves, are inexcusable, because done by one who has no legal right to do them. Yet his usurpation is apparently sustained by public sentiment, and a deep wound is inflicted on the constitution, which will be long in healing.

The danger in this respect is all the greater because it did not originate with the rebellion, but had manifested itself for a long time before. There is a growing disposition on the part of Congress to throw as much of the business of government as possible into the hands of the Executive. The patronage the Executive wields, even in times of peace, is so large that he has indirectly an almost supreme control over the legislative branch of the government. For this, which is, and, if not checked will continue to be, a growing evil, there is no obvious remedy, unless the President is chosen for a longer term of office and made ineligible for a second term, and the mischievous doctrine of rotation in office is rejected as incompatible with the true interests of the public. Here is matter for the consideration of the American statesman. But as to the usurpations of the Executive in these unsettled times, they will be only temporary abuses, and the Southern States, when restored to the Union, will resume their rights in their own sphere, as self-governing communities, and legalize or undo the unwarrantable acts of the Federal Executive.

The socialistic and centralizing tendency in the bosom of the individual States is the most dangerous, but it will not be able to become predominant; for philanthropy, unlike charity, does not begin at home, and is powerless unless it operates at a distance. In the States in which the humanitarian tendency is the strongest, the territorial democracy has its most effective organization. Prior to the outbreak of the rebellion the American people had asserted popular sovereignty, but had never rendered an account to themselves in what sense the people are or are not sovereign. They had never distinguished the three sorts of democracy from one another, asked themselves which of the three is the distinctively American democracy. For them, democracy was democracy, and those who saw dangers ahead sought to avoid them either by exaggerating one or the other of the two exclusive tendencies, or else by restraining democracy itself through restrictions on suffrage. The latter class began to distrust universal suffrage, to lose faith in the people, and to dream of modifying the American constitution so as to make it conform more nearly to the English model. The war has proved that they were wrong, for nothing is more certain than that the people have saved the national unity and integrity almost in spite of their government. The General government either was not disposed or was afraid to take a decided stand against secession, till forced to do it by the people themselves. No wise American can henceforth distrust American democracy. The people may be trusted. So much is settled. But as the two extremes were equally democratic, as the secessionists acted in the name of popular sovereignty, and as the humanitarians were not unwilling to allow separation, and would not and did not engage in the war against secession for the sake of the Union and the integrity of the national domain, the conviction becomes irresistible that it was not democracy in the sense of either of the extremes that made the war and came out of it victorious; and hence the real American democracy must differ from them both, and is neither a personal nor a humanitarian, but a territorial democracy. The true idea of American democracy thus comes out, for the first time, freed from the two extreme democracies which have been identified with it, and henceforth enters into the understandings as well as the hearts of the people. The war has enlightened patriotism, and what was sentiment or instinct becomes reason—a well-defined, and clearly understood constitutional conviction.

In the several States themselves there are many things to prevent the socialistic tendency from becoming exclusive. In the States that seceded socialism has never had a foothold, and will not gain it, for it is resisted by all the sentiments, convictions, and habits of the Southern people, and the Southern people will not be exterminated nor swamped by migrations either from the North or from Europe. They are and always will be an agricultural people, and an agricultural people are and always will be opposed to socialistic dreams, unless unwittingly held for a moment to favor it in pursuit of some special object in which they take a passionate interest. The worst of all policies is that of hanging, exiling, or disfranchising the wealthy landholders of the South, in order to bring up the poor and depressed whites, shadowed forth in the Executive proclamation of the 29th of May, 1865. Of course that policy will not be carried out, and if the negroes are enfranchised, they will always vote with the wealthy landholding class, and aid them in resisting all socialistic tendencies. The humanitarians will fail for the want of a good social grievance against which they can declaim.

In the New England States the humanitarian tendency is strong as a speculation, but only in relation to objects at a distance. It is aided much by the congregational constitution of their religion; yet it is weak at home, and is resisted practically by the territorial division of power. New England means Massachusetts, and nowhere is the subdivision of the powers of government carried further, or the constitution of the territorial democracy more complete, than in that State. Philanthropy seldom works in private against private vices and evils: it is effective only against public grievances, and the farther they are from home and the less its right to interfere with them, the more in earnest and the more effective for evil does it become. Its nature is to mind every one's business but its own. But now that slavery is abolished, there is nowhere in the United States a social grievance of magnitude enough to enlist any considerable number of the people, even of Massachusetts, in a movement to redress it. Negro enfranchisement is a question of which the humanitarians can make something, and they will make the most of it; but as it is a question that each State will soon settle for itself, it will not serve their purpose of prolonged agitation. They could not and never did carry away the nation, even on the question of slavery itself, and abolitionism had comparatively little direct influence in abolishing slavery; and the exclusion of negro suffrage can never be made to appear to the

American people as any thing like so great a grievance as was slavery.

Besides, in all the States that did not secede, Catholics are a numerous and an important portion of the population. Their increasing numbers, wealth, and education secure them, as much as the majority may dislike their religion, a constantly increasing influence, and it is idle to leave them out in counting the future of the country. They will, in a very few years, be the best and most thoroughly educated class of the American people; and, aside from their religion, or, rather, in consequence of their religion, the most learned, enlightened, and intelligent portion of the American population; and as much as they have disliked the abolitionists, they have, in the army and elsewhere, contributed their full share to the victory the nation has won. The best things written on the controversy have been written by Catholics, and Catholics are better fitted by their religion to comprehend the real character of the American constitution than any other class of Americans, the moment they study it in the light of their own theology. The American constitution is based on that of natural society, on the solidarity of the race, and the difference between natural society and the church or Christian society is, that the one is initial and the other teleological. The law of both is the same; Catholics, as such, must resist both extremes, because each is exclusive, and whatever is exclusive or one-sided is uncatholic. If they have been backward in their sympathy with the government, it has been through their dislike of the puritanic spirit and the humanitarian or socialistic elements they detected in the Republican party, joined with a prejudice against political and social negro equality. But their church everywhere opposes the socialistic movements of the age, all movements in behalf of barbarism, and they may always be counted on to resist the advance of the socialistic democracy. If the country has had reason to complain of some of them in the late war, it will have, in the future, far stronger reason to be grateful; not to them, indeed, for the citizen owes his life to his country, but to their religion, which has been and is the grand protectress of modern society and civilization.

From the origin of the government there has been a tendency to the extension of suffrage, and to exclude both birth and private property as bases of political rights or franchises. This tendency has often been justified on the ground that the elective franchise is a natural right; which is not true, because the elective franchise is political power, and political power is always a civil trust, never a natural right, and the state judges for itself to whom it will or will not confide the trust; but there can be no doubt that it is a normal tendency, and in strict accordance with the constitution of American civil society, which rests on the unity of the race, and public instead of private property. All political distinctions founded on birth, race, or private wealth are anomalies in the American system, and are necessarily eliminated by its normal developments. To contend that none but property-holders may vote, or none but persons of a particular race may be enfranchised, is unAmerican and contrary to the order of civilization the New World is developing. The only qualification for the elective franchise the American system can logically insist on is that the elector belong to the territorial people—that is, be a natural-born or a naturalized citizen, be a major in full possession of his natural faculties, and unconvicted of any infamous offence. The State is free to naturalize foreigners or not, and under such restrictions as it judges proper; but, having naturalized them, it must treat them as standing on the same footing with natural-born citizens.

The naturalization question is one of great national importance. The migration of foreigners hither has added largely to the national population, and to the national wealth and resources, but less, perhaps, to the development of patriotism, the purity of elections, or the wisdom and integrity of the government. It is impossible that there should be perfect harmony between the national territorial democracy and individuals born, brought up, and formed under a political order in many respects widely different from it; and there is no doubt that the democracy, in its objectionable sense, has been greatly strengthened by the large infusion of naturalized citizens. There can be no question that, if the laboring classes, in whom the national sentiment is usually the strongest, has been composed almost wholly of native Americans, instead of being, as they were, at least in the cities, large towns, and villages, composed almost exclusively of persons foreign born, the Government would have found far less difficulty in filling up the depleted ranks of its armies. But to leave so large a portion of the actual population as the foreign born residing in the country without the rights of citizens, would have been a far graver evil, and would, in the late struggle, have given the victory to secession. There are great national advantages derived from the migration hither of foreign labor, and if the migration be encouraged or permitted, naturalization on easy and liberal terms is the wisest, the best, and only safe policy. The children of foreign-born parents are real Americans.

Emigration has, also, a singular effect in developing the latent powers of the emigrant, and the children of emigrants are usually more active, more energetic than the children of the older inhabitants of the country among whom they settle. Some of our first men in civil life have been sons of foreign-born parents, and so are not a few of our greatest and most successful generals. The most successful of our merchants have been foreign-born. The same thing has been noticed elsewhere, especially in the emigration of the French Huguenots to Holland, Germany, England, and Ireland. The immigration of so many millions from the Old World has, no doubt, given to the American people much of their bold, energetic, and adventurous character, and made them a superior people on the whole to what they would otherwise have been. This has nothing to do with superiority or inferiority of race or blood, but is a natural effect of breaking men away from routine, and throwing them back on their own individual energies and personal resources.

Resistance is offered to negro suffrage, and justly too, till the recently emancipated slaves have served an apprenticeship to freedom; but that resistance cannot long stand before the onward progress of American democracy, which asserts equal rights for all, and not for a race or class only. Some would confine suffrage to landholders, or, at least, to property-holders; but that is inconsistent with the American idea, and is a relic of the barbaric constitution which founds power on private instead of public wealth. Nor are property-owners a whit more likely to vote for the public good than are those who own no property but their own labor. The men of wealth, the business men, manufacturers and merchants, bankers and brokers, are the men who exert the worst influence on government in every country, for they always strive to use it as an instrument of advancing their own private interests. They act on the beautiful maxim, "Let government take care of the rich, and the rich will take care of the poor," instead of the far safer maxim, "Let government take care of the weak, the strong can take care of themselves." Universal suffrage is better than restricted suffrage, but even universal suffrage is too weak to prevent private property from having an undue political influence.

The evils attributed to universal suffrage are not inseparable from it, and, after all, it is doubtful if it elevates men of an inferior class to those elevated by restricted suffrage. The Congress of 1860, or of 1862, was a fair average of the wisdom, the talent, and the virtue of the country, and not inferior to that of 1776, or that of 1789; and the Executive during the rebellion was at least as able and as efficient as it was during the war of 1812, far superior to that of Great Britain, and not inferior to that of France during the Crimean war. The Crimean war developed and placed in high command, either with the English or the French, no generals equal to Halleck, Grant, and Sherman, to say nothing of others. The more aristocratic South proved itself, in both statesmanship and generalship, in no respect superior to the territorial democracy of the North and West.

The great evil the country experiences is not from universal suffrage, but from what may be called rotation in office. The number of political aspirants is so great that, in the Northern and Western States especially, the representatives in Congress are changed every two or four years, and a member, as soon as he has acquired the experience necessary to qualify him for his position, is dropped, not through the fickleness of his constituency, but to give place to another whose aid had been necessary to his first or second election. Employés are "rotated," not because they are incapable or unfaithful, but because there are others who want their places. This is all bad, but it springs not from universal suffrage, but from a wrong public opinion, which might be corrected by the press, but which is mainly formed by it. There is, no doubt, a due share of official corruption, but not more than elsewhere, and that would be much diminished by increasing the salaries of the public servants, especially in the higher offices of the government, both General and State. The pay to the lower officers and employés of the government, and to the privates and non-commissioned officers in the army, is liberal, and, in general, too liberal; but the pay of the higher grades in both the civil and military service is too low, and relatively far lower than it was when the government was first organized.

The worst tendency in the country, and which is not encouraged at all by the territorial democracy, manifests itself in hostility to the military spirit and a standing army. The depreciation of the military spirit comes from the humanitarian or sentimental democracy, which, like all sentimentalisms, defeats itself, and brings about the very evils it seeks to avoid. The hostility to standing armies is inherited from England, and originated in the quarrels between king and parliament, and is a striking evidence of the folly of that bundle of antagonistic forces called the British constitution. In feudal times most of the land was held by military service, and the reliance of government was on the feudal militia; but no real progress was made in eliminating barbarism till the national authority got a regular army at its command, and became able to defend itself against its enemies. It is very doubtful if English civilization has not, upon the whole, lost more than it has gained by substituting parliamentary for royal supremacy, and exchanging the Stuarts for the Guelfs.

No nation is a living, prosperous nation that has lost the military spirit, or in which the profession of the soldier is not held in honor and esteem; and a standing army of reasonable size is public economy. It absorbs in its ranks a class of men who are worth more there than anywhere else; it creates honorable places for gentlemen or the sons of gentlemen without wealth, in which they can serve both themselves and their country. Under a democratic government the most serious embarrassment to the state is its gentlemen, or persons not

351

disposed or not fitted to support themselves by their own hands, more necessary in a democratic government than in any other. The civil service, divinity, law, and medicine, together with literature, science, and art, cannot absorb the whole of this ever-increasing class, and the army and navy would be an economy and a real service to the state were they maintained only for the sake of the rank and position they give to their officers, and the wholesome influence these officers would exert on society and the politics of the country—this even in case there were no wars or apprehension of wars. They supply an element needed in all society, to sustain in it the chivalric and heroic spirit, perpetually endangered by the mercantile and political spirit, which has in it always something low and sordid.

But wars are inevitable, and when a nation has no surrounding nations to fight, it will, as we have just proved, fight itself. When it can have no foreign war, it will get up a domestic war; for the human animal, like all animals, must work off in some way its fighting humor, and the only sure way of maintaining peace is always to be prepared for war. A regular standing army of forty thousand men would have prevented the Mexican war, and an army of fifty thousand well-disciplined and efficient troops at the command of the President on his inauguration in March, 1861, would have prevented the rebellion, or have instantly suppressed it. The cost of maintaining a land army of even a hundred thousand men, and a naval force to correspond, would have been, in simple money value, only a tithe of what the rebellion has cost the nation, to say nothing of the valuable lives that have been sacrificed—for the losses on the rebel side, as well as those on the side of the government, are equally to be counted. The actual losses to the country have been not less than six or eight thousand millions of dollars, or nearly one-half the assessed value of the whole property of the United States according to the census returns of 1860, and which has only been partially cancelled by actual increase of property since. To meet the interest on the debt incurred will require a heavier sum to be raised annually by taxation, twice over, without discharging a cent of the principal, than would have been necessary to maintain an army and navy adequate to the protection of peace and the prevention of the rebellion.

The rebellion is now suppressed, and if the government does not blunder much more in its civil efforts at pacification than it did in its military operations, before 1868 things will settle down into their normal order; but a regular army—not militia or volunteers, who are too expensive—of at least a hundred thousand men of all arms, and a navy nearly as large as that of England or France, will be needed as a peace establishment. The army of a hundred thousand men must form a cadre of an army of three times that number, which will be necessary to place the army on a war footing. Less will answer neither for peace nor war, for the nation has, in spite of herself, to maintain henceforth the rank of a first-class military and maritime power, and take a leading part in political movements of the civilized world, and, to a great extent, hold in her hand the peace of Europe.

Canning boasted that he had raised up the New World to redress the balance of the Old: a vain boast, for he simply weakened Spain and gave the hegemony of Europe to Russia, which the Emperor of the French is trying, by strengthening Italy and Spain, and by a French protectorate in Mexico, to secure to France, both in the Old World and the New—a magnificent dream, but not to be realized. His uncle judged more wisely when he sold Louisiana, left the New World to itself, and sought only to secure to France the hegemony of the Old. But the hegemony of the New World henceforth belongs to the United States, and she will have a potent voice in adjusting the balance of power even in Europe. To maintain this position, which is imperative on her, she must always have a large armed force, either on foot or in reserve, which she can call out and put on a war footing at short notice. The United States must henceforth be a great military and naval power, and the old hostility to a standing army and the old attempt to bring the military into disrepute must be abandoned, and the country yield to its destiny.

Of the several tendencies mentioned, the humanitarian tendency, egoistical at the South, detaching the individual from the race, and socialistic at the North, absorbing the individual in the race, is the most dangerous. The egoistical form is checked, sufficiently weakened by the defeat of the rebels; but the social form believes that it has triumphed, and that individuals are effaced in society, and the States in the Union. Against this, more especially should public opinion and American statesmanship be now directed, and territorial democracy and the division of the powers of government be asserted and vigorously maintained. The danger is that while this socialistic form of democracy is conscious of itself, the territorial democracy has not yet arrived, as the Germans say, at self consciousness—*selbsbewusstseyn*—and operates only instinctively. All the dominant theories and sentimentalities are against it, and it is only Providence that can sustain it.

Pope Leo XIII
1810-1903

Leo XIII reigned as pope from 1878 to 1903. His pontificate of 25 years is certainly one of the most important in modern times. He manifested great wisdom and patience in addressing major church issues of his time, such as church-state relations, social justice, education and the missions.

Born Gioacchino Vincenza Pecci in 1810, the future pope's life was oriented toward a church career at an early age. After completing his theological and canon law studies at the University of the Sapienza, he was ordained a priest in 1837. He was an archbishop at age 33, a cardinal at 43, and elected pope at 68. Throughout his prepapal years, Pecci manifested a sensitivity toward human problems and a capacity to resolve them well. Three years in Belgium brought him into contact with the industrial conditions of Europe; this knowledge certainly influenced his approach to social issues when he became pope. From 1846 to 1878, Pecci was archbishop of Perugia. Near the end of this tenure he issued pastoral letters insisting that the church must become involved in the shaping of the modern world. He succeeded Pope Pius IX on February 20, 1878.

Leo turned his attention in several directions. His encyclicals on Church and State described both institutions as perfect societies, attempted to re-establish the concept of the divine origin of all authority and encouraged Catholics to participate in political life. With the encyclical Aeterni Patris, *Leo initiated a renewal of philosophy grounded in Thomism and directed that this be the philosophical structure for seminary programs. He labored for the reunion of Rome with the Oriental and Slavic Churches, but did not achieve it. His letter denying the validity of Anglican Orders ended any hopes for reunion with Anglicanism.*

Rerum Novarum, *which is presented below in its entirety, was Leo XIII's most important document on social questions and is the first of the great social encyclicals. The nineteenth century had terribly abused the working classes. "Hence by degrees it has come to pass that working men have been given over, isolated and defenseless, to the callousness of employers and the greed of unrestrained competition." (R.N., 2) Socialism was taking advantage of this tragic situation among the workers. Realizing the imminence of serious conflict between wealthy and poor, capital and labor, Leo chose to speak at length on the condition of labor. The encyclical opened a new era in Catholic social thought.*

Rerum Novarum *begins with an examination and rejection of the socialist movement. The natural right to private property is defended and established as the first and most fundamental principle against the main tenet of socialism, viz., the community of goods. Leo then moves on to assert that no practical solution to the world's social problems can be found without the assistance of religion and the church. He discusses the employer-employee relationship, the right use of money and the dignity of labor. The state is reminded of its responsibility to relieve the suffering of the poor by developing a commonwealth that shall produce public well-being and private prosperity. The poor have a right in justice to be carefully watched over by the state. The questions of workman's rights, hours of labor, child and woman labor and just wages are all considered. The creation of workmen's associations is encouraged. The document closes with a call to all mankind to work for the plenteous outpouring of charity.*

RERUM NOVARUM

O nce the passion for revolutionary change was aroused—
a passion long disturbing governments—it was bound to
follow sooner or later that eagerness for change would
pass from the political sphere over into the related field of
economics. In fact, new developments in industry, new tech-
niques striking out on new paths, changed relations of employer
and employee, abounding wealth among a very small number
and destitution among the masses, increased self-reliance on the
part of workers as well as a closer bond of union with one
another, and, in addition to all this, a decline in morals have
caused conflict to break forth.

2. The momentous nature of the questions involved in
this conflict is evident from the fact that it keeps men's minds
in anxious expectation, occupying the talents of the learned,
the discussions of the wise and experienced, the assemblies of
the people, the judgment of lawmakers, and the deliberations of
rulers, so that now no topic more strongly holds men's interests.

3. Therefore, Venerable Brethren, with the cause of the
Church and the common welfare before Us, We have thought it
advisable, following Our custom on other occasions when We
issued to you the Encyclicals *On Political Power, On Human
Liberty, On the Christian Constitution of States*, and others of
similar nature, which seemed opportune to refute erroneous
opinions, that We ought to do the same now, and for the same
reasons, *On the Condition of Workers*. We have on occasion
touched more than once upon this subject. In this Encyclical,
however, consciousness of Our Apostolic office admonishes Us
to treat the entire question thoroughly, in order that the principles may stand out in clear light, and the conflict may thereby
be brought to an end as required by truth and equity.

4. The problem is difficult to resolve and is not free from
dangers. It is hard indeed to fix the boundaries of the rights and
duties within which the rich and the proletariat—those who

furnish material things and those who furnish work—ought to be restricted in relation to each other. The controversy is truly dangerous, for in various places it is being twisted by turbulent and crafty men to pervert judgment as to truth and seditiously to incite the masses.

5. In any event, We see clearly, and all are agreed that the poor must be speedily and fittingly cared for, since the great majority of them live undeservedly in miserable and wretched conditions.

6. After the old trade guilds had been destroyed in the last century, and no protection was substituted in their place, and when public institutions and legislation had cast off traditional religious teaching, it gradually came about that the present age handed over the workers, each alone and defenseless, to the inhumanity of employers and the unbridled greed of competitors. A devouring usury, although often condemned by the Church, but practiced nevertheless under another form by avaricious and grasping men, has increased the evil; and in addition the whole process of production as well as trade in every kind of goods has been brought almost entirely under the power of a few, so that a very few rich and exceedingly rich men have laid a yoke almost of slavery on the unnumbered masses of non-owning workers.

7. To cure this evil, the Socialists, exciting the envy of the poor toward the rich, contend that it is necessary to do away with private possession of goods and in its place to make the goods of individuals common to all, and that the men who preside over a municipality or who direct the entire State should act as administrators of these goods. They hold that, by such a transfer of private goods from private individuals to the community, they can cure the present evil through dividing wealth and benefits equally among the citizens.

8. But their program is so unsuited for terminating the conflict that it actually injures the workers themselves. Moreover, it is highly unjust, because it violates the rights of lawful owners, perverts the functions of the State, and throws governments into utter confusion.

9. Clearly the essential reason why those who engage in any gainful occupation undertake labor, and at the same time

the end to which workers immediately look, is to procure property for themselves and to retain it by individual right as theirs and as their very own. When the worker places his energy and his labor at the disposal of another, he does so for the purpose of getting the means necessary for livelihood. He seeks in return for the work done, accordingly, a true and full right not only to demand his wage but to dispose of it as he sees fit. Therefore, if he saves something by restricting expenditures and invests his savings in a piece of land in order to keep the fruit of his thrift more safe, a holding of this kind is certainly nothing else than his wage under a different form; and on this account land which the worker thus buys is necessarily under his full control as much as the wage which he earned by his labor. But, as is obvious, it is clearly in this that the ownership of moveable and immoveable goods consists. Therefore, inasmuch as the Socialists seek to transfer the goods of private persons to the community at large, they make the lot of all wage earners worse, because in abolishing the freedom to dispose of wages they take away from them by this very act the hope and the opportunity of increasing their property and of securing advantages for themselves.

10. But, what is of more vital concern, they propose a remedy openly in conflict with justice, inasmuch as nature confers on man the right to possess things privately as his own.

11. In this respect also there is the widest difference between man and other living things. For brute beasts are not self-ruling, but are ruled and governed by a two-fold innate instinct, which not only keeps their faculty of action alert and develops their powers properly but also impels and determines their individual movements. By one instinct they are induced to protect themselves and their lives; by the other, to preserve their species. In truth, they attain both ends readily by using what is before them and within immediate range; and they cannot, of course, go further because they are moved to action by the senses alone and by the separate things perceived by the senses. Man's nature is quite different. In man there is likewise the entire and full perfection of animal nature, and consequently on this ground there is given to man, certainly no less than to every kind of living thing, to enjoy the benefits of corporeal

goods. Yet animal nature, however perfectly possessed, is far from embracing human nature, but rather is much lower than human nature, having been created to serve and obey it. What stands out and excels in us, what makes man man and distinguishes him generically from the brute is the mind or reason. And owing to the fact that this animal alone has reason, it is necessary that man have goods not only to be used, which is common to all living things, but also to be possessed by stable and perpetual right; and this applies not merely to those goods which are consumed by use, but to those also which endure after being used.

12. This is even more clearly evident, if the essential nature of human beings is examined more closely. Since man by his reason understands innumerable things, linking and combining the future with the present, and since he is master of his own actions, therefore, under the eternal law, and under the power of God most wisely ruling all things, he rules himself by the foresight of his own counsel. Wherefore it is in his power to choose the things which he considers best adapted to benefit him not only in the present but also in the future. Whence it follows that dominion not only over the fruits of the earth but also over the earth itself ought to rest in man, since he sees that things necessary for the future are furnished him out of the produce of the earth. The needs of every man are subject, as it were, to constant recurrences, so that, satisfied today, they make new demands tomorrow. Therefore, nature necessarily gave man something stable and perpetually lasting on which he can count for continuous support. But nothing can give continuous support of this kind save the earth with its great abundance.

13. There is no reason to interpose provision by the State, for man is older than the State. Wherefore he had to possess by nature his own right to protect his life and body before any polity had been formed.

14. The fact that God gave the whole human race the earth to use and enjoy cannot indeed in any manner serve as an objection against private possessions. For God is said to have given the earth to mankind in common, not because He intended indiscriminate ownership of it by all, but because He assigned

no part to anyone in ownership, leaving the limits of private possessions to be fixed by the industry of men and the institutions of peoples. Yet, however the earth may be apportioned among private owners, it does not cease to serve the common interest of all, inasmuch as no living being is sustained except by what the fields bring forth. Those who lack resources supply labor, so that it can be truly affirmed that the entire scheme of securing a livelihood consists in the labor which a person expends either on his own land or in some working occupation, the compensation for which is drawn ultimately from no other source than from the varied products of the earth and is exchanged for them.

15. For this reason it also follows that private possessions are clearly in accord with nature. The earth indeed produces in great abundance the things to preserve and, especially, to perfect life, but of itself it could not produce them without human cultivation and care. Moreover, since man expends his mental energy and his bodily strength in procuring the goods of nature, by this very act he appropriates that part of physical nature to himself which he has cultivated. On it he leaves impressed, as it were, a kind of image of his person, so that it must be altogether just that he should possess that part as his very own and that no one in any way should be permitted to violate his right.

16. The force of these arguments is so evident that it seems amazing that certain revivers of obsolete theories dissent from them. These men grant the individual the use of the soil and the varied fruits of the farm, but absolutely deny him the right to hold as owner either the ground on which he has built or the farm he has cultivated. When they deny this right they fail to see that a man will be defrauded of the things his labor has produced. The land, surely, that has been worked by the hand and the art of the tiller greatly changes in aspect. The wilderness is made fruitful; the barren field, fertile. But those things through which the soil has been improved so inhere in the soil and are so thoroughly intermingled with it, that they are for the most part quite inseparable from it. And, after all, would justice permit any one to own and enjoy that upon which another has toiled? As effects follow the cause producing them, so

it is just that the fruit of labor belongs precisely to those who have performed the labor.

17. Rightly therefore, the human race as a whole, moved in no wise by the dissenting opinions of a few, and observing nature carefully, has found in the law of nature itself the basis of the distribution of goods, and, by the practice of all ages, has consecrated private possession as something best adapted to man's nature and to peaceful and tranquil living together. Now civil laws, which, when just, derive their power from the natural law itself, confirm and, even by the use of force, protect this right of which we speak.—And this same right has been sanctioned by the authority of the divine law, which forbids us most strictly even to desire what belongs to another. "Thou shalt not covet thy neighbor's wife, nor his house, nor his field, nor his maid-servant, nor his ox, nor his ass, nor anything that is his."

18. Rights of this kind which reside in individuals are seen to have much greater validity when viewed as fitted into and connected with the obligations of human beings in family life.

19. There is no question that in choosing a state of life it is within the power and discretion of individuals to prefer the one or the other state, either to follow the counsel of Jesus Christ regarding virginity or to bind oneself in marriage. No law of man can abolish the natural and primeval right of marriage, or in any way set aside the chief purpose of matrimony established in the beginning by the authority of God: "Increase and multiply." Behold, therefore, the family, or rather the society of the household, a very small society indeed, but a true one, and older than any polity! For that reason it must have certain rights and duties of its own entirely independent of the State. Thus, right of ownership, which we have shown to be bestowed on individual persons by nature, must be assigned to man in his capacity as head of a family. Nay rather, this right is all the stronger, since the human person in family life embraces much more.

20. It is a most sacred law of nature that the father of a family see that his offspring are provided with all the necessities of life, and nature even prompts him to desire to provide and to furnish his children, who, in fact reflect and in a sense continue

his person, with the means of decently protecting themselves against harsh fortune in the uncertainties of life. He can do this surely in no other way than by owning fruitful goods to transmit by inheritance to his children. As already noted, the family like the State is by the same token a society in the strictest sense of the term, and it is governed by its own proper authority, namely, by that of the father. Wherefore, assuming, of course, that those limits be observed which are fixed by its immediate purpose, the family assuredly possesses rights, at least equal with those of civil society, in respect to choosing and employing the things necessary for its protection and its just liberty. We say "at least equal" because, inasmuch as domestic living together is prior both in thought and in fact to uniting into a polity, it follows that its rights and duties are also prior and more in conformity with nature. But if citizens, if families, after becoming participants in common life and society, were to experience injury in a commonwealth instead of help, impairment of their rights instead of protection, society would be something to be repudiated rather than to be sought for.

21. To desire, therefore, that the civil power should enter arbitrarily into the privacy of homes is a great and pernicious error. If a family perchance is in such extreme difficulty and is so completely without plans that it is entirely unable to help itself, it is right that the distress be remedied by public aid, for each individual family is a part of the community. Similarly, if anywhere there is a grave violation of mutual rights within the family walls, public authority shall restore to each his right: for this is not usurping the rights of citizens, but protecting and confirming them with just and due care. Those in charge of public affairs, however, must stop here: nature does not permit them to go beyond these limits. Paternal authority is such that it can be neither abolished nor absorbed by the State, because it has the same origin in common with that of man's own life. "Children are a part of their father," and, as it were, a kind of extension of the father's person; and, strictly speaking, not through themselves, but through the medium of the family society in which they are begotten, they enter into and participate in civil society. And for the very reason that children "are by nature part of their father . . . before they have the use of

free will, they are kept under the care of their parents." Inasmuch as the Socialists, therefore, disregard care by parents and in its place introduce care by the State, they act *against natural justice* and dissolve the structure of the home.

22. And apart from the injustice involved, it is also only too evident what turmoil and disorder would obtain among all classes; and what a harsh and odious enslavement of citizens would result! The door would be open to mutual envy, detraction, and dissension. If incentives to ingenuity and skill in individual persons were to be abolished, the very fountains of wealth would necessarily dry up; and the equality conjured up by the Socialist imagination would, in reality, be nothing but uniform wretchedness and meanness for one and all, without distinction.

23. From all these considerations, it is perceived that the fundamental principle of Socialism which would make all possessions public property is to be utterly rejected because it injures the very ones whom it seeks to help, contravenes the natural rights of individual persons, and throws the functions of the State and public peace into confusion. Let it be regarded, therefore, as established that in seeking help for the masses this principle before all is to be considered as basic, namely, that private ownership must be preserved inviolate. With this understood, we shall explain whence the desired remedy is to be sought.

24. We approach the subject with confidence and surely by Our right, for the question under consideration is certainly one for which no satisfactory solution will be found unless religion and the Church have been called upon to aid. Moreover, since the safeguarding of religion and of all things within the jurisdiction of the Church is primarily Our stewardship, silence on Our part might be regarded as failure in Our duty.

25. Assuredly, a question as formidable as this requires the attention and effort of others as well, namely, the heads of the State, employers and the rich, and, finally, those in whose behalf efforts are being made, the workers themselves. Yet without hesitation We affirm that if the Church is disregarded, human striving will be in vain. Manifestly, it is the Church which draws from the Gospel the teachings through which the

struggle can be composed entirely or, after its bitterness is removed, can certainly become more tempered. It is the Church, again, that strives not only to instruct the mind but to regulate by her precepts the life and morals of individuals, that ameliorates the condition of the workers through her numerous and beneficent institutions, and that wishes and aims to have the thought and energy of all classes of society united to this end, that the interests of the workers be protected as fully as possible. And to accomplish this purpose she holds that the laws and the authority of the State, within reasonable limits, ought to be employed.

26. Therefore, let it be laid down in the first place that a condition of human existence must be borne with, namely, that in civil society the lowest cannot be made equal with the highest. Socialists, of course, agitate the contrary, but all struggling against nature is vain. There are truly very great and very many natural differences among men. Neither the talents, nor the skill, nor the health, nor the capacities of all are the same, and unequal fortune follows of itself upon necessary inequality in respect to these endowments. And clearly this condition of things is adapted to benefit both individuals and the community; for to carry on its affairs community life requires varied aptitudes and diverse services, and to perform these diverse services men are impelled most by differences in individual property holdings.

27. So far as bodily labor is concerned, man even before the Fall was not destined to be wholly idle; but certainly what his will at that time would have freely embraced to his soul's delight, necessity afterwards forced him to accept, with a feeling of irksomeness, for the expiation of his guilt. "Cursed be the earth in thy work: in thy labor thou shalt eat of it all the days of thy life." Likewise there is to be no end on earth of other hardships, for the evil consequences of sin are hard, trying, and bitter to bear, and will necessarily accompany men even to the end of life. Therefore, to suffer and endure is human, and although men may strive in all possible ways, they will never be able by any power or art wholly to banish such tribulations from human life. If any claim they can do this, if they promise the poor in their misery a life free from all sorrow and vexation

and filled with repose and perpetual pleasures, they actually impose upon these people and perpetrate a fraud which will ultimately lead to evils greater than the present. The best course is to view human affairs as they are and, as We have stated, at the same time to seek appropriate relief for these troubles elsewhere.

28. It is a capital evil with respect to the question We are discussing to take for granted that the one class of society is of itself hostile to the other, as if nature had set rich and poor against each other to fight fiercely in implacable war. This is so abhorrent to reason and truth that the exact opposite is true; for just as in the human body the different members harmonize with one another, whence arises that disposition of parts and proportion in the human figure rightly called symmetry, so likewise nature has commanded in the case of the State that the two classes mentioned should agree harmoniously and should properly form equally balanced counterparts to each other. Each needs the other completely: neither capital can do without labor, nor labor without capital. Concord begets beauty and order in things. Conversely, from perpetual strife there must arise disorder accompanied by bestial cruelty. But for putting an end to conflict and for cutting away its very roots, there is wondrous and multiple power in Christian institutions.

29. And first and foremost, the entire body of religious teaching and practice, of which the Church is the interpreter and guardian, can pre-eminently bring together and unite the rich and the poor by recalling the two classes of society to their mutual duties, and in particular to those duties which derive from justice.

30. Among these duties the following concern the poor and the workers: To perform entirely and conscientiously whatever work has been voluntarily and equitably agreed upon; not in any way to injure the property or to harm the person of employers; in protecting their own interests, to refrain from violence and never to engage in rioting; not to associate with vicious men who craftily hold out exaggerated hopes and make huge promises, a course usually ending in vain regrets and in the destruction of wealth.

31. The following duties, on the other hand, concern rich men and employers: Workers are not to be treated as slaves; justice demands that the dignity of human personality be respected in them, ennobled as it has been through what we call the Christian character. If we hearken to natural reason and to Christian philosophy, gainful occupations are not a mark of shame to man, but rather of respect, as they provide him with an honorable means of supporting life. It is shameful and in-human, however, to use man as things for gain and to put no more value on them than what they are worth in muscle and energy. Likewise it is enjoined that the religious interests and the spiritual well-being of the workers receive proper considera-tion. Wherefore, it is the duty of employers to see that the worker is free for adequate periods to attend to his religious obligations; not to expose anyone to corrupting influences or the enticements of sin; and in no way to alienate him from care for his family and the practice of thrift. Likewise, more work is not to be imposed than strength can endure, nor that kind of work which is unsuited to a worker's age or sex.

32. Among the most important duties of employers the principal one is to give every worker what is justly due him. Assuredly, to establish a rule of pay in accord with justice, many factors must be taken into account. But, in general, the rich and employers should remember that no laws, either human or divine, permit them for their own profit to oppress the needy and the wretched or to seek gain from another's want. To de-fraud anyone of the wage due him is a great crime that calls down avenging wrath from Heaven. "Behold, the wages of the laborers . . . which have been kept back by you unjustly, cry out and their cry has entered into the ears of the Lord of Hosts." Finally, the rich must religiously avoid harming in any way the savings of the workers either by coercion, or by fraud, or by the arts of usury; and the more for this reason, that the workers are not sufficiently protected against injustices and violence, and their property, being so meagre, ought to be regarded as all the more sacred. Could not the observance alone of the foregoing laws remove the bitterness and the causes of conflict?

33. But the Church, with Jesus Christ as her teacher and leader, seeks greater things than this; namely, by commanding

something more perfect, she aims at joining the two social classes to each other in closest neighborliness and friendship. We cannot understand and evaluate mortal things rightly unless the mind reflects upon the other life, the life which is immortal. If this other life indeed were taken away, the form and true notion of the right would immediately perish; nay, this entire world would become an enigma insoluble to man. Therefore, what we learn from nature itself as our teacher is also a Christian dogma and on it the whole system and structure of religion rests, as it were, on its main foundation, namely, that, when we have left this life, only then shall we truly begin to live. God has not created man for the fragile and transitory things of this world, but for Heaven and eternity, and He has ordained the earth as a place of exile, not as our permanent home. Whether you abound in, or whether you lack, riches and all the other things which are called good, is of no importance in relation to eternal happiness. But how you use them, that is truly of utmost importance. Jesus Christ by His "plentiful redemption" has by no means taken away the various tribulations with which mortal life is interwoven, but has so clearly transformed them into incentives to virtue and sources of merit that no mortal can attain eternal reward unless he follows the blood-stained footsteps of Jesus Christ. "If we endure, we shall also reign with Him." By the labors and sufferings which He voluntarily accepted, He has wondrously lightened the burden of suffering and labor, and not only by His example but also by His grace and by holding before us the hope of eternal reward, He has made endurance of sorrows easier: "for our present light affliction, which is for the moment, prepares for us an eternal weight of glory that is beyond all measure."

34. Therefore, the well-to-do are admonished that wealth does not give surcease of sorrow, and that wealth is of no avail unto the happiness of eternal life but is rather a hindrance; that the threats pronounced by Jesus Christ, so unusual coming from Him, ought to cause the rich to fear; and that on one day the strictest account for the use of wealth must be rendered to God as Judge.

35. On the use of wealth we have the excellent and extremely weighty teaching, which, although found in a rudi-

mentary stage in pagan philosophy, the Church has handed down in a completely developed form and causes to be observed not only in theory but in every-day life. The foundation of this teaching rests on this, that the just ownership of money is distinct from the just use of money.

36. To own goods privately, as We saw above, is a right natural to man, and to exercise this right, especially in life in society, is not only lawful, but clearly necessary. "It is lawful for man to own his own things. It is even necessary for human life." But if the question be asked: How ought man use his possessions? the Church replies without hesitation: "As to this point, man ought not regard external goods as his own, but as common so that, in fact, a person should readily share them when he sees others in need. Wherefore the Apostle says: 'Charge the rich of this world . . . to give readily, to share with others'." No one, certainly, is obliged to assist others out of what is required for his own necessary use or for that of his family, or even to give to others what he himself needs to maintain his station in life becomingly and decently: "No one is obliged to live unbecomingly." But when the demands of necessity and propriety have been sufficiently met, it is a duty to give to the poor out of that which remains. "Give that which remains as alms." These are duties not of justice, except in cases of extreme need, but of Christian charity, which obviously cannot be enforced by legal action. But the laws and judgments of men yield precedence to the law and judgment of Christ the Lord, Who in many ways urges the practice of alms-giving: "It is more blessed to give than to receive," and Who will judge a kindness done or denied to the poor as done or denied to Himself. "As long as you did it for one of these, the least of My brethren you did it for Me." The substance of all this is the following: whoever has received from the bounty of God a greater share of goods, whether corporeal and external, or of the soul, has received them for this purpose, namely, that he employ them for his own perfection and, likewise, as a servant of Divine Providence, for the benefit of others. "Therefore, he that hath talent, let him constantly see to it that he be not silent; he that hath an abundance of goods, let him be on the watch that he grow not slothful in the generosity of mercy; he that hath a trade whereby

he supports himself, let him be especially eager to share with his neighbor the use and benefit thereof."

37. Those who lack fortune's goods are taught by the Church that, before God as Judge, poverty is no disgrace, and that no one should be ashamed because he makes his living by toil. And Jesus Christ has confirmed this by fact and by deed, Who for the salvation of men, "being rich, became poor;" and although He was the Son of God and God Himself, yet He willed to seem and so be thought the son of a carpenter; nay, He even did not disdain to spend a great part of His life at the work of a carpenter. "Is not this the carpenter, the Son of Mary?" Those who contemplate this Divine example will more easily understand these truths: True dignity and excellence in men resides in moral living, that is, in virtue; virtue is the common inheritance of man, attainable equally by the humblest and the mightiest, by the rich and the poor; and the reward of eternal happiness will follow upon virtue and merit alone, regardless of the person in whom they may be found. Nay, rather the favor of God Himself seems to incline more toward the unfortunate as a class; for Jesus Christ calls the poor blessed, and He invites most lovingly all who are in labor or sorrow to come to Him for solace, embracing with special love the lowly and those harassed by injustice. At the realization of these things the proud spirit of the rich is easily brought down, and the downcast heart of the afflicted is lifted up; the former are moved toward kindness, the latter, toward reasonableness in their demands. Thus the distance between the classes which pride seeks is reduced, and it will easily be brought to pass that the two classes, with hands clasped in friendship, will be united in heart.

38. Yet, if they obey Christian teachings, not merely friendship but brotherly love also will bind them to each other. They will feel and understand that all men indeed have been created by God, their common Father; that all strive for the same object of good, which is God Himself, Who alone can communicate to both men and angels perfect and absolute happiness; that all equally have been redeemed by the grace of Jesus Christ and restored to the dignity of the sons of God, so that they are clearly united by the bonds of brotherhood not only

with one another but also with Christ the Lord, "the firstborn among many brethren"; and further, that the goods of nature and the gifts of divine grace belong in common and without distinction to all human kind, and that no one, unless he is unworthy, will be deprived of the inheritance of Heaven. "But if we are sons, we are also heirs: heirs indeed of God and joint heirs with Christ."

39. Such is the economy of duties and rights according to Christian philosophy. Would it not seem that all conflict would soon cease wherever this economy were to prevail in civil society?

40. Finally, the Church does not consider it enough to point out the way of finding the cure, but she administers the remedy herself. For she occupies herself fully in training and forming men according to discipline and doctrine; and through the agency of bishops and clergy, she causes the health-giving streams of this doctrine to be diffused as widely as possible. Furthermore, she strives to enter into men's minds and to bend their wills so that they may suffer themselves to be ruled and governed by the discipline of the divine precepts. And in this field, which is of first and greatest importance because in it the whole substance and matter of benefits consists, the Church indeed has a power that is especially unique. For the instruments which she uses to move souls were given her for this very purpose by Jesus Christ, and they have an efficacy implanted in them by God. Such instruments alone can properly penetrate the inner recesses of the heart and lead man to obedience to duty, to govern the activities of his self-seeking mind, to love God and his neighbors with a special and sovereign love, and to overcome courageously all things that impede the path of virtue.

41. In this connection it is sufficient briefly to recall to mind examples from history. We shall mention events and facts that admit of no doubt, namely, that human society in its civil aspects was renewed fundamentally by Christian institutions; that, by virtue of this renewal, mankind was raised to a higher level, nay, was called back from death to life, and enriched with such a degree of perfection as had never existed before and was not destined to be greater in any succeeding age; and that,

finally, the same Jesus Christ is the beginning and the end of these benefits; for as all things have proceeded from Him, so they must be referred back to Him. When, with the acceptance of the light of the Gospel, the world had learned the great mystery of the Incarnation of the Word and the redemption of man, the life of Jesus Christ, God and man, spread through the nations and imbued them wholly with His doctrine, with His precepts, and with His laws. Wherefore, if human society is to be healed, only a return to Christian life and institutions will heal it. In the case of decaying societies it is most correctly prescribed that, if they wish to be regenerated, they must be recalled to their origins. For the perfection of all associations is this, namely, to work for and to attain the purpose for which they were formed, so that all social actions should be inspired by the same principle which brought the society itself into being. Wherefore, turning away from the original purpose is corruption, while going back to this purpose is recovery. And just as we affirm this as unquestionably true of the entire body of the commonwealth, in like manner we affirm it of that order of citizens who sustain life by labor and who constitute the vast majority of society.

42. But it must not be supposed that the Church so concentrates her energies on caring for souls as to overlook things which pertain to mortal and earthly life. As regards the non-owning workers specifically, she desires and strives that they rise from their most wretched state and enjoy better conditions. And to achieve this result she makes no small contribution by the very fact that she calls men to and trains them in virtue. For when Christian morals are completely observed, they yield of themselves a certain measure of prosperity to material existence, because they win the favor of God, the source and fountain of all goods; because they restrain the twin plagues of life—excessive desire for wealth and thirst for pleasure—which too often make man wretched amidst the very abundance of riches; and because finally, Christian morals make men content with a moderate livelihood and make them supplement income by thrift, removing them far from the vices which swallow up both modest sums and huge fortunes, and dissipate splendid inheritances.

43. But, in addition, the Church provides directly for the well-being of the non-owning workers by instituting and promoting activities which she knows to be suitable to relieve their distress. Nay, even in the field of works of mercy, she has always so excelled that she is highly praised by her very enemies. The force of mutual charity among the first Christians was such that the wealthier very often divested themselves of their riches to aid others; wherefore: "Nor was there anyone among them in want." To the deacons, an order founded expressly for this purpose, the Apostles assigned the duty of dispensing alms daily; and the Apostle Paul, although burdened with the care of all the churches, did not hesitate to spend himself on toilsome journeys in order to bring alms personally to the poorer Christians. Monies of this kind, contributed voluntarily by the Christians in every assembly, Tertullian calls "piety's deposit fund," because they were expended "to support and bury poor people, to supply the wants of orphan boys and girls without means of support, of aged household servants, and of such, too, as had suffered shipwreck."

44. Thence, gradually there came into existence that patrimony which the Church has guarded with religious care as the property of the poor. Nay, even disregarding the feeling of shame associated with begging, she provided aid for the wretched poor. For, as the common parent of rich and poor, with charity everywhere stimulated to the highest degree, she founded religious societies and numerous other useful bodies, so that, with the aid which these furnished, there was scarcely any form of human misery that went uncared for.

45. And yet many today go so far as to condemn the Church, as the ancient pagans once did, for such outstanding charity, and would substitute in lieu thereof a system of benevolence established by the laws of the State. But no human devices can ever be found to supplant Christian charity, which gives itself entirely for the benefit of others. This virtue belongs to the Church alone, for, unless it is derived from the Most Sacred Heart of Jesus, it is in no wise a virtue; and whosoever departs from the Church wanders far from Christ.

46. But there can be no question that, to attain Our purpose, those helps also which are within the power of men are

necessary. Absolutely all who are concerned with the matter must, according to their capacity, bend their efforts to this same end and work for it. And this activity has a certain likeness to Divine Providence governing the world; for generally we see effects flow from the concert of all the elements upon which as causes these effects depend.

47. But it is now in order to inquire what portion of the remedy should be expected from the State. By State here We understand not the form of government which this or that people has, but rather that form which right reason in accordance with nature requires and the teachings of Divine wisdom approve, matters that We have explained specifically in Our Encyclical *On the Christian Constitution of States*.

48. Therefore those governing the State ought primarily to devote themselves to the service of individual groups and of the whole commonwealth, and through the entire scheme of laws and institutions to cause both public and individual well-being to develop spontaneously out of the very structure and administration of the State. For this is the duty of wise statesmanship and the essential office of those in charge of the State. Now, States are made prosperous especially by wholesome morality, properly ordered family life, protection of religion and justice, moderate imposition and equitable distribution of public burdens, progressive development of industry and trade, thriving agriculture, and by all other things of this nature, which, the more actively they are promoted, the better and happier the life of the citizens is destined to be. Therefore, by virtue of these things, it is within the competence of the rulers of the State that, as they benefit other groups, they also improve in particular the condition of the workers. Furthermore, they do this with full right and without laying themselves open to any charge of unwarranted interference. For the State is bound by the very law of its office to serve the common interest. And the richer the benefits which come from this general providence on the part of the State, the less necessary it will be to experiment with other measures for the well-being of workers.

49. This ought to be considered, as it touches the question more deeply, namely, that the State has one basic purpose for existence, which embraces in common the highest and the

lowest of its members. Non-owning workers are unquestionably citizens by nature in virtue of the same right as the rich, that is, true and vital parts whence, through the medium of families, the body of the State is constituted; and it hardly need be added that they are by far the greatest number in every urban area. Since it would be quite absurd to look out for one portion of the citizens and to neglect another, it follows that public authority ought to exercise due care in safe-guarding the well-being and the interests of non-owning workers. Unless this is done, justice, which commands that everyone be given his own, will be violated. Wherefore St. Thomas says wisely: "Even as part and whole are in a certain way the same, so too that which pertains to the whole pertains in a certain way to the part also." Consequently, among the numerous and weighty duties of rulers who would serve their people well, this is first and foremost, namely, that they protect equitably each and every class of citizens, maintaining inviolate that justice especially which is called *distributive*.

50. Although all citizens, without exception, are obliged to contribute something to the sum-total of common goods, some share of which naturally goes back to each individual, yet all can by no means contribute the same amount and in equal degree. Whatever the vicissitudes that occur in the forms of government, there will always be those differences in the condition of citizens without which society could neither exist nor be conceived. It is altogether necessary that there be some who dedicate themselves to the service of the State, who make laws, who dispense justice, and finally, by whose counsel and authority civil and military affairs are administered. These men, as is clear, play the chief role in the State, and among every people are to be regarded as occupying first place, because they work for the common good most directly and pre-eminently. On the other hand, those engaged in some calling benefit the State, but not in the same way as the men just mentioned, nor by performing the same duties; yet they, too, in a high degree, although less directly, serve the public weal. Assuredly, since social good must be of such a character that men through its acquisition are made better, it must necessarily be founded chiefly on virtue.

51. Nevertheless, an abundance of corporeal and external goods is likewise a characteristic of a well constituted State, "the use of which goods is necessary for the practice of virtue." To produce these goods the labor of the workers, whether they expend their skill and strength on farms or in factories, is most efficacious and necessary. Nay, in this respect, their energy and effectiveness are so important that it is incontestable that the wealth of nations originates from no other source than from the labor of workers. Equity therefore commands that public authority show proper concern for the worker so that from what he contributes to the common good he may receive what will enable him, housed, clothed, and secure, to live his life without hardship. Whence, it follows that all those measures ought to be favored which seem in any way capable of benefiting the condition of workers. Such solicitude is so far from injuring anyone, that it is destined rather to benefit all, because it is of absolute interest to the State that those citizens should not be miserable in every respect from whom such necessary goods proceed.

52. It is not right, as We have said, for either the citizen or the family to be absorbed by the State; it is proper that the individual and the family should be permitted to retain their freedom of action, so far as this is possible without jeopardizing the common good and without injuring anyone. Nevertheless, those who govern must see to it that they protect the community and its constituent parts: the community, because nature has entrusted its safeguarding to the sovereign power in the State to such an extent that the protection of the public welfare is not only the supreme law, but is the entire cause and reason for sovereignty; and the constituent parts, because philosophy and Christian faith agree that the administration of the State has from nature as its purpose, not the benefit of those to whom it has been entrusted, but the benefit of those who have been entrusted to it. And since the power of governing comes from God and is a participation, as it were, in His supreme sovereignty, it ought to be administered according to the example of the Divine power, which looks with paternal care to the welfare of individual creatures as well as to that of all creation. If, therefore, any injury has been done to or threatens either the

common good or the interests of individual groups, which injury cannot in any other way be repaired or prevented, it is necessary for public authority to intervene.

53. It is vitally important to public as well as to private welfare that there be peace and good order; likewise, that the whole regime of family life be directed according to the ordinances of God and the principles of nature, that religion be observed and cultivated, that sound morals flourish in private and public life, that justice be kept sacred and that no one be wronged with impunity by another, and that strong citizens grow up, capable of supporting, and, if necessary, of protecting the State. Wherefore, if at any time disorder should threaten because of strikes or concerted stoppages of work, if the natural bonds of family life should be relaxed among the poor, if religion among the workers should be outraged by failure to provide sufficient opportunity for performing religious duties, if in factories danger should assail the integrity of morals through the mixing of the sexes or other pernicious incitements to sin, or if the employer class should oppress the working class with unjust burdens or should degrade them with conditions inimical to human personality or to human dignity, if health should be injured by immoderate work and such as is not suited to sex or age—in all these cases, the power and authority of the law, but of course within certain limits, manifestly ought to be employed. And these limits are determined by the same reason which demands the aid of the law, that is, the law ought not undertake more, nor ought it go farther, than the remedy of evils or the removal of danger requires.

54. Rights indeed, by whomsoever possessed, must be religiously protected; and public authority, in warding off injuries and punishing wrongs, ought to see to it that individuals may have and hold what belongs to them. In protecting the rights of private individuals, however, special consideration must be given to the weak and the poor. For the nation, as it were, of the rich, is guarded by its own defences and is in less need of governmental protection, whereas the suffering multitude, without the means to protect itself, relies especially on the protection of the State. Wherefore, since wage workers are

numbered among the great mass of the needy, the State must include them under its special care and foresight.

55. But it will be well to touch here expressly on certain matters of special importance. The capital point is this, that private property ought to be safeguarded by the sovereign power of the State and through the bulwark of its laws. And especially, in view of such a great flaming up of passion at the present time, the masses ought to be kept within the bounds of their moral obligations. For, while justice does not oppose our striving for better things, on the other hand, it does forbid anyone to take from another what is his and, in the name of a certain absurd equality, to seize forcibly the property of others; nor does the interest of the common good itself permit this. Certainly, the great majority of working people prefer to secure better conditions by honest toil, without doing wrong to anyone. Nevertheless, not a few individuals are found who, imbued with evil ideas and eager for revolution, use every means to stir up disorder and incite to violence. The authority of the State, therefore, should intervene and, by putting restraint upon such disturbers, protect the morals of workers from their corrupting arts and lawful owners from the danger of spoliation.

56. Labor which is too long and too hard and the belief that pay is inadequate not infrequently give workers cause to strike and become voluntarily idle. This evil, which is frequent and serious, ought to be remedied by public authority, because such interruption of work inflicts damage not only upon employers and upon the workers themselves, but also injures trade and commerce and the general interests of the State; and, since it is usually not far removed from violence and rioting, it very frequently jeopardizes public peace. In this matter it is more effective and salutary that the authority of the law anticipate and completely prevent the evil from breaking out by removing early the causes from which it would seem that conflict between employers and workers is bound to arise.

57. And in like manner, in the case of the worker, there are many things which the power of the State should protect; and, first of all, the goods of his soul. For however good and desirable mortal life be, yet it is not the ultimate goal for which we are born, but a road only and a means for perfecting, through

knowledge of truth and love of good, the life of the soul. The soul bears the express image and likeness of God, and there resides in it that sovereignty through the medium of which man has been bidden to rule all created nature below him and to make all lands and all seas serve his interests. "Fill the earth and subdue it, and rule over the fishes of the sea and the fowls of the air and all living creatures that move upon the earth." In this respect all men are equal, and there is no difference between masters and servants, between rulers and subjects: "For there is the same Lord of all." No one may with impunity outrage the dignity of man, which God Himself treats with great reverence, nor impede his course to that level of perfection which accords with eternal life in heaven. Nay, more, in this connection a man cannot even by his own free choice allow himself to be treated in a way inconsistent with his nature, and suffer his soul to be enslaved; for there is no question here of rights belonging to man, but of duties owed to God, which are to be religiously observed.

58. Hence follows necessary cessation from toil and work on Sundays and Holy Days of Obligation. Let no one, however, understand this in the sense of greater indulgence of idle leisure, and much less in the sense of that kind of cessation from work, such as many desire, which encourages vice and promotes wasteful spending of money, but solely in the sense of a repose from labor made sacred by religion. Rest combined with religion calls man away from toil and the business of daily life to admonish him to ponder on heavenly goods and to pay his just and due homage to the Eternal Deity. This is especially the nature, and this the cause, of the rest to be taken on Sundays and Holy Days of Obligation, and God has sanctioned the same in the Old Testament by a special law: "Remember thou keep holy the Sabbath Day"; and He Himself taught it by His own action: namely the mystical rest taken immediately after He had created man: "He rested on the seventh day from all His work which He had done."

59. Now as concerns the protection of corporeal and physical goods, the oppressed workers, above all, ought to be liberated from the savagery of greedy men, who inordinately use human beings as things for gain. Assuredly, neither justice

nor humanity can countenance the exaction of so much work that the spirit is dulled from excessive toil and that along with it the body sinks crushed from exhaustion. The working energy of a man, like his entire nature, is circumscribed by definite limits beyond which it cannot go. It is developed indeed by exercise and use, but only on condition that a man cease from work at regular intervals and rest. With respect to daily work, therefore, care ought to be taken not to extend it beyond the hours that human strength warrants. The length of rest intervals ought to be decided on the basis of the varying nature of the work, of the circumstances of time and place, and of the physical condition of the workers themselves. Since the labor of those who quarry stone from the earth, or who mine iron, copper, and other underground materials, is much more severe and harmful to health, the working period for such men ought to be correspondingly shortened. The seasons of the year also must be taken into account; for often a given kind of work is easy to endure in one season but cannot be endured at all in another, or not without the greatest difficulty.

60. Finally, it is not right to demand of a woman or a child what a strong adult man is capable of doing or would be willing to do. Nay, as regards children, special care ought to be taken that the factory does not get hold of them before age has sufficiently matured their physical, intellectual, and moral powers. For budding strength in childhood, like greening verdure in spring, is crushed by premature harsh treatment; and under such circumstances all education of the child must needs be foregone. Certain occupations likewise are less fitted for women, who are intended by nature for the work of the home—work indeed which especially protects modesty in women and accords by nature with the education of children and the well-being of the family. Let it be the rule everywhere that workers be given as much leisure as will compensate for the energy consumed by toil, for rest from work is necessary to restore strength consumed by use. In every obligation which is mutually contracted between employers and workers, this condition, either written or tacit, is always present, that both kinds of rest be provided for; nor would it be equitable to make an agreement otherwise, because no one has the right to demand of, or to

make an agreement with anyone to neglect those duties which bind a man to God or to himself.

61. We shall now touch upon a matter of very great importance, and one which must be correctly understood in order to avoid falling into error on one side or the other. We are told that free consent fixes the amount of a wage; that therefore the employer, after paying the wage agreed to would seem to have discharged his obligation and not to owe anything more; that only then would injustice be done if either the employer should refuse to pay the whole amount of the wage, or the worker should refuse to perform all the work to which he had committed himself; and that in these cases, but in no others, is it proper for the public authority to intervene to safeguard the rights of each party.

62. An impartial judge would not assent readily or without reservation to this reasoning, because it is not complete in all respects; one factor to be considered, and one of the greatest importance, is missing. To work is to expend one's energy for the purpose of securing the things necessary for the various needs of life and especially for its preservation. "In the sweat of thy face shalt thou eat bread." Accordingly, in man labor has two marks, as it were, implanted by nature, so that it is truly *personal*, because work energy inheres in the person and belongs completely to him by whom it is expended and for whose use it is destined by nature; and, secondly, that it is *necessary*, because man has need of the fruit of his labors to preserve his life, and nature itself, which must be most strictly obeyed, commands him to preserve it. If labor should be considered only under the aspect that it is personal, there is no doubt that it would be entirely in the worker's power to set the amount of the agreed wage at too low a figure. For inasmuch as he performs work by his own free will, he can also by his own free will be satisfied with either a paltry wage for his work or even with none at all. But this matter must be judged far differently, if with the factor of *personality* we combine the factor of *necessity*, from which indeed the former is separable in thought but not in reality. In fact, to preserve one's life is a duty common to all individuals, and to neglect this duty is a crime. Hence arises necessarily the right of securing things to sustain life, and only

a wage earned by his labor gives a poor man the means to acquire these things.

63. Let it be granted then that worker and employer may enter freely into agreements and, in particular, concerning the amount of the wage; yet there is always underlying such agreements an element of natural justice, and one greater and more ancient than the free consent of contracting parties, namely, that the wage shall not be less than enough to support a worker who is thrifty and upright. If, compelled by necessity or moved by fear of a worse evil, a worker accepts a harder condition, which although against his will he must accept because the employer or contractor imposes it, he certainly submits to force, against which justice cries out in protest.

64. But in these and similar questions, such as the number of hours of work in each kind of occupation and the health safeguards to be provided, particularly in factories, it will be better, in order to avoid unwarranted governmental intervention, especially since circumstances of business, season, and place are so varied, that decision be reserved to the organizations of which We are about to speak below, or else to pursue another course whereby the interests of the workers may be adequately safeguarded—the State, if the occasion demands, to furnish help and protection.

65. If a worker receives a wage sufficiently large to enable him to provide comfortably for himself, his wife, and his children, he will, if prudent, gladly strive to practice thrift; and the result will be, as nature itself seems to counsel, that after expenditures are deducted there will remain something over and above through which he can come into the possession of a little wealth. We have seen, in fact, that the whole question under consideration cannot be settled effectually unless it is assumed and established as a principle, that the right of private property must be regarded as sacred. Wherefore, the law ought to favor this right and, so far as it can, see that the largest possible number among the masses of the population prefer to own property.

66. If this is done, excellent benefits will follow, foremost among which will surely be a more equitable division of goods. For the violence of public disorder has divided cities into two

classes of citizens, with an immense gulf lying between them. On the one side is a faction exceedingly powerful because exceedingly rich. Since it alone has under its control every kind of work and business, it diverts to its own advantage and interest all production sources of wealth and exerts no little power in the administration itself of the State. On the other side are the needy and helpless masses, with minds inflamed and always ready for disorder. But if the productive activity of the multitude can be stimulated by the hope of acquiring some property in land, it will gradually come to pass that, with the difference between extreme wealth and extreme penury removed, one class will become neighbor to the other. Moreover, there will surely be a greater abundance of the things which the earth produces. For when men know they are working on what belongs to them, they work with far greater eagerness and diligence. Nay, in a word, they learn to love the land cultivated by their own hands, whence they look not only for food but for some measure of abundance for themselves and their dependents. All can see how much this willing eagerness contributes to an abundance of produce and the wealth of a nation. Hence, in the third place, will flow the benefit that men can easily be kept from leaving the country in which they have been born and bred; for they would not exchange their native country for a foreign land if their native country furnished them sufficient means of living.

67. But these advantages can be attained only if private wealth is not drained away by crushing taxes of every kind. For since the right of possessing goods privately has been conferred not by man's law, but by nature, public authority cannot abolish it, but can only control its exercise and bring it into conformity with the commonweal. Public authority therefore would act unjustly and inhumanly, if in the name of taxes it should appropriate from the property of private individuals more than is equitable.

68. Finally, employers and workers themselves can accomplish much in this matter, manifestly through those institutions by the help of which the poor are opportunely assisted and the two classes of society are brought closer to each other. Under this category come associations for giving mutual

aid; various agencies established by the foresight of private persons to care for the worker and likewise for his dependent wife and children in the event that an accident, sickness, or death befalls him; and foundations to care for boys and girls, for adolescents, and for the aged.

69. But associations of workers occupy first place, and they include within their circle nearly all the rest. The beneficent achievements of the guilds of artisans among our ancestors have long been well known. Truly, they yielded noteworthy advantages not only to artisans, but, as many monuments bear witness, brought glory and progress to the arts themselves. In our present age of greater culture, with its new customs and ways of living, and with the increased number of things required by daily life, it is most clearly necessary that workers' associations be adapted to meet the present need. It is gratifying that societies of this kind composed either of workers alone or of workers and employers together are being formed everywhere. But it would be greatly desired that they grow in number and in active vigor. Although We have spoken of them more than once, it seems well to show in this place that they are highly opportune and are formed by their own right, and, likewise to show how they should be organized and what they should do.

70. Inadequacy of his own strength, learned from experience, impels and urges a man to enlist the help of others. Such is the teaching of Holy Scripture: "It is better therefore that two should be together, than one: for they have the advantage of their society. If one fall he shall be supported by the other; woe to him that is alone, for when he falleth he hath none to lift him up." And this also: "A brother that is helped by his brother, is like a strong city." Just as man is drawn by this natural propensity into civil union and association, so also he seeks with his fellow citizens to form other societies, admittedly small and not perfect, but societies none the less.

71. Between these latter and the large society of the State, there is, because of their different immediate purposes, a very great distinction. The end of civil society concerns absolutely all members of this society, since the end of civil society is centered in the common good, in which latter, one and all in due proportion have a right to participate. Wherefore, this society is called

public, because through it "men share with one another in establishing a commonwealth." On the other hand, societies which are formed, so to speak, within its bosom are considered *private* and are such because their immediate object is private advantage, appertaining to those alone who are thus associated together. "Now a private society is one which is formed to carry out some private business, as when two or three enter into association for the purpose of engaging together in trade."

72. Although private societies exist within the State and are, as it were, so many parts of it, still it is not within the authority of the State universally and *per se* to forbid them to exist as such. For man is permitted by a right of nature to form private societies; the State, on the other hand, has been instituted to protect and not to destroy natural right, and if it should forbid its citizens to enter into associations, it would clearly do something contradictory to itself because both the State itself and private associations are begotten of one and the same principle, namely, that men are by nature inclined to associate. Occasionally there are times when it is proper for the laws to oppose associations of this kind, that is, if they professedly seek after any objective which is clearly at variance with good morals, with justice or with the welfare of the State. Indeed, in these cases the public power shall justly prevent such associations from forming and shall also justly dissolve those already formed. Nevertheless, it must use the greatest precautions lest it appear to infringe on the rights of its citizens, and lest, under the pretext of public benefit it enact any measure that sound reason would not support. For laws are to be obeyed only in so far as they conform with right reason and thus with the eternal law of God.

73. Here come to Our mind for consideration the various confraternities, societies, and religious orders which the authority of the Church and the piety of Christians have brought into being; and history down to our own times speaks of the wonderful benefit they have been to the human race. Since societies of this character, even if judged in the light of reason alone, have been formed for an honest purpose, it is clear that they have been formed in accordance with natural right. But in whatever respect they concern religion, they are properly subject to the

Church alone. Therefore those in charge of the State cannot in justice arrogate to themselves any right over them or assume their administration to themselves. Rather it is the office of the State to respect, to conserve, and as occasion may require, to protect them from injustice. Yet we have seen something entirely different being done, especially at the present time. In many places the State has violated associations of this kind, and in fact with manifold injury, since it has put them in the bonds of the civil law, has divested them of their lawful right to be considered legal persons, and has robbed them of their property. In this property the Church possessed her rights, and individual association members possessed theirs, as did also the persons who donated this property for a designated purpose as well as those for whose benefit and relief it had been donated. Consequently, We cannot refrain from deploring such vicious and unjust acts of robbery, and so much the more because We see the road being closed to Catholic associations, which are law-abiding and in every respect useful, at the very time when it is being decreed that most assuredly men are permitted by law to form associations, and at the very time when this freedom is being lavishly granted in actual fact to men urging courses of conduct pernicious at once to religion and to the State.

74. Certainly, the number of associations of almost every possible kind, especially of associations of workers, is now far greater than ever before. This is not the place to inquire whence many of them originate, what object they have, or how they proceed. But the opinion is, and it is one confirmed by a good deal of evidence, that they are largely under the control of secret leaders and that these same leaders apply principles which are in harmony with neither Christianity nor the welfare of States, and that, after having possession of all available work, they contrive that those who refuse to join with them will be forced by want to pay the penalty. Under these circumstances, workers who are Christians must choose one of two things; either to join associations in which it is greatly to be feared that there is danger to religion, or to form their own associations and unite their forces in such a way that they may be able manfully to free themselves from such unjust and intolerable oppression. Can they who refuse to place man's highest good in imminent

jeopardy hesitate to affirm that the second course is by all means to be followed?

75. Many of our Faith are indeed to be highly commended, who, having rightly perceived what the times require of them, are experimenting and striving to discover how by honest means they can raise the non-owning working class to higher living levels. They have championed their cause and are endeavoring to increase the prosperity of both families and individuals, and at the same time to regulate justly the mutual obligations which rest upon workers and employers and to foster and strengthen in both consciousness of duty and observance of the precepts of the Gospel—precepts, in truth, which hold man back from excess and prevent him from over-stepping the bounds of moderation and, in the midst of the widest divergences among persons and things, maintain harmony in the State. For this reason, we see eminent men meeting together frequently to exchange ideas, to combine their forces, and to deliberate on the most expedient programs of action. Others are endeavoring to unite the various kinds of workers in suitable associations, are assisting them with advice and money, and making plans to prevent a lack of honest and profitable work. The bishops are giving encouragement and bestowing support; and under their authority and auspices many from the ranks of the clergy, both regular and diocesan, are showing zealous care for all that pertains to the spiritual improvement of the members of these associations. Finally, there are not wanting Catholics of great wealth, yet voluntary sharers, as it were, in the lot of the wage workers, who by their own generous contributions are striving to found and extend associations through which the worker is readily enabled to obtain from his toil not only immediate benefits, but also assurance of honorable retirement in the future. How much good such manifold and enthusiastic activity has contributed to the benefit of all is too well known to make discussion necessary. From all this, We have taken auguries of good hope for the future, provided that societies of this kind continually grow and that they are founded with wise organization. Let the State protect these lawfully associated bodies of citizens; let it not, however, interfere with their private concerns and order of life; for vital activity is set in

motion by an inner principle, and it is very easily destroyed, as We know, by intrusion from without.

76. Unquestionably, wise direction and organization are essential to these associations in order that in their activities there be unity of purpose and concord of wills. Furthermore, if citizens have free right to associate, as in fact they do, they also must have the right freely to adopt the organization and the rules which they judge most appropriate to achieve their purpose. We do not feel that the precise character in all details which the aforementioned direction and organization of associations ought to have can be determined by fast and fixed rules, since this is a matter to be decided rather in the light of the temperament of each people, of experiment and practice, of the nature and character of the work, of the extent of trade and commerce, and of other circumstances of a material and temporal kind, all of which must be carefully considered. In summary, let this be laid down as a general and constant law: Workers' associations ought to be so constituted and so governed as to furnish the most suitable and most convenient means to attain the object proposed, which consists in this, that the individual members of the association secure, so far as is possible, an increase in the goods of body, of soul, and of property.

77. It is clear, however, that moral and religious perfection ought to be regarded as their principal goal, and that their social organization as such ought above all to be directed completely by this goal. For otherwise they would degenerate in nature and would be little better than those associations in which no account is ordinarily taken of religion. Besides, what would it profit a worker to secure through an association an abundance of goods, if his soul through lack of its proper food should run the risk of perishing? "What doth it profit a man, if he gain the whole world, but suffer the loss of his own soul?" Christ Our Lord teaches that this in fact must be considered the mark whereby a Christian is distinguished from a pagan: "After all these things the Gentiles seek—seek ye first the kingdom of God and His justice, and all these things shall be given you besides." Therefore, having taken their principles from God, let those associations provide ample opportunity for religious instruction so that individual members may understand their duties to God,

that they may well know what to believe, what to hope for, and what to do for eternal salvation, and that with special care they may be fortified against erroneous opinions and various forms of corruption. Let the worker be exhorted to the worship of God and the pursuit of piety, especially to religious observance of Sundays and Holy Days. Let him learn to reverence and love the Church, the common Mother of all, and likewise to observe her precepts and to frequent her Sacraments, which are the divine means for purifying the soul from the stains of sin and for attaining sanctity.

78. When the regulations of associations are founded upon religion, the way is easy toward establishing the mutual relations of the members so that peaceful living together and prosperity will result. Offices in the associations are to be distributed properly in accordance with the common interest, and in such a way, moreover, that wide difference in these offices may not create discord. It is of special importance that obligations be apportioned wisely and be clearly defined, to the end that no one is done an injustice. Let the funds be disbursed equitably in such way that the amount of benefit to be paid out to members is fixed beforehand in accordance with individual needs, and let the rights and duties of employers be properly adjusted to the rights and duties of workers. If any one in these two groups feels that he has been injured in any way, nothing is more to be desired than that prudent and upright men of the same body be available, and that the association regulations themselves prescribe that the dispute be settled according to the decision of these men.

79. It must also be specially provided that the worker at no time be without sufficient work, and that the monies paid into the treasury of the association furnish the means of assisting individual members in need, not only during sudden and unforeseen changes in industry, but also whenever anyone is stricken by sickness, by old age, or by misfortune.

80. Through these regulations, provided they are readily accepted, the interests and welfare of the poor will be adequately cared for. Associations of Catholics, moreover, will undoubtedly be of great importance in promoting prosperity in the State. Through past events we can, without temerity,

foresee the future. Age presses hard upon age, but there are wondrous similarities in history, governed as it is by the Providence of God, Who guides and directs the continuity and the chain of events in accordance with that purpose which He set before Himself in creating the human race. In the early ages, when the Church was in her youth, We know that the reproach was hurled at the Christians that the great majority of them lived by precarious alms or by toil. Yet, although destitute of wealth and power, they succeeded in winning the good will of the rich and the protection of the mighty. All could see that they were energetic, industrious, peace-loving, and exemplarily devoted to the practice of justice and especially of charity. In the presence of life and conduct such as this, all prejudice vanished, the taunting voices of the malevolent were silenced, and the falsehoods of inveterate superstition yielded little by little to Christian truth.

81. The condition of workers is a subject of bitter controversy at the present tine; and whether this controversy is resolved in accordance with reason or otherwise, is in either event of utmost importance to the State. But Christian workers will readily resolve it in accordance with reason, if, united in associations and under wise leaders, they enter upon the path which their fathers and their ancestors followed to their own best welfare as well as to that of the State. For, no matter how strong the power of prejudice and passion in man, yet, unless perversity of will has deadened the sense of the right and just, the good will of citizens is certain to be more freely inclined toward those whom they learn to know as industrious and temperate, and who clearly place justice before profit and conscientious observance of duty before all else. Under these circumstances there will follow also this great advantage, that no little hope and opportunity for developing a sound attitude will be afforded those workers who live in complete disdain of the Christian Faith or in a manner foreign to its profession. These men indeed, for the most part, know that they have been deceived by illusory hopes and by false appearances. They are conscious of being most inhumanly treated by greedy employers, that almost no greater value is being placed on them than the amount of gain they yield by their toil, and that in the

associations, moreover, in whose meshes they are caught, there exist in place of charity and love, internal dissensions which are the inseparable companions of aggravating and irreligious poverty. Broken in spirit, and worn out in body, how gladly many would free themselves from a servitude so degrading! Yet they dare not because either human shame or the fear of want prevents them. It is remarkable how much asssociations of Catholics can contribute to the welfare of all such men if they invite those wavering in uncertainty to their bosom in order to remedy their difficulties, and if they receive the penitents into their trust and protection.

82. These, Venerable Brethren, are the persons, and this is the procedure to be employed in dealing with this most difficult question. Everyone according to his position ought to gird himself for the task, and indeed as speedily as possible, lest, by delaying the remedy, the evil, which is already of vast dimensions, become incurable. Let those in charge of States make use of the provision afforded by laws and institutions; let the rich and employers be mindful of their duties; let the workers, whose cause is at stake, press their claims with reason. And since religion alone, as We said in the beginning, can remove the evil, root and branch, let all reflect upon this: First and foremost Christian morals must be re-established, without which even the weapons of prudence, which are considered especially effective, will be of no avail to secure well-being.

83. So far as the Church is concerned, at no time and in no manner will she permit her efforts to be wanting, and she will contribute all the more help in proportion as she has more freedom of action. Let this be understood in particular by those whose duty it is to promote the public welfare. Let the members of the Sacred Ministry exert all their strength of mind and all their diligence, and Venerable Brethren, under the guidance of your authority and example, let them not cease to impress upon men of all ranks the principles of Christian living as found in the Gospel; by all means in their power let them strive for the well-being of peoples; and especially let them aim both to preserve in themselves and to arouse in others, in the highest equally as well as in the lowest, the mistress and queen of the virtues, Charity. Certainly, the well-being which is so longed

for is chiefly to be expected from an abundant outpouring of charity; of Christian charity, We mean, which is in epitome the law of the Gospel, and which, always ready to sacrifice itself for the benefit of others, is man's surest antidote against the insolence of the world and immoderate love of self; the divine office and features of this virtue being described by the Apostle Paul in these words: "Charity is patient, is kind . . . is not self-seeking . . . bears with all things . . . endures all things."

84. As a pledge of Divine Favor and as a token of Our affection, most lovingly in the Lord We bestow on each of you, Venerable Brethren, on your clergy and on your people, the Apostolic Blessing.

85. Given in Rome, at St. Peter's, the 15th day of May, in the year 1891, the fourteenth of Our Pontificate.

John Ireland
1838-1918

The Catholic Church in America is not too many genera-
tions removed from being a population of poor immigrants from
Europe. Lost in a land that was often culturally and linguistically
foreign to them, often experiencing open hostility and abuse,
the newly arrived Catholic immigrants tended to flounder, give
up hope, and feel inferior. Men such as James Cardinal Gibbons
of Baltimore and Archbishop John Ireland of St. Paul, Minnesota,
stand out as brilliant lights in the darkness that surrounded the
Church at the close of the nineteenth and beginning of the
twentieth centuries.

In the selection that follows, "The Church and the Age,"
the reader will get a taste of what these two men were all about.
It is taken from Archbishop Ireland's book, The Church and
Modern Society *(1896).*

"I am tired of the common, I am angry with it ... I wish
to see men rise far above their fellows ... The common never
puts humanity forward, never begets a great movement; nor
does it save humanity when grave peril threatens ... The one
man of sufficient firmness of hand and grandeur of soul saves a
whole nation; the one man saves the whole Church." Men of
Ireland's stature see further than ordinary men. He himself saw
a new age dawning. He boldly told the Catholics of America
how they should welcome the modern era by intellectual vigor,

sound patriotism, active involvement in social movements, ready acceptance of the achievements of material progress. He allowed no room for the timid and the half-hearted; Catholics of this type deserve failure. Ireland challenged the Church to move ahead with the times, taking no heed of opposition that worries about change and innovation. For him, to hold the age to truth and justice, Catholics must be in it and of it.

Ireland's teaching must have been refreshing to Catholics who looked for a way to integrate themselves into pluralistic America in a positive manner and without fear of losing their religious orientation. But he also had his severe critics. Too American, said some, too Catholic said others. History, however, has proven him to have been a sound spokesman and capable churchman. America and the Catholic Church are still trying to catch up with his fearless and innovative statements on issues such as education, social movements, race relations, modern science, and Church and State.

Archbishop Ireland was born in Ireland in 1838. He immigrated to America in 1848 with his parents. He was sent to France by the Bishop of St. Paul to study for the priesthood in 1853. Ordained in 1861, Ireland served briefly as a chaplain in the War between the States. As Archbishop of St. Paul, he was recognized as one of the leaders of the American hierarchy. While vigorously building up the Church in the midwestern states, he found time for scholarly writing and active participation in the resolution of several key national problems of his time. What he said of Cardinal Gibbons describes John Ireland as well: "He is large-minded; his vision cannot be narrowed to a one-sided consideration of men or things. He is large-hearted; his sympathies are limited only by the frontiers of humanity."

THE CHURCH
AND MODERN SOCIETY

F ive and twenty years in exalted office, a bishop, a chieftain among bishops, in the Catholic Church, in America, in the latter days of this nineteenth century of the Christian era! Great the opportunities and weighty the responsibilities!

Of those years what would the record be that I, who revere and love the Cardinal Archbishop of Baltimore, would fain write? Would it be that they went by without harm done, or good prevented, without blemish or reproach? This, whatever be its value along the dark lines of frail humanity, would be, at best, but the story of the talent wrapped up in napkin folds and securely guarded from misuse. Not this record did Christ expect from His apostles, and from this pulpit I will not speak it.

Would the record be of common duties performed in zeal and loyalty, of useful ministry in blessing and ordaining, in building temples and asylums, in exhorting souls into their salvation? This would be the story of the ten hundred; it merits no special praise; it teaches no special lesson, and it shall not be my theme this evening.

Let others tell of the many; I would tell of the few. I am tired of the common; I am angry with it. If I am, myself, compelled to plod its wearisome pathways, I wish, at least, to see others shun them; I wish to see men rise far above their fellows, and by their singular thoughts and singular deeds freshen human life and give to it the power to place itself in those lofty altitudes where progress is born. The common never puts humanity forward, never begets a great movement; nor does it save humanity when grave peril threatens. The common! We are surfeited with it; it has made our souls torpid and our limbs rigid. Under the guise of goodness it is a curse. The want in the world, the want in the Church, to-day as at other times, but to-day as never before, is men among men, men who see farther than others, rise higher than others, act more boldly than others. They need not be numerous. They never were numerous. But, while the few, they take with them the multitude and save humanity. The one man of sufficient firmness of hand and grandeur of soul saves a whole nation; the one man saves the whole Church.

This evening, it is my privilege to honor a man among men. The record of the Cardinal Archbishop of Baltimore! I speak it with pride and exultation. It is the record I should have traced for the ideal bishop and leader of men in these solemn times through which the Church is passing.

The times are solemn. In no other epoch of history, since the beginning of the Christian era, did changes so profound and so far-reaching take place. Discoveries and inventions have opened to us a new material world. Social and political conditions have been transformed. Intellectual curiosity peers with keenest eye into the recesses of sky and earth. Intellectual ambition, maddened by wondrous successes in many fields, puts on daring pinions and challenges all limitations of knowledge. The human heart is emboldened to the strangest dreams, and frets itself into desperate efforts before all barriers to the fulfillment of its desires. Let all things be new, is the watchword of humanity today, and to make all things new is humanity's strong resolve. To this end are pledged its most fierce activities, which, wherever in the realm of man they are put forth, are exemplified in the steam and electricity of the new material creation.

In the midst of times so solemn the Catholic Church moves and works, purposing, under the terms of her charter, to conquer to Christ minds and hearts, individuals and society. Her mission to the world is the same as it has been during nineteen hundred years; but the world has changed and is changing. With the new order have come new needs, new hopes, new aspirations. To conquer the new world to Christ, the Church must herself be new, adapting herself in manner of life and in method of action to the conditions of the new order, thus proving herself, while ever ancient, to be ever new, as truth from heaven is and ever must be.

Now is the opportunity for great and singular men among the sons of God's Church. To-day, routine is fatal; to-day the common is exhausted senility. The crisis demands the new, the extraordinary, and with it the Catholic Church will score the grandest of her victories in the grandest of history's ages.

The Church and the age are at war. I voice the fact with sorrow. Both Church and age are at fault. I explain my words. When I speak of Church and age in conflict one with the other, I take the age as portrayed by many representatives of the age, and I take the Church as portrayed by many representatives of the Church. Church and age, rightly understood, are not at war.

I blame the age. Elated with its material and intellectual successes, it is proud and it exaggerates its powers. It imagines that the natural, which has served it so well, is all sufficient; it tends to the exclusion of the supernatural; it puts on the cloak of secularism. In its worship of the new, it regards whatever is old with suspicion. It asks why its church may not be new, as well as its chemistry, or its biology. A church bearing on her front the marks of nineteen centuries is, in its eyes, out of date and out of place. Pride and thoughtlessness are the evil and misleading characteristics of the age.

I blame the Church. I speak as a Catholic. I know the divine elements in the Church. I have full faith that those elements are at all times guarded by the abiding presence of the Holy Spirit. But I know, also, the human elements in the Church, and I know that upon those human elements much of the Church's weal depends. The Church has had her more brilliant epochs of light and glory, according as pastors and people scanned the world with clearer vision and unsheathed the spiritual sword with greater alacrity. The dependency of the Church upon her human elements is too easily forgotten, although the Church herself authoritatively teaches that undue reliance upon divine grace is a sin of presumption.

I am not afraid to say that, during the century whose sun is now setting, many leaders of thought in the Church have made the mistake of being too slow to understand the new age and too slow to extend to it the conciliatory hand of friendship. They were not without their reasons. The Church, in her divine elements, is unchangeable, supremely conservative; her dread of change, so righteous in a degree, is easily carried beyond its legitimate frontier, and made to cover ground where change is proper. The movements of the age were frequently ushered into existence under most repellent and inauspicious forms. The revolution of 1789, whose waters, rushing and destructive as the maddest mountain torrent, were crested with the crimson of blood, was the loud signal of the new era. The standard-bearers of the age often raised aloft the insignia of impiety and of social anarchy. Certain Catholics, indeed, as Lamennais, sought to establish an alliance between the church and the age; but they were imprudent in speech, and, in their impatience, they invoked failure upon themselves and discouragement upon their allies. But with all these excuses, churchmen thought and acted too slowly. They failed to grasp the age, to Christianize its aspirations, and to guide its forward march. The age passed beyond them. There were a few Lacordaires, who recognized and proclaimed the duties of the hour: but timid companions abandoned them; reactionaries accused them of dangerous liberalism, of semi-heresy; and they were forced to be silent. The many saw but the vices of the age, which they readily anathamatized; its good and noble tendencies they either ignored or denied. For them the age was the dark world against which Christ had warned His followers. The task of winning it to the gospel was a forlorn hope. It was a task to be accomplished only through some stupendous miracle from heaven, and, until the miracle would come, the ministers of Christ must withdraw into winter quarters, sacristies, and sanctuaries, where, surrounded by a small band of chosen souls, they might guard themselves and their friends from the all-pervading contagion. The age, abandoned to itself and to false and mischievous guides, irritated by the isolation and the unfriendliness of the Church, became hardened in its secularism, and taught itself to despise and hate religion. This deplorable condition was prevalent in some countries more than in others; but from none was it wholly absent. The Church had seemingly furled her flag of battle, her flag of victory.

It was a mistake and a misfortune. "Go, teach all nations," Christ had said once for all time. In obedience to this command the first apostles hastened through the Roman Empire, preaching to the sages of Athens on the Hill of Mars, to the patricians and senators of Rome in the courts of emperors, to the slaves in their huts, and the Roman Empire was Christianized. Even if our age

John Ireland

had been radically evil and erring, the methods and the zeal of the early apostles would have won it to the Saviour. But, in veriest fact, the present age, pagan as it may be in its language and in its extravagances, is, in its depths, instinct with Christian emotions; it worships unwittingly at Christian shrines, and only awaits the warm contact of Christ's Church to avow itself Christian.

I indicate the opportunity for the great and singular churchman. His work is to bridge the chasm separating the Church from the age, to dispel the mists of prejudice which prevent the one from seeing the other as it is, to bring the Church to the age, and the age to the Church.

Men must be taught that the Church and the age are not hopelessly separated.

The age has, assuredly, its sins and its errors, and these the Church never will condone. But sins and errors are the accidentals, not the essentials, of the age. For my part, I see in the present age one of the mighty upheavals which, from time to time, occur in humanity, producing and signalizing the ascending stages in its continuous progress. Humanity, strengthened by centuries of toil and of reflection, nourished and permeated by principles of Christian truth, is now lifting its whole mass upward to higher regions of light and liberty, and demanding full and universal enjoyment of its God-given rights. All this is praiseworthy; all this is noble and beautiful. This is what we are asked to accept when we are asked to accept the age. When we accept the age, we reserve to ourselves the right to rebuke it for its defects; in accepting it we put ourselves in a position to correct it.

The Church, too, has her accidentals and her essentials. We should distinguish accidentals from essentials; we should be ready, while jealously guarding the essentials, to abandon the accidentals, as circumstances of time and place demand. What the Church at any time was, certain people hold she must ever remain. They do her much harm, making her rigid and unbending, incapable of adapting herself to new and changing surroundings. The Church, created by Christ for all time, lives in every age and is of every age. We find, consequently, in her outward features the variable and the contingent. The Church, at

399

one time imperialistic in her political alliances, was, at another, feudalistic; but she never committed herself in principle to imperialism or to feudalism. She spoke Greek in Athens and Latin in Rome, and her sons wore the chlamys or the toga; but she was never confined to Greece or to Italy. In later days she lisped the nascent languages of Goth and Frank, and, in her steppings through their lands, showed not a little of their uncultured bearing and of their unformed civilization; but she was never limited in life and conditions to the life and conditions of Goth or Frank. Her scientific knowledge was scant as that of the epoch; her social legislation and customs, as rude and tentative. She was merely partaking, in her human elements, of the life of her epoch, her divine elements always remaining the self-same. Two or three centuries ago she was courtly and aristocratic under the temporal sway of the Fifth Charles of Spain, or of the Fourteenth Louis of France; but this again was a passing phase in her existence, and at other times she may be as democratic in her demeanor as the most earnest democracy would desire. Her canon law, which is the expression of her adaptability to environment, received the impress, now of Charlemagne, now of Hapsburgh or Bourbon edicts; but never was she herself mummified in Justinian or Bourbon molds, and her canon law may be as American as it was Roman, as much the reflection of the twentieth century as it was of the middle ages. Were not all this true, the Church would not be Catholic, as her founder was Catholic, the teacher and Saviour of all ages and of all nations. Let us be as broad and as Catholic in our conception of the Church as Christ was, and we shall have no difficulty in recognizing her fitness to all lands and to all ages—past as well as present, and present and future as well as past.

What! the Church of the living God, the Church of ten thousand victories over pagans and barbarians, over heresies and false philosophies, over defiant kings and unruly peoples—the great, freedom-loving, truth-giving, civilizing Catholic Church—this Church of the nineteenth century afraid of any century! not seeing in the ambitions of the nineteenth century the fervent ebullitions of her own noble sentiments, and in its achievements for the elevation of mankind the germinations of her own Christlike plantings! this Church not eager for the fray, not precipitating herself with love irresistible upon this modern world to claim it, to bless it, to own it for Christ, to foster and encourage its hopes or to rectify and remedy its defects, and with her impetuous arm to lift it to the very summit of its highest aspirations —to which by the Church's aid alone this doubting, quivering, hoping, despairing world can ever attain! Far, far, from Catholics be the chilling, un-Catholic thought!

I preach the new, the most glorious crusade. Church and age! Unite them in the name of humanity, in the name of God.

Church and age! They pulsate alike: the God of nature works in one, the God of supernatural revelation works in the other—in both the self-same God.

Let us note the chief characteristics of the age. The age is ambitious of knowledge. Its searchings know no rest and submit to no limitations. Be it so. The Catholic Church proclaims that all truth, natural as well as supernatural, is from God, and that the mind grows more Godlike as it absorbs truth in more generous proportions. Two sources of knowledge there are, according to Catholic teaching, both from God—the reason of man and the voice of God in revelation. Between reason and revelation there can never be a contradiction; the so-called war between faith and science is a war between the misrepresentations of science and the misrepresentations of faith, or, rather, between the ignorance of some scientists and the ignorance of some theologians. The Church has no fear of natural truth; yea, from it strongest proofs came to her of the truth of supernatural revelation. The discoveries of the age, whether in minute animalcules or in vast fiery orbs, demonstrate God. Through all the laws of the universe they show forth an absolute cause, all-wise, all-powerful, eternal. The fruits of all historical research, of all social and moral inquiry, give us Christ rising from the dead and raising the world from the dead. They give us Christ's Church as the enduring embodiment of Christ's mission. The knowledge of the age! The age has not a sufficiency of knowledge; and the need of the hour, the duty of the Church, is to stimulate the age to deeper researches, to more extensive surveyings, until it has left untouched no particle of matter that may conceal a secret, no incident of history, no act in the life of humanity, that may solve a problem. The knowledge of the age! The Church blesses it; the

Church promotes its onward growth with all her might, with all her light.

It is an age of liberty, civil and political; it is the age of democracy—the people, tired of the unrestricted sway of sovereigns, and exercise with more or less directness the power which was primarily theirs by divine ordinance. The age of democracy! The Catholic Church, I am sure, has no fear of democracy, this flowering of her own most sacred principles of the equality, fraternity, and liberty of all men, in Christ and through Christ. These principles are found upon every page of the gospel. From the moment they were first confided to the Church they have been ceaselessly leavening minds and hearts towards the full recognition of the rights and the dignity of man, towards the elevation of the multitude, and the enjoyment of freedom from unnecessary restrictions, and of social happiness mingled with as few sorrows as earth's planet permits. The whole history of the Catholic Church is the record of the enfranchisement of the slave, the curbing of the tyranny of kings, the defense of the poor, of woman, of the people, of all the social entities that pride and passion choose to trample upon. The great theologians of the Church lay the foundations of political democracy which to-day attains its perfect form. They prove that all political power comes from God through the people, that kings and princes are the people's delegates, and that when rulers become tyrants the inalienable right of revolution belongs to the people. The Church is at home under all forms of government. The one condition of the legitimacy of a form of government, in the eyes of the Church, is that it be accepted by the people. The Church has never said that she prefers one form of government above another. But, so far as I may from my own thoughts interpret the principles of the Church, I say that the government of the people, by the people, and for the people, is, more than any other, the polity under which the Catholic Church, the church of the people, breathes air most congenial to her mind and heart.

It is an age of battlings for social justice to all men, for the right of all men to live in the frugal comfort becoming rational creatures. Very well! Is it not Catholic doctrine that birth into the world is man's title to a sufficiency of the things of the world? Is not the plea for social justice and social well-being the loud outburst of the cry which has ever been going up from the bosom of the Church since the words were spoken by her founder: "Seek first the kingdom of God and His justice and all these things shall be added unto you?" It is not sufficiently understood that the principles which underlie the social movement of the times in its legitimate demands are constantly taught in schools of Catholic theology; as, for instance, the principle which, to the surprise of his fellow-countrymen, Cardinal Manning proclaimed: that in case of extreme necessity, one may use, as far as it is needed to save life, the property of others. We have, of late, been so accustomed to lock up our teachings in seminary and sanctuary that when they appear in active evolution in the broad arena of life they are not recognized by Catholics; nay, are even feared and disowned by them.

It is an age of material progress, of inventions, of the subjugation of nature's forces to the service of man, of the building up of man's empire over all irrational creation. Will the Church condemn the age for this? It is her teaching that the earth was given to man that he dominate over it. Progress along lines of all human activity is the divine ordering. That the stagnation of human energies provokes God's anger, is the lesson of the parable of the talents.

I have described the intellectual attitude which it befits us to assume towards the age. What should our practical relations with it be? Let them be all that the warmest apostolic zeal and the best human prudence counsel. We desire to win the age. Let us not, then, stand isolated from it. Our place is in the world as well as in the sanctuary; in the world, wherever we can prove our love for it or render it a service. We cannot influence men at long range; close contact is needed. Let us be with them in the things that are theirs—material interests, social welfare, civil weal—so that they may be with us in the things that are ours—the interests of religions. Let us be with them because their interests are ours, and ours are theirs, because nature and grace must not be separated.

The age loves knowledge: let us be patrons of knowledge. Let us be the most erudite historians, the most experienced scientists, the most acute philosophers; and history, science, and philosophy will not be divorced from religion. The age demands liberty with good government: let us be models of patriotism, of civic virtue, of loyalty to the country's institutions; and no suspicion will ever rest on us that we are the advocates of buried regimes, the enemies of liberty, civil or political. The age pleads for social justice and the amelioration of the masses: in social movements let us be most active, most useful; and men will recognize the truth that religion, having the promises of the life to come, has those, too, of the life that is, and seeing in the Church the friend and the protectress of their terrestrial interests, they will put faith in her pledges of supernatural rewards. The age exults in its material progress, its inventions, and discoveries; let us exult with it and recognize its claims to stupendous achievements; let us, books of history in hand, show to the age that the earliest leaders in modern material progress were sons of the Church; let us embrace every opportunity to work for further victories of mind over matter; and no man will dare speak to the Church a word of reproach in the name of progress.

And in all that we undertake or do, let us labor earnestly and energetically. The world succeeds in its enterprises through tireless perseverance and Titanic labors. It is in such wise that we shall succeed in our task. The half-hearted manner in which we evangelize the age deserves and entails failure. Steam and electricity in religion coöperating with divine grace will triumph; old-fashioned, easy-going methods mean defeat. We have not heretofore won the age; let us not put all the blame upon the age.

But I am afraid, one will say, of the opposition that I shall encounter if I speak as you speak this evening, if I act as you advise me to act. Do not, I pray, lose time in thinking of opposition that may come to you. If you dread opposition, you are not "of the seed of those men by whom salvation is brought to Israel." Opposition is sure to come. In every historic transition there are reactionaries, who would feign push back into Erie the waters of Niagara—men, to whom all change is perilous, all innovation damnable liberalism, or, even, rank heresy. Heed them not; pass onward with Christ and His Church.

But the age, another says, is wedded to its idols; it is turned away from the Church and will not listen. The age will listen, if minds and hearts properly attuned speak to it. Men are always convertible to God; the age is convertible to Him. I know as well as you the errors and the evils of the age, and you and I condemn them, even as God and His Church condemn them. I know that movements, holy and legitimate in themselves, are directed towards things false and pernicious, and that by many advocates of the age natural truth is made a protest against revealed religion; liberty becomes license and anarchy, and social justice means the violation of private right to property. Against this misdirection of the movements of the age, Catholics should labor with all their might. But to do so effectively, Catholics must first prove that they are heart and soul in sympathy with the movements themselves, and actively devoted to the advancement of all that is good and true in them. No one will say that during the nineteenth century Catholics have not, in loud speech and brave acts, made opposition to all the bad tendencies visible in the movements of the age. If, however, their opposition failed to arrest those tendencies, may not the cause be that they did not make clear their love for what is good in the age, while expressing their hatred of what is bad in it? The age believed that it was attacked in all its aims and activities; it regarded as its enemies those who spoke, and it refused to hearken to them. To hold the age to truth and justice, Catholics must be in it and of it; they must be fair to it, recognizing what is good no less than what is bad in it; they must love what is good in it, and work in aid of all its legitimate aspirations.

The Church and the age! Their union is assured. The nineteenth century has seen in its latter days men "by whom salvation is brought to Israel." I name a few: Von Ketteler, of Mayence; Lavigerie, of Carthage; Manning of Westminster; Gibbons, of Baltimore; Leo, of Rome. Two we especially revere.

Leo, I hail thee, pontiff of thy age, providential chieftan of the Church in a great crisis of her history! How true it is that God has care of His Church! It seemed to be a supreme moment in her life among men. The abyss between her and the age was widening; governments warred against her; peoples distrusted her; the intellectual and social movements of humanity ignored her. Catholics, priests and laymen, terrified and disheartened, isolated themselves from the active world and made of their isolation a rule, almost a dogma. Humanly speaking, the horizon was dark with fateful forebodings. Leo comes to the helm; quickly he discerns the dangers from angry elements, from shoals and breakers, and, under his hand, the ship moves in new courses; she surmounts the highest billows, fearless of their fury; she reaches calm seas, where tirumphantly she ploughs the waters— the peerless queen.

Leo speaks to the age in its own language, and the age understands him. He tells the age what the mind of the Church is in regard to its hopes and aspirations, and the age wonders and admires. He acts, and demands that others act, for the furtherance of those hopes and aspirations under all their legitimate forms, and the age praises and loves the name of Leo.

Leo charges the age to go forward in its discoveries and inventions. He writes: "Because all that is true must of necessity have come from God, whatever of truth human investigation brings out, is recognized by the Church as a reflection of the divine mind. The Church is not opposed to the discovery of new things; she is not opposed to the searching for things that will add to the elegance and the comfort of life: nay rather, the Church, as the enemy of apathy and idleness, ardently desires that the minds of men be exercised and cultivated and made to produce rich fruits."

He opens to the scholarship of the world the archives of the Vatican, establishes universities in Europe and America, raises the standard of studies in the schools of the Church, and thus strives to place the Church in the van of the world's race for knowledge.

By his encyclical on "The Condition of Labor," he makes himself the pontiff of the working man; he gives to labor its charter, teaching labor not only its duties, of which it had heard so much, but, also, its rights, of which it had heard so little. The poor, the oppressed, the masses of the people now know that the Church is with them, not merely as their counselor, but as their defender and their champion.

Leo's encyclical to the Catholics of France tenders to democracy the long-coveted approval of the Church. Empires and monarchies had claimed as exclusively their own the smiles of the church: these smiles are now bestowed upon the republic, the highest embodiment of popular rights. God be praised that we have lived to know and to love Leo!

In letters, in private conversation, Leo urges bishops, priests, and laymen to be ambassadors of the Church, to bear in her name to peoples and governments, not the sword of war, but the olive branch of amity and concord. His letters to Decurtins and De Mun are examples of his enlightened zeal. "I try to do everything, everywhere, for the Church," said Leo to me, "and so would I have bishops do, whatever circumstances permit." Nor does Leo restrict for Catholics the lines of action to confraternities and religious associations. In his letter to the Bishop of Grenoble, he counsels Catholics to work for truth and virtue wherever they are allowed to work and with men who, though not themselves Catholics, are led by their good sense and their natural instincts of righteousness to do what is right and to oppose what is evil.

Leo has the courage of his high mission. Pope as he is, he has opponents within the Church; men whose sickly nerves suffer from the vibrations of the ship moving under his hand with accelerated velocity: reactionaries, who think that all the wisdom and all the providential guidance of the Church are with the past; obstinate advocates of self-interest, who place their own views and their own likings above the welfare of the Church of Christ. But in spite of all opposition Leo works, and Leo reigns. The Roman Pontificate is to-day invested before governments and peoples with prestige and moral power unknown to it for years; the Church is out upon the broad world, esteemed and listened to as she has not hitherto been in this century. Whole nations are saved! Leo is doing for France what France is unable to do; he is uniting her people, giving to her a durable government, and staying the hand of religious persecution. Say what some may, such are in France the results of the Papal encyclicals in favor of the Republic.

Leo shows forth in especial splendor the Church's catholicity—her divinely-begotten fitness for all ages and all nations. He withdraws the Church from political and social entanglements, makes her independent of the transient traditions of the past, and sets her before the world radiant in her native beauty and freedom, prepared to embrace and bless the new humanity of the twentieth century, as she embraced and blessed the humanity of preceding centuries, the Church of to-day as of yesterday, the Church of to-morrow as of to-day.

True, much is yet to be done before the union of Church and age is complete; but the work has been begun and is progressing. May Leo live yet many years! May Leo's spirit long dominate in the Vatican! All will then be well. Meanwhile, in America, let us be loyal to Leo, and work as earnestly as he does for the welfare of Church and of humanity, and in full accord with his teachings. We are especially favored by Leo. He lives among us in the person of his chosen friend and representative, one who makes the pontiff known to us as none other could, and who, in the acts and discourses by which he interprets Leo's mind, proves daily to us that Leo is, indeed, the pontiff of the age. The Church and the age! Rome and America! Their intimate union is heralded in the command of Monsignor Satolli to the Catholics of America: "Go forward on the road of progress, bearing in one hand the book of Christian truth—Christ's gospel— and in the other the Constitution of the United States."

Gibbons, of Baltimore: I cannot give to my words the warmth of my heart; I will give to them its sincerity. I have spoken of the providential Pope of Rome. I speak now of the providential Archbishop of Baltimore. Often have I thanked God that in this latter quarter of the nineteenth century Cardinal Gibbons has been given to us as primate, as leader. Catholic of Catholics, American of Americans, a bishop of this age and of his country, he is to America what Leo is to Christendom. Aye, far beyond America does his influence extend. Men's influence is not confined by the frontiers of nations, and Gibbons is European as Manning is American. A special mission is reserved to the American Cardinal. In America, the Church and the age have fairest field to diplay their activities, and in America more speedily than elsewhere is the problem of their reconciliation to be solved. The world has a supreme interest in this reconciliation, and watches intently the prelate who in America leads the forces of the Church. The name of Cardinal Gibbons lights up the pages of nearly every European book which treats of modern social and political questions. The ripplings of his influence cross the threshold of the Vatican. Leo, the mighty inspirer of men, is himself not seldom inspired and encouraged by his faithful lieutentants, from whom he asks: "Watchman, what of the night?" And this historic incident of the Knights of Labor, whose condemnation by the Roman Congregations Cardinal Gibbons was able to avert, exercised, I am sure, no small influence upon the preparation of the encyclical "The Condition of Labor."

But Cardinal Gibbons belongs to America; let him be judged by his work in America.

The work of Cardinal Gibbons forms an epoch in the history of the Church in America. He has made the Church known to the people of America; he has demonstrated the fitness of the Church for America, the natural alliance existing between the Church and the freedom-giving democratic institutions of America. Thanks to him the scales have fallen from the eyes of non-Catholics; prejudices have vanished. He, the great churchman, is also the great citizen. In him Church and country are united, and the magnetism of the union pervades the whole land, teaching laggard Catholics to love America, teaching well-disposed non-Catholics to trust the Church. Church and country, Church and age, modern aspirations and ancient truths, republican liberty and spiritual princedom—harmonized, drawn into bonds of warm amity, laboring together for the progress and happiness of humanity! How great the mission assigned to Cardinal Gibbons! How precious the work done by him in fulfillment of it!

I need not tell what qualities of mind and heart have brought the reward of success to the labors of Cardinal Gibbons. The nation knows them. He is large-minded; his vision cannot be narrowed to a one-sided consideration of men or things. He is large-hearted; his sympathies are limited only by the frontiers of humanity. He is ready for every noble work, patriotic, intellectual, social, philanthropic, as well as religious, and, in the prosecution of it, joins hands with laborer and capitalist, with white man and black man, with Catholic, Protestant, and Jew. He is brave; he has the courage to speak and to act according to his convictions; he rejoices when men work with him; he works when men fall away from him. Cardinal Gibbons, the most outspoken of Catholics, the most loyal co-laborer of the Pope of Rome, is the American of Americans. I desire to accentuate his patriotism, for it has been a wondrous factor in his success. We have heard it said that frequent declarations of patriotism are unseeming in loyal citizens, whose silent lives ought to give sufficient evidence of their civic virtue. Then let it be said, too, that frequent declarations of religious faith are not in place among devoted Christians; then, let the *Credo* be seldom repeated.

I have spoken my tribute to the Cardinal Archbishop of Baltimore. A wide field remains ungleaned from which others may gather other tributes.

My whole observation of the times, and in particular of this memorable Columbian year, convinces me that the Church has now her season of grace in America, and I often put to myself the anxious question: Will she profit by it? At times my soul sinks downward to the borderland of pessimism. I hate pessimism; I believe it to be one of the worst crimes against God and humanity; it puts an end to progress. Yet it tempts me, when I read in so many souls indifference and inertia, when I hear of the trifles with which soldiers of truth busy themselves, when I perceive the vast crowd looking backward lest they see the eastern horizon purpled by the rays of the new sun, and moving at slowest pace lest perchance they leave the ruts of the past and overtake the world, whose salvation is their God-given mission. But this evening, far from me is pessimism driven. I feel that religion will surely conquer. My soul throbs with hope. For I remember the God above me; I remember the leaders He has given to the Church—in Rome, Leo XIII.; in America, Cardinal Gibbons. What one man can do is wondrous; what could not ten men—a hundred men do? O Catholic Church, fruitful mother of heroes, give us in unstinted measure men, sons of thy own greatness and of thy own power!

The jubilee of Cardinal Gibbons is not a celebration of song and tinsel; it is a lesson to bishops, priests, and laymen of God's Church in America.